Tantra Illuminated

THE PHILOSOPHY, HISTORY, AND PRACTICE OF A TIMELESS TRADITION

Tantra Illuminated

THE PHILOSOPHY, HISTORY, AND
PRACTICE OF A TIMELESS TRADITION

Second Edition

-Christopher D. Wallis-

with illustrations by Ekabhūmi Ellik

MATTAMAYŪRA PRESS

Mattamayūra Press
3950 Colorado Ave, Unit B
Boulder, CO 80303
tantrikainstitute.org

10 9

Publisher's Cataloging-In-Publication Data
(Prepared by The Donohue Group, Inc.)

Wallis, Christopher D.
Tantra illuminated : the philosophy, history, and practice of a timeless tradition / Christopher D. Wallis ; with illustrations by Ekabhūmi Ellik. -- 2nd ed.
p. : ill. ; cm.
First edition published in 2012.

Includes translations from primary Sanskrit sources.
Includes bibliographical references and index.

ISBN: 978-0-9897613-0-7 (pbk.)
ISBN: 978-0-9897613-1-4 (hardcover)
1. Saivism. 2. Tantrism. I. Ellik, Ekabhūmi. II. Title.
BL1280.54 .W35 2013
294.5/513 2013946524

Cover Art: Greg R. Perkins
Book Design: Chris Todd
Copyediting: Margaret Bendet and Anne Malcolm
Indexing: Eve Rickert
Illustrations: Ekabhūmi Ellik
Managing Editor: Eve Rickert

Printed in the United States of America

Contents

PART TWO:
A History of Śaiva Tantra

PART THREE:
An Introduction to the Practice of Śaiva Tantra

CONCLUSION

NONDUAL INVOCATION TO THE DIVINE

Ātmā tvaṃ Girijā matiḥ sahacarāḥ prāṇāḥ śarīraṃ gṛham
Pūjā te viṣayopabhoga-racanā nidrā samādhi-sthitiḥ |
Sañcāraḥ padayoḥ pradakṣiṇa-vidhiḥ stotrāṇi sarvā giraḥ
Yad-yat karma karomi tat-tad-akhilaṁ Śambho tavārādhanam ||

Ātmā tvam	You are my Self, my core, my essence.
Girijā matiḥ	The Goddess is my mind.
sahacarāḥ prāṇāḥ	My prāṇas are Your attendants.
śarīraṃ gṛham	My body is Your temple.
pūjā te viṣayopabhoga-racanā	Enjoying the objects of the senses is my worship of You.
nidrā samādhi-sthitiḥ	My sleep is Your state of samādhi.
Sañcāraḥ padayoḥ	Wherever I walk,
pradakṣiṇa-vidhiḥ	I am performing *pradakṣiṇa* of You.
stotrāṇi sarvā giraḥ	All my words are hymns of praise to You.
Yad-yat karma karomi	Whatever actions I perform,
tat-tad-akhilaṁ	they are all worship of You,
śambho tavārādhanam	O Benevolent One!

Jaya jaya Karuṇābdhe Śrī Mahādeva Śambho!

Hail! Hail! O ocean of compassion! O reverend Great Divinity! O Benevolent Lord!

DEDICATION AND BENEDICTION

Namas te, reverent greetings to you.

Reverent greetings to the One who dwells within you, as you.

Reverent greetings to the divine Light of Consciousness that manifests as this entire universe of tangible and intangible things; that makes all experience possible; and that shines forth in the form of true wisdom, the spontaneously blissful intuition of its own self-luminous nature.

May all apparent obstacles to the unfolding of our path and the completion of this work be dissolved through the realization that they are not separate from Consciousness—that they are the Path, and they are the Work.

May diving into the nectarean ocean of the Tantrik teachings support you in the journey to awareness of your own true nature, joyously raising you far beyond what your mind ever thought possible for you, into a whole new expansive world of wonder.

Knowing your own Self, may you shine the light of that sublime Awareness out to include all beings. May you thus become a manifestation of divine grace in this world for the benefit of all beings.

This book is dedicated to You.

May all beings be free! May all beings be free! May *all* beings be free!

Hariḥ Oṃ Tat Sat

ACKNOWLEDGMENTS

Gratitude to my gurus and a brief life-sketch.

First I will acknowledge those who made this book possible in the broadest sense, which will also entail a brief autobiography. Swāmī Muktānanda ("Bābā") probably did more than anyone else in the 20th century to make the teachings of Śaiva Tantra known in the West, from incorporating them into his own teachings[1] to influencing major publishers (specifically Motilal Banarsidass in India and SUNY Press in the United States) to bring out some of the major texts of Kashmīr Shaivism. My father brought me to meet Bābā in Santa Monica at the age of eight, which made a big impression on me.

My mother brought me to meet Bābā's successor, Swāminī Chidvilāsānandā (better known as Gurumayī), when I was sixteen. She granted me *śaktipāt* initiation, forever altering the direction of my life. Studying and practicing at Gurumayī's āshram (until the age of twenty-four) and receiving her sublime teachings, I started to fall in love with the texts of Shaivism from which she quoted. At her Catskills āshram, I met two great practitioner-scholars of the Tantra, Paul Muller-Ortega and Douglas Brooks.

Contact with these scholars led me to commit to attending university to study this tradition full time. The instruction and loving mentorship I received from Muller-Ortega and Brooks at the University of Rochester provided an invaluable foundation. There being no graduate program in Sanskrit at Rochester, I next attended the University of California at Berkeley, where I was taught Sanskrit grammar by two masters of the subject, Robert Goldman and Sally Sutherland-Goldman. I also did a year at U.C. Santa Barbara, where I studied with David Gordon White. The watershed in my academic education, though, came when I enrolled in the Master of Philosophy program in Classical Indian Religions at the University of Oxford (United Kingdom), where I was fortunate to be tutored (often one-on-one) by the greatest living scholar of Śaiva Tantra and one of the finest Sanskritists in the world, Alexis J. G. S. Sanderson, Spalding Professor of Eastern Religions and Ethics at All Souls College.

Returning to U.C. Berkeley, I was extremely blessed to have as a visiting professor one of Sanderson's foremost students, Dr. Somadeva Vasudeva, the breadth of whose knowledge of Sanskrit literature and Śaiva Tantrik* yoga is quite beyond my comprehension. I have learned much from this great scholar and truly fine man.

* Note that this publication uses the more correct spelling "Tantrik," derived from the Sanskrit adjective *tāntrika*, instead of the anglicized "Tantric."

This book owes its greatest debt, though, to Professor Sanderson, whose influence can be felt on nearly every page (especially in the history section). His example formed my ideal of absolute intellectual integrity, which entails relentless pursuit of the truth as part of a community of scholars engaged in longitudinal study that prioritizes the field as a whole over personal glory. He taught me the value of admitting when I don't know, of sacrificing my own agenda and sense of how I would like things to be in deference to the truth, and of striving to be as transparent a mediator as possible in the act of transmitting the words and ideas of the ancient masters to students of the present day. I bow to the vast ocean of his knowledge. I am not at all sure that he will approve of the synthesis of historical scholarship and constructive theology that this book presents (see the Foreword). In the act of making these ancient spiritual teachings relevant to the lives and needs of modern spiritual seekers (my community and my student base), I have striven to not distort those teachings. If I have done so inadvertently, I apologize and refer the reader to Sanderson's extensive academic writings. It is to these and his patient, personal instruction that I owe nearly all of my understanding of the history of Tantra.

In terms of my spiritual understanding of the philosophy, that is due to all of the teachers named above. It has been further enhanced recently by my contact with two excellent practice teachers, Ādyashānti and Dharmabodhi Sarasvatī. The former is not educated in the Tantrik view, yet his teachings are perfectly aligned with it, and sitting with him in retreat has powerfully affected me. The latter is highly educated in the Tantrik tradition and its yogas, and his insight into practice, based on extensive personal experience, has been extremely helpful in clarifying for me aspects of this path. He has been very generous in supporting the writing of this book, reviewing the manuscript, and hosting me at his āshram in Thailand. These two teachers helped me bring my practice and understanding to a whole new level.

The North American yoga community has showered me with incredible love and support, inspiring me to bring these teachings to a wider audience. Without it, this book would not have been written.

At the deepest level, the one without whom none of this would have happened is Gurumayī. The spiritual awakening I had through her grace catalyzed a process of unfolding that allowed me to encounter the words of the Tantrik master Abhinava Gupta as palpably living energy, not mere fossils. Without Gurumayī's unfailing love and grace, I would likely be a mere intellectualist, dessicated of spirit, wondering what it might be like to experience that which the ancient masters describe. I will never forget the blessing she gave me in 1997, when I left her āshram to attend university to study this tradition full time. To her, to my parents (of course), and to all my beloved teachers, one thousand humble *pranāms.*

PREFACE

UNIQUENESS OF THE PRESENT VOLUME

The book you hold in your hands is the first of its kind. That is, it is the first introduction to the history of Tantra and its philosophy written for a general audience.[2] The present volume is unique in combining these three characteristics: 1) it is intended for a readership other than professional scholars, that is, both spiritual practitioners (*yogīs*) and undergraduate students; 2) it provides a thorough overview of classical Tantra (8th–12th centuries); and 3) it is based on the original manuscript sources in Sanskrit and the best of the scholarship produced over the last thirty years, especially the major research breakthroughs in Tantrik studies in the last ten years.

NEED FOR THIS BOOK

This book meets a specific need, for outside of a relatively small circle of scholars, awareness of the huge impact of the Tantrik religions on the development of Asian spiritual thought is still virtually unknown. In university courses on Indian religion, it is either not taught, or it is touched on briefly in a grossly distorted manner. And in countless popular books like the recent *American Veda*, doctrines that come out of Tantra are mistakenly identified as belonging to other streams of Indian religion.[3] A book for the wider readership is needed to set the record straight, give credit where credit is due, and provide accurate answers to the many questions that the more thoughtful practitioners of modern yoga are starting to ask about "the real Tantra."

THE PURPOSE OF THIS BOOK

The purpose of this book is to clearly and effectively answer the following questions:

- What is Tantra?
- What are its basic spiritual and philosophical ideas?
- What is its history and who are its main figures?
- What are its fundamental practices?
- What is the significance of Tantra to the broader history of Indian yoga?
- To what extent is it possible to incorporate Tantrik teachings and practices into a modern Western yoga practice?

The book has an additional purpose as well—to offer the reader an immersion into a spiritual worldview that can trigger radical personal transformation and permanently expanded awareness.

SCOPE OF THE PRESENT VOLUME

You may wonder what the phrase "classical Tantra" refers to. It distinguishes our subject matter from the later Hindu Tantra and *haṭha-yoga* traditions, and also from modern Western neo-Tantra. The classical Tantra treated in this volume is associated with a specific religious tradition, the religion of Śiva-Śakti, also known as Shaivism, the dominant religion of India throughout the medieval period. But there is also the important category of Buddhist Tantra; thus some readers will wish to know its relation to what I am calling classical Tantra. (If you are not interested in this question, please skip to "How to read this book," below.) To answer the question briefly (since more detail is given later on), I believe that this book is a good introduction to Tantra, even for those interested in its Buddhist form, because the latter is so very similar to classical Śiva-Śakti Tantra. This is not coincidental; the practices of Buddhist Tantra that are not found in earlier (non-Tantrik) Buddhism were directly adopted from classical Śiva-Śakti Tantra.[4] Furthermore, much of the spiritual philosophy of Buddhism that is unique to its Tantrik phase is extremely similar to the nondual Tantrik teachings at the core of the present volume.[5] I believe that future scholarship will show that the Tantrik tradition that flourished in the Himālayan region transcended the rigid religious boundaries that are of such importance to religious conservatives and scholars.[6] Therefore, this book, though it focuses on Śaiva (= Śiva-Śakti) Tantra, can indeed function as an adequate orientation to Tantra in general, i.e., to the worldview and practices shared by the various Tantrik religions.

HOW TO READ THIS BOOK

This is not exactly like other books you have read. It uses a couple of different voices, since it attempts to bridge the gap between those who have a serious spiritual interest in the subject and those who have a scholarly interest in it but cannot read Sanskrit well. Much of the time it is informal and easy to read, and occasionally it is a little more difficult and philosophical. Therefore it is written in a way that makes it possible to skip ahead or even skip around. Don't get bogged down in a difficult passage. You will enjoy the book more and be more successful at understanding it if you make it through once, skipping whatever seems too dense for you, and then go back for a more thorough second read. There are also many Sanskrit words in parentheses, which are not necessary to pay attention to at first. In fact, most things in parentheses are adding nuances that you needn't worry about the first time through. The same goes for the endnotes: they provide more information and discussion for those already familiar with the material in the main body of the text. Some of the endnotes are scholarly; others simply add more detail.

Since the subject matter of the book is difficult to present in a linear form, and since some readers will skip around anyway, the book is cross-referenced throughout. You will find notes in the margins referring you to other pages that will further illuminate the current topic of discussion. You can also use the index to help you grapple proactively with what is being presented. Let yourself engage in a conversation with this book, and the potentially mind-altering or even life-changing experience it offers to you will be of a much fuller quality.

This book is an introduction to the history as well as the philosophy of classical Tantra. The standard scholarly format would be to present the history first, since it provides the context for what follows, but the historical material can be dense for anyone not already motivated by love for the philosophy. We have chosen, then, to place the spiritual philosophy up front, after an introduction that explores the definition of the term *tantra*. If the quasi-scholarly introduction seems too dense, and you want to dive right into the spiritual teachings, feel free. On the other hand, if you are already somewhat educated in Shaivism, the introduction and the history sections may hold the greatest interest for you, since the research presented there is cutting-edge and may very well surprise you.

Once you have read through the book once or twice, I invite you to return to especially difficult or profound passages so you can contemplate them further. Such passages are marked with a special symbol (see the key on page 13). You also may wish to select quotes that move or intrigue you and work with them in a spiritual process, as described on pages 370–371.

NOTE FROM THE ILLUSTRATOR

"Art enables us to find ourselves and lose ourselves at the same time."
— Thomas Merton

Essence manifests form. When patterns arise, consciousness may see something we call a personality, just as a pattern of sounds can be called a "song." Over time, traditional personalities emerged. When a desire arose to share these personalities on paper, there was a challenge: how does one draw a song-of-Consciousness? Not just as a pretty picture, but as a guide for others to hear and play the music? One might use symbols that could be read like sheet music by one's intended audience.

So over many centuries, a rich system of symbols was developed in the East to illustrate deities as patterns in essence, like songs are patterns in space. These images are not Art in the Western sense of expressing a personal vision. They're Sacred Art as a vehicle, as a yantra or device to transmit essence. It's tempting to consider this iconography as depicting something "out there." However, this view may prevent us from "hearing the music" inside ourselves. The music, symbols, musician, and audience are all the same song played in different keys.

The images in this book exactly match descriptions in texts translated by Christopher Wallis. Those descriptions did not contain all the necessary details, so manuscripts, statues, and paintings as far back as the 10th century were also consulted. Though the source materials are ancient, my artwork is flavored by the modern Newar style of Nepal (that of my primary teacher in Sacred Art) and my own preference for humanistic anatomy. Months were spent in research, but when it was time to draw, I followed my heart.

Many thanks to Dinesh Shrestha, Mavis Gewant, and Pieter Weltevrede for sharing teachings from their Sacred Art traditions.

Friends from around the world collaborated via social websites, adding depth and richness to my work. The books created by Harish Johari and Robert Beer were invaluable not only as references but also as tools for transforming the task of drawing into the joy of sadhana. Most of all, I am grateful to Dharmabodhi Saraswati for his insights, guidance, and encouragement.

Ekabhūmi Ellik
August 2011, Berkeley, CA

LIST OF ILLUSTRATIONS

KEY TO SYMBOLS

 Passage translated from original Sanskrit source

Contemporary reference

Key point

Cross-reference

QUICK 'N' EASY PRONUNCIATION GUIDE FOR SANSKRIT WORDS

(a full guide can be found in the back of the book)

- c is always pronounced as "ch," as in the Italian *cioccolato*; so *candra* = chandra and *vāc* = vaach
- ph is always as in upheaval, never as in phrase
- ś and ṣ are both pronounced "sh" as in sugar
- jñ is pronounced gnya, so yajña is "yag-nya" and jñāna is "gnyaana"

FOREWORD

FOR SCHOLARS AND ACADEMICS

This section addresses concerns primarily of interest to scholars. It is a defense of the identity of the "scholar-practitioner" and of a new way of doing religious studies, to which this book is a contribution.

One of the most interesting things about the mastery of a body of knowledge is the extraordinary flexibility it grants. Once well understood, it can be variously inflected depending on the context, audience, and purpose of articulation. Those who study the field called "semiotics," which, in its pragmatic dimension, refers to the collective process of meaning-making, are familiar with the seemingly spontaneous process by which distinct spheres of discourse are generated by specific contexts, and the fact that that apparent spontaneity does not equate with cultural transparency. In academic writing and teaching in the humanities, and most especially in religious studies, there is a tacit normative metadiscourse around "objective knowledge" and "knowledge for its own sake" that pushes a forced consensus, one which almost completely prohibits the examination of religious ideas from a personal or pragmatic perspective. This is an institutionally imposed consensus in the sense that it is not shared by any undergraduates I have taught, certainly not by the general public, and it only appears in the discourse of graduate students because they have learned to conceal their personal religious commitments in order to conform to the normative concept of so-called objectivity, an intellectual pretense glamorized as an academic ideal. (Show me a religion grad student, and I'll show you a deeply religious person "in the closet," or someone who's had their religiosity weeded out of them by the reductionist discourse intellectually privileged by academia.) As the respected Buddhist scholar-practitioner José Cabezón has noted,

"[T]here is still a widespread reticence to engage the question of the religious identity of the scholar within religious studies as a whole."[7]

This situation has, in my view, brought about the current atrophying of the academic study of religion. The fashionability the field enjoyed in the 1960s and '70s has long since waned, and the field has been rightly criticized for failing to develop methodologies or hermeneutic strategies that justify its existence independent from departments of history, sociology, anthropology, philosophy, etc. (I am reminded of Ninian Smart's self-mocking characterization of religious studies as "polymethodological doodling all the time.") But none of this would matter, I think, if undergraduate students could study religion the way they want to, an approach that would, coincidentally, also constitute the unique methodology that religion departments are lacking. By this I mean a serious engagement with the worldviews expressed by religions in acts of body, speech, and mind, in a manner that would entail a range of thought experiments (and even body experiments) that allow the student to make his own embodied consciousness the locus for consideration of the question, *What does reality actually look like and feel like from within this religious worldview?* Such experimentation clearly does not involve an actual conversion to the given religion, nor does it necessitate the instructor's personal adherence to the religious object of experimentation, and yet it is rarely practiced in the university setting. This despite the fact that this sort of process is, in my experience, what students drawn to the study of religion are most interested in, and despite the fact that such an open and real exploration would be the most authentic engagement with the original ideals of academia one could imagine.

Though I am an academic scholar, I am also a spiritual practitioner. The book I have chosen to write as my first is not one that is likely to gain me credibility in the academic world, despite the fact that in order to write it I had to earn three degrees and become competent in the reading and interpretation of a wide variety of primary and secondary sources. My endeavor here is not to profit from the current popular interest in something called Tantra, nor is it a bid for notoriety by watering down and "making ready for prime time" ideas that are chiefly comprehensible to trained professionals, as academics often view mainstream books in their field. Rather, this book is something more interesting to me: it is an exercise in what Cabezón calls "academic theology," or what I would call a *self-conscious experiment in well-grounded constructive theology.* It weds together the interests and needs of two diverse communities of readers in a way that, I here argue, *only* a scholar-practitioner is capable of doing. In such an individual, two realms of discourse—one rooted in intellectual claims of objectivity, the other in personal religious experience and concomitant beliefs—may either exist separately, forcing him to maintain a kind of split personality, or they may cohere into unity as he permits intellectual insight to inform his spiritual being and spiritual experience to guide his intellectual inquiry without relinquishing his commitment to truth. For me, this process of coalescence did not arise within the academic context, in which the only good religious scholar is a dis-integrated religious scholar, but within a very different context to which I was initially driven by financial need: freelance teaching in yoga studios. This environment, derided by some academics as being anti-intellectual and woefully ignorant of "real yoga," not only welcomed the process of sustained and engaged reflection on the philosophy and practice of yoga but pushed me to reflect in more productive ways on the material I had studied. Questions of how philosophy related to practice, and of what the religious life of those who authored the ancient texts might have really looked like, were forced into the center of my awareness as my audience relentlessly pushed the discourse away from intellectual abstraction and textual literalism and toward concerns about why the original historical actors held the views they did, what experiences informed those views, what it would mean for modern people to hold those views, and how our own cultural context might alter, organically, the ways in which those views might be held. These nonacademic teaching engagements have compelled me to understand the knowledge systems of ancient Indian religion *as what they originally were:* ways of interpreting reality that were embedded in practice contexts and grounded in the real-life concerns of human beings *who worked with these religious understandings as ways of purposively refashioning their approach to daily lived existence.* To avoid discussion of how religious ideas might personally impact us is thus to avoid confronting, in any real way, the original purpose and function of those ideas: for, I argue, it is only in actually applying religious ideas to our own lives that they can take on their real power and significance, and only in this way do they become accessible to us as authentic and meaningful objects of inquiry.

Introduction

AN ORIENTATION TO TANTRA

Tantra is now a buzzword in the modern Western world. We see it on the covers of popular magazines and books, usually linked suggestively with the notion of superlative sexual experience. Though almost everyone has heard this word, almost no one—including many people claiming to teach something called tantra—knows anything about the historical development of the Indian spiritual tradition that scholars refer to as Tantra. What these academics study as Tantra bears little resemblance to what is taught under the same name on the workshop circuit of American alternative spirituality. It is not the main purpose of this book to explain why that gap is so wide—a deeply complex issue of historical transmission and strange misunderstandings. Here we simply present a comprehensive overview of the original Indian spiritual tradition that was articulated in Sanskrit scriptures called tantras (which is where the name came from). Why would this be of interest to modern Westerners? There is one outstanding reason: millions of Westerners are today practicing something called yoga, a practice which, though much altered in form and context, can in many respects be traced back to the Tantrik tradition.[8]

Given the widespread terminological confusion, I ask you as the reader to simply clear your mind of whatever you think you know about Tantra, however valuable that knowledge may or may not have been to you, and to start afresh. In this way, I have a chance to effectively orient you to the original Tantrik worldview: a way of seeing and understanding reality that can challenge and illuminate you to the deepest levels of your being.

Yoga is a living tradition profoundly influenced by the Tantra, yet it has forgotten much of its own history. This book is part of a new wave of work by scholars who are also practitioners, and whose goals are to rediscover and reintegrate some of what has been forgotten; to clarify the roots of many ideas and practices that are floating around (thereby grounding them and enhancing their richness); and to chart clearly the vast and varied landscape of Indian spiritual thought, with a view to what it can contribute to our lives today. For it is certainly the case that most 20th-century teaching and writing on Indian thought was either exciting but incoherent and ungrounded (the practitioner context) or systematic but dry, boring, and insipid (the academic context). It's time to rectify that—and no Indian tradition has been more misunderstood, relative to its deep influence on global spirituality, than Tantra.

Part of this book is historical. As a scholar, I help people to distinguish between new ideas and those that have been around for a while, not in order to suggest that the old is better or inherently more legitimate than the new but so that readers may be equipped to accurately identify which ideas are persistent and widespread in the Tantrik traditions, and therefore central, and which ones are more peripheral. Why might this be an important point of discernment? From the practitioner's point of view, the enterprise of learning to identify the central tenets of a given spiritual tradition is based on the axiom that any tradition preserves over time the most effective teachings and practices and tends to discard those that have proven ineffective.[9] Therefore, to identify the most prevalent Tantrik practices and ideas over the course of centuries of historical development is to identify practices and ideas that have been effective for countless practitioners. This process of identification allows us to innovate on a firm foundation of understanding, rather than—as many modern yoga teachers have done—filling the gaps in our knowledge by simply making up ideas that sound good based on idiosyncratic individual experience. Again, I do not mean to imply that a traditional way of thinking or technique will necessarily be more effective for you as an individual than a new one. But it is true that only time will tell if a new technique or teaching has sufficient efficacy to become an enduring part of a living spiritual tradition.

You may ask (and I think you should) how I am qualified to represent the original Tantrik tradition. Twelve years of intensive study at the university level have served to acquaint me with the Sanskrit language and the contents of some of the Tantrik texts written in this language. This academic study is, in my view, complemented by twenty-six years as a spiritual practitioner in a tradition influenced by several of these original Tantrik texts. Though I am hardly a master, I have spent many years of my life in the full-time occupation of simply trying to understand the ancient Tantrik masters sufficiently well to accurately represent them in my own English words. The effect reading this book has on your life will be a testament to whether I have accomplished this goal in some measure.

See pages 4–6

See page 438

WHY STUDY THE HISTORY OF TANTRA?

Unlike the history you might have been forced to learn in school, the history of the Tantrik traditions is a fascinating story that consists not merely of information, but of inspirational and powerful ideas—some of the most original ideas ever conceived concerning human potential.

Historically, these ideas were inextricably wedded to transformative spiritual practices, some of which you may already be practicing. You see, some practices that originated within Tantra were handed down to the present but became unmoored from their original philosophical anchor points. (For example, the tradition of *haṭha-yoga*, the basis for modern yoga, originally grew out of Śaiva Tantra.) The Tantrik masters evolved their teachings and techniques as an unbroken whole, a well-crafted interconnected matrix designed to free you permanently from ignorance and suffering. So when you understand the profound and exquisite vision of reality that was originally taught in connection to these yogic practices, this knowledge empowers your practice, keeps you inspired about your path, and gives you great clarity and focus. It is therefore practically useful for you to become more educated in the traditions that nurtured the practices of yoga that you cherish today.

See pages 308–316

There is tremendous misunderstanding in the yoga world today about the historical facts of the development of the yogic and Tantrik traditions. While we all agree that historical facts are not the most important aspect of studying this tradition, it is also true that learning them helps us replace our fantasies about how things are (and were) with the reality of things. This is a process that challenges us in at least three important ways. It challenges us to accept the world as it is, rather than how we would like it to be. It grounds us in an awareness of the very human difficulties involved with learning, teaching, and living a spiritual path, thereby helping us to cultivate compassion for others and patience with ourselves. Finally, it prevents us from using shaky or downright incorrect historical claims to justify what we think is the best path or the most correct form of yoga practice. When knowledge of the real history keeps us from this error, we are forced to rely on our own experience of our practice when justifying it to others—which is a far more stable basis. Arguments about which path is best or most authentic are fruitless endeavors. Even worse, when these arguments are "supported" by spurious facts and a confused and partial knowledge of history, they merely antagonize others and make us look bad. On the other hand, openly sharing your experience and what works for you as an individual, without an agenda, helps to connect you with others and invites them to contemplate their own experience. This is *yoga*, beneficial connection.

Now a word about the methodology of good scholarly research and the results it produces. Some people, influenced by so-called postmodern thought, regard with suspicion any claim about facts or history. They prefer to see everything as a subjective narrative and refuse to grant any authority to truth claims, saying that everyone's "truth," though different, is equally valid. Though this may be the case as far as our individual psychological experience of the world goes, social science and the hard sciences have shown that there *is* such a thing as a real fact. How have they shown this? Simple: by drawing on a sufficient quantity of evidence, weighing it carefully, and then using it to make a prediction about something not yet known. When new evidence comes to light showing that prediction to be correct, the information and the method used for prediction is shown to be valid. We have many examples of this in the hard sciences. Black holes were predicted on the basis of mathematical models long before they were observed by astronomers. What physicists knew *must* be true as a result of their accurate understanding of the physical laws of the universe was vindicated, almost as an afterthought, by observational evidence.[10] There are also examples of this in the "soft" sciences, including the study of India, though these are too complex to get into here.[11] Let me hasten to add that unlike some authors, I will *not* present as fact anything for which strong evidence or scholarly consensus is wanting. In the absence of the latter, the former is needed.

Accepting that there are such things as facts requires you to be humble and to have the flexibility to relinquish your position when it is shown to be wrong. This too is part of the tradition of yoga. Of course, there is also plenty of room for an individual to develop her own beliefs, as these philosophical traditions partially concern themselves with metaphysical issues, about which we are not in a position to provide definitive proof one way or the other. That is, while the Tantra actively engages the higher mind, it also attempts to transcend the level of the intellect on which "proof" is an operative term. Here your own contemplated experience becomes primary in formulating your understanding of reality. When the wisdom of well-considered experience is joined coherently to well-grounded factual knowledge, you have a strong foundation from which to successfully navigate both the path of yoga and the world in general.

WHAT'S IN A NAME?

THE MEANING OF THE WORD TANTRA

In this section I will explain the development of the word "tantra," starting from its simple and general meanings and working up to its more complex and specific applications. First off, *tantra* is a Sanskrit word with various straightforward meanings, including "theory," "doctrine," or simply "book." Though the word sometimes designates any sort of book, it more commonly refers to scriptural texts that are purported to have been divinely revealed by God or the Goddess. These tantras began appearing in India around the 6th century of the common era and continued to be composed in large numbers for the next thousand years. These scriptural texts also went by other names, such as *āgama* ("what has come down to us"). Therefore, the tantric tradition could equally be called the āgamic tradition. You will find out more about them and their contents later.

"Tantra" has a more specific meaning in the context of these revealed scriptures: it can refer to the system of practice presented by them, and this is the meaning in which we are usually using the word. In general, we may say that each tantra presented a more-or-less complete system of spiritual practice. So a given guru would work primarily with a single tantra (though he would sometimes supplement it with related and subsidiary texts) and would teach his disciple on the basis of that specific tantra. In this sense, then, *tantra* would simply mean "a system of spiritual practice articulated within a specific sacred text," and people in the original tradition would thus ask each other, "Which tantra do you follow?" Western spiritual teachers often state that "tantra" means "loom" or "weave," and these meanings are indeed found in the dictionary under "tantra"—but that usage is merely a homonym. None of the Tantrik texts cite this as the meaning of "tantra," which incidentally signals one of the pitfalls of definitions offered by non-Sanskritists. However, the tradition does offer some interpretive etymologies of the word "tantra." An interpretive etymology is a way of breaking down the word into component parts that allows an unpacking of the inner meaning of the word. The most commonly found etymology of "tantra" follows. It breaks down the word into the verbal roots √*tan* and √*tra*, the former meaning "propagate, elaborate on, expand on," and the latter, "save, protect":

Kāmikā-tantra

> *Because it elaborates copious and profound matters, especially relating to the principles of reality* [tattvas] *and mantras, and because it saves us [from the cycle of suffering], it is called a* tantra.[12]

In other words, Tantra spreads (*tan*) wisdom that saves (*tra*). Here the second verbal root has a double meaning, for it alludes to the fact that Tantrik practices give us a means of strengthening and protecting ourselves from worldly harm, as well as bestowing the ultimate spiritual liberation (more on this later). We could equally well say that a tantra is a device (*tra*) for expanding (*tan*), as a mantra is a device for working with the mind (*man*), and a yantra is a device for controlling (*yan*). Modern teachers like to mention that the verbal root √*tan* means "stretch, expand," saying that Tantra is so called because it stretches our awareness and expands our capacity for joy. This is a good example of a modern interpretive etymology, and though it is not found in the original sources, it is very much in their spirit.

In premodern India, those people who received Tantrik initiation usually received it from a single guru in a specific lineage and performed the daily practice given by that guru on the basis of a single tantra. So for each individual practitioner, Tantra as a spiritual movement was not something highly complex, for he did not concern himself with what other tantras or gurus might be saying. By contrast, the Western mind likes to have a sense of the whole landscape and formulate general definitions based on it, so unlike their Indian counterparts, Western scholars have striven to define Tantra as a phenomenon, a religious movement, by looking at what its various streams had in common. This effort has not been entirely successful, primarily due to a failure to consult a wide enough range of sources, but it is still worth looking at its results so far, which we will do after considering the tradition's own definition of the word.

THE TRADITION'S OWN DEFINITION

Though it is true that most premodern Indian people didn't care for formulating abstract general definitions, a few of their scholars did. And when we investigate thoroughly enough, we find just such a definition in the original sources. In my mind a definition of a tradition from *within* that tradition takes precedence over definitions offered by academics from a foreign culture a thousand years later (though those too are useful, as we will see). So let's look at what the Tantrik scholar and guru named Rāma Kaṇṭha, who lived around a thousand years ago, says Tantra is:

> *A Tantra is a divinely revealed body of teachings, explaining what is necessary and what is a hindrance in the practice of the worship of God; and also describing the specialized initiation and purification ceremonies that are the necessary prerequisites of Tantrik practice. These teachings are given to those qualified to pursue both the higher and lower aims of human existence.*[14]

Rāma Kaṇṭha's commentary on the *Sārdhatriśati-kālottara*

I should note here that the language of this definition is colored by the fact that the author is a dualist (which might surprise you, since all the Tantrik teachings that have come to the West are from nondualist sources). However, since Tantra was (as we shall see) a coherent spiritual system regardless of sectarian differences such as dualism versus nondualism, the points of Rāma Kaṇṭha's definition are more or less applicable across the board. Furthermore, the definition is important as the only known indigenous attempt to define Tantra. Let's get clear on the four main points Rāma Kaṇṭha makes.

First, he mentions the requirement of proper initiation to the Tantrik path, which originally took the form of a ritual ceremony that destroyed karmic barriers to successful practice, brought the goal of spiritual liberation within the reach of a single lifetime, and (on the immediate practical level) gave the initiate access to the scriptures and the secret practices they contained. We will discuss in the conclusion of this book whether this requirement of initiation means that Westerners cannot properly undertake a real Tantrik practice. Here it suffices to note that initiation was regarded as crucial and required in original Tantra.

See page 332–339

See page 423

Second, his definition highlights what many people in the original Indian context saw as the key element of daily Tantrik practice: "ritual worship" of a form of the Divine. Now, the English phrase "ritual worship" will probably give the wrong idea to a Westerner with a very different religious background. Let me clarify that here "worship" means—at the very least—*the actual evocation of the power of the Deity* and interaction with it. More commonly, it means *becoming* that deity through techniques of ritualized meditation and/or meditative ritual, either temporarily or as part of a process by which any perception of difference between oneself and the Deity is eventually permanently eradicated. As we will see later on, there are also forms of the Tantra that dispense with ritual altogether and emphasize direct intuitive awareness of divine reality brought about through simple practices connected with the elements of daily life. Though originally these forms were greatly in the minority, I will argue later that these are the forms that Westerners can most successfully and authentically engage with.

See page 431

Third, Rāma Kaṇṭha's definition states that there are two goals of all Tantrik practice, the "higher" and the "lower" goals. The first refers to a state of spiritual freedom, release from all suffering, salvation or beatitude, the nature of which we will discuss in more depth. This state is usually called *mokṣa* or *mukti* in Sanskrit (both of which mean "release" or "liberation" or "freedom"). The second refers to the goal of worldly enjoyment and prosperity, which encompasses pleasure, power, and all good things of the tangible world; it is usually called *siddhi* or *bhukti* or *bhoga*. The fact that the Tantra is legitimately directed at *both* of these goals is one thing that sets it apart from other Indian religious traditions, or indeed most religions in the world. Though it is true that there are Tantrik texts devoted almost exclusively to either the goal of *mukti* or of *bhukti*, in general Tantrik spiritual technology was designed to secure both goals, with that of pleasure subordinated to that of liberation. Note carefully here that Rāma Kaṇṭha's definition tells us we cannot call any practice Tantrik that is only directed toward the lower goal. For example, if the goal of a practice is simply to improve one's sex life, then however spiritual-sounding it may be, it cannot be called Tantra. If, on the other hand, that goal is part of a practice in which it is consistently subordinated to the goal of complete spiritual freedom and awakening to the true nature of reality, then it can be called Tantra.

Fourth and lastly, Rāma Kaṇṭha's definition says that the Tantra is something given in scriptures that are divinely revealed, which means, in this worldview, that Tantrik teachings and instructions on practice are sanctioned by divine authority. The Tantrik scriptures themselves are always said to be spoken by a form of God or the Goddess, Śiva or Śakti; or, in Buddhist Tantra, a celestial Buddha or Bodhisattva, which arguably amounts to the same thing. The "fact" of whether these tantras were "really" divinely revealed was not a question that much interested the classical writers; issues of faith and belief were simply not as significant to them as those of efficacy and practice. Since one received the scriptural teachings from a trusted authority (the guru), one simply got on with the practice, and faith naturally increased as that practice started to show results.

It should be added here that the scriptural corpus of Tantrik texts is almost entirely unpublished so far, in India or the West. That is, they exist largely only in manuscript form (see image to the right), physically and linguistically inaccessible to most. What the general public has some limited access to in English is in fact not the Tantrik scriptures themselves, but rather the commentaries on those scriptures, and other works inspired by them, written by great Tantrik masters.[15] These commentaries came, over time, to be treated like scriptures themselves, and this is how they are presented by some modern gurus. Such a presentation is possible because of the high degree of sophistication and spiritual wisdom exhibited by these commentarial texts, which in many cases seem considerably greater than that of the original scriptures. The part of the Tantra that today is called Kashmīr Shaivism consists entirely of these commentaries and associated writings, written by a series of masters from Kashmīr. These materials are what preoccupy most discussions of Tantrik philosophy, since the scriptural texts are themselves almost wholly concerned with practice.

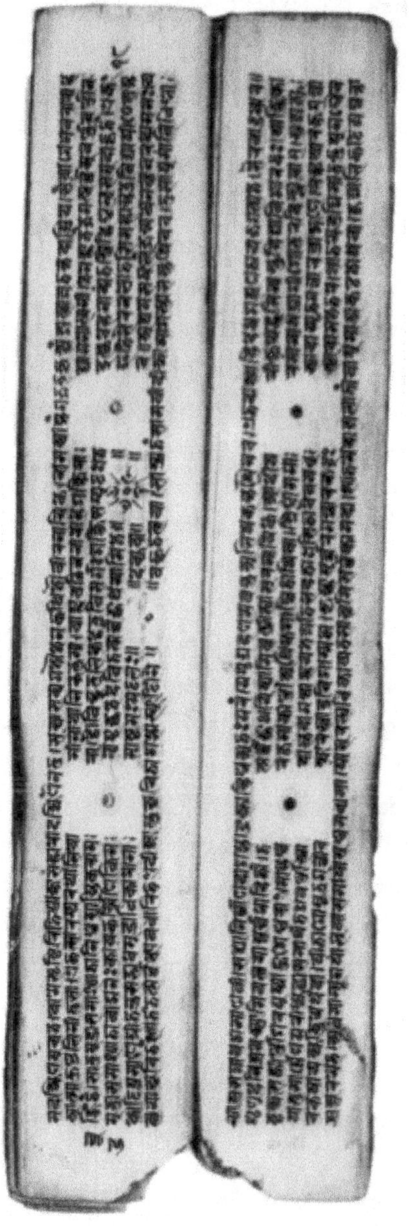

Ancient manuscript of a Tantrik scripture (rotate book 90º clockwise to view correctly)

Tantra is a mode of practice that affected all the Indian religions to some degree.

WESTERN DEFINITIONS AND CATEGORICAL LISTS

Earlier I said that Western scholarly attempts to define Tantra are also valuable. Though Rāma Kaṇṭha's definition gives us some crucial information, the modern reader needs additional parameters to recognize what original Tantra really looks like. The scholarly definitions give us this information in the form of lists of features and elements that are typically found in Tantrik thought and practice. We will now examine some of these lists. First, though, I should mention that the scholarly attempt to define the Tantra is rooted in the understanding that it was a spiritual phenomenon that affected all the Indian religions to some degree. It was a new way of doing spiritual practice that was deeply influential, though it was undertaken by a small percentage of the total population. An argument can be made that the Tantra is a mode of practice (and associated mode of viewing reality) that is not of any one religion, though it is found as the esoteric dimension of many religions.[16] The Indian religions that it influenced, in order of degree of influence, were Shaivism, Buddhism, Vaishnavism, Jainism, and Indian Islam.[17] The innovations of Tantra were developed almost entirely within the first two religions in this list, then transmitted to the others. Between these two, Shaivism has historical priority, because many of the Buddhist Tantrik texts drew directly or indirectly on Śaiva tantras, while the reverse was rarely if ever the case.[18] Though Shaivism was therefore the Tantrik religion *par excellence,* Buddhism eventually became thoroughly "Tantricized," and in this form, it was transmitted to Tibet. Thus Tibetan Buddhism is almost completely Tantrik. Any attempt to define the Tantra as a general category, then, ought to encompass both Śaiva Tantra and Buddhist Tantra. Indeed, there is little discernable difference between the most "Buddhistic" school of Śaiva Tantra (the Krama) and the most "Śaivist" school of Buddhist Tantra (Dzogchen). The commonalities that lead us to argue for the validity of "Tantra" as a

See page 439

general concept will become more obvious as we examine a list of characteristics that match both Śaiva and Buddhist variations.

Scholars have attempted to ascertain what Śaiva Tantra, Buddhist Tantra, and Vaiṣṇava Tantra all have in common, and thus what constitutes Tantra per se. Here I wish to combine the lists presented by five different scholars (Tribe, Hodge, Goudriaan, Brooks, and Lopez) to create a master list of Tantric features. In no particular order, the features that characterize Tantra as a spiritual movement are:

- alternative path / new revelation / more rapid path
- centrality of ritual, esp. evocation and worship of deities
- proliferation in the number and types of deities (compared to the antecedent tradition)
- visualization and self-identification with the deity
- centrality of mantras
- installation of mantras on specific points of the body (nyāsa)
- ontological identity of mantras and deities
- necessity of initiation and importance of esotericism/secrecy
- yoga (usually referring to meditation and visualization practices)
- ritual use of maṇḍalas and *yantras*, especially in initiation
- spiritual physiology (i.e. subtle body and cakras) and kuṇḍalinī
- mapping deities and pilgrimage sites onto the practitioner's body
- linguistic mysticism
- importance of the teacher (guru, ācārya)
- addition of worldly aims, achieved through largely magical means
- lay/householder practitioners dominate the tradition, rather than the ascetics
- bipolar symbology of god/goddess
- nondualism
- revaluation of the body

- revaluation of 'negative' mental states
- importance of śakti (power, energy, goddess)
- revaluation of the status and role of women
- transgressive/antinomian acts
- utilization of "sexual yogas"
- the cultivation of bliss
- spontaneity (sahaja, a technical term)
- special types of meditation that aim to transform the individual into an embodiment of the divine after a short span of time

Yogic meditation, mantras, *maṇḍalas*, guru, initiation, and ritual worship are the six most prominent features of Tantra.

The last ten features really only apply to nondualist or "left current" Tantra (a term that will be explained further). There are six elements that constitute the most prominent features of classical Tantra: yogic meditation, mantras, maṇḍalas, guru, initiation, and ritual worship of the divine (using fire, water, flowers, scented pastes, and so on). Yet, despite their universality, these features cannot be taken to completely define Tantra by themselves, because all of them are also found to some degree in non-Tantrik Indian religions.

These six aspects are usually organized and given their specific form by the seventh universal feature of the Tantra, that of "deity yoga," which entails working with the power of a particular aspect of the Divine to which one has been linked through initiation. This work takes place through use of the deity's associated mantra, *yantra*, visualization, and/or consecrated image. Thus we return full circle to the beginning of our discussion: what distinguishes a practice as indisputably Tantrik is that it involves deities and their mantras that are revealed in explicitly Tantrik scriptures. Having said this, it is perfectly appropriate to call *any* teaching or practice Tantrik (or "tantric") if it appears in an original Tantrik source (whether scripture or commentary). If we wish to preserve any specific meaning to the word, however, the label is not otherwise appropriate.

IMPLICATIONS

The definitions we are considering are entirely focused on the historical reality of the Tantra in its original Indian context. As a Western student of the Tantra, you may be dismayed by them, because they don't seem to describe a practice that you can engage with as part of *your* yoga and philosophy of life. However, though it may or may not be true that you cannot undertake a Tantrik practice of the type most frequently found in medieval India, that does not mean that *no* form of Tantrik practice is available to you. As you will see, there are Tantrik teachings and practices that are both accessible and powerfully effective for the Westerner. The most important thing about any Tantrik practice you learn is that you receive it from someone experienced in it who has navigated some or all of its pitfalls and received some or all of its benefits.

It is impossible to describe the whole field of Tantra in one book. The present volume therefore focuses almost exclusively on the teachings and practices of **nondual Śaiva Tantra** (defined on page 48). Aside from the need for brevity, there are three reasons for this.

- First, nondual Śaiva Tantra is the area of my expertise.
- Second, despite its massive historical and contemporary significance, Śaiva Tantra is not yet well known compared to Tibetan Buddhist Tantra, which already has a substantial following in the West.
- Third, and most importantly, I have seen first-hand how powerfully the teachings of nondual Śaiva Tantra resonate with Western yoga practitioners. I have come to believe that this tradition possesses some of the most effective teachings and technologies for human transformation, and that it is particularly relevant for our time.

QUESTIONS AND ANSWERS

HOW DOES ALL THIS FIT INTO "HINDUISM"?

Most of us have been taught that the indigenous religion of India (which used to be called Hindustan) is something called Hinduism. What is Hinduism, and how does it relate to Shaivism and Tantra? This question, which should be a simple one, is confused by a profound series of misunderstandings.

Let me start by clarifying the biggest misunderstanding: there is no such thing as "Hindu*ism*." That is, until recently. Bear with me and I'll explain. When European culture began interacting with India in a sustained manner, starting in the 16th century, it encountered a bewilderingly complex culture of dozens of languages and a wide range of religious and cultural traditions. Overwhelmed by this complexity, Europeans simply referred to all non-Muslim Indian people as *Hindoos* (derived from the Persian term for "people east of the Indus River") and, a little later, started grouping all their various religious practices under the name Hinduism.[20] Part of the reason for this is that Europeans at that time did not care to investigate the various Indian spiritual traditions and come up with more accurate terminology. What is certain is that prior to the colonial period, the term Hinduism is not accurate: what we find instead are religious traditions that regarded themselves as mutually distinct, called (in English) Brāhmanism, Shaivism, Shāktism, Vaiṣhṇavism, Buddhism, and Jainism (plus a few non-religious spiritual traditions, like Sānkhya and Pātañjala Yoga).[21] So, the term "Hinduism" in origin is a European one.

The term Hinduism is inappropriate for another important reason; it was not used by Indian people themselves until the colonial period. Modern scholarship increasingly (though still not fully) respects the object of its study and strives to understand things from the inside as well as the outside. From that perspective, we can say that something called Hinduism authentically began to exist when the first Indian used the word to refer to his own religion (this happened for the first time in the early 1800s).[22] As more educated Indians began to use the term, they had to come up with a definition for it. They decided that "Hinduism" denotes all those lineages, sects, and traditions that regarded the Vedas (India's first holy books) as the ultimate spiritual authority. This excluded Buddhism—which distanced itself from other Indian traditions by repudiating the Veda—despite the fact that Buddhism derived from the same religious culture and played a crucial role in the development of Indian spirituality in all periods. Some other Indian traditions (such as Shaivism) *were* included in the definition of Hinduism, though they were not directly based on the Vedas, and they granted the Vedas no special religious authority.[23]

Nowadays, we can certainly say that Hinduism exists: though originally an artificial concept, it has now—for better or for worse—become "reified." This is not only because the word is used extensively today by Indian people themselves, but more importantly because previously separate Indian religions have come together over the last five hundred years to make a new religious "stew," erasing many old boundaries, making meaningless many of the old debates, and imparting more or less the same flavor throughout. This has necessarily meant the loss of the more distinct and unique flavors; the unique doctrines and practices of the religions that coalesced to make Hinduism have mostly been forgotten.[24]

This modern Hinduism is as much a cultural identity as it is a religious one, which is why it is not, generally speaking, something one converts to but rather something one is born into.

SO AS A PRACTITIONER OF YOGA OR TANTRA, I'M NOT SOMEHOW CONVERTING TO HINDUISM?

The foregoing discussion explains why it is the case that a Westerner who wishes to practice yoga or Śaiva Tantra does not necessarily need to adopt a new religious and cultural identity. It is true that membership in some Indian religious traditions requires that you be part of a specific caste or clan, or undergo specific Vedic rites of passage. However, the practice of Tantrik yoga involves transcending one's ordinary identity, and therefore does not require initiates to belong to any specific caste, class, gender, or ethnic group. To be more precise, Tantrik practice involves the creation (or realization) of an esoteric divine identity within your earlier, cultural-specific identity. So you can remain a cultural Christian, Jew, or Buddhist and still be a Tāntrika.[25] Śaiva Tantra in particular articulated the idea—unique in India—that all followers of its tradition form a single community regardless of birth, and that therefore it is better to initiate a sincere foreigner than an insincere brāhmin.[26] Though in the 21st century people can do what they like, to me it's important to know that the spiritual path I want to walk sanctions my walking on it.[27]

You can remain a cultural Christian, Jew, or Buddhist and still be a Tāntrika.

See page 430

WHAT'S THE CONNECTION BETWEEN TANTRA AND YOGA?

That really depends on what you mean by "yoga." I'll address two main meanings. The first is the original meaning of the word "yoga," referring to a comprehensive set of psycho-physical practices (emphasizing meditation) intended to discipline and integrate body, mind, and spirit with the aim of attaining the highest spiritual goal. Yoga in this sense began around the time of the Buddha or a little before. A thousand years later, the Tantra incorporated yoga as an important part of its systems of practice. Tantra also expanded on the previously existing body of yogic practice, adding hundreds of new techniques: more complex *prāṇāyāmas*, detailed visualization practices, and mantra-science, as well as many body-based practices, especially yogic postures, sacred hand gestures, and the activation of energy centers (*cakras*) in the body.

We see the significance of yoga to the Tantrik tradition when we simply list the four main topics found in the Tantrik scriptures:

- wisdom teachings (*jñāna*),
- ritual worship (*kriyā*),
- mystical or meditative practice (*yoga*), and
- daily conduct and vows (*caryā*).

A number of elements of Tantrik yoga have survived into the present day, though usually separated from their original context. We will present some information on the practice of Tantrik yoga in Part 3 of this book.

On the other hand, if you mean "yoga" in the modern sense of a comprehensive *āsana* practice, plus one or two other simplified practices (i.e., what scholars call "modern postural yoga"), it too is connected to the Tantra, if only tenuously. Modern yoga is the latest phase of a historical development that may be traced all the way back to Śaiva Tantrik yoga. We can briefly summarize the salient facts here: the religion of Shaivism and its Tantra or esoteric teachings, which comprised an enormously detailed system with a vast institutional base, became unwieldy with the loss of state patronage after the Muslim conquests, and thus was later simplified into (and mostly replaced by) a grassroots system of practice called *haṭha-yoga*.

See pages 308–320

Haṭha-yoga traced itself back to the most well-known Śaiva Tantrik guru, Matsyendra or Macchanda. It presented itself as a complete spiritual path, consisting of *prāṇāyāma*, meditations on the centers of the subtle body, and the use of three *bandhas** and more than eighty-four different yogic postures or *āsanas*, all in service of activating and raising the spiritual energy called *kuṇḍalinī*. Though nearly all of these

See page 309

* Mūla bandha, uḍḍīyāna bandha, and jālandhara bandha; the last two are named after Tantrik pilgrimage sites.

elements were explicitly derived from Śaiva Tantra, *haṭha-yoga* was not fully Tantrik because its texts did not teach Tantrik mantras, Tantrik ritual, or require full Tantrik initiation (the three indispensable elements of mainstream classical Tantra). It preserved some of the earlier practices of Tantrik yoga with admirable success, though it also continued the process of dilution and simplification of the Tantra. In the early 20th century, *haṭha-yoga*'s *āsanas* and *prāṇāyāmas* became the inspiration for the synthesis of the system of modern postural yoga.[28] Thus modern yoga has its roots in ancient Śaiva Tantra.

The three indispensible elements of mainstream classical Tantra are mantras, ritual, and initiation.

WHAT IS THE KĀMA-SŪTRA? WHAT DOES IT HAVE TO DO WITH TANTRA?

Nothing. The *Kāma-sūtra* is part of a branch of literature called *Kāma-śāstra*, or the science of pleasure. Its overall goal is the maximization of sensual pleasure as a valid end in itself. By definition, it is not Tantrik, because in the Tantra, the goal of pleasure, when present, is always subordinated to the goal of final spiritual liberation and awakening, which does not figure into the *Kāma-sūtra* at all. Simply reading the original texts will immediately reveal that they belong to a completely different class of literature. Nor do any of the public erotic temple carvings seen in India (such as in Khajurāho) relate to Tantrik practice in any way.

BUT TANTRA IS ABOUT DIVINE SEXUALITY, RIGHT?

Only if you are interpreting that phrase very broadly indeed. If we survey the Tantrik literature as a whole, we see that sex *per se* is virtually absent as a topic. There is one lineage group in Śaiva Tantra, the Kaula lineages, that teach sensual practices and have what we might call a "sexualized" view of the world, seeing the whole of reality as the harmonious and joyous pulsating union of various sets of complementary opposites.

In the original Tantrik sources, we do find some techniques for working with sexual energy and using it to activate *kuṇḍalinī,* but we find absolutely no physical techniques aimed at prolonging orgasm, maximizing pleasure, and so on. While there *is* such a thing as a Tantrik sexual ritual in the Śaiva tradition, it was taught in only one text out of many hundreds, and it is there called a secret and esoteric doctrine meant for a very few. The Tantrik sexual ritual was primarily a meditative exercise, not a pleasure-maximizing exercise. For more on the difference between original Tantra and the American new-age "Tantric sex" workshops, see page 427. Those workshops are about spiritualized sexuality (not necessarily a bad thing *per se*), whereas original Tantra is about a sensual and embodied *spirituality* (and even then, only in the Kaula schools). What original Tantra is all about will become clear as you continue reading.

OUTLINE OF THE REST OF THE BOOK

In Part 1, after briefly defining nondual Tantra, we will explore all the basic teachings in the philosophy of nondual Śaiva Tantra, especially as they apply to spiritual practitioners in the 21st century. In Part 2, I will give a historical overview of the development of the major branches or schools of Śaiva Tantra—that is, the systems dedicated to Śiva and/or Śakti—with an outline of the characteristics of each branch. Following that, in Part 3, I will delineate the main practices and lived reality of this Tantrik tradition in an introductory manner. All three sections include new translations of passages from the original Sanskrit texts. Finally, there is a conclusion discussing "Undertaking a Tantrik spiritual practice in the modern world" with an afterword on "Survivals of Śaiva Tantra; or, where do I learn more?" You will also find various appendices of interest to the serious student of Tantra.

1
The Philosophy of Nondual Śaiva Tantra

PREFACE

WHAT YOU'RE GETTING YOURSELF INTO

To step into the world of Śaiva Tantra is to enter a world of magic and mystery. Mind-expanding philosophy and arcane rites, pantheons of fierce goddesses embodied in mystic syllables, energy diagrams that map the many dimensions of reality, visualizations of power centers within the body, gestures that express the purest forms of consciousness, nectarean experiences of the sheerest ecstasy, wielders of supernatural power, and concepts that challenge the fundamental norms of ordinary society: these are just some of its features. In short, it is a world that encompasses the entire range of human spiritual and religious activity, from the most elevated and sublime contemplations of our inner nature to the strangest of superstitions. (We'll be focusing on the former more than the latter.) Some people today are interested only in the high philosophy of the Tantra, others in the purely practical techniques, others are curious about the entire historical picture.

Whomever you are, to fully delve into this world, you must not only relinquish any notions of what you think Tantra is but also some of your deeply held assumptions about reality itself. Otherwise, you will never be able to truly understand this particular worldview. Any alternative worldview can function as a critique of the status quo view of reality in our society, but for it to do so in a real and productive way we must—at least temporarily—lay open to question even the fundamental principles by which we create interpretations of phenomena; in other words, we must question the very frameworks with which we create a world for ourselves to live in.

One way to initiate this process is to begin cultivating an awareness that we all live in a world of stories, or narratives. Narratives are the more or less coherent stories that we are told, and we tell ourselves, about the events and people around us in order to make sense of them. All generalizations, statements of value judgment, and verbal representations of reality constitute narratives in this sense. All narratives are *false* in the sense that they are necessarily distortions of reality and *true* in the sense that they bear some relationship to reality, one that can often tell us much about ourselves. For example, if someone says, "The San Francisco Bay Area is a great place to live," we don't usually assume that they have done a careful study of dozens of places to live, cross-referenced against a survey of ordinary people about what constitutes a great place to live. Rather, we know that they have had some specific good experiences living in the Bay Area and have generalized these into a story. Usually, however, we aren't so clear minded about our own stories. When you say, "I have an issue with ____" or "I'm good/bad at ____," you are selectively representing to yourself and others a complex array of past experiences in a way that reduces them to an apparently factual proclamation and implies a permanent state of affairs. Similarly, if you say to someone, "I'm happily married," you are representing and reducing a set of experiences that, if known by the person to whom you are speaking, might not necessarily be described by them as a happy marriage. However, to try to arrive at the "truth" of whether or not the marriage is in fact happy is missing the point entirely—for the only truth is the nature and content of the specific, individual experiences themselves.

Everything else is a story being told about these experiences. So, what type of question does not miss the point? Perhaps one that addresses how and why we represent our experiences with a given narrative about them, and whether or not that narrative is serving us well. For each narrative about the past shapes our experience of the present. While it is true that some narratives better approximate reality than others, the primary value narratives have lies in their usefulness for helping us create the world we want to live in. When they are not doing that, their value is highly questionable.

The Real cannot be adequately captured by language, and therefore all attempts to do so are approximations that have a relative utility.

So like everyone, you have sold yourself a set of stories about how things are and how you are. When a set of stories doesn't meet a person's deepest needs, that person eventually starts seeking new ones. This is where religion or spirituality comes in. A religion is a complex structure of narratives about reality intended to accomplish a specific goal (often labeled as "salvation" or "liberation"). A religion, then, is a metanarrative. When you engage with a spiritual tradition such as Śaiva Tantra, you are inquiring into whether its narratives about reality are sufficiently compelling and effective to warrant overwriting some of your narratives with some of its. (Of course, you are also enquiring into the efficacy of its practical techniques, but these are inseparably joined to its narratives.) According to Śaiva Tantra, embracing a more uplifting interpretation of reality is a necessary step on the way to complete transcendence of all narratives. Unlike the way it is seen by many religions, some branches of Tantra explicitly acknowledge that nothing that can be said in words is complete or absolute Truth. The Real cannot be adequately captured by language, and therefore all attempts to do so are approximations that have a relative utility. An approximation in language (i.e., a narrative) is useful insofar as it ultimately leads you beyond language to a desired *experience* of reality, which is itself a wordless, immediate state of personal revelation.[29] If this is not your goal, then what follows can at least have an intellectual interest for you.

DEFINITION OF NONDUAL ŚAIVA TANTRA

While we will address other Tantrik traditions in the following historical overview, this book takes as its exemplar and focal point the lineages of nondual Śaiva Tantra (pronounced *SHY-vuh TUN-truh*), most clearly typified by the Kaula Trika lineage. Later on, as we move through the history, you will understand how this specific tradition fits into the big picture of the Tantra. To begin, though, I want to define nondual Śaiva Tantra (NŚT for short) as clearly as possible, so you can get oriented to where we're headed and what we're going to focus on (please note in the period we are looking at, the Goddess traditions, sometimes called Śākta Tantra, were not separate from Shaivism. They were considered part of the same religion).

Definition of nondual Śaiva Tantra

My definition of nondual Śaiva Tantra is
A spiritual movement originating in northern India that reached its peak in the 9th to 12th centuries, primarily characterized by

1 Emphasis on direct experience of a divine reality that has transcendent and immanent aspects, called Śiva and Śakti respectively, with Śiva primarily understood as the pure consciousness that is the ultimate ground of being and Śakti as the flowing energy making up the entire manifest universe.

2 Initiation into a guru-disciple relationship and an egalitarian kula (spiritual community).

3 Spiritual practice in four aspects: contemplation of View teachings, meditative ritual, yogic techniques of the subtle body, and the aesthetic cultivation of the senses, all aimed at accessing and assimilating the divine energy in all things, in order to achieve both worldly success and spiritual liberation.[30]

This definition also applies to other forms of nondual Tantra, such as Buddhist forms (though they of course use names for the Divine reality other than Śiva and Śakti, such as Buddha-nature or Dharmakāya). This rather condensed definition will be explained simply now and elaborated later.

NŚT holds that one thing alone exists: the Divine, in various permutations. To say that God alone is real is the same as saying everything that exists is God, everything is divine. In NŚT, to experience this divinity in and as all things is the goal of the practice. The Divine is here taught as having two aspects, the transcendent and the immanent. The transcendent aspect is called **Śiva** (*SHEE-vuh*) and personified as male divinity (sometimes, God). Though Śiva is represented mythologically as having certain characteristics, Tāntrikas (followers of the Tantra) understand Śiva as pure Consciousness: nonpersonal, utterly transcendent of all limitations or qualities, beyond the reach of senses, speech, and mind—in short, the singular Light of Awareness that makes possible all manifestation; the quiescent and peaceful ground of all that is.

To experience divinity in all things is the goal of Tantrik practice.

The immanent aspect of the divine ("immanent" means perceivable through the senses and the mind) is called **Śakti** (*SHUCK-tee*) and personified as female divinity (Goddess). That is, the entire manifest universe is the Goddess, and therefore ought to be reverenced as such. Now, Śiva and Śakti are actually one, not two, but are represented as two because they correspond to two interdependent aspects of reality, one of which is predominant in any given moment of experience. The two different experiences of the Divine represented by Śiva and Śakti are the *enstatic*, in which we turn within, surrender everything, and reach the quiescent and transcendent ground of our being; and the *ecstatic*, in which we express our divine nature in creative, dynamic, outward-going, and embodied ways. According to NŚT, both modes are necessary to fully know the Divine, and a harmonious balance of both is the only true spiritual liberation.

The cultivation of this state of awakened freedom originally took place in the context of a spiritual community guided by a spiritual master. (He was called a master not because he was everyone's boss but because he had completely mastered himself.) Though people were required to take initiation formally in order to have access to the guru and to the scriptures, it is important to note that initiates were not required to renounce their jobs, possessions, or family life. That is to say, the Tantra was mostly a "householder" path, and renunciates were the minority. The practitioners of Tantra were people like you and me, and they dealt with many of the same challenges of everyday life that we face today. They joined a *kula*, or spiritual community that rejected the significance of caste, class, and gender divisions, and they practiced a life-affirming spiritual discipline. This is part of the definition above because NŚT emphasizes the crucial importance of having a teacher, of proper initiation, and of the role of community. We could even say these are indispensable.

The third element of the above definition concerns the type of practice NŚT taught. While meditation, mantras, and ritual are central, these are also found in many other forms of Indian spirituality. What NŚT added was its innovative yogic techniques of the subtle body, plus the revolutionary notion that virtually *anything* can become a form of spiritual practice. This idea is based on the teaching that all things are manifestations of the Goddess. Therefore the body was seen not as a locus of sin and impurity, as in the pre-Tantrik tradition, but rather as a vehicle to realize divine reality. This led to a new emphasis on practices focused on the body and its energies and to the detailed mapping of the structure of the universe onto the body, which was seen as a microcosm of the whole. Likewise, the experiences of the senses were not viewed as distractions from spirituality but as opportunities to engage in divine worship. This was a more effective approach for people living in the world, for spiritual practice was no longer limited to ritual acts or ascetic renunciation. Thus this path was sometimes called "the new and easy method." NŚT teaches that even mundane daily actions like washing the dishes and walking the dog are opportunities for experiencing the joy that flows naturally from the holistic awareness of being in full Presence.

Again, this is just a brief and simplified summary of the attitude NŚT takes to the world and to practice. It is also a definition in the sense that it helps us to know what we're looking at and to differentiate it from other paths. Though NŚT shares many similarities with other nondual mystical paths, we honor the tradition by reserving the word Tantra for the lineage teachings that were based on the revealed scriptures called *tantras*.

ORIENTATION TO THE VIEW

This section serves to summarize the vision of reality that is central to the nondual Śaiva Tantra and which undergirds and empowers all the practices that constitute the path. In the Indian tradition, the first and most crucial step on the spiritual path is getting oriented to the View (*darśana*) of the path that you will walk. The Sanskrit word *darśana* is often translated as "philosophy," but the connotations of that English word miss the mark. *Darśana* means worldview, vision of reality, and way of seeing; it is also a map of the path you will walk. We may understand the importance of View-orientation through an analogy: You might have all the right running gear, a snappy outfit and the best shoes, and you might be in great shape, but none of that will matter if you are running in the wrong direction. By contrast, if you first get properly oriented so that you are moving in the right direction, even if you go slow or have a funny walk, you'll still get there in the end. Thus, orientation to the View is crucial even for those whose interest in the Tantra is entirely practical, for practice

Darśana means worldview, vision of reality, and way of seeing; it is also a map of the path you will walk.

that is not founded on and aligned with right View (*sad-darśana*) is said to be fruitless. Note that "right View" is also the first step of the Noble Eightfold Path of Buddhism.

Now this teaching is not very popular in the West, partially because we value not telling people what to think or believe, but also because the View teachings are not well understood. The popular opinion, then, is that yoga will do its work regardless of what viewpoint you hold, since yoga transcends the mind. This is true but to a very limited extent. It is also true that yoga can only take you so far if its attainments are being used to reinforce a skewed or misaligned view of reality. This explains why some great yogis in medieval India became sorcerers, drunk on power; and why some prominent yogis today, similarly deluded, have manipulated their students and wielded their power for personal gain. Yoga (and even more so Tantrik Yoga) gives power, and that power can magnify whatever is present: it makes a good person into a saint and a jerk into an even greater and more effective jerk. Realizing this fact, which accounts for so much otherwise disillusioning behavior in the world of yoga, we may begin to take a leaf out of ancient India's book and require students to be well-versed in right View before they are considered intermediate, let alone advanced.

Let's get clear: Having right View does not mean the ability to recite doctrine accurately. It means having marinated your mind and heart in the spiritual teachings until they illuminate your experience of reality. It means holding the teachings close until they become your beloved friends and allies, your unfailing supports. It means being able to offer them to others in your own way, through your own unique words and actions. (Note well though, being a good speaker of the View does not necessarily indicate inner attainment.) Finally, it means having seen through the pitfalls of wrong understanding that drain the teachings of their uplifting power.

Of course there is not only *one* right View. Each practice tradition has a range of possibilities for right View (a broader range on some issues and a narrower range on others), straying from which will take you off the path sooner or later. As a deceptively simple Chinese proverb has it, "Be careful where you're going, because you might end up there." If you stop and think about it, you'll see this makes sense. Just as wrong alignment in a yoga pose will cause damage to your body sooner or later, in the same way having an understanding which is not aligned with your real goal will be at best ineffective and at worst will take you into deep delusion. Since practice happens every day, misalignments have a slow but huge cumulative effect over time. There must be alignment of View, practice, and fruit for this path to work. If you know anyone who has practiced for years and is not a highly developed, stable, kind, clear, relaxed, and open person, it is because of a lack of alignment of these three, view, practice, and fruit. It is never too late, but the longer the misalignment has been there, the harder it can be to correct.

There must be alignment of View, practice, and fruit for this path to work.

An objection that is sometimes raised concerning the process of learning and imbibing View teachings is that as practitioners we wish to become free of all mental constructs, so why would we add more to the already considerable load of ideas we are carrying? The ancient teachers were very much aware of this objection and clarified that we cannot leap from a flawed foundation straight into freedom from mental constructs. Right View, in alignment with our goal, is precisely that View which can empower us to first release our distorted views and then to go beyond constructed views altogether. As we proceed, you will start to understand how this is possible.

I will conclude these prefatory comments by giving just one real-life example to help to dissolve any remaining skepticism about the value of View teaching. The great master Abhinava Gupta suggests to us that if you practice yoga from the perspective that you are not good enough as you are, or that there is something wrong with you that needs fixing, then your yoga cannot fulfill its ultimate purpose because it is a practice founded on wrong understanding. It can only go as far as fulfilling the limited purpose that has been conceived by your limited ego-mind. However, if you undertake the practice of yoga with the right View of yourself, that you already are a perfect and whole expression of the Divine and that you are doing yoga to realize and then fully express what is already true, then you have empowered your practice to take you all the way. This shift into right View can happen at any time; and when it does, the rocket fuel added to your progress will be proof enough of what I have said about the value of right View. In fact, only experiential proof is valid in this domain; I make arguments with words only to satisfy your mind that the experiment is worth conducting.

Now that we have been oriented to the necessity of View-orientation, we are ready to encounter the core View of nondual Śaiva Tantra. First I will present a condensed, high-octane paragraph that contains the whole of the View in seed form. After that, I will unpack that paragraph in more detail. Engage your intuitive and poetic faculty more strongly as you read the seed paragraph, reading slowly and carefully, letting the words sink in regardless of whether you fully understand them mentally. Your intellectual faculty can engage more fully for the unpacking of this initial paragraph. You may wish to reread this orientation section more than once; at the same time, don't feel that you have to understand everything before moving on.

Now let's dive in together, beginning at the very core: what is the true nature of reality?

THE VIEW

All that exists, throughout all time and beyond, is one infinite divine Consciousness, free and blissful, which projects within the field of its awareness a vast multiplicity of apparently differentiated subjects and objects: each object an actualization of a timeless potentiality inherent in the Light of Consciousness, and each subject, you and I, the same plus a contracted locus of self-awareness. This creation, a divine play, is the result of the natural impulse within Consciousness to express the totality of its self-knowledge in action, an impulse arising from love. The unbounded Light of Consciousness contracts into finite embodied loci of awareness out of its own free will. When those finite subjects then identify with the limited and circumscribed cognitions and circumstances that make up this phase of their existence, instead of identifying with the transindividual overarching pulsation of pure Awareness that is their true nature, they experience what they call "suffering." To rectify this, some feel an inner urge to take up the path of spiritual wisdom and yogic practice, the purpose of which is to undermine their misidentification and directly reveal within the immediacy of awareness the fact that the divine powers of Consciousness, Bliss, Willing, Knowing, and Acting comprise the totality of individual experience as well—thereby triggering a recognition that one's real identity is that of the highest Divinity, the Whole in every part. This experiential insight is repeated and reinforced through various means until it becomes the nonconceptual ground of every moment of experience, and one's contracted sense of self and separation from the Whole is finally annihilated in the incandescent radiance of the complete expansion into perfect wholeness. Then one's perception fully encompasses the reality of a universe dancing ecstatically in the animation of its completely perfect divinity.

UNPACKING THE VIEW

All that exists, has ever existed or will ever exist, is one infinite divine Being, free and blissful, whose body is the universe and whose soul is consciousness. This philosophy, then, can be called *theistic monism,* which means

1) the view that only one thing really exists—i.e., that every person and object exists as a form or aspect of one basic reality (monism)—and
2) that that basic reality has an innate capacity for self-awareness, and therefore it can be called a being, a being whose nature is unbounded by any form of limitation (theism).

All sentient beings, seen and unseen, are simply different forms of one divine Consciousness.

Though problematic, the only word we have in English to denote a completely unbounded conscious being is "God." Thus all sentient beings, seen and unseen, are simply different forms of one divine Consciousness, which looks out at the universe that is its own body through uncountable pairs of eyes. To make it personal: you are not separate from God/dess, the Divine, and never have been. *Indeed, you are the very means by which She knows Herself.*

This philosophy holds that the basic principle of reality—the foundation of all that is, that to which all things are reducible and which is not itself reducible to anything else—is conscious Awareness. This is argued for in the following manner: We cannot demonstrate the existence of any reality that is not the content of some being's experience, and all experiences by definition take place within awareness and are permeated by awareness. Thus everything and anything we can point to as having any existence whatsoever—whether commonly held realities, like what we call the external world, or your own personal reality, such as your dreams and visions—all of that exists within the field of awareness. To posit the existence of something that no one is aware of is nonsense, for as soon as you posit it, you are necessarily aware of it. (If you say, "Well, what about things out there in the universe that scientists have proven the existence of but no one has ever seen?" then you have confused consciousness with perception. If the physicist has modeled the outer-space object mathematically, then he is necessarily aware of it.)

So far the proposition is quite logical; the specific spiritual assertion here is that all limited consciousnesses (e.g., you and me) are merely vantage points within *one* all-encompassing and unbroken field of awareness. Actually, this too is logical, because if we were each separate islands of consciousness, discontinuous with the rest, we would not be able to communicate with each other or even share the same reality. There could not be any coherence by which we could call reality a *universe* if it was perceived by more than one perceiver. Thus there is only one Perceiver and only one Doer in all of existence. Still, I call this assertion "spiritual" because there is no way to prove it except through your inner spiritual experience, which will prove it to you and you alone.

Each of us is a vantage point within one all-encompassing and unbroken field of awareness.

In other words, the nature of Consciousness is such that each given embodiment of it can, through empowered reflection, come to realize its nature; but there is no proof of its nature other than this individual internal process, precisely because this Consciousness is prior to, and the basis of, all "proofs." From the perspective of the nonduality of Consciousness, then, the attempt to scientifically prove or validate our spirituality is absurd, because all science presupposes Consciousness but not the other way around.

Another way of explaining this teaching is to say that all things are part of one vast field of energy, called the Light of Creation or the Light of Consciousness *(prakāśa)*. This field of energy, vibrating at an incalculable number of different frequencies, is all that really exists. It is also called the Ocean of Awareness. Though we are experiencing it (and nothing but it) all the time, we do not realize that we are. We are like the fish in the story, asking skeptically, "What is this thing called water?" The last thing a fish would contemplate is the very medium of its existence. *An ordinary being notices least that which is the greatest constant in his life.* So, we pay little attention to the nature of the one thing present in every single experience: Consciousness. We don't perceive the fullness and potency of the divine reality in which we constantly partake because we exist in a state of contracted awareness, our powers limited and our perception narrowed to a tiny bandwidth.

All things are part of one vast field of energy, called the Light of Creation or the Light of Consciousness.

To put it briefly, our brains synthesize an experience of reality through our limited senses, each of which functions as a different type of frequency analyzer directed at this fluxing field of energy all around us (and which we are not separate from). Sentient beings like us are simply nodal points of self-awareness, recursive movements of energy in an otherwise undifferentiated dynamic field. As thinking beings, we perform analytic and synthetic mental operations in our contemplation of reality. Some of those operations rigidify, becoming more or less durable and persistent mental constructs, which we then use as filters to select and interpret what we think is significant in reality, thereby narrowing further our already limited spectrum of perception. Then we make the final error of believing that the interpretive constructs we superimpose on reality *are* reality itself, instead of what they actually are, imperfect representations that served a particular need at a particular time. This wrong understanding causes us untold suffering. Indeed, it is the only cause of suffering.

If the last paragraph was dense for you, don't worry, it will be unpacked further as we go along.

THE NAMES OF THE ULTIMATE REALITY

This divine Consciousness is called by various names in the texts of the tradition. When talking about it as God, it is called Śiva or more commonly Parameśvara, "the highest Divinity." But the nondualist scriptures usually prefer other names for it, because this is a principle that far transcends (even as it includes) any notion of a personal God. Some of these follow.

The names of the nondual Divine (= Śiva-Śakti in perfect fusion)

the Heart (*hṛdaya*)	Potency (*sāmarthya*)
the Essence (*sāra*)	Experience (*bhoga*)
the Vibration (*spanda*)	the Fierce One (*caṇḍī*)
Absolute Potential (*visarga*	the Supreme Power (*parā śakti*)
the Bliss of Awareness (*cidānanda*)	the Devourer of Time (*kālakarṣiṇī*)
the All-Pervasive (*vibhava*)	the Word (*vāk*)
the Totality (*kula*)	the Wave (*ūrmi*)
Intimate Fusion (*saṅghaṭṭa*)	the Eternal (*nityā*)
Vision (*dṛk*)	the Nameless (*anākhya*)

We are told that the Absolute has many names so that at least one of them will spontaneously penetrate the inner awareness of the practitioner. Of these, NŚT's preferred name for the supreme principle of reality is the Heart.*

* We must distinguish Heart, the core of being, from the emotional center. See page 92.

However, since the Tantrik masters do frequently use the word "God" or "Divinity," it is important to define exactly what that means in this context, for it is something quite different from what the word means in the minds of many Westerners. Abhinava Gupta offers us a nondual definition of "God" in his *Essence of the Tantras:*

Essence of the Tantras

In actuality it is only the unbounded Light of Consciousness, reposing in innate bliss, endowed with the Powers of Willing, Knowing, and Acting, that we call God.

This profound statement will be unpacked in the pages to come.

THE ESSENTIAL NATURE OF THE DIVINE

Now, this infinite all-pervading Divine Consciousness is absolutely free and independent (*svatantra*) and, in its self-aware mode, is spontaneously blissful (*ānanda*). Because you are not separate from That, your true nature is also free and blissful, though you are usually not aware of it, for reasons we will come to. Suffice to say now that the process of *sādhanā* (spiritual practice) is simply about removing the impediments to your ability to see yourself as you really are and accessing the blissful freedom that is always already your real being.

THE ACTIVITY OF THE DIVINE

Creation is a projection within the infinite field of a single Consciousness.

We have established that the fundamental nature of all beings is divine, and we have established what the Divine is—a completely autonomous blissful awareness. So, what does it actually do? Its activity is also fundamental to its identity, and that activity is of course the creation (and dissolution) of the manifest universe. But what is creation, really? It is nothing but the projection, the flowing forth, *within* the infinite field of Consciousness, of a vast multiplicity of apparently differentiated subjects and objects. Let's define this subject-object pole, this basic apparent twoness that the One appears as. Each object (= something that can be known) is an actualization of a timeless potentiality inherent in the Light of Consciousness (*prakāśa*). That is to say, each object is an embodiment of some facet of the One's infinite being. Each subject (= any knower, a sentient being like you) also embodies that Light of Consciousness, but is further a reflexive movement of self-awareness, a specifically defined mode of the One's self-reflection (*vimarśa*). That is, you (and every sentient being) incarnate a unique way for the One to reflect on its Self.

REFLECTION (VIMARŚA) AND RECOGNITION (PRATYABHIJÑĀ)

A few more words about this crucial principle. We said above that everything that exists is a manifestation of the one Light. Some embodiments of that Light, then, also have the capacity to enfold awareness and reflect on themselves or on other aspects of the Light in relation to themselves. These are what we call sentient beings, those nodal points of the energy field that can, as it were, fold light back onto itself in the act of self-reflection or self-representation (*vimarśa*). And we can understand the term "self-reflection" both figuratively and literally here, for the self-aware being realizes that all other beings are reflections of herself, as she is also a reflection of them, and that all are reflections of the one Self. For this reason, *vimarśa* can also be translated as "representation," for it is the process by which Consciousness *re-presents* itself to itself in various forms, as part of its overarching play of self-awareness and self-love.

Sentient beings are those that can self-reflect and can see others as reflections of themselves.

Thus for a sentient being, every encounter with any other being is an opportunity for reflecting on his own total nature. Recognizing yourself in the other being, and the other being in yourself, necessarily involves an expansion of your sense of identity. That is, it entails a realization that you have artificially limited yourself to a set of mental constructs (such as any set of "I am" statements), and this realization is simultaneously an opportunity for the expansion of that limited sense of identity. The process of expansion continues until you experience yourself in *all* things, and all things in yourself—the unbounded state of absolute fullness (*pūrṇatā*) that is oneness with the Divine and final realization. Then, you no longer perceive yourself as a mother or an American or a doctor or a yogī but rather as the pattern of the whole universe currently playing a given role and no more identified with it than the actor on stage believes he is really Hamlet, even as he plays his part passionately.

This perspective brings a sense of meaning and presence to even the simplest acts. For when you sit and contemplate a pebble, what is really happening is that *the universe is contemplating itself in that form.* Your perception of yourself as somehow separate from the Whole is nothing but ignorance. This was the revelation had by a certain physicist who one day realized that, though he studies fundamental particles (protons, electrons, neutrons), he himself was composed of the very same particles. He saw that because the universe is one continuous whole, his study of physics is nothing other than the universe contemplating itself. Yet to accomplish this act, the universe must temporarily alienate part of itself from the whole in order to turn and look at itself; and the process is not complete, he saw, until that portion turns its capacity for contemplation upon itself, collapsing subject and object, and thus reintegrating itself with the Whole, which it actually never left.[31]

The act of creation is called a divine play since it is a free and joyous act of self-expression.

To recap, then, this infinite Consciousness chooses not to remain static homogenous formless nothingness but rather condenses itself into form, manifesting itself (within the field of its own awareness) as a vast multiplicity of *apparently* differentiated subjects and objects, thus initiating a vast dance of self-exploration. Now, this act of creation is called a **divine play** or game (*krīḍā*), in the sense that this activity is fundamentally a free and joyous act of self-expression, done entirely for its own sake. The word "play" is simply used to indicate an activity that has no purpose outside of itself, as well as pointing toward the notion that joy and love underlie and motivate the whole process. (For God so loved Herself, we could say, that She gave form to every aspect of Her being. For God so loved the world, that She became it.) The doctrine of play shows us that the Tantrik View is *not* evolutionary, that it does not hold that reality will be intrinsically better or more beautiful at some future point (though your individual capacity to experience its beauty *is* always evolving!). The whole of divine reality is expressed fully in each moment. Rather than "play," the Tāntrikas could have used the word "art" to express this understanding—for that word has connotations of creativity and beauty that are central to their vision of reality—except that art is often thought of as representing something else, and the universe stands for nothing but itself. Furthermore, "art" implies artifice, while "play" or perhaps "artful play" better expresses the organic, spontaneous, dynamic quality with which the universe unfolds and, as well, alludes to the childlike wonder experienced by those who see it as it really is. Our discussions here are neatly summarized by the verse that concludes chapter 1 of *Essence of the Tantras:*

> *This Self is an embodiment of the Light of Consciousness; it is Śiva, free and autonomous. As an independent play of intense joy, the Divine conceals its own true nature [by manifesting plurality], and may also choose to reveal its fullness once again at any time.*[32]

Essence of the Tantras

Thus, this play of manifest creation, in which the Divine freely bodies itself forth as the universe, is the result of an impulse, a natural creative urge (*icchā*) within the Divine to express the totality of its self-knowledge (*jñāna*) in action (*kriyā*). These, then, are the three primary Powers (*śaktis*) of God, the three that denote what Śiva-Śakti *does*, as opposed to the even more basic triad above that denotes what Śiva-Śakti *is* (i.e., Consciousness, Bliss, and Freedom). The three Powers of Willing, Knowing, and Acting naturally unfold in precisely that sequence, for the precognitive creative impulse toward joyful self-expression (*icchā*) must come first, surging up from the core of Being; and then it must equip itself with understanding (*jñāna*), i.e., with information about how energy flows most effectively in embodied forms; and then it can engage in empowered activity (*kriyā*), inevitably achieving its consummation. This process unfolds in each instant on all scales.

Śiva-consciousness rejoices equally in happiness and sorrow, for both poles equally express its divine Being.

The natural question that most people have at this point is something like, "If this whole world is nothing but the free and voluntary self-expression of the divine Light, why is life so hard?" The problem with this question is that it demonstrates a lack of understanding of nonduality, for it can only be asked by a mind that does not include "hard" as an aspect of divine Light, one that is as beneficial and blessed in its own way as "easy" or "happy." To put it another way, divine consciousness rejoices equally in pain or pleasure, in happiness or sorrow, for both poles equally express its divine Being. God loves the whole of the creation that is himself, and since you are not separate from God, you have the capacity to love the whole of reality as well. This, of course, is the "tough nut" of nondual philosophy, and it cannot be resolved through intellectual understanding (which is rooted in duality), but only through a state of nondual experience brought about by dedicated spiritual practice. With this in mind, let's explore a little more the perspective on suffering in NŚT.

Suffering is a result of your ignorance of your own true nature.

The View states, "When that divine Consciousness contracts into finite embodied loci of awareness, out of its own free will, and those finite subjects then identify with the limited and circumscribed cognitions that make up this phase of their existence, instead of identifying with the transindividual overarching pulsation of pure Awareness that is their true nature, they experience what they call 'suffering'."

Let's break that statement down. It is simply saying that suffering is a result of your ignorance of your own true nature. Here we must distinguish suffering from pain. There's nothing wrong with pain; it is both natural and beautiful. Natural in that it is a feedback mechanism by which nature protects us, and beautiful when it shows us our aliveness. For example, the intensity of the pain you feel when a loved one passes away is another form of your love for them—experienced in that way, it becomes a thing of sharp beauty. Suffering, however, is a mental state we could represent with statements like "This sucks!" "I hate this," "I wish this wasn't happening," or "I don't deserve this!" Most of what is unpleasant about human existence is not pain, but mind-created suffering. And we can be free of this suffering, for the Tantric scriptures tell us it is entirely a product of ignorance, of *not seeing things as they truly are.* The primary form of this ignorance is our misidentification of ourselves. This misidentification is a kind of forgetting: God incarnates as you, and in order to specifically become you, She has to forget the rest of her vast all-encompassing being. In other words, to fully manifest the particular aspect of herself that you are, She has to temporarily let go of all the other aspects of herself. This is the self-concealment mentioned in Abhinava's verse above.

So, here you are: What you see of yourself, what you know of yourself, is simply the tip of a massive iceberg (to use one analogy). You look around, and all you can see is what shows above the water, so you assume that's all there is. Yet, the sages tell us, the pattern of the whole universe, of all that is, is imprinted on the deepest level of your being. You are not only part of the whole, *you are the Whole.* Realizing this brings the experience of joyous freedom because you perceive that with infinite options available to Her, *Consciousness chose to become you.* And furthermore, you are not a static entity but a dancing pattern of energy, an unfolding process—a perfect and integral instantiation of the divine process by which God reflects on herself and expresses herself.

You are not only part of the whole, *you are the Whole.*

To attain all the fulfillment you've ever dreamed of and more, you simply need to see the truth of your own Being: that infinite potential exists within you, for you are an expression of the Divine, and whatever manifests through you in this life, though not infinite, is to be honored as what you alone can add to the ever-expanding process of God's grand self-exploration. Suffering will automatically fall away when you are able to simultaneously honor what is currently manifesting through you (the tip of your iceberg) as well as the whole of your divine being, a fullness you may not be able to "see" but can learn to palpably feel. Abhinava gives this teaching in the summary verse of the introduction to his *Essence of the Tantras:*

Essence of theTantras

> *Tradition teaches us that ignorance is the sole cause of bondage: it is taught under the name "impurity" in scripture. When the power of all-encompassing insight arises, it is completely uprooted. With the arising of the full consciousness of the Self, by which all apparent impurity is destroyed, there is automatically liberation.*[33]

Those who gain an intimation of the fact that they are not seeing the full picture of reality will at some point feel an inner urge (*icchā*) to take up the path of the cultivation of spiritual wisdom (*jñāna*) and practice (*kriyā*). The purpose of walking the spiritual path, from the nondual Tantrik perspective, is simply to undermine your misidentification and directly reveal within the immediacy of your awareness the fact that the divine Powers of Consciousness, Bliss, Willing, Knowing, and Acting comprise the totality of your individual experience as well—thereby triggering a recognition that your true identity is that of the highest Divinity, the Whole in every part.

Let's unpack that. The purpose of spiritual practice could not be to attain union with God, for you already are one with the divine reality, and it couldn't be otherwise. Neither is its purpose to make you more beautiful or more perfect, for nothing exists that is not God, so you cannot be more beautiful or more perfect than you already are in this moment. Yet you are not currently experiencing reality that way, due to your misperception of yourself. So, the primary purpose of spiritual practice is to destabilize deep-seated, skewed mental constructs about yourself, constructs that you also project onto others in your life. These visions of reality are not in alignment with the Truth and therefore debilitate you. The process of undermining false views through practice continues until they are seen for what they are and begin to fall apart. When your obscuring mental constructs fall away, you automatically see yourself as you really are: a free being of blissful consciousness, playing with your powers of intent, understanding, and action.

When you see yourself clearly, there comes a flash of recognition: you are a microcosmic expression of precisely the same divine powers that create, maintain, and dissolve this whole universe. When you *experientially* realize that the same beautiful and awesome powers that orchestrate the intricate and wondrous display of this entire creation are flowing within you, creating you even as you create with them, providing the very foundation of your whole experience of reality, there is a profound shift. Your fear and pettiness drop away as you harmoniously fall into the dance of life energy, realizing that you have been the only one who has ever limited your potential. An explosion of joy accompanies the realization that there is nothing to do, nothing to achieve, other than to fully embrace the divine powers that seek to manifest through you by expressing the entirety of your authentic being in the fullness of each moment, in an endless flow of such moments.

This state of awareness in which you are completely in tune with reality, immersed in your divine nature, is called *samāveśa*. You have touched this state, however fleetingly or incompletely, many times in your life. Recognize it as that state in which you are fully present with yourself and your surroundings, relaxed yet focused, expansive and

Samāveśa is the state of awareness in which you are immersed in your divine nature.

free yet grounded in your real situation—embracing the reality of what is in the now. What is important about this state, from the Tantrik perspective, is not so much how good it feels but what you learn from it and how you grow from integrating it.

Is it really possible to be in such a state—that we may call Presence—all the time, or are the uppermost reaches of human potential impossible to sustain? The answer given by the Tantra is that it is, indeed, possible for Presence to become your default state. This does not imply that it is a static condition or that it does not need refreshing. Nevertheless, just as your default perception of reality is currently one of subject/object duality, with occasional revelations of the unity of being, that situation can become reversed, even permanently reversed, because unity is in fact the more fundamental reality. So, we may say that spiritual practice serves to repeat and reinforce experiential knowing of the Truth through various methods, until this vision of reality becomes the nonconceptual ground of every moment of your experience. That means it has passed beyond the level of philosophy and religion, beyond the level of words and thought, and has become a vibrating reality at the foundation of your being, spontaneously illuminating all that you experience. When this happens, your contracted sense of self and separation from the Whole is finally annihilated in the incandescent radiance of complete expansion into all-embracing perfect wholeness (*pūrṇatā*). Then, as Abhinava Gupta tells us, *your perception fully encompasses the reality of a universe dancing ecstatically in the animation of its completely perfect divinity.* This is liberation. This is awakening to the Truth. This is why you took birth.

Let your perception fully encompass the reality of a universe dancing ecstatically in the animation of its completely perfect divinity.
— Abhinava Gupta

THOUGHTS TO LIVE BY

THE BASIC PHILOSOPHICAL FRAMEWORK OF NONDUAL ŚAIVA TANTRA

Philosophers use a handful of special terms to denote the central questions contemplated by those who wish to understand reality. We will learn them now because they are conveniently precise and concise, and besides, you can impress your friends with them.

ONTOLOGY – What is the fundamental nature of reality? What is "being"? What can we say about existence?
EPISTEMOLOGY – How do we know anything? What are the valid means of knowledge? How can we test what we think we know?
TELEOLOGY – Is there a specific purpose to existence? Is it evolving toward an end point? Are things progressing?
PHENOMENOLOGY – What is the nature of conscious experience? Does the content and quality of our moment-to-moment experiences give us any access to enduring truth(s)?
THEODICY – If there is a God, how do we explain suffering? What is the purpose of evil? How can evil and suffering exist if the all-pervasive Divine is fundamentally good?

We will explore each of these questions briefly in plain and accessible language. I should mention that the mode of our discussion here is not straight philosophy but what is called *philosophical theology* because it includes the Divine as an axiom, or at least a variable, in the mix.

Furthermore, some of these questions—which are all central to Western philosophy as well—are not addressed in a systematic manner in the Tantrik literature but through a variety of sometimes cryptic statements that I have wrestled with over the years. So, I am particularly grateful to one of my teachers, Ādyashānti, for clarifications of several of these issues, explanations that deeply connected to both my contemplated experience and my scriptural study.

ONTOLOGY

The topic of ontology (and the related ones of cosmology and metaphysics) is partially covered in the summary of the View, and it will be further explored in "The Categories of Tantrik Thought," so we will not address it separately here.

See page 91

EPISTEMOLOGY

One of the central concerns of philosophy is to investigate how we know what we know, if there is such a thing as certain knowledge, and, if so, how it is attained. This is a topic of concern to the Tantra as well, and it is explored in depth by the scholar-sages Utpala Deva and Abhinava Gupta. The difficult and abstruse nature of these discussions invite us to focus on a simpler formulation offered by the second author in his *Essence of the Tantras*. There Abhinava tells us that the process of creative contemplation or holistic meditative inquiry (*bhāvanā-krama*) that leads to experiential knowing of reality is based on these three supports:

- sound and careful reflection on your experience (sat-tarka)
- the guidance of a great teacher (sad-guru) who is skilled in meditative enquiry and has attained its fruit
- the wisdom of the scriptures (sad-āgama)

When these three come together in agreement, Abhinava suggests, we know we have arrived at truth. Your own contemplated experience, the words of your teacher and the wisdom of the scriptures. When these three are in agreement, we know we've arrived at truth. One or two of them is insufficient for certainty. In fact, allowing ourselves to abide in uncertainty about anything not supported by all three keeps us open and in a process of learning that closes down if we prematurely decide that we know how things are.

Usually in Indian philosophy, the first two valid means of knowledge that are argued for are direct perception and valid inference; those two are here combined into *sat-tarka*, which means the process of drawing sound conclusions based on one's experience. In logic (both Western and Indian), a conclusion is "sound" when the premises are true and the structure of thought leading to the conclusion is valid. To give a slightly modified version of the standard Indian example of a logical argument:

> **Premise 1:** Where there is smoke, there is fire (axiom based on the aggregate of one's experiences).
> **Premise 2:** There is smoke on the mountain over there (direct observation).
> **Conclusion:** Therefore, there is fire on the mountain.

The foundation of all philosophy is a sense of wonder and openness.

The argument is called *valid* structurally because if the premises are true, the conclusion must also be true. But it is only *sound* (= correct) if the premises *are* in fact true. And this particular argument is an example of inference because there is no way to be one hundred per cent sure that there is always fire whenever and wherever there is smoke. The standard argument in the Indian system of logic is not deduction, which seeks to establish irrefutable certainty, but inference. Unlike in Western philosophy, in the Indian system you never decide that you know for sure, and so you never completely close yourself to unguessed possibilities. Thus the sense of wonder and openness that is the foundation of all philosophy is maintained. Just because all the swans you've seen are white doesn't mean that there's no such thing, for sure, as a swan that's not white. This is the open-endedness of inferential reasoning.

The problem of direct experience as a means of knowledge is that people often draw conclusions based on their experience that are logically invalid. They don't realize they are doing so because their assumptions and the process by which they draw their conclusions usually go unexamined. Even more basically, they are often unable to separate their experience from their interpretation. People can get ruffled when their interpretation of their experience is questioned, saying, "But that's my experience!" In fact, anything you can say in words about your experience is an interpretation, not the experience itself. On the path of inquiry into truth, we never devalue or dispense with reflection on our personal experience (note that Abhinava mentions it first), yet since we cannot be one hundred per cent certain about the conclusions we draw or how universally applicable they are, we soften our iron grip on our apparently safe and comfortable sense of certainty and seek to corroborate it or test it with trusted authorities: the teacher and sacred scripture.

To some Westerners, having the spiritual teacher and scripture as the other two legs of this epistemological tripod seems redundant. But this system of checks and balances is well worked out. Scripture exists as a representative document of a whole community; because even if a given scripture was written by just one person, it is transmitted (copied and recopied) for centuries if and only if some of its contents are effective for a wider group of people. As a document of collective wisdom perpetuated by community, scripture protects you from an aberrant teacher who preaches his own idiosyncratic experience as if it were universal, thereby potentially leading you astray. Of course, for this setup to work, you must read a scripture with your own judgment, your own critical faculty, not solely on the basis of the teacher's interpretation of it.

On the other hand, though scriptures are presumed to have been written by an awakened master, a healthy skepticism is maintained by requiring their wisdom to be corroborated by the other two sources of knowledge. Further, the requirement of the living teacher means that you are protected from an off-the-wall interpretation of scripture that you might arrive at in your own head. Such an interpretation might make sense to you, might even feel good, but is seen by a teacher with insight and clear long-term view to be one that will eventually take you off track. Such a teacher will rarely say, "You're wrong," but will more likely challenge you to contemplate deeper, beyond the limits of your conditioned mind.

This system of double corroboration for valid knowledge allows us to come up with seeds of wisdom that we can count on and build a spiritual life on. But the process is not completed until these seeds come to life as living, vibrating wisdom within us. That is, in the Tantra, we seek not just to know wisdom but to fully embody it. The evidence that you have done so is that you no longer need the external form of the teaching (the words or concepts); it has simply blossomed into living experience, unsupported by any reminders. When this happens, then no matter how beautiful the words of the teaching are, they seem to be flat or pale or inadequate in comparison with the actual experience. We discuss this final, subtle criterion for true wisdom elsewhere in the book.

In Tantra we seek not just to know wisdom but to fully embody it.

See page 356 and following

TELEOLOGY

Many religions are *teleological*, that is, they say there is a purpose to life, a purpose to the creation of the universe, a Grand Plan. This vision of things usually entails the notion that things will one day be better, both for you personally (such as when you die and go to heaven) and for the whole world (such as when the savior comes). NŚT is unusual, then, in denying and/or challenging teleology. It clearly denies teleology of the second kind, on the universal scale, for it teaches that the fullness of divine reality is present here and now: there is no future moment when God will be more fully revealed than it already is. This antiteleological stance is called the doctrine of divine play, Lila, or *krīḍā*, mentioned above. The universe is said to be a divine play

There is no future moment when God will be more fully revealed than S/He already is.

Joy (*ānanda*) is loving acceptance of any and every present-moment reality.

not in the sense that it is always fun (obviously) but rather in the strict sense of the word "play," that is, anything done *for its own sake* rather than for an after-the-fact result. And it is a play in another sense, in that there exists the *possibility* for joy (*ānanda*) in any and every experience, though some yield up that potential more easily than others. By joy here I do not mean "extreme happiness," but rather a kind of loving acceptance of any given present-moment reality. The Heart has an innate capacity to grant a deep affirmation of whatever is going on in this moment, to envelop the whole of each experience in loving awareness (even experiences that the mind might despise). When the heart exercises that capacity, it is called *ānanda.*

See pages 105–107

It is not all that surprising that the Tantra denies universal teleology, since Indian philosophy has always seen time as cyclical rather than linear. However, there is a kind of individual teleology in this tradition, seen in the claim that spiritual awakening and the initiation that follows it guarantee your eventual liberation. This is on the one hand a claim intended to ensure the success of the religion, but on the other hand it acknowledges a deep truth: the process of awakening to your real divine nature, once set in motion, will inevitably bear its fruit. Even if you reject and scorn the path totally, it is argued, eventually divine grace will prevail and you will find your way back to the path, even if it's in a future life. This is partially because once the power of full awakening has been glimpsed, even if the memory of it lies dormant, nothing else will seem totally worthwhile in comparison.

See pages 321–341

This notion of the inevitability of the process gives rise to two possible misunderstandings. First, that nothing need be done by one who desires liberation, and second, that the process leading to liberation is necessarily a gradual progression. These misunderstandings are corrected by two teachings. The first is that the process unfolds through a combination of grace and self-effort. Grace ensures that the conditions for its unfolding are met; self-effort determines the speed and efficiency of the process. Self-effort takes the form of the cultivation of insight or yogic practice or (more commonly) both. Without self-effort, the blossoming of your awakening occurs at an infinitesimal rate. At the same time, if your effort has the quality of striving hard toward a distant goal, you are wasting a lot of energy. The effort in question here is the gentle effort required to no longer hold on to your limited knowledge and self-images.

Awakening to your real nature is not the result of a certain specific amount of spiritual practice.

The second teaching is linked to the first. Though the process of your liberation unfolds gradually, at any moment it may complete itself through a sudden leap of all-encompassing insight. This is possible because awakening to your real nature is not the result of a certain specific *amount* of spiritual practice. Furthermore, if we consider full awakeness as a far distant goal, to be attained after much striving, then that is what it will be. Instead, we are invited to gently hold the awareness, that it could be as close as our next breath—and then to take the next breath as an opening to that possibility.

But, we protest: it can't be that close, because I have so much work on myself to do, so many unresolved issues and unhealed wounds. In so protesting, we forget that our real nature, by definition, is always available to us in some measure. Accessing it does not depend on solving any problem or healing any wound. (Though it is also true that those wounds, or rather our beliefs about them, can impede the recognition that this divine core is our real being—and this recognition is necessary to end our habitual return to the limited story of the separate self.) This understanding is crucial, for when people hear about the possibility of liberation, they almost always imagine that such a thing could only be the result of solving their problems and healing their wounds. But your real nature was never wounded, so why should accessing it be dependent on completing your therapy? This misunderstanding leads to putting the cart before the horse, and devoting an inordinate amount of energy to figuring out and fixing a "self" that is not the real you.

In fact, what often happens is this: you wake up out of the false belief that the limited, conditioned self is you, and *then* that limited self—whose locus is the mind—slowly begins to reflect the new state of affairs. That is, the mind begins to align itself to the vibration of your real nature, now that the power of your awareness is focused there instead of on the mind. Though awakening can happen in a moment, there is a (sometimes lengthy) period of integration as the mind dissolves some belief structures and reorganizes others to come into harmony with the new realization that it is not what it thought it was—that it is not the real you. Depending on the type of awakening you've had, this process can be easeful or deeply disorienting and unsettling. If the latter, there needs to be frequent remembering that it is just the mind that is unsettled, for in your real Self or essence-nature, you are always completely okay.

At this point, we need some clarification to avoid the problem of "spiritual bypassing," whereby some people say, "I don't need to work on myself at all because my real nature is unconditioned Light, not this messy mind that has nothing to do with the real Me." This is a near-enemy to truth that turns into a dangerous delusion, and it is countered by the following teaching. As described above, you first wake up to your individual essence-nature, that is, the way God vibrates uniquely in and as you, unaffected by all your conditioning. Second, the mind or conditioned self needs to come into alignment with this essence-nature or else you end up with a kind of split personality: a divine you and a messed-up you. There is no integration. No matter how good you are at accessing the divine you, the messed-up mind keeps getting triggered by life situations, and that is what other people experience from you. So, even if you have access to your divine core, if its energy is not flowing forth and blessing your mind and body and others around you, you are not liberated. Tantra utterly rejects the goal of Patañjali's yoga, that of retreating to and dwelling in a divine soul that is safely removed and cut off from the world and other people. Therefore, awakening is not complete until the body-

Your individual essence-nature is the way God vibrates uniquely in and as you.

mind is clear and strong and healed enough to be a vessel for the flowing forth of the divine energy of the Core. Tantra seeks to develop a "healthy ego," which is a servant of the divine Core. But as mentioned, that strengthening and healing of the body-mind is far easier and more joyful once there has been some degree of awakening to your essence-nature, which is why the latter is given priority. When your individual awakening and corresponding liberation of the body-mind are complete (called *āṇava-samāveśa*), only then can you properly proceed to the next level of awakening, that of unity with all things, in which your individual divinity is realized as an expression of universal divinity, and thus dissolves into the universal field of energy (a realization called *śākta-samāveśa*).

Tantra seeks to develop a "healthy ego" which is a servant of the divine Core.

For the Tantra, awakening (*bodha*) and liberation (*mokṣa*) are real, and they are the key concepts that drive the whole of the spiritual life. But there is a subtle and significant point here: as concepts, as goals, as destinations, they must eventually be transcended. After reaching a certain level of development, we discover that the simple teleology implied by the concept of liberation was actually a teaching tool. That is, the teaching that there is such a thing as "liberation" galvanizes a new seeker on the spiritual path and sets in motion a process that is inevitably beneficial, even though the seeker's concept of liberation as a "thing" that she will one day attain is itself false. What we discover is that instead of walking a path to reach a specific final destination, we are walking it to learn how to walk it. The moment we fall into complete harmony with the walking, dissolving ideas about our destination or our identity as a walker, path and goal merge into one. In other words, liberation is complete when we are no longer waiting to be liberated. But that is not a teaching that is useful for beginners, since it can undermine their beneficial dedication to practice and encourage spiritual bypassing in some. Rather, it is a teaching the guru presents to individuals who have been successful in their practice but are still striving after their concept instead of surrendering into what's already there for them.

In this sense, then, even individual "progression" on the path, in the sense of progressing from point A to point B, is an illusion. You are moving through a process, yes, and there is a kind of directionality to your movement, but it is not an evolution to some better state of being as much as it is a dissolving of that which prevents you from recognizing the truth that has always been right in front of you as it were, right within you. So, to conclude, future-focused teleology as conceived by most religions is downplayed or at least deeply nuanced by NŚT, even as it is affirmed that 1) there is such a thing as awakening; 2) if you're not yet fully awake and free, you can be (indeed, you will be, if that is your heart's desire); and 3) NŚT offers you the necessary guidance to experientially actualize that reality.

PHENOMENOLOGY

Phenomenology asks, what is the truth-value of experience? What and how far can our subjective experience tell us about reality? Here I will not be exploring a favorite subject of phenomenology, how consciousness encounters the world, since I will do that later. Instead I will address the role of experience, especially spiritual experience, in a nondual philosophy.

See page 116 and following

Quite simply, since reality is One, and everything is equally an expression of that one divine Light of Consciousness, every experience by definition is an experience of God. As the scriptures say, "Śiva is the substance of every experience whatsoever." Now, some interpreters of the tradition say, "Everything is God, but some things are more God than others." This is as nonsensical as the famous quote from *Animal Farm,* "Everyone is equal, but some are more equal than others." If we propose that some things are more God than others, like concentrated orange juice versus watered-down orange juice, then we must also propose the existence of something that is *not* God that waters down divinity. But no

Śiva is the substance of every experience whatsoever.

such thing can be found, at least in this philosophy, because 1) the definition of God here is the unbounded Light of Consciousness, 2) everything that is known to exist is an object of experience, and 3) every experience is by definition pervaded by consciousness.

Therefore, this—whatever is happening *right now*—is as God as it gets. Now, if you are in a miserable or banal life situation, you may be disappointed by this announcement. But notice I said, "This is as God as it gets," not, "This is as free as it gets." Freedom means actually experiencing the divinity in each moment, which is the same as not wanting the present moment to be any different from the way it is. When you don't want any moment to be any different, when you give your heart's consent to what is, then you are no longer struggling (or even waiting) for a better situation, and therefore you are free to fully show up for what is actually happening now. Paradoxically, this reveals the inherent joy of consciousness, because by not struggling against some part of reality, you see and meet the whole of the moment, and you naturally enjoy it to the maximum extent you are capable of in that moment.

Whatever is happening right now is as God as it gets.

Ultimate freedom, then, is not an experience or a state of mind. It can't be, because no experience or state of mind is permanent. An experience, however great and wonderful, cannot be the goal of the spiritual path, for as soon as it is gone, you want it again, and then you are not free—and radical freedom is the avowed goal of all forms of yoga. So, this leads us to the necessary conclusion that *pleasurable experience, however refined and pure, cannot be more divine than anything else.* The pursuit of spiritual "highs" is not the path of yoga, Tantrik or otherwise. Nor is final liberation the result of a high experience. It is the result of total surrender of all your grasping, total opening to what is beyond all your stories about it.

Pleasurable experience, however refined and pure, cannot be more divine than anything else.

So, what's all this talk about *ānanda*, or bliss, in the Tantrik tradition? Simple: *ānanda* is the most common by-product of this deep surrender and opening to reality as it is. In fact, it is more than that:

ānanda is a very important feedback mechanism for consciousness. If you believe you have given up your struggle and accepted what is and you do *not* experience *ānanda* (joy, relief, profound contentment, or similar) as a result, then that means you have actually surrendered to your dominant story about reality, rather than to reality itself. Surrendering to your story makes you feel defeated and depressed. Seeing things as they really are, and giving the full heart's consent to reality as it is, always results in some form of *ānanda,* whether subtle, soft, sweet relief or astonishing, ecstatic, expansive joy. *Ānanda* in whatever form is what tells you that you have had a true seeing and a true dying away of your grasping limited self into divine reality. But, and this can hardly be said too many times, *ānanda* is simply the chief by-product of realization, it is not the goal of the path, and it is not more divine than anything else. If you think otherwise, you will starting grasping after it and building a new "spiritual" self-image around it, and then you are caught again. Probably the greatest pitfall on the spiritual path is confusing the by-products of realization with that which produces them, and this is why nondual Tantra clearly posits the goal of the path as Truth, not happiness. Make true seeing your goal, and more bliss than you can imagine will arise as a by-product of that journey; but the moment your sights shift to bliss or pleasure as the goal, delusion begins to reassert itself. This is the key teaching that shortens the duration of the whole spiritual process more than any other single teaching, so I strongly advise you to work it deep inside.

Ānanda is what tells you that you have had a true seeing and a true dying away of your grasping limited self into divine reality.

The greatest pitfall on the spiritual path is confusing the by-products of realization with that which produces them.

THE ROLE OF DESIRE IN A NONDUAL VIEW

You may object that Tantra famously legitimates human desire, even viewing it as a means to liberation, instead of negating it as other yogas do. Desire is, of course, just as divine as anything else, but for it to become a means to liberation, there must be right View toward it. Why would the Tantra bother to legitimate the common variety of delusion-based desire, seeing that it has never brought true and lasting freedom to anyone? As we will explore later, ordinary desire is binding for it reinforces the false view that you are not already complete as you are, that you are something separate from the object of your desire. Desire becomes a vehicle to your liberation when you trace it back to its source and realize that your desire for some external situation (whether a car, a spouse, whatever) is really a desire for the feeling, the flavor of consciousness, that having that thing or person will bring you; or, to be more accurate, the feeling that you *believe* having that thing will bring you. All desire boils down to the fundamental desire for the fullness of being; in other words, all longing is longing for God. As suggested above, this fullness of being is not accomplished by a quantitative accumulation of good experiences. It is your natural state, and in terms of desire, it is accessed by finding the primal root of your desire, far deeper than any particular wanting, and letting it explode with the realization that ultimately you simply desire to be the whole of what you are. The intensity of this desire has the power to shatter the confines of the constructed self, for it is not satisfied until it is connected to everything. In this way, desire does become a vehicle of your liberation. You discover that what the mind really wants is to stop wanting. And that will never happen until you realize and experience the whole of what you are.

See pages 137–138

All desire boils down to the fundamental desire for fullness of being.

Whenever you are centered in the real core of your being, a completely different kind of desire can arise: the "pure desire" that is a natural flowing forth of your essence-nature into embodied action. It does not seek to grasp something and bring it in. It is the opposite movement: an impulse to share yourself, to connect your innate vibration with the world. This desire does not limit or contract you, for it does not arise from self-image but from a much deeper place. This is the kind of desire that the Tantra honors unreservedly, the longing not only to be your Self but to act in the world as a beautiful expression of that Self.

The longing to not only be your Self but to act in the world as a beautiful expression of that Self.

So first the longing to know and experience the fullness of your being takes you deep inside. And then upon experiencing that fullness, the pure desire to share and express that fullness in the world carries you out again in embodied, compassionate action. These are the movements of desire that the Tantra honors as the primary engine of the spiritual process.

THEODICY

One of the most difficult—and interesting—questions in the study of spiritual philosophy is often phrased like this: "If God is wholly good and all-powerful, how can there be evil, how can there be suffering?" This form of the question of *theodicy* presumes an all-powerful personal deity separate from his creation who could intervene to prevent suffering but chooses not to. Who could ever worship such a God, I wonder, without simultaneously resenting him? The whole orientation to the question is fundamentally different for nondualism, which simply denies that kind of separate deity. Let's explore how this question can be meaningfully answered in a nondual context.

"Evil" and "good" are relative degrees of ignorance of the true nature of reality.

First off, Tantrik philosophy shifts the terms of the discussion by denying that evil exists at all. That is, both "good" and "evil" are conceptual structures that people overlay onto reality; they are not inherent in reality itself. But why do these concepts arise, and to what aspect of reality do they relate? "Good" is a label that we give to human beings or human institutions that perform actions that, in our estimation, benefit others or in some way make life more wonderful for people. Conversely, "evil" is a label we give to those whose actions, in our estimation, are detrimental or make life more painful for others. But both of these oversimplifying, reductionist labels alienate us from the real humanity of those that we are labeling by sanctifying or demonizing people who are, in actuality, doing exactly the same thing that you are doing every day of your life: that is, trying to find some happiness and freedom *in the best way they know how.*

That phrase is the key to the issue, for the factor that is actually operative here, differentiating those we wish to call "evil" from those we wish to call "good," is their relative degree of ignorance of the true nature of reality. Two types of ignorance are operative here: the nonconceptual ignorance that is simple disconnection from essence-nature, and the conceptual ignorance that is a set of interpretations of reality that is not actually in alignment with reality. These two forms of ignorance are related because the second is built on the foundation of the first.

Those who are deeply disconnected from their own real nature, and are thus unable to tap into the inexhaustible wellspring of joy, love, and inspiration at their core, will express this inner disconnection and alienation in actions that others find difficult and painful. Furthermore, the disconnected person will evolve a worldview corresponding to their inner experience, one in which happiness is something they have to obtain from outside, something they have to fight for. Being disconnected from themselves, they are likewise disconnected from others, and therefore it seems perfectly logical to such a person to try to obtain wealth and happiness for themselves at any expense to others. Society and religion try to change such people by telling them that they will reap what they sow, that harm to others will come back on them, but such moralizing misses the point: that is not the way disconnected individuals are experiencing reality. They don't feel their connections to all other living things, so such moralizing appears to them as a thinly veiled attempt to control their actions and limit their freedom, and they rebel against it. When we label such people as "evil," we shut down the possibility of understanding their experience, and we shut down the possibility of compassion, which is particularly sad because *only* acts of compassion and love furnish the compelling counter-evidence to a disconnected person that might begin to change his view. In other words, the only way for this disconnected self-concealment and concomitant misalignment to start to correct itself is for the individual to have an experience that gives him concrete evidence of another way of seeing and understanding reality, a way that demonstrates greater value because it is more effective in meeting his deepest needs. This is why we call love a transcendent principle: it is the appropriate response to both love and hate.

Love is a transcendent principle: it is the appropriate response to both love and hate.

There are others whom we praise and call saints or heroes: those who can love unconditionally, those whose actions uplift others and make life more wonderful for many who come into contact with them. But such people are simply expressing their inner experience of profound connection to the source of love and insight. When we put them on the pedestal of sainthood or greatness, we distance ourselves from our capacity to access that same source. If you seek "the good" for yourself and for others, the only sustainable way of actualizing that goal is through a palpable, living connection to a level of being on which contributing to the well-being of others is the easiest and most natural thing you could possibly do. This is why, from a spiritual perspective, the most effective political, social, or environmental activism is awakening to your true nature and helping others awaken. Indeed, in the long run, it is the only effective method, for awakened ones naturally exist in harmony with their total environment (because they never use their personal will to resist the larger pattern, because by definition they *are* the larger pattern). All our political, social, and environmental controls are simply attempts to compensate for our lack of awakeness, and as external superimpositions, they ultimately fail in exact proportion to the degree of unawakeness in the people they aim to control.

So, everyone, everywhere, is doing exactly the same thing: living in precise accordance with their view of reality and trying to maximize their happiness and freedom *in the most effective way they can see from within their worldview*. And their view is built upon the basis of their experience, so arguing with it does no good (unless maybe you know them well enough to base your argument on elements of *their* experience instead of your own). Since everyone is doing the same thing, how can we call some evil and others good? We *can* say that some are more ignorant and others less so, because it is factually true that the strategies by which disconnected persons pursue their happiness will not be successful, but they believe that they will be successful. Thus, it is fair to say that they are in a temporary state of misalignment. As the teaching states: *All beings are Śiva, in relative degrees of self-concealment or self-revelation.*

All beings are Śiva, in relative degrees of self-concealment or self-revelation.

This brings us to the question of suffering. Having granted that there is no such thing as evil, we naturally turn to the question of why there must be suffering. Why not create a universe in which suffering is not a possibility? This form of the question presumes a dualism between creator and created that is not operative here. If we alter it to the question of why the universe is created in such a way as to allow for the full range of possibilities, from the most horrific to the most sublime, then we have the sort of question that was of greater interest to the Tantrik thinkers.

Consciousness, we learn, is innately autonomous by nature. Since it is the first principle of reality, it is subject to no limitations; rather, any and all limitations are produced by it as the framework in which it moves. It is free to exist in any mode, which is why no one else has the power to determine your inner state. Naturally, when Consciousness embodies itself as a universe, that universe will also display the same nature of openness to any and every possibility: a wide-open playing field. What mechanism could there be to impede the expression of contracted forms of consciousness while simultaneously allowing the expression of expanded forms? In fact, it is crucial that all forms of consciousness have the power of self-expression, because that is the primary mode through which consciousness learns about itself. If the consequences of ignorance were not permitted to arise, how would it mature into wisdom?

If the consequences of ignorance were not permitted to arise, how would it mature into wisdom?

You might think, "Well, I'd rather people have less autonomy, less freedom, than see all this suffering." That is of course the principle on which laws are enacted and prisons are filled: given the amount of ignorance about, we'd better curtail people's ability to act on their ignorance. One way to show the flaw in this thinking is to take it to its logical conclusion. A friend of mine in college, where we both studied religion, thought up a parable to demonstrate that we will always ultimately choose freedom and the full range of possibilities it includes, even if it means suffering. It's called the parable of the Dream Machine. He said, "Imagine you live in a dimension where you have total control. Nothing happens without your permission, and everything you want to happen happens. For a while, you'd probably enjoy innumerable pleasures and luxuries. Then, after not so very long, you'd get bored, and you'd invent adventures for yourself that seemed to include challenge, such as rescuing a damsel from a fire-breathing dragon. But even that would pale eventually, because you're always in control. The challenge isn't real, because there is no possibility of failing. Sooner or later, you fall into boredom, ennui, and jaded lassitude—in other words, all the signs of a consciousness in stagnancy. Then one day, a magical machine appears that you didn't put there. There's a big button on it and next to the button a sign. The sign says,

> *The Dream Machine*
> *"If you push this button, anything could happen: joys beyond your wildest dreams, and fears beyond your darkest nightmares; or more probably, both. If you push it you will forget you pushed it and be plunged into a world of infinite possibility. Will you take the chance? Will you go on the adventure?"*

At this point my friend turned to me and said the phrase that gave me chills of recognition: "The question is not whether you'll push the button. It's just, *how long will you wait?*" And, in a certain sense, we've already pushed that button. That's why we're here.

This story shows so effectively that as much as we think we would be happy bending the world entirely to our individual will, we would not. It is only by giving full range to the all the possibilities within consciousness that it can discern the true pattern of its being. As one of my teachers says, it is only by granting the whole world its freedom to be exactly as it is that you can be free.

Having explored the innate autonomy of Consciousness that allows for both wisdom (full self-awareness) and ignorance (partial self-concealment) and for the aligned and misaligned actions that arise from them respectively, we are still left with the question of why there is ignorance in the first place. Why does the mode of concealment arise at all? Almost all Indian philosophy evades this question, stating that ignorance is beginningless and thus we cannot address the question of a cause. That which is beginningless is uncaused. Tantrik philosophy, however, has an interesting answer for those who care to dig for it. It observes that when the universal, the formless Absolute, moves into the particularity of form, each form is necessarily limited; that is, it expresses certain qualities by negating others. To manifest X is to suppress or withdraw all that is not X. To manifest Steve is to withdraw into the formless ground all that is not Steve. The problem comes when a self-aware bit of consciousness like you or me or Steve surveys its manifest limited being and makes the assumption that this is all there is to it. But this is not all there is to it because the formless ground of infinite possibility is always in you as well—as the very root of your being. In other words, orienting to the most tangible and obvious level of reality (your body, thoughts, etc.), which is also the level of maximal difference from other forms, you start to identify with that level and thereby lose awareness of the subtle dimensions of your being wherein the pattern of the whole universe is encoded. Seeing only part of the whole but taking it to be the Whole is what we mean by ignorance, and ignorance gives rise to suffering because it entails a misalignment with reality as it is.

Why does this assumption, which leads to limited identification, which leads to suffering, get made? We could say that the motive force of the universe is love. It is out of love for itself that Consciousness bodies itself forth as a universe, and it is out of love that it allows for the total range of possibilities in that universe (because to negate any possibility would be to reject that aspect of itself). The beginning point of limited identification is therefore also love: when Consciousness finds itself in a body, it is as it were so enamored of its creation that it temporarily forgets the rest of itself. It then is no longer seeing the whole and gets caught in partial (limited) identification. (An innocent mistake with not-so-innocent consequences down the line.) That limited form of consciousness then receives (as it were) "signals" from reality that it is out of alignment, signals we often characterize as "suffering." Being a limited form of consciousness, it takes a while for the real import of these signals to sink in, at which point Consciousness starts to wake up to the whole of itself. This entire process, which seems to us to take so long, is really just a brief moment, a blip of misunderstanding, on the larger timescale of the universe.

So, most pain and all suffering is part of a feedback mechanism that the universe uses to warn you of a misalignment. We do not object to having bodies that feel pain when we touch something that's really hot, because we know that pain protects us from further damage. Mental suffering can be more acute and difficult to bear than physical pain because it points us toward deep misalignments in our thought-structures. As it turns out, most human suffering is mind-created suffering, that is, it arises from clinging to stories that are not in alignment with reality. If a way of looking at a situation causes you to suffer and brings you into division and conflict, then that's all the evidence you need to mark that perspective as misaligned and begin to release it. "But surely some forms of pain are perfectly natural," the objectioner says. "You can't think that the pain of losing a loved one is indicative of a misalignment." If the pain in question is unbearable despair and depression, then yes; it indicates that there is a misaligned story in place such as "I'll never be happy without him." When there is no story to turn pain into suffering, the pain of loss is a thing of sharp beauty, fully welcomed by the clear and awake one as another form of her love. It passes through her without resistance and therefore does not get stuck and turn into despair or depression.

Most pain and all suffering is part of a feedback mechanism that life uses to warn you of a misalignment.

Since all suffering, from a twinge of anger to agonizing guilt, is a feedback mechanism, all suffering is welcomed by the awake one as a gift and a blessing. Not in the artificial Pollyanna sense of "Oh, it's really okay, I'm fine, let's look on the bright side, somehow it'll turn out okay," but rather in the sense that no matter how much it hurts in the moment, she knows that it is part of a honing process which is perfectly calibrated to eventually center her in her unconditional freedom and love. It is a process that works insofar as we look into what the feedback is asking us to be aware of. Often we do not. We just try to get past the suffering; in which case it will arise again, and again, until we look into what we are being shown about the way we are holding reality. The moment you see clearly how *you*—and no one else—are responsible for your suffering, and how your view of things creates it, an irrevocable process has begun that will not stop until it has brought to an end all mind-created suffering.

Reality is intrinsically auspicious (*śiva*)—anything can be for a blessing.

Because everything contributes to this process, which tends only to your benefit, the awakened ones have always said, "Everything is a blessing," or, to translate more accurately, "Anything can be for a blessing." The very word "Śiva" means blessing, so when the scriptures say that the world is *śiva*, they mean both that it is divine and that it is a blessing (since there are actually no capital letters in the Sanskrit language, *śiva* as a name for god and *śiva* meaning "blessing" are always one and the same word). It is in this sense that we can say that reality is intrinsically auspicious (which means "conducive to eventual success"), that reality is intrinsically good—not in the sense of good versus bad, rather in the deeper sense that anything can be for a blessing, and every experience offers itself to you as a guru, teaching you something about the deeper pattern. You don't have to understand this with your mind; you simply open to it in full awareness and without resistance, whether it is painful or pleasurable, and the learning happens automatically.

Now, the final objection: "All that sounds fine, but what happens to all your high-flown spiritual philosophy when humanity manifests the worst it has to offer? What about war and concentration camps?" Well, no spiritual philosophy is worth its salt that breaks down just because the degree of suffering has increased. The point here is this: everything points us to the deeper pattern, and sometimes consequences get drastic indeed before humans choose to learn about that pattern and act on their learning. But in every case that consequences became drastic, there were smaller signs of the misalignment long before that point. "So," the objectioner says, "do you think war is a blessing?" No, not if by "blessing" you mean "a good thing"; but yes, if you mean "a powerful opportunity to wake up." One of the great beings of our time Thich Nhat Hanh woke up in the midst of the Vietnam War, and his insight and compassion have been flowing ever since, benefitting hundreds of thousands of people. And the great humanistic psychologist Victor Frankl tells us that he discovered the power of love in a Nazi concentration camp: he found the deepest meaning, and a connection to God he had not known before, in maintaining his humanity and supporting his fellow inmates in the worst of circumstances. He later wrote,

Victor Frankl

> *We must never forget that we may also find meaning in life even when confronted with a hopeless situation, when facing a fate that cannot be changed. For what then matters is to bear witness to the uniquely human potential at its best, which is to transform a personal tragedy into a triumph, to turn one's predicament into a human achievement. When we are no longer able to change a situation—just think of an incurable disease such as inoperable cancer—we are challenged to change ourselves.*

Some say Frankl was the exception, a man gifted by his natural constitution to take the best out of the worst. Actually, he was a normal man who transformed radically when he realized, on the very brink of despair, "Everything can be taken from a man but one thing, the last of the human freedoms: to choose one's attitude in any given set of circumstances—to choose one's own way." This power of autonomy exists in everyone in equal measure, in you just as much as in Victor Frankl; in exercising it, you make the worst thing that ever happened to you into the greatest gift, thereby joining the legion of those who have gone before you who can honestly say, "My life has sometimes been filled with challenge and pain. I'm so grateful for all of it and I wouldn't change a single thing."

THE CATEGORIES OF TANTRIK THOUGHT

The Five Layers of the Self—The Five Acts of God—The Five Powers

The 36 Tattvas—The Three Impurities—The Four Levels of Speech

The Five States of Awareness—The Seven Perceivers

INTRODUCTION TO THE CATEGORIES

Like all Indian philosophical systems, nondual Śaiva Tantra (NŚT) presents what seems at first a bewildering array of lists of various aspects of reality, all of which attempt to describe the experience of embodied consciousness in its various phases. Such categorical lists are a primary teaching tool for the tradition. Before you read this section, it is important to understand that *each* of these lists gives a more or less complete account of reality from one particular angle. To use an (imperfect) analogy, it's like cutting a marbled cake from several different angles: each cut produces a different pattern of one and the same thing. Without understanding this, those who like to get the basic gist of a teaching may find the categories redundant or repetitive; while those interested in details may feel overwhelmed by the wealth of distinct types of information. Both problems can be corrected by understanding first that each of these various lists provides a different roadmap to practice, a viewpoint that orients the unfolding of *sādhanā*. If you understood any one of them completely, you wouldn't need any other map. Yet a variety of maps are presented, because some will make sense to some people, others to others. My recommendation is that after reading them all, you focus on contemplating deeply whichever one makes the most sense to you. Then later you can contemplate another one, for cultivating an understanding of any one of these lists serves to illuminate the others. First we turn our attention to the Tantrik vision of the nature of an embodied conscious being. This section will answer the question "What are you?"

NESTED LAYERS OF CONSCIOUSNESS: THE TANTRIK FIVE-LAYERED SELF

One of the central questions of Indian philosophy has always been "Who or what am I?" What are the dimensions of the self? What are the contours and constituents of a human being? Or, to be more precise, "What is the referent of the 'I'-cognition?" NŚT has its own unique answer to this question, one that like many Tantrik teachings will seem familiar yet provide fresh insights.

The Tantrik vision of the self may be compared to a *matryoshka* or Russian doll: nested layers, proceeding from the more superficial to the more subtle, the less essential to the more essential, as we move from the periphery to the core. There are, in total, five layers of the self in the Tantrik analysis:

- the physical body (deha),
- the heart-mind/energy body (citta, puryastka),
- the *prāṇa* or life-force,
- the transcendent Void (sunya), and
- the Power of Awareness (cit-sakti).

The last of these is your essential nature, the innermost Self within the conditioned self.[34] We should understand right at the beginning that these layers are not rigidly separated; in fact, as one Tantrik master tells us, "It is the nature of each layer to be pervaded by all the layers deeper than it." The subtler the layer is the more it can pervade other layers, which is why Consciousness, the power of awareness, the subtlest of all, is all-pervasive.

The body is the only layer of the self where *all* the layers can be experienced simultaneously.

But this schema does not denigrate the body; in fact, the body is the only layer where *all* the layers of self can be experienced simultaneously.

Some sources add a sixth, most peripheral layer: the material expression of your being that surrounds you, your "stuff," or vastu in Sanskrit.

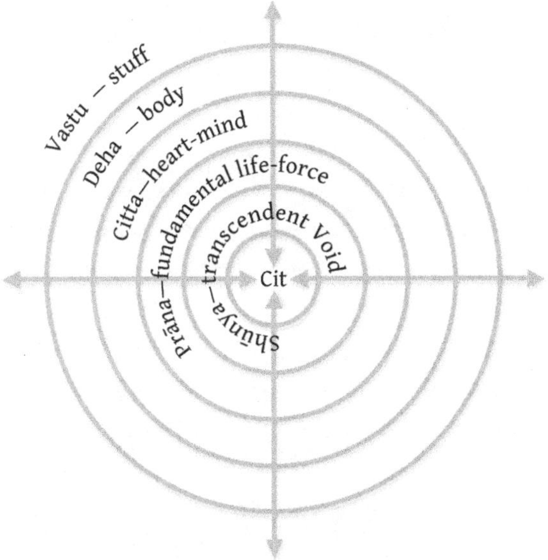

The point to this map of ourselves is that suffering arises as a result of a failure to perceive the whole of your being and its natural hierarchy. This inability to perceive the whole comes from mistakenly identifying your "self" as only one or two of the layers we have described. Let's analyze the layers from the outer to the inner.

Stuff

If you are identified with the outermost layer, your "stuff" (vastu), that identification expresses itself in such thoughts or statements as "I am rich," or "I am poor," and so on. In these statements, we are literally equating our I-ness with our economic status, because the verb "am" (to be) functions as an equals sign. As another example of stuff-identification, consider how we equate ourselves with our cars, such as when someone else's car bumps ours and we yell, "You hit me!" I need hardly point out how identifying ourselves with the material layer brings suffering, for material wealth and status is neither stable nor certain. Though vastu includes our self-expression in the selection and arrangement of objects in our home environment, it does not necessarily follow that delighting in this form of expression indicates attachment to the vastu layer. There is nothing wrong with loving material objects per se; it is forming an identity dependent on that dimension that we are concerned about. Here for example, if others' opinions about your home feed your pride or self-hatred, then the unhealthy form of attachment is present. Discernment is necessary to tell the difference, on this and all the other layers.

Body

The next layer is that of the physical body or *deha.* Our identification with the body is expressed in many thoughts or statements like "I am fat," "I am thin," "I am young," "I am old," "I am pretty," "I am ugly," "I am fit," "I am out of shape," and so on. Thoughts such as these indicate a belief that your identity is defined by your physicality. If you are identified with the body to the exclusion of the deeper layers of your being, then you will necessarily base your self-worth on your own and others' opinions of your body. In this case, you are definitely setting yourself up for suffering, for the one universal truth of the body is that it will break down, age, decay, and die. If you believe you are this body and nothing more, that truth is terrifying. In ancient Indian tradition, yogīs would contemplate the impermanence of the body by going to cremation grounds and practicing open-eyed meditation, gazing at the burning bodies for days or weeks on end. This was a powerful way to get the truth of mortality through their heads, and it resulted in decreased attachment to the body and an increased sense of the preciousness of life. It is no coincidence that in our culture that celebrates the physical dimension of life to the point of obsession, death is hidden away. Crowds are diverted from seeing a body in public; examples of extreme old age are sequestered away in old folks' homes. Thus we propagate a fantasy of our immortality, setting ourselves up for greater suffering when the fantasy is inevitably shattered. We do not know how to age and die gracefully in our culture. But if we believe and experience that we are something more than this physical body, dying gracefully becomes a possibility.

Note that for each layer, I give the expressions of identification with that layer in the form of pairs of opposites; this is because according to yoga psychology, it is impossible to identify with one side of a pair without also identifying with the other side. In other words, if the thought "I'm pretty" gives you pleasure, then the thought "I'm ugly" will give you equal amounts of pain. Attachment to one side *necessitates* attachment to the other, which shows that they are flip sides of the same coin, part of the same paradigm.

Heart-mind

The next layer is that of the heart-mind, or *citta,* which is nothing but pure Consciousness contracted into thoughts and feelings. We express our identification with the mind-layer in thoughts or statements such as "I am smart," "I am stupid," "I am competent," "I am incompetent," "I am happy," "I am sad," and so on. The last two may surprise you as examples of mind-identification. In Indian philosophy (as expressed in the Sanskrit language), the mind and the heart are not two different things, if by those terms we mean the locus of thought and the locus of emotion. Both thoughts and feelings are vibrations of *citta,* or the "mind-stuff." They are actually two ends of a single spectrum. If this were not true, we could never talk about our feelings or feel strongly about our ideas. The difference between thoughts and feelings is simply that thoughts are vibrations (*vṛttis*) with a greater linguistic or logical component, while feelings are vibrations with a greater affective charge. The difference is not absolute but one of degree. For example, when we feel sad, that feeling is nearly always strongly tied to a specific thought or story, often unconscious. Becoming aware of that thought can help us become unstuck, tapping the latent energy of the feeling and allowing it to flow.

When we are identified with our mind—that is, with our thoughts and feelings—to the exclusion of the other layers of our being, we suffer. For the mind changes even more rapidly than the body, a kaleidoscopic shifting display of imagery, words, ideas, and feelings, in which apparently sure ground turns out to be total fantasy. In an attempt to stabilize this mental emotional domain, we repeat certain patterns of thought until they become ingrained habits. These are often not healthy patterns, but we prefer the comfort of their familiarity to the wide-open possibility that can seem like terrifying uncertainty. We can become very attached to creating a sense of security by rigidly defining how things "ought to be"; in reality, we are staving off the fear that comes with the realization that nothing is certain and we are very much not in control even of our own mind, let alone what happens to us. By contrast, the most amazing relief and sense of freedom come when we no longer see our identity and reality as defined by our thoughts and feelings. When we are not overly identified with the mind, we ride the flow of its energy, learning its flow like the surfer learns to ride the waves. We are merely amused by its foibles and petty fears and draw power from its intense feelings, whether "positive" or "negative."

Most of us are most strongly identified with the mind out of all the layers. Remember, every time I say "mind" I mean heart-mind, citta, the locus of both thought and emotion. Becoming free of the bondage of this identification is of course impossible without increasingly grounded direct experience of the deeper layers of self. Such disengagement from the mind (which does not imply devaluing its usefulness) is crucial in all forms of yoga, whether Tantrik or non-Tantrik. You see, when we overidentify with the mind, we cannot help but believe its stories. The mind creates oversimplified, overgeneralized, and distorted representations of reality (called *vikalpas* in Sanskrit). When we take these mental constructs *as* reality—instead of the distorted second-order representations that they are—we suffer. (Remember that according to NŚT, all suffering comes from not seeing things as they really are.) When we are not overidentified with the mind, we are naturally more skeptical of the stories it makes up about reality, which are spun out of

See page 357 and following

hopes and fears based on past pleasurable and painful experience, rather than any clear assessment of the real situation in front of us or within us. Free of mind-identification, we don't take ourselves too seriously, and we certainly don't believe everything we think. We understand that the mind is just one of many sources of input that an awakened being takes note of as part of her self-aware loving embrace of her whole being. It's like a mother who lovingly listens to the stories of all her children, not necessarily believing any of them literally but taking note of them when they point to a deeper reality or issue.

Vital Energy

The next layer of the self is that of the *prāṇa,* which is usually translated as "vital energy" or "life-force." At this layer, individuality is transcended, for we share this layer with all living beings. The movement of *prāṇa,* which is intimately connected to the breath, is vital for life to continue. In fact, *prāṇa* serves as the interface between the physical body and the mind and is the key to the mind-body connection, though it is subtler and more fundamental than either. It is, in a sense, the *means* by which the mind extends itself throughout the body in the form of what is called the "subtle body." (More on that later.) *Prāṇa* constitutes a subtler and more essential layer of our being than the mind. Our identification with *prāṇa* is expressed in such statements as "I am energized," "I am drained," "I feel alive," "I feel blah." The amplification and depletion of *prāṇa,* which is connected to diet, exercise, sleep, and thought-patterns, is responsible for our general energy level and many of our moods as well. If you find yourself cranky or irritable or listless, with no clear external reason for it, it is often due to the energy-state of your *prāṇa* and can thus be addressed through food, exercise, sleep, or relaxation. Though it may be "natural" to be more strongly identified with the *prāṇa* layer than with any of the more external layers, over-identification with *prāṇa* puts us at the mercy of our moods. Taking our moods too seriously can prompt impulsive action that our mind- or body-layer may later regret (such as when you snap at a loved one because you're irritable due to simple hunger). We take *prāṇa*-based moods too seriously when we believe they are arising from the layer of the mind instead of simple *prāṇa* depletion or amplification (this is the widespread problem in our culture of reducing everything to our psychology).

We may take a moment here to define the five basic subtypes of *prāṇa.* Somewhat confusingly, the first subtype has the same name as that of the general category, being called *prāṇa-vāyu,* (the "outward-moving wind"). This is the *prāṇa* that governs exhalation. *Apāna-vāyu* (the "downward-moving wind") is linked to inhalation and governs all downward movement in the body, such as moving food through the digestive tract and eliminating waste. *Samāna-vāyu* (the "equalizing wind") is linked to the digestive fire in the stomach and to the fusion of the in-breath and the out-breath in the yogic practice of *prāṇāyāma. Udāna-vāyu* (the "uprising wind") is linked to belching, vomiting, sneezing, speech, and the rise of *kuṇḍalinī* through yogic practices. Lastly, *vyāna-vāyu* (the "pervasive wind") is linked to the movement of the limbs and the distribution of nutrients throughout the body. As you can see, all the five *prāṇa*s must be in good working order to have a healthy and enjoyable experience of being in the body.

the Void

The penultimate layer in our analysis of the self is that of the transcendent Void (*śūnya).* The Void, which is all-pervasive, is empty of all form and energy, absolutely still. It is, in a sense, Śiva without Śakti, or rather with Her existing as unexpressed potentiality. This is the layer our awareness occupies in the state of deep dreamless sleep. We can also access this layer while awake through meditation. Most people don't identify with this layer; but many meditators who have reached the place of the transcendent and profoundly peaceful Void decide (upon emerging from it) that this is their real nature, declaring their identification with phrases like "I am the transcendent Void," or, more commonly, "I am not of this world; my true Self transcends all things." They might not say that out loud, but they may have that inner feeling. Such people renounce all identification with the material world, body, and mind, becoming what we call transcendentalists. They can attain deep states of peace but often cannot integrate these states into daily life, and thus they may fail to adequately take care of their body and become unable to relate to others easefuly. They may even become escapist and turn away from the beneficial work of engaging in relationships and improving the health of the ordinary mind and body. This is not the Tantrik path; a Tāntrika renounces nothing and seeks tirelessly to realize the Divine on all layers of being.

the Core

In the Tantrik View, the ultimate center of our being is absolute nondual nonlocal Consciousness (*cit* or *saṃvit* in Sanskrit), beyond all other layers yet pervading them, making awareness of them possible. Consciousness is the secret pulsating core of your whole existence, mysterious because it is omnipresent and yet you don't notice it. It is the most difficult "layer" of your self to grasp, because it is the power by which all grasping is done (grasping in the sense of comprehension here). It is the most difficult to perceive, for it is the power behind all perception. It is the core in the sense that it is the only aspect of yourself that is impossible to objectify. This Awareness is absolutely not different from the supreme Divinity that is the essence of all things. It is all-embracing, present in all forms of consciousness, including even the most contracted forms of self-identification with any of the previous layers. Because this core Awareness is by definition simultaneously transcendent and immanent, when we are identified with it, we can experience any state as divine, not just the ones that are radically elevated from our ordinary experience. In other words, identification with our core Awareness enables us to experience divinity in all things, because it *is* the divinity in all things. It is the perfect fusion of Śiva and Śakti, pure consciousness and all the forms of energy that it embraces. Therefore this "level" of your being cannot be pictured as topping the hierarchy of the layers of the self, or at the bottom of it, because it pervades and subsumes the entire hierarchy. So this divine awareness is simultaneously the deeper layer of your being, but pervades all the layers. It's not really at the bottom or top of the list; it's to the sides and in all the cracks, and everywhere else, too. This is where the conceptual mind finds it difficult to grasp, and yet the subtlest principles are the most true.

Identification with this Core takes the form of the experience (*not* the thought), "I am blissfully free self-aware Consciousness!" This is sometimes expressed with the mantra *śivo'ham* ("I am the Divine"). For nondual Tantra, this state of liberated awareness in which we know our true nature *by being it* is most perfectly summed up by the phrase *pūrṇo'ham,* which we may translate as "I am the whole," or "I am complete and perfect," or (less poetic but more technically accurate) "I am that 'I' which encompasses all things." The great master Utpala Deva describes the spiritual state of *samāveśa*—total immersion into the Divine—precisely in terms of this five-layered self we have discussed:

Stanzas on the Recognition of the Divine

> *Experientially realizing the primacy of the Conscious Self as the true Knower and Agent, and realizing that the other layers of individuality—from the Void to the body—are mere attributes of it; this is what characterizes immersion into the divine samāveśa.*[35]

In other words, the deepest spiritual experience of reality consists of the full realization that this divine Consciousness is your true essence, and that all the layers of your being that you are accustomed to identifying yourself with—your stuff, body, mind, *prāṇa*, and the Void—are in fact the ever-changing expressions of that core Consciousness.[36] To put it yet another way, Consciousness vibrates forth into manifestation as all the more peripheral layers of your being, from the Void outward. Those other layers are epiphenomena of the core Consciousness, not the other way around.

The Tantrik model of the self invites us to ask where the locus of our constructed identity lies. On what level do we habitually fixate our awareness? In Paul Muller-Ortega's phrase, what is our "individual identity assemblage point"? If it is on one of the more peripheral layers, we have more work to do. In working with this five- or six-layer model of the self in actual practice, we see the classic Tantrik twofold movement of transcendence followed by pervasion. That is, we are asked to engage in a contemplation practice of negation followed by a deeper affirmation. First, we reject identification of our real Self with our stuff, then with our body, then our mind, then the *prāṇa*, then the Void. When we realize our real Self as core divine Consciousness, the simultaneously transcendent and immanent blissfully free Self-awareness, then we also realize that we are in fact *all* the layers of the self that we had previously negated. All those layers are seen as expressions of that nondual Consciousness. Identifying with the body, etc., ceases to be a problem when it is superseded by a deeper and truer identification. Thus we move from the erroneous perception "I am (only) this body," to "I am divine Consciousness, vibrating in the form of this body." Or, "I am all of these layers of being, and yet I am inexpressibly more than that!" (Note that as a statement in language, these experiences sound egotistical or ostentatious; but as deep wordless experience, they are anything but.) Negation is thus simply a tool to reach a deeper affirmation; transcendence is merely a preliminary to a fuller expansion into our embodied wholeness. In the contemplation of the Tantrik five-layered self, we find our center, we plunge into our core, we "hug into the midline of our being" that we may expand outward fully and joyously in a balanced way.

THE FIVE (+1) POWERS OF GOD

The five Powers, or *śakti*s, are the primary way in which the nondual Śaiva Tantra describes the fundamental nature of the Divine. They are the following:

- **CHIT-ŚAKTI**—the Power of Consciousness or the Power of Awareness (note that I use these two terms interchangeably throughout the text)
- **ĀNANDA-ŚAKTI**—the Power of Bliss
- **ICCHĀ-ŚAKTI**—the Power of Will or creative impulse
- **JÑĀNA-ŚAKTI**—the Power of Knowing
- **KRIYĀ-ŚAKTI**—the Power of Action

To put it another way, God/dess is simply the blissful conscious agent of all knowing and doing. There is also a sixth, all-important "meta-power" that encompasses the other five: *Svātantrya-śakti*, the Power of Freedom. This power is "meta" because it provides the context for the operation of the other five. In other words, the Divine exercises its five powers as an expression of its innate freedom and total autonomy.

These six Powers pervade all reality, and nothing exists separate from them. NŚT invites us to recognize the Powers as our own. The experiential realization that we are truly not different from God is triggered by the recognition that the five Powers and five Acts of God (see below) also comprise the totality of our individual experience of embodiment.

We have already discussed that the Power of Consciousness (*cit-śakti*, pronounced CHIT, like all c's in Sanskrit) is the foundation of all reality, the only factor present in any experience whatsoever. The only question is whether it is predominant in any given experience. That is, at any given moment, either you are predominantly aware of some particular contracted reality, some particular object of consciousness, or you are predominantly aware of your subjectivity, of yourself as a conscious being, of the fact of consciousness itself. In the latter case, contraction may still be present; it is simply subordinated in our awareness. For example, you may be experiencing something difficult or enjoyable, such as a painfully stubbed toe or an exquisite sunset, and enveloping that is the feeling-sense "I am a conscious being experiencing such-and-such a vibration in my awareness." This perspective can be predominant in such a way that you are not any less present with the sunset or the stubbed toe. When you are predominantly aware of awareness itself, you do not experience any form of contraction (such as a thought, pain, or pleasure) as a *limitation.* Whereas if you are predominantly aware of the contraction, you will necessarily be limited by identification with the body, mind, *prāṇa*, etc.—that is, with whichever layer of your being is predominant in that given experience. Society and culture condition you to pay attention more to what you're aware of rather than to the power of awareness itself. But when, through practice, we shift the focal point of our awareness from the objects of consciousness to the power of consciousness itself several times throughout our day, a whole different experience of life begins to open up.

As Lord Kṣemarāja teaches us in his sublime text *The Heart of the Teachings on Recognition* (*Pratyabhijñā-hṛdayam*), being predominantly aware of our Awareness comes about either spontaneously or through a spiritual practice. We do have spontaneous experiences of this expansive and encompassing Self-awareness from time to time because it is our true being. Perhaps you have felt it walking silently in nature. Perhaps connecting deeply with a friend while still being centered in yourself. Perhaps at a profound crossroads in your life, wondering which path to take. Perhaps realizing that you are falling in love. Perhaps at a moment when you're plunged in grief. In these moments, we feel more expanded, our awareness is intensified, and our surroundings may seem more vivid, more sharply real (or sometimes more dream-like) than usual. These moments feel charged with meaning and with power, even if there is nothing specifically happening externally. They are tiny intimations of our inner potency. They hint at the experience of reality we may have if we invest in cultivating Awareness.

We cultivate Awareness through meditation-focused spiritual practice, by which we progress in stages toward the state of constant awareness of our real nature, with our powers and potencies fully expanded—an awareness that is ever arising, ever new, ever refreshing itself (*nityodita*). Now, it is important to note that in the context of NŚT, the practice of meditation is primarily *destructive* in nature—that is, it allows you to strip away all your false limited notions about what you are, revealing your true nature, the core of being that is all you have ever been. As Abhinava Gupta teaches, if the false mental constructs about ourselves are destabilized then dissolved, the Heart will stand revealed in its fullness. Since you are already That, nothing need be added to make you perfect, though it is also the case that most of us will need to strengthen our capacities through exercising them if we wish to maintain our connection to our innate perfection. The process of uncovering the core reality of your being is very different from the kind of therapy aimed at making you feel better or behave more functionally. For some, this process can be very difficult, even searingly painful; it involves surrendering the self-images in which a lot of energy has been invested; but it will invariably result in a much greater intimacy of reality and therefore a far vaster joy in being. The central tool in this process of dissolution, which is simultaneously the process of Self-revelation, is the practice of discernment (*tarka*), for it is what allows us to distinguish between reality and the mental constructs (*vikalpas*) that we project onto reality. Through discernment, we examine and discard ever more refined conceptualizations of reality, until finally we come up with one that is so refined that when it falls away we are face-to-face with reality itself without any intermediate conceptualization or interpretation. In terms of the six Powers mentioned above, this is simply Consciousness exercising its Power of Knowing in order to access its Powers of Bliss and Freedom. For when we see things as they really are, we are naturally suffused with joy and a sense of our freedom to choose how to experience them.

If the false mental constructs about ourselves are dissolved, the Heart will stand revealed in its fullness.

Discernment is the primary tool for dissolving untruth.

The Power of Bliss

Let us then define the second of these Powers more precisely: Ananda-sakti, the power of bliss. When we are able to activate, intensify, and expand our Power of Consciousness, to ground ourselves in the very center of it, and then repose in that center, even just for a few moments, we naturally access the fullness of *ānanda-śakti*, the Power of Bliss. Bliss inheres in Consciousness like heat in fire. Now, we must be careful to distinguish Bliss (*ānanda*) from ordinary happiness or pleasurable feeling (*sukha*). Ordinary happiness arises only when our needs are met, only when the circumstances are just so; otherwise we experience its opposite, dissatisfaction, discontent or misery (*duḥkha*). By contrast, *ānanda* designates a way of experiencing and loving reality that is completely independent of circumstance. Therefore it is difficult to translate into English—but we get close if we describe it as a state of absolute contentment, acceptance, and quiet yet sublime joy: the peace that passeth all understanding. This state, which is far more fulfilling than ordinary happiness, can exist in any circumstance. For example, you could be feeling intense grief or pain and still experience *ānanda* in the form of a fierce joy at being alive at all to experience pain. We begin to tap into our Power of Bliss when we simply become fully aware of what we are feeling in this moment and accept it totally, resisting no part of it. The more we practice this loving self-awareness, the more complete is the experience of *ānanda* that arises through it.

Common sense says there are many possible sources of happiness. However, when it comes to the experience of true Bliss that we all seek, of which happiness is a mere shadow, this tradition argues that it has one and only one cause. To understand this, reflect for a moment on the times in your life when you have felt totally free and contented, cut loose from all your cares and worries, when all seemed right with the world, and you fit perfectly into it—in other words, times when you felt *ānanda*. You might think that each such moment had a different cause: in one case the beauty of nature, in another the applause and recognition of your peers, or the perfect ski slope, or the perfect lovemaking, or an awesome band, or the kindness of a friend, and so on. Is it the case that many different causes can bring about precisely the same result, that same joyous fullness, or do all these experiences have something in common? Upon reflection, you may see that all those moments *did* have one common element: you allowed yourself to be fully present and aware—you gave yourself over to the reality of the present moment and opened to its beauty. But there was nothing intrinsically more beautiful about that moment than any other, as others who were there will attest (otherwise, everyone would have had the same experience as you and to the same degree). It was just that you opened and connected with reality, rather than a concept of reality in that moment. In other words, the Power of Consciousness was activated and expanded, allowing you to feel your total connection with the universe, which is always present. *This openness, this conscious Presence, is the sole means of unveiling your innate Bliss.* We disempower ourselves when we believe the cause of our greatest joy is something outside of ourselves, such as another person or a particular circumstance. Those external things can (at best) trigger an expanded and intensified awareness, which itself is the cause of bliss.

Openness, or conscious Presence, is the sole means of unveiling your innate Bliss.

Consider that most of us dwell in a world of our own thoughts, concepts, and projections; we are not fully connected with reality and thus are less likely to tap into the innate power and beauty of reality. Usually we are not fully present because we fear the vulnerability entailed by such engagement with reality or because we find the present moment boring compared to our fantasy world. This explains why it is only when circumstances are either safe enough (for example, when we are sure of the love and good opinion of those around us) or exciting enough (for example, peak experiences) that we fully connect with the present moment. This leads us to the natural but false conclusion that such experiences are only possible in those conditions. The spiritual path teaches us how to open in all circumstances and thus discover that it is being open, connected and aware that gives rise to true bliss, and nothing else.

The first step toward innate repose is to take a long, deep, slow breath.

Developing this crucial insight helps us understand that to access that bliss, we need only become more aware. To achieve that end, we can adopt any one of a number of tools. These tools are always available to us! This realization empowers us by rescuing us from falsely fixating on a particular person or thing as the source of our joy. In fact, the whole spiritual path can be characterized as the development of internal triggers for this blissful awareness, so that we become totally free of the need for external circumstances to be anything other than what they are.

Abhinava Gupta teaches that Bliss arises naturally and spontaneously when we repose in Consciousness. The Sanskrit word *viśrānti*, repose, is quite beautiful. It means to rest in the peaceful ground of being, that state of real connectedness, which is as refreshing and delightful as the cooling rays of the moon after a scorching day. The first step toward this repose, in any situation, is to take a deep, long, slow breath. You can greatly increase the effect of the deep breath by imagining the cooling, silvery-white, lunar inhale flowing into the space of the Heart and landing you there in a place of exquisite rest at the base of your heart. After several such in-breaths, remain centered in your Heart while extending your awareness out with a warming solar out-breath that connects you to the reality of your current situation. This can become a powerful meditation: to use the in-breath to release everything but the sense of coming to rest in the space of the Heart, and the out-breath to illuminate your total environment with intensified awareness. With practice, *ānanda* will arise and flood your whole being.

The Power of Will

The third of the Powers is *icchā-śakti*, the Power of Will. In ordinary Sanskrit usage, the word *icchā* can mean desire; but one can only desire something after knowing about it, and in the context of NŚT *icchā* is instead defined as a *precognitive* creative urge toward self-expression. It is the impulse behind the manifestation of a universe and behind all artistic expression that is done for its own sake. It is contingent on the first two Powers because it is precisely when Consciousness reposes in blissful self-awareness that the dynamic impulse toward self-expression arises. As a microcosm of the divine, you too can tap into the Power of divine Will, the source of the infinite energy behind all creation. In order to do so, you must first let yourself repose in Self-awareness. The more we access our real innate nature, the more we can draw on the unfailing power of the divine Will. The Will seeks self-expression for no reason other than the joy inherent in the act of self-expression. If you are tapping into *icchā-śakti* in your pursuits in life, be they dancing or computer repair, you will have a vast reservoir of energy to draw upon. This is because when you are pursuing an activity as a form of self-expression, it replenishes you instead of draining you. Thus a yogī must find a way to express his innate nature through his career and life activities, and if he cannot, he must change them or become internally desiccated, devoid of juice and sweetness in life.

The Power of Knowing

For *icchā-śakti* to successfully flow into action, it must first be fused with *jñāna-śakti,* the Power of Knowing. The inspirational energy of *icchā-śakti* must be poured into the structured patterns of *jñāna-śakti* if it is to be made use of; otherwise the inspiration fizzles out. *Jñāna-śakti* is the organic patterning of Consciousness, expressed as the deep structures of reality. Without *jñāna-śakti* there would be no consistent laws of physics (for example), no cohesive form to the universe, no pattern in the interaction of living beings. As a microcosm of the Divine, if you wish to express your creative impulse in action, whether as a stockbroker or a musician or a chef, you must first equip yourself with knowledge. You must cultivate profound understanding of the specific ways in which energy flows in your chosen field of activity—that is its deep structures and laws of operation. The seeming paradox is that by submitting yourself to the discipline of mastering the knowledge of form and structure, you become capable of joyously free expression in that arena. For example, a great jazz musician or modern dancer is only able to improvise with such consummate virtuosity, with such freedom and focused passion, because she or he has mastered the forms and structures within which music operates and the body moves. It is in submitting ourselves to a discipline that we become truly free and capable of real self-expression; otherwise our creative energy is not sufficiently directed to accomplish anything. Similarly, no matter how much passion you have for walking the spiritual path, for that fervor to serve you, you must equip yourself with knowledge about the path, for example drawing on the wisdom of the masters who have themselves walked the path and successfully navigated its many pitfalls.

The Power of Action

All of these powers would add up to nothing without *kriyā-śakti*, the Power of Divine Action. Nothing would actually come into being in any concrete way without *kriyā-śakti*, for the structures spoken of in the context of *jñāna-śakti* above are purely subtle, the intangible patterns in which energy naturally flows. Thus *kriyā-śakti*, though the "lowest" of the Powers, is celebrated as the final culmination of the movement of Consciousness into the diverse forms of its self-expression. Though from the absolute perspective, all activity is a form of *kriyā-śakti*, from our limited perspective there is an important distinction to be made between "*kriyā*" and "karma." Both words mean "action," but karmic actions (defined as volitional actions motivated by an expected result) bind the individual soul and restrict her freedom, whereas actions that partake of *kriyā-śakti* are, like all the *śakti*s, absolutely free and thus not part of the usual karmic system. In other words, karma is conditioned and conditional action while *kriyā* is spontaneously arising action that expresses our natural being. What are examples of such actions? Any action done for its own sake, pure and selfless, with no agenda, as a spontaneous expression of your being, is a manifestation of *kriyā-śakti* and thus does not bind you further into the karmic cycle. One of my teachers says that when anyone wants to do something for him, he cautions them, "Please do this for me only if you can do it with all the delight of a child feeding a dog, because I don't want to have to pay for it later." That is his way of saying that he wants his relationships with others to be expressions of *kriyā-śakti*, not karmic bondage. The spiritual practices, unless they are done in a spirit of grasping after results, are all expressions of *kriyā-śakti*. That is why spiritual practice is most successful when you enjoy it for its own sake, experiencing it as a celebration of the Divine you nature rather than as a means to an end.

Karma is conditioned and conditional action, while *kriyā* is spontaneously arising action that expresses our natural being.

Śiva as Lord of the Dance (Naṭarāja)

THE FIVE ACTS OF GOD

If the five, or rather six, Powers describe what the divine is, the five Acts describe what the divine *does*. In this sense they are expressions of the Power of Action (which of course never operates separately from Will, Knowing, Freedom, Consciousness and Bliss). Kṣemarāja, the disciple of Abhinava Gupta, refers to the five Acts in the opening verse to his masterful treatise *The Heart of the Teachings on Recognition* (*Pratyabhijñā-hṛdayam*):

Oṃ namaḥ śivāya satataṃ pañca-kṛtya-vidhāyine |
cidānanda-ghana-svātma-paramārthāvabhāsine ||
Reverence to the Divine, who ceaselessly performs the Five Acts,
and who, by so doing, reveals the ultimate reality of one's own
Self, brimming over with the joy of Awareness!

The Heart of Recognition

The five divine Acts (*pañca-kṛtya*) are not only what the divine does; in fact, they are all that it *ever* does. So, everything that is happening in the universe expresses one or more of these Acts. They are the following:

- **SṚṢṬI**—creation, emission, the flowing forth of Self-expression
- **STHITI**—stasis, maintenance, preservation
- **SAṂHĀRA**—dissolution, resorption, retraction
- **TIRODHĀNA**—concealment, occlusion, forgetting
- **ANUGRAHA**—revealing, remembering, grace, revelation

These five Acts take place on all scales: from the grand macrocosmic processes of the creation and dissolution of this entire universe to the moment-to-moment processes that create and dissolve your subtle inner experience of reality. Kṣemarāja teaches us in the above verse that it is the performance of these five Acts that reveals the ultimate reality of the Self as the pure dynamism of blissful Consciousness. We will investigate how this is so.

We may use the image of Śiva as Lord of the Dance (*Naṭarāja*) to orient us to the five Acts, for His four hands and upraised foot express the Acts perfectly. The first of the five Acts is *sṛṣṭi*, creation, represented by Śiva's upper right hand, holding the *ḍāmaru* drum. The drum represents the rhythmic pulsation that gives rise to the whole of reality. Since the universe is nothing but *spanda,* the dynamic pulsation of interlaced movements of expansion and contraction, the beat of the drum sets the tone for all that follows. Now, *sṛṣṭi* is usually translated as "creation," but in the Tantrik context, it is better rendered as "emission" (which is in fact closer to the root meaning of the word) for the act of creation is nothing other than the flowing forth of the Divine into manifest form, the projection of its self-reflection into embodiment.

The second Act is *sthiti,* the maintenance of something that has been created for a specific duration of time. Thus we may also translate it as "stasis." This act is represented by Śiva's lower right hand, held in *abhaya-mudrā,* the palm-outward gesture that traditionally indicates, "Do not fear. I am in support."

The third Act is *saṃhāra*, usually translated as "dissolution" or even "destruction." It is represented by Śiva's upper left hand, holding fire. (In mainstream Hinduism, destruction is considered the special purview of Śiva when He is placed on par with Viṣṇu and Brahmā. This is because of Śiva's association with the power of Time (*mahākāla*), seen as a primarily destructive force.) However, in Śaiva Tantra, *saṃhāra* is understood not as destruction so much, but as "reabsorption" or "retraction"; it is simply the drawing back into himself of what God has created, the reabsorption of into His unmanifest formless being. What seems to us as destruction is truly just reabsorption into the luminous, indescribable ground of pure potentiality into which all things ultimately dissolve.

The fourth Act is *tirodhāna*, which means "occlusion, concealment, forgetting." It is expressed by the arm that crosses Naṭarāja's chest with the palm facing down, concealing His heart from view. Of all the Acts, this Act of self-forgetting is the most difficult to understand. The process by which

Consciousness moves from the unmanifest state of absolute potential into manifest particularity necessarily involves concealment or forgetting. For in order for Consciousness to manifest itself in one particular form, it must conceal or suppress all other possible forms. In order for God to fully become you, and thereby embrace Herself as you, She must temporarily forget everything about Herself that is not you. Thus the coalescence of Consciousness into embodied form is necessarily an act of *self-limitation*—but one that is freely chosen. The movement from total expansion into contracted embodiment is an "auspicious squeeze," to use my friend Sianna Sherman's felicitous phrase. In the expanded state of absolute potential, there is total homogeneity and stillness and thus no possibility for dynamic action and creative self-expression. Since the latter qualities are potencies that are inherent in divine Consciousness, there was (and is) no possibility of failing to express them. To fail to express any part of Her being would be an act of self-negation on the part of God, and since Her very nature is love and reverent self-awareness, that would be impossible.

The coalescence of Consciousness into embodied form is an act of self-limitation—but one that is freely chosen.

Thus the act of creation, of particularization and diversification, is necessarily also one of concealment. This can be difficult to accept for us, because suffering is one corollary of such self-forgetting on the part of God. When we do not see the whole reality, we suffer, since true bliss is predicated on seeing things as they really are. Therefore the fourth Act is naturally balanced and resolved by the fifth, that of *anugraha*, self-revelation or grace. This Act is symbolized by Śiva Naṭarāja's upraised foot, because in Indian tradition the feet of the Guru are the most sacred part of his body and are associated with the outflow of his grace. Note that Śiva's hand of concealing points directly at the upraised foot of grace: one implies the other. Grace, the blessing of the divine, is nothing but the act of remembering or self-revealing that cancels out the previous act of forgetting or self-concealing; or more accurately, it brings the latter to fruition by revealing its deeper purpose. Grace is fundamentally an act of *reconciliation* in this tradition. It is through the blessing of this revelation that an individual, limited manifestation of the divine (such as you) is reconciled with the pattern and purpose of the Whole. Such reconciliation is thus also a reintegration; through it, you experientially realize yourself as a complete and perfect expression of the deep pattern of the one Consciousness which moves and dances in all things. The act of grace is about showing you who you really are. This revelation does not negate what you already know of yourself but simply shows it to be the most superficial layer of your vast being.

This then is another example of the pattern of contraction as a necessary precursor to further expansion. That's what we call *spanda* in this tradition. The contractive movement into embodiment that expresses the particular facets of the Divine (such as yourself) is completed and consummated by an expansion back into the awareness of the fullness of your divine nature. But, and this is crucial, this expansion does not necessarily involve any relinquishment of your individuality; rather, that very individuality is experienced as a unique expression of the pattern of the Whole. Such an experience is the result of grace.

Through grace, your individuality can be experienced as a beautifully unique expression of the pattern of the Whole.

The use of the word "grace" might trigger the wrong associations for some; for example, some people think of grace as a blessing that must be earned through good works or by being a "good person." The implication that God is one who bestows favor on those who are worthy and withholds it from others, says Abhinava Gupta, is simply the "nonsensical prattling of the dualists." In a nondualist system, such an understanding is impossible. So, what activates the power of grace in an apparently limited individual such as ourselves? It can only be the exquisitely subtle yet profound movement within us by which we begin to open ourselves to a greater reality. To use a metaphor, as soon as we make space within our hearts, the power of grace moves in to fill the vacuum. When we have had enough of the pleasures and pains, the ups and downs, of the ordinary existence, we turn toward our final expansion and open to divine reality, which underlies and pervades all of that. Then *anugraha,* divine grace, inexorably flows into us in proportion to our ability to open to it. The etymology of *anugraha* is "that which follows grasping," which seems a bit strange. I have not yet seen an explanation of this in any primary source, but I take it to allude to the experience of blessedness that follows upon our grasping of our own innate divine potential. When we glimpse, however briefly, the magnificence of our true nature, we begin to inherit our birthright. The gratitude that wells up in response to the inexpressible sweetness of this experience of awakening is such that we can say nothing but "I am so blessed!" This is grace.

The five Acts of creation, sustenance, dissolution, concealment, and grace might seem to be grand cosmological processes, distantly removed from your everyday life. So, how is it that the performance of all five Acts reveals the ultimate reality of your very own Self, as Kṣemarāja claims? See page 111 NŚT teaches that our universe exhibits self-similarity, like a snowflake or a fractal, with the same patterns repeating on all levels. As above, so below. As without, so within. As here, so elsewhere. Thus the five Acts that are involved in the universal process are precisely the movements of our individual process as well. Our moment-to-moment experience of reality can be described in terms of these five Acts. (Things are going to get a bit more philosophical and dense soon, so feel free to skip a bit if you get bogged down. The text gets less philosophical again in about six pages.)

The Krama school of NŚT teaches that we can observe the divine acts of *sṛṣṭi*, *sthiti*, and *saṃhāra* (emission, statis and retraction) in the arising and falling away of each and every cognition. Whether the object of awareness is something we are thinking about (a concept) or something we are currently perceiving (a percept), it undergoes the same process. The cognition of it emerges out of an apparently blank or neutral "void" state, persists for a short time, then dissolves again into the void. Most cognitions trigger another related cognition so quickly that we cannot perceive any space between them—but we can perceive it at least at the end of what we call a "train of thought." The dissolution of the last of a connected series of cognitions gives way to a perceptible space between thoughts, often experienced as a kind of "coming back to yourself"—a natural return to greater awareness of yourself and your environment in the present moment, which is simultaneously an expansion into open possibility. It is in this moment of connecting to reality, which provides an opportunity for self-reflection, that we choose to conceal or reveal to ourselves the fact of our agency in the whole process—that it is not something happening to us but a process in which our own consciousness is both agent, meaning the actor, the author of the process, and the ground of the whole process. The Krama-influenced Recognition school (Pratyabhijñā) teaches that this process of cognition, by which the field of our consciousness contracts into particular thought-forms and releases them again, something that happens countless times each day, holds the key to the liberating recognition of ourselves as a microcosmic expression of the whole of divine reality. Let us investigate this more fully.

Ābhāsa Theory Part One: The Status of "External" Objects

Investigating how the Act of creation unfolds within us will take us on a little journey. In order to understand how an object of awareness manifests, we must understand the relation between the perceiver and the perceived and the nature of the existence of apparently external objects.

The process begins when Consciousness manifests an object of awareness. This is described as a "descent" of Consciousness from a fully expanded state of absolute potential—a densification of the energy of Consciousness whereby it begins to vibrate on the more limited wavelength of the object. In other words, Consciousness coalesces and contracts in conformity with the object to be perceived and thus creates a representation of it in awareness. Now, an object of awareness could be anything, such as a hovering dragonfly or your memory of a loved one. The traditional examples that are given for an object of awareness are the color blue or the feeling of happiness. The important thing is that all "objects" of awareness are in fact just particular vibrations of the one field of Consciousness. They all arise out of a state of pure potentiality, the infinite void of pure Consciousness, out of which, theoretically, anything could emerge.[37]

The manifestation of an object of awareness necessarily requires the manifestation of a limited subject as well: the perceived implies a particular perceiver. This is what we generally call "the mind." What we do not realize, however, is that the mind and its object are only an apparent bifurcation of one principle: the Goddess Consciousness who is the ground of the whole process. It divides into two mutually correlated and coordinated contractions, reflections of each other as it were, manifesting in two spheres that we have labeled as "internal" and "external." These labels conceal the fact that no "external" reality can be shown to exist that is independent of a corresponding "internal" reality. This invariable concomitance proves that they are aspects of each other. Invariable concomitance simply means that the two things always arise together and cannot be shown to ever arise separately. When two things always arise together and never arise separately, we say they must be two aspects of the same thing. Modern cognitive science can accept that we create a mental image that is a representation or reflection of an actual external object and that mirrors it; but from the perspective of NŚT, *the object is equally a reflection of the internal cognition.* In other words, the apparently external object does not have existential priority. But an objectioner might reply here, the object must have priority, because multiple different people perceive it and describe it similarly. No, this tradition replies, it need not have priority if those different perceivers are all aspects of *one* Perceiver, which differentiates itself precisely in order to view the object from different perspectives. (For of course no two people can have precisely the same perspective on anything, literally or figuratively, and this lack of redundancy is, in a sense, precisely what justifies each individual's existence.)

The mind and its object are an apparent bifurcation of one principle: the Goddess Consciousness.

Well, what about the opposite case, the objectioner asks—in cognition of a concept (as opposed to a percept). Surely then the subject has priority over the object, since the concept I contemplate is part of my own private reality. Not so, comes the reply: can you think of any concept that you could contemplate that has not also been contemplated by others? The very creation of a concept is a social act, a collective act of meaning-making, that from the perspective of this tradition is only possible because the individuals involved are all aspects of one being. Furthermore, in this philosophy, not only any concept but equally any object known by more than one individual is said to be co-created by all those who perceive it. This of course explains both why no single individual has complete autonomy in the creation of her reality and why, to experience such unlimited autonomy, one must subsume one's individuality in one's universality (that is, one's divinity). So, we have shown that the manifestation of the cognition of any object, however simple, is a process that cannot be separated from the manifestation of an "external" object, and vice versa—the two are aspects of one object and cognition, mirroring each other as part of the dialectical process by which divine Consciousness reflects on itself and on the various dimensions of its being. Pondering this truth as a meditative exercise is an example of the Tantrik practice called *bhāvanā*, which means "creative contemplation," or meditation, or feeling into something. As it is said in the sacred *Vijñāna-bhairava-tantra*:

Vijñāna-bhairava-tantra

> *The awareness of the knower and the known is common to all embodied beings; but for yogīs, this is the difference: they pay careful attention to the connection.* || 106 ||

So the *Vijñāna-bhairava-tantra* in verse 106 says what a yogi *is* is one who pays careful attention to the connection between knower and known. The interdependence, the unity of these apparently separate aspects of reality. And indeed, for the Tantrik yogī, the most fascinating thing to do is observe the process by which Consciousness creates reality by dividing itself into three: a perceived object, a perceiver of that object whose experience of herself in that moment is colored by that object, and a process of perception that links the two. All three aspects of consciousness are expressed in a simple sentence like "I see a pot." By providing three separate terms with distinct grammatical functions, language programs us to believe that the three *are* separate, the "I," the "seeing" and the "pot"—but reflection shows they must be part of one continuous process, for not one of them can exist without the other two. To be more precise, the *limited* "I," the sense of one's self as a perceiver, cannot exist without the other two, but the unlimited "I" can, for it is the indescribable ground of all three (more on that later). For a yogī who is fully aware of all that is entailed in making the statement, "I see a pot," it is both a profound philosophical realization *and* a spiritual experience.

Ābhāsa Theory: Part Two
Many Shinings of the One Light

One more note on the nature of external objects. To fully understand how they manifest in Consciousness, we much touch on what is called *ābhāsa* theory. In this understanding of reality, all manifestation is a projection or "shining" (*ābhāsa*) of the one Light of Consciousness. Each object has its various characteristics, such as "tall," "round," "blue," "male," or "made of sandalwood." Each of these various characteristics is called an *ābhāsa*, literally "a shining" within Consciousness. They are each a vibration of that one Light. (Note that "shine" and "manifest" and "vibrate" are different meanings of the same word in Sanskrit: whether √*ābhā* or √*prakāś*.) The mind, in this theory, is said to be a *synthesizer,* for it constructs an object it calls "pot" insofar as it perceives the various *ābhāsas* of "short," "round," "blue," "hard," and so on as pertaining to a single object.[38] It's the mind that sees those characteristics as pertaining to that object, which is why it's called a synthesizer. However, there are less tangible *ābhāsas* that are even more important to our individualized perception of an object, and without these we would be no different from a robot. The most important of these "subjective" *ābhāsas* are 1) how much you like or dislike the object, 2) how useful or useless it is to you, and 3) what prior education and experience you have concerning the object. When we perceive an object, our mind is synthesizing all of these *ābhāsas* into a unified experience of a single "thing." But there is no such thing as a pot in general; there are only particular pots, each one unique due to being composed of different *ābhāsas*. The idea of a

In abhasa theory, the mind is a synthesizer.

pot in general is just that, a mental concept with no corresponding reality. Here we are using this simpler example of a tangible object; needless to say, the act of synthesizing an experience of an intangible object (like, say, "justice" or "love") is even more complex.[39]

The practical application of *ābhāsa* theory is that it helps you to encounter reality as it is: various vibrations of energy analyzed by the different sense faculties and synthesized into an object by the mind, and then made the object of various judgments. Observing this process requires a step back and expansion into a meta-awareness that is considerably closer to our real nature, allowing us to hold a much bigger yet more subtle and more sensitive picture. I said *closer* to our real nature because ultimately we seek the ability to hold that broader perspective without the sense of detachment connoted by the phrase "step back." Indeed, in the Tantra we seek that holistic meta-awareness even while fully engaged with the world.

To conclude our excursus on *ābhāsa* theory, I want to note that our Western materialistic society (if I may usefully overgeneralize for a moment) grants greater reality to the traits of an object that everyone agrees on (such as its physical parameters), calling those traits "objective reality." Less significance is given to our "subjective" experience of an object—despite the fact that those dimensions are never absent from anyone's experience of the object and are invariably more important to each real individual experiencer. NŚT implicitly argues that the so-called subjective traits (the appeal and utility of the object and so on) are just as much a part of the reality of the object as its physical properties, for nobody experiences it without those subjective traits, even though they vary from person to person. "Why bother to make this point?" you may ask. Because, by focusing attention on the so-called "objective" consensus about a given object, our culture takes the most superficial layer of reality to be the primary one and thus fails to realize that it is the sum total of the *different* perspectives on the object that constitute its total multidimensional reality. It is the so-called subjective dimension that we argue over, and even kill each other over, without realizing that these different experiences of the thing or person or situation in question are *all* part of its reality. All co-created by the one consciousness. Acknowledging this, our differences of opinion invite us into a cooperative process of inquiry by which we come to understand the way in which Consciousness creates reality.

The sum total of the different perspectives on each object constitute its total reality.

We have taken some time to explore the various facets involved in the manifestation of an object of awareness (and remember, *all* objects are necessarily objects of awareness). We have seen that the very act of perceiving or thinking of something implies a whole interconnected theory of the nature of reality. But let us return to the sequential flow of a simple act of cognition, such as the awareness of the color blue or the feeling of happiness. First, the object emerges into conscious awareness: we are performing the act of creation or emission. Even if it is a familiar object, you never experience it exactly the same way twice; thus we are creating it anew each time. Now, the object must have some duration for it to be experienced as a reality. Thus, we perform the act of stasis (*sthiti*) when we hold a thought or percept in awareness, however briefly. It may mutate, unfolding as a series of connected ideas or images (each with their own mini reiteration of the cyclical flow), but still we stay with a particular line of thought, sustaining it until we release it.

When we feel "done" with that object of awareness, we release it, and it dissolves, merging back into the indescribable ground out of which it came—the Goddess Consciousness in Her fully expanded and all-encompassing form. This is the act of *saṃhāra,* dissolution or retraction. As mentioned above, just after the moment of dissolution, when we return to the timeless ground of all thought, there is a moment of opportunity. At that moment in which we have, however briefly, been returned to the ground of awareness, we have a choice: self-revealing or self-forgetting. We have the opportunity to recognize that this still, expansive, ground state of pure Consciousness in which we rest for but a moment is our true nature, the inherently blissful and free Self, the author of all five Acts.

This is the great secret: we touch down in our fundamental nature many times a day—every single time we have released one thought or

We have a choice: self-revealing or self-forgetting.

experience and before we turn to the next—yet we do not know how to repose in that divine state, we do not know how to savor its divine *rasa*, its sweetness, its juice; indeed, we do not even recognize the opportunity oftentimes. Usually, when confronted with this moment of choice, we do not perform the Act of *anugraha* (revealing) but rather that of *tirodhāna* (forgetting or concealing). Instead of surrendering to the opportunity for ineffable self-awareness, we unreflectively initiate another train of thought as soon as possible, one that often begins as an evaluation of the previous train of thought. Needless to say, the likelihood of recognizing the opportunity in the moment of choice, the moment of "touchdown," is greater the longer that moment lasts. Thus the yogī seeks to prolong the space between the thoughts, even just by a little bit. That's where a meditation practice comes in. It allows everything to slow down a bit so we can see our golden opportunities more clearly.[40]

The yogini seeks to prolong the "space between the thoughts".

So, you are performing the five Acts of God within yourself all day, every day. You create thoughts, hold them, dissolve them, and choose to reveal or conceal what's really going on and who is really in charge, and then you do it again. You're always doing one of these five Acts! Whether you are responding to external or internal stimuli, *you* manifest the objects of awareness that create your specific experience, *you* hold onto them, *you* let them go, and then *you* choose: to repose in your true nature and thus recognize yourself as the divine author of the whole process or to overlook your Self and, instead, look to the next thing that might give you pleasure, in an endless cycle. If you choose the former self-revelation, you choose empowerment. To recognize that the space of expanded self-awareness between thoughts is their unchanging ground—to recognize that there is one eternal Perceiver of the arising and dissolving of this cognitive process, and you are It—is supremely empowering and liberating, for in so doing you realize that you are always choosing your experience of reality, and you can also choose differently. You are not and never have been a victim of circumstance, for no one else can determine your inner state for you. True, choosing differently can be quite difficult at first because of the power of your *saṃskāras* (subliminal impressions of past experiences that influence how you see the present). We tend to repeat old familiar patterns rather than making new choices. Even so, identifying yourself as the ground of the process of thought and experience instead of as your thoughts means that you are no longer at the mercy of those thoughts. You can choose to alter the way you experience reality, for you are the only one who creates and dissolves the cognitions through which you experience reality. Let's take a moment to clarify this. Of course, it's easy to think that you are the thinking mind. That you are the thinker, or the stream of thoughts. But it's obvious once you take a moment to look at it that that's not what you are. You are the one who is aware that there are thoughts or not in any given moment. And that awareness persists whether there's thoughts or not. So how could you be the thought-stream? Since you are not the stream of thoughts, the contents of the mind have very little to tell you about who you really are. Awakening is, in a very real sense, waking up out of the notion that the contents of the mind tell you something about who you really are. When you wake up out of that notion you naturally begin to look deeper, to feel deeper into a more expansive sense of your being within which thoughts arise and subside just like tiny bubbles on the surface of a vast ocean.

You are not and never have been a victim of circumstance.

In conclusion, let's return to the verse that started this whole discussion:

> *Reverence to the Divine, who ceaselessly performs the Five Acts, and who, by so doing, reveals the ultimate reality of one's own Self, brimming over with the Bliss of Consciousness!*

The Heart of Recognition

Kṣemarāja assures us that by accessing our root nature, our core essence, the One who constantly performs the five Acts—not different from the divine Author of the whole cosmic process—we will discover a level of awareness which is densely replete with the bliss of pure Being, the bliss of being aware (cit ananda), the bliss of being embodied Consciousness, of being the absolutely free agent in the creation of our moment-to-moment experience of reality.

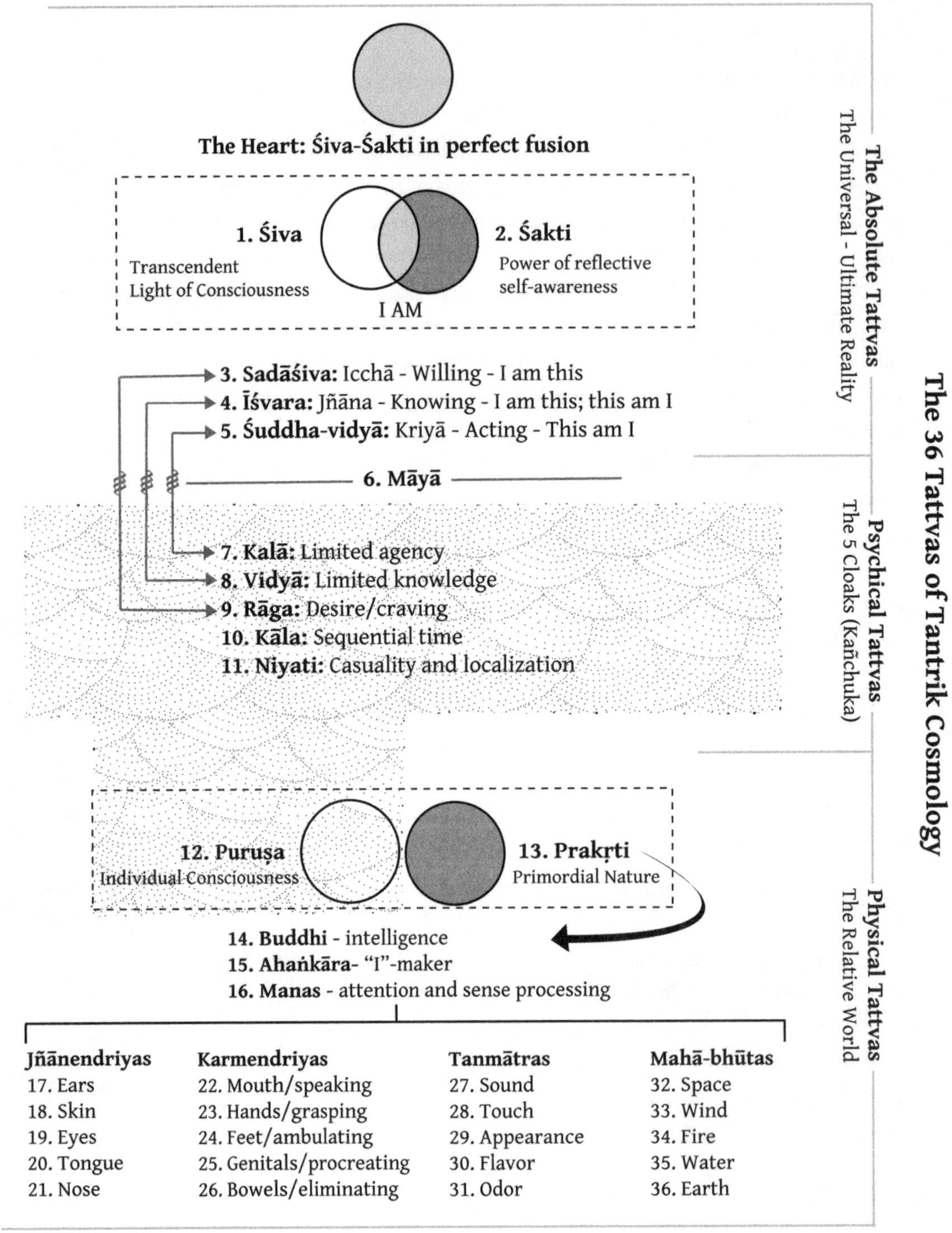

The 36 Tattvas of Tantrik Cosmology
The Heart: Śiva-Śakti in perfect fusion
1. Śiva
Transcendent Light of Consciousness
2. Śakti
Power of reflective self-awareness
I AM
The Absolute Tattvas
The Universal - Ultimate Reality
3. Sadāśiva: Icchā - Willing - I am this
4. Īśvara: Jñāna - Knowing - I am this; this am I
5. Śuddha-vidyā: Kriyā - Acting - This am I
6. Māyā
7. Kalā: Limited agency
8. Vidyā: Limited knowledge
9. Rāga: Desire/craving
10. Kāla: Sequential time
11. Niyati: Casuality and localization
Psychical Tattvas
The 5 Cloaks (Kañchuka)
12. Puruṣa
Individual Consciousness
13. Prakṛti
Primordial Nature
14. Buddhi - intelligence
15. Ahaṅkāra- "I"-maker
16. Manas - attention and sense processing
Physical Tattvas
The Relative World
Jñānendriyas
17. Ears
18. Skin
19. Eyes
20. Tongue
21. Nose
Karmendriyas
22. Mouth/speaking
23. Hands/grasping
24. Feet/ambulating
25. Genitals/procreating
26. Bowels/eliminating
Tanmātras
27. Sound
28. Touch
29. Appearance
30. Flavor
31. Odor
Mahā-bhūtas
32. Space
33. Wind
34. Fire
35. Water
36. Earth

THE 36 TATTVAS:
PRINCIPLES OF REALITY

Central to Tantrik philosophy and cosmology is the system of the *tattvas* or "levels of reality," or "principles of reality." The *tattva* system is a kind of map of the conscious being's experience of the world. (Please refer to the Tattva Chart to the left) The earlier non-Tantrik Sānkhya philosophy (followed by Patañjali among others) articulated a system of twenty-five *tattvas*; when Śaiva Tantra took over and reworked the Sānkhya system, it added eleven more levels of reality on top, which it claimed the Sānkhyas had failed to discover.

Tattvas 1 -> 36 is the order of creation; 36 -> 1 is the order of liberation or return to the Source.

It's difficult to define the word *tattva*; it literally means "that-ness." We often translate it as "principle of reality," but Abhinava Gupta offers a more precise definition that is helpful if you can understand it: "A *tattva* is that which, by virtue of its reality, enables conscious agents to subsume the categories within it." It's easier to understand the concept if you familiarize yourself with the specific *tattvas*. The *tattvas* can be enumerated from the bottom up or the top down. The top down order (Śiva -> Earth) is the order of creation (*sṛṣṭi-krama*). The bottom up order (Earth -> Śiva) is the order of liberation or return to Source (*saṃhāra-krama*). We'll examine them in the latter sequence, i.e., from the bottom up.The first five *tattvas* are the five great elements of materiality, or *pañca mahā-bhūtas*. Each is accompanied by its traditional Tantrik symbol, used in visualization exercises.

TATTVA #36: EARTH (*pṛthvī*)

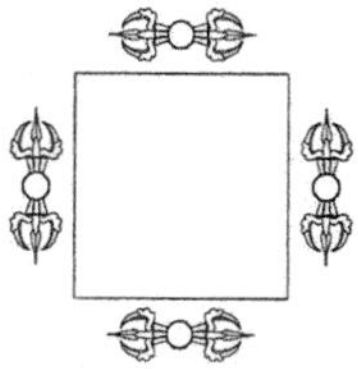

Earth, at the bottom of the *tattva* hierarchy, is not seen by the Tāntrikas as the "lowest" of the principles, but rather the most complete: that level of reality on which all the *tattvas* are fully manifest. In other words, at the top of the *tattva* hierarchy (Śiva-*tattva*) all the principles are present in potential form, while at the bottom (Earth-*tattva*) all those potentialities inherent in the Divine are fully expressed.

Earth element by itself is the principle of solidity, density, resistance, and groundedness. The exoteric *bīja* mantra (seed-syllable) commonly used to evoke and activate it is *lam.*[41] Now, there is a common misconception that the *bīja* mantra *lam* is associated with the mūlādhāra cakra. In fact, it is the *bīja* mantra of earth element which happens to be installed at the level of mūlādhāra cakra in the subtle body, which will come to later. With earth element, all five senses are engaged in perceiving it so, it is a full embodied experience. The traditional abstract symbol used in Tantric visualization for earth element is a golden yellow square marked by vadras in all four sides, or a golden yellow cube or prism.

TATTVA #35: WATER (*āp* or *āpaḥ*)

Water is the principle of liquidity and solvency. The senses of hearing, touch, sight, and taste are engaged in perceiving it, especially the latter. The *bīja* mantra commonly used for it is *vam*. The abstract symbol for the water element is a silvery crescent moon with its points pointing upward, a silvery white crescent moon, or a silvery white silver bowl with water inside of it and sometimes pictured with two lavender water lilies to either side of that bowl of silvery water.

TATTVA #34: FIRE (*tejas*)

Fire is the principle of combustion and transformation. (Āyurveda speaks of the "digestive fire" within the human body as a way of describing the process by which the digestive system transforms food into energy, which is a kind of combustion.) The senses of hearing, touch, and sight are engaged in perceiving it, especially the latter. The *bīja* mantra commonly used for it is *ram*. The abstract symbol for the fire element is an upward pointing red triangle wreathed in flames, or in three-dimensional visualization it is a red pyramid.

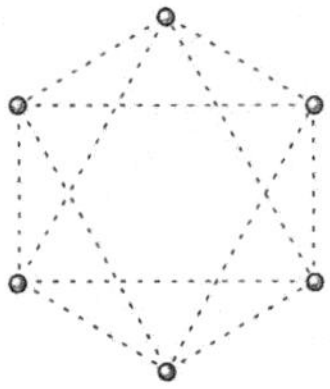

TATTVA #33: WIND (*vāyu*)

Wind is the principle of mobility (note that "air" and "wind" are the same word in Sanskrit, but the latter would be the more accurate translation). The primary characteristic of *vāyu* is the way it moves to fill a partial vacuum, constantly seeking to even itself out. So the wind element is primarily marked by its mobility, which is why "wind" is a better translation than "air." The senses of hearing and touch are engaged in perceiving it, especially the latter. The *bīja* mantra commonly used for it is *yam.* And you can hear and feel wind especially the latter it activates the touch element mostly.

The abstract symbol is six smoky black dots or six smoky black spheres that are rotating round arranged on the points of a Star of David.

TATTVA #32: SPACE (*ākāśa*)

Space is the principle of vacuity and of extension (three-dimensionality). It is sometimes mistranslated in English as "ether" (a concept of the interstellar medium that was debunked around a hundred years ago). Really, *ākāśa* means "space." Space provides the context for the manifestation of all matter/energy. The sense of hearing is engaged in perceiving it, in the sense that sound resonates through space and requires space to resonate in. The *bīja* mantra commonly used for it is *ham.* The visualization of the Space element, as you might imagine, is simply black space or a black sphere sometimes visualized as studded with multicolored points of light.

The next five *tattvas* are the *tanmātras* or so-called "subtle elements," that is to say, the properties of things that make them perceptible by our senses. Sentient beings live in worlds that are smellable, tastable, visible, tangible, and audible. By virtue of these qualities, sentient beings developed senses corresponding to these qualities (see below).

TATTVA #31: ODOR (*gandha*)
TATTVA #30: FLAVOR (*rasa*)
TATTVA #29: APPEARANCE (or form; *rūpa*)
TATTVA #28: TACTILITY (*sparśa*)
TATTVA #27: SOUND VIBRATION (*śabda*)

The next five are the five "action capacities" or *karmendriyas*. These are the five fundamental functions of a human being in relation to his or her environment.

TATTVA #26: EVACUATION (bowels)
TATTVA #25: REPRODUCTION (genitals)
TATTVA #24: LOCOMOTION (feet)
TATTVA #23: MANIPULATION (hand)
TATTVA #22: SPEECH (mouth)

The next five are the "sense capacities" or *jñānendriyas*. They are the internal correlates of the five "subtle elements" above, the sensory energies that have evolved in conformity with the manifold sensibility of reality. Since all that really exists of course is a single field of energy, the senses (even touch) are essentially frequency analyzers that translate specific kinds of vibrations into the apparently tangible and static realities perceived by our brain, such as the visual appearance, color, texture, or sound of something.

TATTVA #21: SMELLING (*ghrāṇa*)
TATTVA #20: TASTING (*rasana*)
TATTVA #19: SEEING (*cakṣus*)
TATTVA #18: TOUCHING (*tvak*, lit. "skin")
TATTVA #17: HEARING "*śrotra*"

The four sets of five that constitute the twenty lower *tattvas* we have enumerated so far may be aligned this way, bringing out their correspondences more clearly:

Dense Elements	Subtle Elements	Perceptive Energies	Active Energies
Earth	Odor	Smelling	Evacuation
Water	Flavor	Tasting	Pleasure/Reproduction
Fire	Appearance	Seeing	Locomotion
Wind	Touch	Feeling	Manipulating
Space	Sound	Hearing	Speech

Most of these alignments may seem common sense, but in fact a correct and complete meeting between the energies of senses and their respective sense objects such as the Tāntrikas seek is more rare than it seems. That is, most of us live in a mental world of our own making to such an extent that we are not well grounded in the sensual world. When we do pay attention to it, it is "through a glass, darkly," filtering it through that mentally constructed world. This is why the Tantra stresses sensual meditations—meditative savoring of food and music, as well as slowed down and ritualized acts of refined awareness like the Japanese tea ceremony—that allow us to cultivate our ability to let the senses meet their objects fully. In nondual Śaiva Tantra, this is called "feeding the goddesses of the senses." When fed properly, the "goddesses" reward you by suffusing your awareness with aesthetic rapture (*chanakara*), increasing your capacity to experience beauty. The whole world becomes more vivid and real, more radiantly lovely, more full of life-energy, not the relatively dull and lifeless world perceived by one living primarily in the mind, or the insubstantial shadow world perceived by a transcendentalist meditator (one who takes the transcendent realm of the void as ultimately "Real," and this world as unreal). The latter are the worlds of one who starves the goddesses of the senses.

Now we move into the higher and subtler *tattvas*, and here it gets more interesting. The next three are the aspects of what in the West are generally called "the mind." The Sanskrit collective term for these faculties is the *antaḥ-karaṇa*, the "inner instrument," meaning the mind.

TATTVA #16: MIND (*manas*, faculty of attention and sense processing)

This tattva is similar to Prana, which is an overarching category with five subtypes, the first of which is called Prana. Here also is the overarching category of mind, within which one aspect of the three aspects of mind is also translated as "mind." So Tattva #16 is really *manas,* which we could translate as "mind" but more accurately is the faculty of tension and sense processing.

The *manas* is the common functional mind, processing and synthesizing the data collected by the senses. It is also the faculty of attention, and thus it is the *manas* that needs to be gently trained and lovingly disciplined when learning to meditate.

The ego is a persistent contraction of awareness in the form of a collection of self-images that causes suffering through artificial self-limitation.

TATTVA #15: EGO (*ahaṅkāra*, lit. "identity-maker")

The *ahaṅkāra* is the part of mind that identifies what is "me" and "mine." It appropriates certain things and experiences, assimilating them into its constructed sense of identity. Simply put, it is what you think you are. So, it is the ego that declares, "I am fat," "I am thin," "I am clever," "I am stupid," "I am independent," "I am a victim," and every other "I" statement (*ego* literally means "I am" in Latin). The aggregation of all these thoughts constitutes the egoic identity, so the ego is nothing more than a raft of self-images bound together by the power of your belief in them. The egoic identity is a fictitious construct, consisting primarily of self-images that persist because they are believed and attached to. Each such self-image is based in a particular moment or moments of past experience that generated a mental construct (a "story") that was taken as a static reality. For example, the moment when you are praised or condemned for some aspect of your being, and by buying that story, you acquired a self-image to add into this forming ego that became the static reality. But the ego is essentially a fiction, because all that really exists is the flux of phenomena in each present moment. But it seems very real because you believe in it, you believe in that raft of self-images, and belief shapes experience of reality. Ego, then, to define it very precisely, is *a persistent contraction of awareness in the form of a collection of self-images that causes suffering through artificial self-limitation.* Since it is part of the inherent dynamism of consciousness to pulsate continually through cycles of expansion and contraction, whenever we get "stuck" in one or the other, we lose alignment and experience suffering. The ego should be a fluid entity but instead becomes a static prison.

Many spiritual traditions view the ego as an enemy on the spiritual path because its voice seems opposite to the divine voice, the voice of our innermost Self. However, in the Tantrik tradition, an enemy is simply an ally viewed in the wrong way. Thus the ego is not to be annihilated in Tantrik yoga but rather purified and infinitely expanded until it simply melts into all that is. Since the ego simply means "what you think you are," expanding it means expanding your sense of self, including more and more reality in your self-definition. Ultimately, when the ego expands infinitely, you experience all things in yourself and yourself in all things. There are no more boundaries to selfhood. You have acquired an all-encompassing "I." When you experience all beings as part of yourself, you naturally act with compassion and wisdom. This is the state of *pūrṇo'ham vimarśa,* which can be translated several ways: "the perfect 'I'-consciousness," or "the awareness 'I am full and complete and whole'" or "the awareness 'the real I encompasses everything'." It is the state of complete all-inclusive expansion. Just as the mass of any object accelerated to the speed of light increases to infinity, in the same way when the ego reaches the state of complete expansion, it merges into the ocean of Consciousness. Obviously, there is a pitfall in this particular strategy: you expand you ego to become very large, but not infinite; you may find that becomes a problem if you get stuck there.

The most important form of discernment on the spiritual path is discerning between what is to be held close and what is to be laid aside.

TATTVA #14: DISCERNING FACULTY (*buddhi*, commonly translated as "intellect")

This is the most important mental faculty for all schools of yoga philosophy. It is a key term in the *Bhagavad-gītā* and in Patañjali's *Yoga-sūtra.* The *buddhi* is the faculty of reason by which we formulate conceptions and make decisions and judgements, also the power of imagination. It is, most importantly for yogīs, the faculty of discernment, by which we decide what is beneficial for us and what is not. Abhinava Gupta argues that discernment (*tarka*) is the highest of all the limbs of yoga, and the only one that directly leads to liberation. The most important form of discernment on the spiritual path, he tells us, is discerning between what is to be held close (*upādeya*) and what is to be laid aside (*heya*)— that is, what is ultimately beneficial for you and what is not.

And there's the rub: what guarantee do we have that the *buddhi* is accurate in its discernment? In fact, we have ample evidence of its inaccuracy, for many times we choose what we think is beneficial, and it turns out not to be so. Of course, this is not as huge a problem as it seems because on the path of Tantrik yoga most, if not all, "mistakes" become advantages when regarded as growth opportunities. But since the learning from some mistakes is harder, more painful, and more time-consuming than strictly necessary, we wish to constantly refine and improve our ability to choose what is beneficial, and thereby increase our efficiency of movement on the path. Why does that seem so difficult?

In yoga philosophy, the *buddhi* is impaired in its function by the presence of what are called *saṃskāras*, or the subliminal impressions of past experiences. In common Sanskrit usage, a *saṃskāra* is literally an impression, like a footprint in the sand at the beach. Now, if there is a series of deep footprints and other impressions in the sand, when the tide comes in and the water flows over them, it will flow differently than if the sand were perfectly smooth. In precisely the same way, when the energy of the world flows through your mind, it is affected by the deep impressions of past experiences that are lodged there, and therefore it flows differently for you than for someone else. Thus based on our experience of the past, we formulate projections and make assumptions that too often are misaligned with the reality of the present. Our brains are good at pattern matching—perhaps too good, for even a superficial resemblance of the current situation to a past situation will cause you to unconsciously assume that the present is like the past in most of its details. This act of unconsciously projecting the past onto the present is the primary reason we are unable to be aware of the reality of the current situation as it is and, thereby, make good choices. So, the presence of *saṃskāras* impair the natural ability of the *buddhi* to discern what is beneficial and what is not.

The spiritual path is very much about developing clear vision, about cultivating the ability to see things as they really are. In classical yoga philosophy, the practices of yoga (especially meditation) have the primary purpose of dissolving the *saṃskāras*, these impressions, in order to bring about this clear vision, and the clear discernment that results from it. The analogy that is often given is that of polishing a dirty mirror. When, through yoga, the mirror of the *buddhi* becomes clear, it can perfectly reflect the light of the divine Self. Thus, the more you practice yoga, the more accurate your intuition and discernment become. Sometimes people think great yoga masters can read minds or have other psychic abilities. In fact, they just see with much less obstruction, something so rare in our world that it seems like a magical or psychic power. And indeed, knowledge *is* power—the only kind that cannot be taken away. A yoga master with a purified *buddhi* can always see the most beneficial course of action in any given situation, giving him or her a great power to change situations and uplift human beings. Of course, if this accurate power of discernment is used to build and reinforce a new spiritual ego, then it can become a pitfall.

Finally, we should note that in Tantrik philosophy, the *buddhi* is not localized in the brain but extends throughout the body. Thus *saṃskāras* of different kinds are distributed throughout the body and can be released by the physical as well as the mental practices of yoga. We experience the *buddhi* on different levels of the body; for example, when we speak of "gut instinct," we refer to an aspect of the *buddhi*'s intentionality associated with very deep, unconscious *saṃskāras*, which we tend to feel in the viscera, the enteric nervous system. However, without the practice of yoga, the gut instinct in which we place so much trust might in fact be based in fear and lead us badly astray.

TATTVA #13: SECONDARY MATERIALITY (*prakṛti*)

Prakṛti, sometimes translated as "nature," sometimes as "materiality," really refers to the entire physical universe of matter/energy. (Matter and energy were recognized as aspects of each other by the early Indian philosophers, whereas in the West the discovery is still so recent (Einstein, about 110 years ago) that we don't have a single word for matter/energy as Sanskrit does: *prakṛti.*) In the human microcosm, *prakṛti* refers to the body/mind field. Just as matter and energy are aspects of each other, the body and mind are not separate, but on a continuum: the mind is the subtlest aspect of body and the body the most tangible manifestation of the mind. This is why disease in the mind affects the body, and vice versa.

Prakṛti can also refer to the unmanifest field of primordial materiality at the beginning of the universe, out of which all the lower *tattvas* are created. In this form, *prakṛti* consists of perfect balance of the three *guṇas* or qualities of nature: *sattva,* lucidity and lightness; *rajas,* energy and passion; and *tamas,* darkness, heaviness, and inertia. These three *guṇas* recombine in various proportions to make all the *tattvas* 14–36 (above). The field of *prakṛti,* then, is everything that can become an object of consciousness; i.e., everything except the *tattvas* we have yet to address (1–12 below). However, note that in the Tantra, *Prakṛti* is defined as "secondary materiality" because there is a higher principle, Māyā, which is the primary source of the material universe (see *tattva #6* below).

TATTVA #12: INDIVIDUAL "Soul" (*puruṣa,* the knowing subject, the Self, the witness, pure consciousness, the embodied knower of the field = *ātman, jīva, kṣetrajña*)

The *puruṣa,* the innermost self, soul, or pure witness consciousness, sits at the top of the hierarchy of *tattvas* in the system of Sāṅkhya and the classical yoga of Patañjali. For those non-Tantrik systems, it is the ultimate principle, a transcendent reality: spirit as *opposed* to matter/energy. These systems propose that there are a plurality of divine Souls (each sentient being having his own), that are not part of one overarching conscious entity. For Tantrik philosophy, it naturally follows, the *puruṣa* is not the highest principle for it does not express an all-encompassing View. Rather, *puruṣa* is correctly understood in the Tantrik view as contracted form of the universal Consciousness. So, in the Tantrik view, there are not a plurality of selves, as in Patañjali, but rather one self. So *puruṣa* is individuated consciousness, defined as Śiva veiled by five types of limitation (see below). In some systems of Indian philosophy, the individual soul is a permanent entity, but in Tantrik Shaivism it is a phase of contraction, and every contraction gives way to expansion—in this case, the expansion back into the absolute fullness of unlimited divine Awareness. So, the individual soul is not permanent in the system: though it may last for many thousands of lifetimes, it is still a wave on the ocean of being. But how does Śiva, the absolute Consciousness, manifest itself in the form of an individual soul? By concealing its fullness with five "veils."

THE FIVE SHELLS OR VEILS (*kañcukas*)

Though we have been so far proceeding from the bottom up, it doesn't make sense to discuss the *kañcukas* that way, so we will proceed to *tattvas* 7 through 11, then move on to 6. The five *kañcukas* unfold directly from Māyā (*tattva* #6). They are usually discussed as the veils that contract Śiva's self-awareness into that of the limited individual (*jīva*). However, in the original Tantrik tradition, the understanding is this: Prior to manifesting himself as a limited individual, fully expanded Śiva first contracts himself down to a single point of absolute limitation, *anu*, shedding his omnipotence, omniscience, and omnipresence completely. Then, in order to manifest as an embodied sentient being, he equips himself with five limited capacities. These are the *kañcukas*, and the term literally means "shell" or "armor," for these are the capacities necessary for experience and action in the world of duality. However, it is true that *kañcuka* can also mean "covering" or "veil," and the most common way of presenting the *kañcukas* is as the coverings that conceal the fullness of divine reality. Thus we can say that Śiva + *kañcukas* = *jīva* ("individual soul").[42] (Note that when I say "Śiva" above, I really mean "Śiva-Śakti," but the problem with pronouns makes it easier to talk about Śiva.) Let us now explore these five *kañcukas*.

TATTVA #7: LIMITED POWER OF ACTION (*kalā*)

This is the fundamental *kañcuka;* the others all follow from God's self-imposed limitation on his power of action, his omnipotence. Note that kalā does not mean "powerlessness" but rather "limited power." *Kalā* is in fact that principle which animates the individual soul's capacities to a greater or lesser degree. Each of the five *kañcuka*s, far from being a negative force, is the limited form of a divine Power. We seek to cultivate them, expanding them through spiritual practice. Thus *kalā* in its fully expanded form is simply *kriyā-śakti,* the Power of divine Action. Note that in other contexts *kalā* also means a sliver of the moon, i.e., the amount that the moon grows in a single day. On the spiritual path, we are waxing from a mere sliver of divine power toward the total fullness of our capacity to express our innate divinity.

TATTVA #8: LIMITED POWER OF KNOWLEDGE (*vidyā*)

The second veil is not ignorance but incomplete knowledge. The problem of this *kañcuka* is not that we know nothing but that we know a little bit and assume that that is all there is to know. The "shell" (*kañcuka*) of *vidyā* protects us by allowing us to understand something about our world. But when we believe that we know what life is like, that we have an understanding that is more or less complete except in the trivial details, when in fact we are seeing only the tiniest fragment of the true reality, in this case we disallow the possibility of divine illumination. As I once read in a college philosophy book, "When a man looks at the horizon of his own knowledge and believes he sees the horizon of knowledge itself, then he is truly lost." Yet, this very limited knowledge that binds us to a contracted experience of what reality is, is itself simply a limited form of the divine Power of Knowing or *jñāna-śakti.* Thus, it is usually not the case that what we know about life is simply wrong but rather that it needs to be situated in a larger context, integrated into a more all-encompassing vision. On the spiritual path we seek to ever expand our understanding; this may be why Abhinava Gupta calls this same power *unmeṣa-śakti,* the

Desire is not a problem but an opportunity to follow that desire back to the source.

Power of Unfolding. This unfolding is fueled by our intention and our practice of self-aware reflection, supported by the contemplation of the scriptures and the words of our teachers. But in the expansion of our limited power of knowledge, we of course seek to move beyond words to an inner knowing, an embodied experiential knowledge that the word-based understanding of the intellect can only approximate.

Desire teaches us about those areas of life in which we may need to expand and express ourselves more fully or authentically.

TATTVA #9: DESIRE (*rāga*)

When the fully expanded Consciousness contracts into the form of an individual, it experiences itself as incomplete or imperfect and therefore desires whatever it thinks it needs for completion. This desire is called *rāga,* most accurately translated as "the nonspecific craving for worldly experience" in an attempt to fill an inner void.[43] It is nonspecific in the sense that it is a craving for *something* not quite known that gets rationalized as a specific desire based on each individual's life experience, e.g., love, sex, admiration, money, power. But in fact all craving is truly craving for only one thing: the fullness of knowing your true being, the fullness divine Consciousness. Therefore, when any other desire gets fulfilled it is found to be unsatisfactory; the craving still remains.

The literal meaning of the word *rāga* is "color," for like dye these desires saturate and even stain the mind, influencing how we see things and people. In the Tantra, however, desire is not a problem but an opportunity, an opportunity to follow that desire back to the source and realize that what we really crave is fullness, wholeness—that we will be satisfied by nothing less than knowing (and being) our diving self. Thus we come to understand that *rāga* is the limited form of the divine *icchā-śakti* or the Power of Will, the deep impulse to express the fullness of our authentic being. From this perspective, desire teaches us about those areas of life in which we may need to expand and express ourselves more fully or authentically. We can choose to activate our *icchā-śakti* in those areas, flowing forth our intentionality from a place of fullness, not of lack. But as long as you are ignorant of the true nature of desire, as long as you believe that acquiring, attaining, or possessing something outside of yourself (whether tangible or intangible) will somehow permanently or completely fulfill you, you will continue to experience an insatiable void, an emptiness that cannot be filled, and an inexplicable angst that will burden you until the last day of your life. It is primarily this *rāga,* our craving for more, that propels us into another birth and another round of suffering. But again, *rāga* should, in the Tantric view, not be rejected but transmuted. In the mythological tales, even Lord Śiva had an addiction to gambling and wine, a craving that he transformed into an addiction to "shattering the fear of all beings in all worlds."* The first step in such transmutation is tracing desire back to its source and realizing your longing for divine fullness, letting that longing soften your heart and compel you again and again to seek true connection to the One, the source.

That which causes us suffering is also the means of our fulfillment when we shift our attitude toward it.

* Śiva-mahimnaḥ Stotram. See also Ka by Roberto Calasso.

TATTVA #10: TIME (*kāla*)[44]

The fourth of the prerequisites for embodied experience is Time. Instead of the timeless simultaneity of absolute Consciousness, for which the entire universe is a single complex creation including all times, embodied beings generally experience time at the slow crawl of one second per second. This also means that we experience time sequentially, with one thing following another in a process of continual change (though some Tantric sources tell us that change is mere appearance and what really happens is that the Goddess Kālī devours the whole universe each instant and then recreates it anew in a slightly different form, hundreds of times each second).

We are often burdened by our awareness of past and future—endless regrets and hopeful expectations, worry and anxiety—yet it is because of that very awareness of time that we can grow. As the great German philosopher Martin Heidegger says, we are beings who always have our past with us and are always growing toward our future. That is what makes us different from other animals. So, as usual in Tantrik philosophy, the very thing that causes us suffering is also the means of our fulfilment once we shift our attitude toward it and our understanding of it. We do not seek to be entirely in the present moment the way animals are, with no conscious awareness of past and future. Rather, we seek to be centered in the present moment, aware of our past behind us and our future ahead of us *while being free of the four modes of escaping the experience of the now*—guilt, reverie, fantasy, and anxiety. This is to transcend time even while being in time.

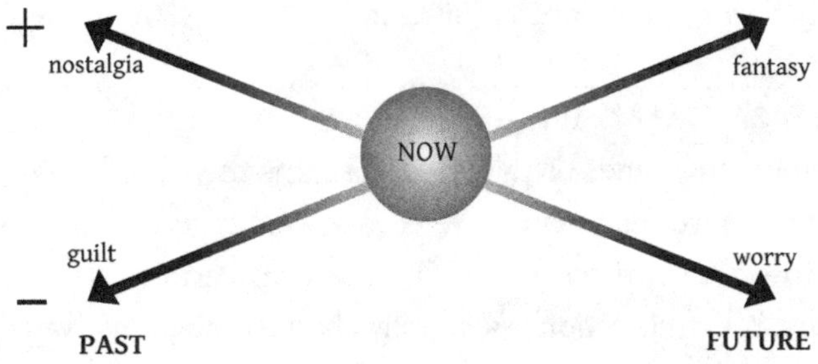

When you look at the chart, if you're like most people, you'll acknowledge the stress and disease caused by guilt and worry but think there is nothing wrong with nostalgia and fantasy. Yoga psychology challenges this notion, telling us that losing ourselves in fantasy is as detrimental to us as being obsessed by worry because fantasizing is equally effective in removing us from full awareness of the present. The present is what is real, and it is what we are called to respond to. In fact, the only way your hopes for the future can ever become a reality in the present is by careful attention to the details of present-moment reality, moment to moment. A more accurate perspective would be to accept that there is no future *per se* but only a constantly flowing present, which, through close and reverent attention, reveals its divinity ever more fully to the yogī. In this way we can learn to experience ourselves as a whole being, with our past and future part of our *present*, without grasping toward either. This grasping takes four primary forms. In the past we grasp towards positive memories, which is called nostalgic reverie, and we grasp after painful memories in the form of guilt and regret. We grasp future imaginary possibilities, which is called fantasy, and future negative possibilities, which is called worry or anxiety. These four different forms of grasping are all ways we depart immersing ourselves in the fullness of the present moment. So when we let go of the four forms of grasping, that is how we let past and future become part of our present and experience the fullness of the present, which has much more to offer us than the mind could ever imagine. In this way we can become free of the net of Time, entering into eternally flowing simultaneity (*nityodita*).

Māyā is the Divine's power to project itself into manifestation.

TATTVA #11: CAUSALITY (*niyati*)

Niyati is the force that binds us to our karmas; it is the law of cause and effect that ensures we shall reap as we have sown. Because of *niyati,* you are certain to experience the results of your own karmic actions, not someone else's. A karmic action is a morally charged action motivated by a desire to attain or avoid a particular result. When we learn to perform actions as service or sacrifice, investing in the process but letting go of our attachment to the final outcome, those actions have no karmic charge and therefore do not bind us, whatever the result may be. Thus the liberated being is no longer bound by *niyati,* fate, and is free from karma, though he or she may still undergo the fruits of karmas accrued before liberation.

Niyati is also associated with specific place (*deśa*), because it is your unique set of karmas that determines your location. That is, because of your karmas, you are born on the Earth, living where you do and not in some other city, country, or planet. Thus the inverse of *niyati,* or rather its full expansion, is all-pervasiveness or nonlocality, the tradition tells us.

TATTVA #6: MĀYĀ

Now we come to the top of the hierarchy of manifest reality, the highest principle that is not the Absolute itself. In other traditions, *māyā* means illusion or delusion, but not so in Tantra. Māyā is rather the "world-source" (*jagad-yoni*), the Divine's power to project itself into manifestation. It is also the power of differentiation by which the One appears as many.

Māyā is not given a negative valuation in the Tantra, even though it does in a sense delude us into seeing duality where there is only unity; for seeing dualistically is a necessary part of the process of Self-exploration that the Divine has freely chosen by manifesting a universe in the first place. Māyā is the power the Divine uses in the creative expression of its nature. The paradox of Māyā is that the power that creates the apparent differentiation that causes so much trouble is the very same power God that uses to glorify Himself. Māyā is the form of the Goddess that constitutes all manifest reality, blessing us with the opportunity for the more challenging—and therefore deeper—realization of *unity-in-diversity*. Look around you right now and see a flash of the truth: everything that is happening is Her play. Just as we form different ornaments out of pure gold and call them earrings, necklace, bracelet, anklet, and so on, in the same way all things of this universe are made of one substance, the energy-body of the Goddess, and differ from one another only in name, form, and function, not in essence.

THE PURE UNIVERSE (*śuddhādhvan*)

The so-called Pure Universe comprising the top five *tattvas* is not a place; it is the divine Reality that pervades the whole of the manifest universe. The top five *tattvas* are essentially a description of the divine. Though divided into five levels, they are all aspects of the Divine and are referred to as phases of God's awareness. The differences between them are differences of perspective and emphasis. To reach any of the five *tattvas* of the Pure Universe is to attain complete liberation and awakening.

TATTVA #5: PURE MANTRA-WISDOM (*Śuddha-vidyā*)

The level of Pure Wisdom is also the level of mantra (because besides meaning "wisdom," *vidyā* is also the feminine word for "mantra"). The wisdom spoken of here is not any type of intellectual knowledge but rather the various phases of Śiva-Śakti's self-awareness expressed in the form of the seventy million mantras—all the mantras that have ever existed or will ever exist. For the Tantrik tradition, mantras are actually conscious beings, analogous to angels in the Western religions. Someone who attains liberation on the level of *tattva* #5 becomes a mantra-being. We know that this doctrine, that mantras are conscious entities, was taken seriously because the texts tell us that if a guru grants initiation into the Tantra to someone who subsequently falls from the path, then that guru must perform a special ritual to apologize to the mantras for putting them to work needlessly.

Īśvara is a generic, non-sectarian term for God.

It is absolutely crucial to understand that in this tradition a mantra, its deity, and its goal are all one and the same. Thus, for example, Lakṣmī's mantra *Oṃ śrīṃ mahālakṣmyai namaḥ is* the Goddess Lakṣmī in sound form; it is her sonic body. Nor is her mantra something separate from the goal for which it is repeated, i.e., to cultivate abundance, for it is the very vibration of abundance (and, as well, the other qualities of Lakṣmī: elegance, charm, grace, beauty, prosperity, and auspiciousness). So, all the various "deities" of Indian spirituality exist on the level of the *Śuddha-vidyā tattva* as phases of divine awareness, the many facets, if you will, of the One jewel, phases of Śiva-Śakti's awareness of herself. Further, there are countless mantra-beings on the *Śuddha-vidyā* level that do not correspond to known Indian deities; perhaps we can suppose that the deities of all spiritual traditions exist on this level, insofar as they can be understood as having vibrational forms.

One who reaches liberation on this level will see the entire universe as a diverse array of energies, but with a single essence. She sees no static matter, experiencing everything as interacting patterns of vibration. The wonder of that which she sees takes precedence over her I-sense, though there is unity between them: "I am *this!*" (*idam evāham*).

The divine Power that corresponds to this level is *kriyā-śakti,* the Power of Action. This is so because the primary characteristic of mantras is that they are agents of transformative change, i.e., of action.

TATTVA #4: THE LORD (*Īśvara*)

This is the level of the personal God, God as a being with specific qualities, that is, the Deity that can be named in various languages (whether the name be Krişhņa, Allāh, Avalokiteśvara, YHWH, Jehova, etc.) This is the level of reality that most monotheistic religions presume to be the highest level of reality. *Īśvara* is a generic, nonsectarian term for God (also found in Patañjali's *Yoga-sūtra*).

This level is associated with *jñāna-śakti,* the Power of Knowing, for Īśvara holds within His being the knowledge of the subtle pattern that will be used in the creation of the universe. He empowers His regents on *tattva* #5 (who are really aspects of Himself) to stimulate the primordial homogenous world-source (Māyā, *tattva* #6) with this pattern he holds within himself, "churning" her so that she begins to produce the differentiation of the lower *tattva*s, starting with the contractions called the *kañcukas* (#7 and below, see pages 135–140).

At the level of Īśvara there is a balanced equality and identity between God and His incipient creation. The Sanskrit phrase said to express the experience of reality at this level is *aham idam aham,* or "I am This; This am I."[45] There is a fascinating and purely "coincidental" parallel here with the self-declaration of the God of the Hebrew Bible, who when asked for His name (at Exodus 3:14), replied simply, *ehyeh Asher ehyeh,* "I am That I am."

In Śaiva Tantra, it is not only God who exists at this level; so do any beings who have reached that same awareness. Thus the difference between Īśvara and other beings abiding at *tattva* #4 is one of office, not of nature.

TATTVA #3: THE EVER-BENEVOLENT ONE (*Sadāśiva*)

The word "God" is no longer applicable at this level, for this level transcends any form of a Deity with identifiable names or attributes. This is the level on which only the slightest subtle differentiation has just begun to emerge between the absolute Deity and the idea of the universe, the universe that S/he will create out of Him/Herself. (When I say "just begun to emerge," I mean the top-down perspective, not the bottom-up perspective.) Thus, it is the level of *icchā-śakti,* the divine Will Power, the creative urge or primal impulse toward Self-expression. The Sanskrit phrase said to express the experience of reality at this level is *aham idam,* "I am this," or "This incipient totality is my own Self," where there is identity between the Divine and the embryonic universe held within it. The sense of "I" has clear priority here, wholly enveloping the "this"; so all beings who attain unity-consciousness with emphasis on the "I" pole abide at this level.

The Sadāśiva-*tattva* is the first movement into differentiation, from the top-down perspective, for at the level of *tattvas* #1 and 2, there is absolute nonduality. Abhinava Gupta tells us that the Divine at this level is called Sadāśiva, "eternally Śiva," to remind us that even as a universe begins to come into being through the power of the Will, the Absolute loses none of its divinity in that process, it is "still Śiva," which of course also means "still a blessing," Sadāśiva.

See page 216

Historically, Sadāśiva is also the name of the high deity of one form of Śaiva Tantra, a form that was later surpassed by the worship of the conjoined and co-equal pair of Śiva-Śakti. He is also pictured as the form of Śiva that sprouts the five faces that speak the five streams of sacred scripture. Thus Sadāśiva is sometimes considered the first ray of divine compassion.

While Shakti is immanent, omniform, and dynamic, Shiva is transcendent, formless, and still.

TATTVA #2: POWER / THE GODDESS (*Śakti*)

In the traditional *tattva* hierarchy, Śakti is #2, but in the nondual schools, care is taken to emphasize that Śiva and Śakti switch places, for they are two sides of the same coin. That is, neither Śiva nor Śakti has priority—it is a matter of which aspect is dominant in any given experience.

The word *śakti* literally means "power, potency, energy, capacity, capability." In NŚT, all powers are worshipped as goddesses, or rather as forms of *the* Goddess (*Mahādevī*). Śakti can no more be separated from Śiva than heat can be separated from fire. All forms of energy are Śakti, and since matter is energy (as the Tāntrikas well knew), the whole manifest universe is seen as the body of the Goddess, and the movements of all forms of energy are Her dance. The various aspects of Śakti are covered in detail above.

See page 101 and following

The term *śakti* is often used to specifically denote spiritual energy, or God's transformative power. In the scriptures, this meaning is often conveyed with the special term *rudra-śakti,* which refers to the primal, awe-inspiring divine Power that flows through us in spiritual experience. An infusion of this divine Power is called *rudra-śakti-samāveśa,* where *samāveśa* refers to the spiritual experience comprising an expansion of consciousness, a dissolution of the boundaries between self and other, a sharing of self-hood with God and/or with the whole universe, and that accompanied by a blissful influx of energy. It so happens that the phrase *rudra-śakti-samāveśa* is the subject of my doctoral thesis.

Śiva is spaciousness, Śakti is energy.

TATTVA #1: THE BENEVOLENT ONE (*Śiva*)

In the context of NŚT, Śiva is not the name of a god. Rather, the word is understood to signify the peaceful, quiescent ground of all Reality, the infinite silence of transcendent Divinity, or, in the poet's phrase, the "still point at the center of the turning world." While Śakti is extroversive, immanent, manifest, omniform, and dynamic, Śiva is introversive, transcendent, unmanifest, formless, and still. Śiva is the absolute void of pure Consciousness.

The word *śiva* is traditionally interpreted as "that in which all things lie (since the verbal root *śī* means "to lie")." Thus Śiva is the ground of being, that which gives reality its coherence, that in which all things find their repose. His nature is beyond any qualities and is, therefore, difficult to express in words, but in *Essence of the Tantras,* Śiva is described as the coherence and unification of all the various *śakti*s. Thus, He is called *śaktimān,* the one who holds the Powers, or rather "holds space" for their unfolding. However, since Śiva is literally nothing without the Powers of Consciousness, Bliss, Willing, Knowing, Acting, and so on, it is usually Śakti who is worshipped as the highest principle in NŚT. Śiva is that which grounds and coheres the various powers; He is the Lord of the Family (*kuleśvara*), the center axis of the spinning wheel of Powers. As the coherent force, Śiva hardly has an insignificant function, but as he is not an embodiment of potency himself, he is less likely to attract worship in a spiritual system that is focused primarily on the *empowerment* of its adherents. You may notice that in the imagery of NŚT we often see a dynamic image of the goddess and a static image of Śiva, Śiva lying down in *śavāsana* with a goddess sitting or standing upon him.

The previous paragraph defined Śiva primarily as spaciousness, the hosting space for the energy that is Śakti. This space/energy polarity is the one given in a Trika text called *Vijñāna-bhairava*, among other sources. The *Vijñāna-bhairava* prefers to define Śiva as "spaciousness" and Śakti as "flowing energy." We should note that in other contexts, the roles are defined differently. For example, the influential Recognition school (a subset of the Trika) defines Śiva-Śakti as the two complementary aspects of one divine Consciousness: Śiva is the Light of Manifestation (*prakāśa*), also known as the Light of Consciousness (*cit-prakāśa*), and Śakti is blissful Self-reflective awareness (*vimarśa*). This pairing is sometimes concisely abbreviated as *cid-ānanda* (Awareness-Bliss). In this way of understanding Śiva-Śakti, He is the illuminative power of Consciousness that manifests and shines as all things, and She is the power by which that same Consciousness folds back on itself and becomes self-aware and thus can enjoy itself. While new students of the Tantra often want a simple, cut-and-dried definition of the polarity of Śiva-Śakti, the tradition does not offer us one. Indeed, as this paragraph has shown, we get different definitions within the very same school sometimes. These need not be seen as contradictory, however, for the ultimate reality of Śiva-Śakti transcends all thought; the diverse explanations are just varying orientations or angles of approach to that

See page 61

one Reality, serving different students in different contexts.

In another schema, that of the radical Krama school, Śiva disappears entirely, for there the two aspects of the One are represented as different facets of one Goddess: the indescribable Void of absolute potential, the formless ground of all reality (Śiva's usual role) is represented as the dark and emaciated, terrifyingly attractive Goddess Kālī, who devours all things and makes them one with Herself; and the infinite Light that encompasses all things and beings with loving compassion and insight is represented as white and full-bodied Goddess Parā, overflowing with boundless nectar. But, as Abhinava Gupta stresses, these apparent opposites (black and white, empty and full) are simply the two forms of the one great Goddess beyond all representation. The Krama school simply wishes to avoid the inevitably dualistic implications of the image of Śiva-Śakti as two beings joined together.

See page 269

How to reconcile these different presentations? The answer is simple: they need no reconciliation, for they are each perfectly fitted to the system in which they occur; and the absolute Reality beyond words can be represented by any of these schemas or by none.

It is important to note that the term Śiva or "God" never loses its importance in this tradition. Some might construe the more refined philosophies of NŚT as atheistic because they wholly repudiate the notion of God as a separate person, "a guy in the sky," or indeed as anything separate from your essence-nature as dynamic free Awareness. Yet it is significant that these very traditions continue to use the term "God" and its synonyms (such as *maheśvara*, "the Great Lord," and *parameśvara,* "the Supreme Divinity"). It seems to me that they do not want to dispense with the love and devotion that is inspired in so many by this personalizing of the Absolute. They want a path of intimate relationship, even though ultimately we can relate with nothing but our own self. At the same time, remember that the tradition gives us a beautiful nondual definition of the word "God," one worth repeating:

Essence of the Tantras

> *...in actuality it is the unbounded Light of Consciousness, reposing in its innate Bliss, fully connected to its Powers of Willing, Knowing, and Acting, that we call God.*

It is in the context of this definition that we may understand such scriptural statements as "Nothing exists that is not God."[46] But here we are anticipating the next section: for "beyond" even *tattva* #1 is that which unfolds all the *tattvas*, from 1 to 36, within itself as the expression of its blissful self-awareness.

TATTVA #0: THE HEART (Śiva/Śakti in perfect fusion)

This secret *tattva*, taught only in the esoteric nondual Tantrik sources, is the key to understanding the whole philosophy of nondual Tantra. It is #0 because it does not crown the hierarchy, for as we have seen, the "highest" *tattva*, #1, is absolutely transcendent Śiva. But the Ultimate Principle (*paramārtha*), *tattva* #0, is not transcendent; for to transcend is to go beyond and, thus, to exclude. In nondual understanding, the Ultimate must be that which simultaneously transcends *and* encompasses all things, excluding nothing. It is the supreme paradox, for it expresses itself *as* the very substance of all things while simultaneously being something more than simply the sum of all perceptible realities. This absolute principle cannot be written in the *tattva* list, for it pervades the whole as the indefinable essence of all the *tattvas*, and everything manifest or unmanifest. It is absolutely incomprehensible by the mind, this ground of being. Abhinava says:

Essence of the Tantras

> *This whole universe is One Reality—unbroken by time, uncircumscribed by space, unclouded by attributes, unconfined by forms, inexpressible by words, and impossible to understand with the ordinary means of knowledge.*

This all-pervasive and ultimate Reality, subtler than the subtlest, beyond the highest transcendent Śiva and yet closer to you than your own breath, equally present in the most sublime refined pure awareness of infinite openness and in the scent of the foulest excrement, its radiantly beautiful divine nature never tainted though it shines equally in the form of all that is called pure and impure—this is what Abhinava's lineage calls the Heart (*hṛdaya*) or the Essence (*sāra*) of Reality. He also gives it more mysterious names, citing the scriptures: he calls it *Visarga*, the Absolute Potential, *Spanda,* the Vibration, *Ūrmi,* the Wave, and *Yāmala*, the Couple: the perfect fusion of Śiva and Śakti as one. It is this same ultimate principle that is worshipped in radically nondual Goddess Tantra as Kālī Kāla-sankarṣaṇī: the radiant Dark, the resounding Silence, the Devourer of Time—by which is meant the timeless ground of the cycle of creation, stasis, and reabsorption.

See pages 59 & 292

Kālī is the radiant Dark, the resounding Silence, the timeless ground of all.

This is the doctrine of "the higher nonduality" (*paramādvaya*), which subsumes both duality and ordinary nonduality. It is all-encompassing, including even duality as a level within the Real, whereas ordinary nonduality simply negates duality as wrong or false. But duality *is* a level of reality, an undeniable experience, and a meaningful term of discourse, so no system is complete that simply denies it. And just as duality is superseded by the more encompassing truth of nonduality, that too is superseded, and subsumed, by the all-encompassing truth of the higher nonduality.

This Heart, this Vibration, this Essence, is the light by which all things are illuminated, the reality by which all things are real. It is the omnipresent divinity, manifest *equally* in all things, from the horrific to the sublime. Philosophers tend to object to this articulation of the nature of reality, saying that if everything is equally divine, the word "divine" loses its meaning and value, because something has value only in opposition to something else that doesn't. While this objection is perfectly rational, it is operating on a level of understanding that for Tāntrikas is superseded by the immediate mystical experience that initiates share—an experience in which everything is indeed perceived as equally suffused with beautiful divine radiance, in which the total freedom and joy of being permeate the entire sphere of perception, and in which no phenomena whatsoever can be perceived as anything less than absolutely perfect. This vision of reality has been labeled "transrational" by some because of the fact that it cannot be fully understood by the ordinary mind, despite the fact that the one who has had the experience usually considers it the most intensely real experience of her life. (Even this experience, though, is merely a pointer to the state of abiding in oneness with the ground of reality, which is not an experience per se, since all experiences come and go. Nothing can be said in words about the non-state of *nirvāṇa,* permanently abiding in the Heart of reality.)

This is *not* to say that in this expanded mode of perception, everything is considered the same. In is not the case that everything is considered equally good, for example. In fact, diversity is very much a part of this aesthetic mode, as this way of seeing celebrates all things as *different* expressions of one reality. In fact, everything is beautiful to the Tāntrika precisely *because* each thing expresses the One principle differently. Every sentient being is worthy of reverence because she expresses her divinity in a unique manner, never seen before and never to be seen again. Still, though this awakened consciousness sees everything as equally divine, one puts one's hat on one's head and one's shoes on one's feet, and not the other way around, as one great teacher said. Though every being that one meets is worthy of reverence for expressing infinity divinity in a unique manner, that doesn't necessarily mean that the awakened being has no discernment about who is beneficial to associate with and who is not.

One Divinity pulsates joyously in all that exists.

The spiritual experience of one Divinity pulsating joyously in all that exists, as well as paradoxically present in the repose in the non-state of complete stillness and emptiness, is considered a gift of divine grace. Yet it can only be fully understood, cultivated, and firmly rooted as abiding realization through spiritual practice.

THE THREE IMPURITIES (WITH AN EXCURSUS ON THE DESCENT OF POWER)

Though the *tattva* schema purports to be a complete account of all the principles of reality, there are three important principles not enumerated in that list. (Some sources consider them as aspects of *māyā-tattva*; others suggest they are not in the list because they are not truly real.) These are the three *malas*, or "impurities" (not to be confused with *mālā*, which is a garland or rosary). The three *malas* constitute our experience of bondage. From the nondual viewpoint, they are not truly impurities or stains; they are simply ignorance, or rather limited perception, which Consciousness has taken on in order to become a finite individual, and which it can choose to relinquish at any time. The first and most basic of the three is the *āṇava-mala* or "Impurity of Individuality"; the second is the *māyīya-mala* or "Impurity of Differentiation", and the third is the *kārma-mala* or "Impurity of Action." We will look at each in turn.

THE IMPURITY OF INDIVIDUALITY

The Impurity of Individuality is fundamental because the other two Impurities could not exist without it and also because it constitutes the very basis of the limitation that makes us finite beings. This is the fundamental form of ignorance. It consists of the deep unconscious belief that you are incomplete and imperfect, a tiny insignificant creature, certainly not the Divine. It is the belief that you are limited and powerless, unworthy and meaningless. Even more basically, it is the belief that something is *missing* or else deeply *wrong* with you, a belief that prevents you from knowing and revering yourself as what you truly are. I called it an unconscious belief, but it is more accurate to say it is *pre*conscious, for it informs all our thoughts and perceptions; it is a way of seeing reality held very close to the deepest level of our individual being. *Āṇava-mala* is the primary cause of our suffering, the ignorance (= skewed or partial view) from which all other errors of perception stem. Remember that in this system, to hold a vision of reality that is not in alignment with the actual nature of reality is the only cause of suffering. Believing that we are incomplete and imperfect and separate from God, which is the most untrue thing that we could possibly believe, causes us terrible suffering for precisely that reason: it does not allow us to experience reality, that is, to access the universal Consciousness that is always already flowing in us and in all things and whose nature is freedom and bliss.

Here I'm using the word "belief." But we must take care not to misunderstand. This is not a matter of correcting an intellectual misapprehension or adhering to the correct doctrine. For *āṇava-mala* is not a mental construct programmed into us by society. It is the limited sense of individuality that makes possible the whole process of the formation of dualistic thought. Thus, it cannot be countered by merely attempting to believe the opposite. You must have the actual experience of *pūrṇatā*—of fullness, completeness, divine perfection—deep within your own being, and you must have it so frequently or powerfully that it displaces *āṇava-mala* and becomes your basic reference point for who you are.

As you might expect, in Tantrik philosophy the very condition of contracted individuality contains within it the seed of the possibility for expanding back into our natural state of absolute fullness. Everyone has this so-called impurity of individuality, this *āṇava-mala*, so as soon as they are self-aware, everyone has the feeling that "something's missing" or "something's not quite right" or "there's more to life, there must be more to life, more to *me,* than this!" That *mala*-driven perception points to a real truth: you are not accurately perceiving the whole of your real nature. For most of us, the spiritual path begins when we perceive that something *is* missing, and also we realize that it is not romance or money or power or fame that will be able to fill the void within. We become seekers on the path when we feel this acutely and realize that it will only be addressed by a fundamental shift in our very experience of reality. When we begin to feel that there is a reality beyond what we have known or even suspected, beyond what we have been taught to believe—something vast and all-encompassing and deeply real—then we open ourselves to that greater reality. In other words, the process of contraction comes to an end when we no longer believe, way deep down, that our limited experience of reality is all there is to know. At that moment, we begin turning toward expansion, initiating a new arc in the movement of the soul, an arc that will necessarily terminate in the all-encompassing fullness of being that alone can satiate the hunger of Consciousness.

Śaktipāta is triggered by a turn toward expansion deep within your being.

Though it is absolutely true that your belief that there is something wrong with you as you are—or that you are missing something to be complete—is the deepest form of ignorance, it is nonetheless real. You cannot simply be convinced out of it. Otherwise, just reading this book would be all you needed to do. Since this ignorance is not intellectual but rather is the very organizing principle of your limited individuality, only a powerful revelation can begin to dislodge it. This initiatory experience, this initial awakening, is called *śakti-pāta,* or the Descent of Power (also translated as "the Descent of Grace"). It is your initial awakening to your real nature. Without it the *āṇava-mala* holds sway over your experience of life, and without it the practices of yoga cannot bear their full fruit.

ŚAKTIPĀTA: THE DESCENT OF POWER

The scriptures clarify that the Descent of Power is not a literal descent of energy from heaven or some higher place, though for some it can feel like that; rather, it is an awakening of the divine Power (*śakti*) within you that will lead you to your ultimate liberation. It is in fact more like an ascent than a descent; but the term *śaktipāta* is used both because it is inherited from earlier Śaiva tradition and because the word "*pāta*" ("descent") has a connotation of a sudden, forceful fall, a startling experience that comes out of the blue, as it were. *Śaktipāta* is unprecedented, a primordial opening to a deeper level of being. Furthermore, the language of descent (or ascent) connotes that the awakening in question is truly a vertical movement, because it takes us out of the endless fruitless horizontal circling of our "normal" life, deepening us into our own innate being, opening us to the greater reality.

As mentioned above, there comes a moment in the existence of an embodied soul (perhaps after many lifetimes) when it is done with the phase of contraction and begins to turn toward its own expansion. This turning may take place so deep inside your being that you may not even be aware of it at first. But things that seemed exciting or fulfiling before—like gaining wealth, having lots of friends, getting wasted, making sexual conquests, being praised by others—no longer seem to do it for you. For most this "world-weariness" is a necessary step in opening to a deeper reality. The longer the gap of time between the subtle turn inward, toward expansion and the occurrence of actual *śaktipāta,* or initial awakening, the more intensely felt that awakening is. So, some people receive a very intense *śaktipāta,* consisting often of a mystical experience of their oneness with all reality, or of their true nature as unborn, uncreated, eternal Essence, or of all reality bathed in the unitary light of compassionate love, or of energy shooting up their spine and exploding in their head, or of waves of bliss surging in their body, and so on. Others receive a *śaktipāta* so subtle that it is almost imperceptible. Now, the difference between these two is not that the former person is more blessed, more worthy, than the latter. It is simply that that person waited longer for their *śaktipāta,* perhaps lifetimes longer, and thus their longing (whether conscious or unconscious) became ever more intense and thereby, when the conditions were right, triggered a more intense awakening. (It's just like firewood—the longer it dries out, the more quickly and completely it catches fire when a flame comes near.) *But the awakening is the same in both cases,* fire is fire, so in the sense that it sets a person irrevocably on the path to total integration with divine reality, no matter the strength of that awakening in terms of your subjective experience of it. The person with the imperceptible *śaktipāta* also has her life transformed as a result; but because she didn't wait as long for it to happen, her belief that worldly enjoyments might fulfill her is stronger, and thus she draws a less intense *śaktipāta* to her. (Note that this doctrine corrects the false view that those with more intense *śaktipātas* are more spiritual or special or worthy.) The important thing, however, is that the awakening has occurred.

If you've had an imperceptible *śaktipāta,* you might wonder whether it has happened at all. The most significant thing about it, again, is not the experience but its effect on your life. I will briefly describe some signs and symptoms of this awakening. One of the most important signs is subtle but significant: when you close your eyes, take some slow, deep breaths, and turn your attention within, there is immediately a sense of presence, a kind of sweetness in just being with your inner self. Those who have not received *śaktipāta* have little patience for turning within; they don't see the point, for they don't sense the Divine there. Furthermore, those who have received the Descent of Power manifest substantial changes in their lives, including some or all of these:

- You find worldly forms of "fun" are less satisfying.
- You are fascinated by spiritual teachings, even if you don't quite understand them.
- You find yourself drawn to eat healthier food or otherwise honor your body.
- You feel respect or reverence towards spiritual teachers or anyone who seems to have authentically dedicated themselves to the path.
- Tears of joy or gratitude well up spontaneously, especially when witnessing acts of compassion or devotion.
- Your creative capacity maybe is unleashed.
- Mantras are effective for you.
- Yogic practices, especially meditation, yield a significant benefit, even if they are challenging.
- You experience yourself as more vulnerable and sensitive, yet somehow more strong at the same time.

- ❖ You find it harder (for a time) to relate to friends who have no apparent spiritual sensitivity.
- ❖ When you read the words of a great spiritual master, they resonate on a deep level of your being, and you "get" them, even if you can't explain them.
- ❖ When you get quiet and turn within, you feel a subtle "presence."

Everything is one infinite Light of Consciousness vibrating at different wavelengths in a joyous interconnected dance.

The experience of *śaktipāta*, when it is medium or strong grade, gives a taste of what the final state of liberation is like. It is a temporary immersion—whether for a few moments or days—into our true nature. From this perspective you see things as they really are: the one infinite Light of Consciousness vibrating at different wavelengths in a joyous interconnected dance. Often it takes the form of experiencing yourself as profoundly connected to the Divine in some way. People who receive a strong *śaktipāta* of this variety often make the mistake of believing that they are now enlightened, that the beginning of their path is in fact the end. This mistake can be very hard on the person's loved ones, and if s/he clings to it, it can even occasionally bring about a temporary psychotic break that might take some time to heal. It is important to see the value of what you have received while retaining the humility of realizing that this gift of grace is simply to show that the fully expanded state is real and worth striving for; it is not the final attainment. Otherwise, it would be abiding, naturally ever refreshing itself with no effort on your part, and it would entail the dissolution of your self-images, your ego. For a more detailed explanation of the results of *śaktipāta*, see part 3, beginning on page 321.

THE UNFOLDING OF ONE'S AWAKENING

In fact, you need to be shown that the goal is worth striving for precisely because of how challenging the path can be. In order to complete the process of expanding back into the fullness of your divine nature, you will have to let go of everything you think you are. You will have to let go of every image or idea you have of yourself, the "positive" ones as well as the "negative" ones. Why should this be the case? Because the state of all-encompassing fullness and wholeness (*pūrṇatā*) that is the goal of the path—your already existent ultimate nature—is by definition one in which you experience that the pattern of the *whole* of reality exists within you and that your identity is not defined by one part more than by any other. In other words, to experience identity with the all-encompassing divine Absolute, you must necessarily relinquish identification with some limited aspect or fragment of it—that aspect you habitually call "me." It is your clinging to your limited identity that is precisely what prevents you from experiencing the Whole within yourself.

When I say that you will have to let go of "positive" self-images as well as negative ones, I do not mean to imply that you discard your positive virtues; rather, you let go of the story about yourself that is based on those virtues. This is necessary because the self-image that you are a "good person" carries with it a raft of "shoulds" and "should nots" that ironically prevents you from expressing your innate virtue in a way that is organically responsive to the actuality of the present situation. Your real virtue is not based on a story about yourself; it is a natural expression of your essence-nature. So you do not need to regard yourself as a good person, or indeed any kind of person.

You will ultimately have to let go of all your self-images to be free.

Nor does this process of letting go of everything you think yourself to be entail abandoning your roles and responsibilities in life. For what is at issue is not whether you are a wife, or mother, or doctor, or teacher, but whether you identify yourself as that and that alone—and thus define and limit and circumscribe your experience of reality through those identifications. In other words, you don't need to run away from all those responsibilities to obtain liberation, because liberation in the Tantrik sense means going from the experience of being trapped in your life situation to the experience of continuously perceiving that you are the infinite creative Light of divine Presence, joyously playing the *role* of a wife, or mother, or doctor, and in so doing providing service to all beings. The metaphor of the actor and his role is perfect here: Does an actor feel miserable playing a role on stage, even the part of a tragic figure? No, because he knows that he will relinquish the role, that he is not bound by it, and that he will return to what he has never forgotten: his real identity. In fact, even as on one level the actor does experience the sadness of his character, on a deeper level he experiences great joy in playing his part well! And he can have that experience simultaneously feeling the sadness of his character and the joy of playing the part well. Imagine what your life would be like if you had that experience of joy in *all* your roles, if you retained a wordless awareness of your fundamental expansive, all-encompassing, complete, and perfect nature even as you went about performing the most mundane of tasks.

So, the whole process of *sādhanā,* walking the spiritual path, is the process of removing the *āṇava-mala,* the Impurity of Individuality, of limited identity and lack of wholeness. Its final removal is the state of liberation. Though it is the primary "stain" or obscuration of the transparent light of our being, preventing our clear vision, it is also the beneficial nagging sense of missing something important that prompts us to seek and find the Truth. So, as always in Tantric philosophy, nothing is downright bad; everything, even the *āṇava-mala,* serves a divine purpose.

The Impurity of Differentiation

The Impurity of Differentiation is that form of ignorance that causes us to perceive dualistically, that is, to see differences but not the underlying unity. It is the *māyīya-mala* that causes us to feel separate from all other beings, and from that which we perceive. The fundamental form of the *māyīya-mala* is subject-object differentiation. This means that you perceive the objects of your awareness as something separate and different from yourself. This wrong view leads either to a sense of the world as a persecuting threat or as a source of things to acquire or conquer. This is ignorance, for as we have seen, anything that exists within your consciousness is necessarily already an aspect of yourself. True seeing is seeing all beings within yourself and yourself within all beings. Only when we are focused on the most superficial layer of reality does difference seem to be the most fundamental truth.

Imagine, if you will, a massive continent with many mountains, a continent mostly submerged under an ocean but with many of the mountain peaks poking above the surface of the water. A person who had never gone below the surface would see those mountains as separate unconnected islands. But someone who had made the effort to explore the inner depths of the ocean would realize that there was only one landmass, extruding at various points into the air. In the same way, all manifest, conscious beings are extrusions into the tangible world of the singular, continuous Being that alone exists. This analogy is imperfect (as all are) because, in truth, that one Being has become the ocean of the tangible, perceptible world as well as the beings within it. The analogy often used in the original tradition is that all perceptibles, anything that is perceivable, constitute the single body of that one Being, and all perceivers constitute its single soul.

See the other as a different form of yourself.

A person who is not aware of this truth will see an object of her perception as something separate from her. But in reality, anything you perceive is nothing other than a vibration of conscious energy within your awareness. The consequences of *not* realizing this are tremendous. When you perceive other beings as different and separate from you, you do not bother to understand things from their point of view, failing to realize that to do so would also give you insight into yourself. In an us-versus-them view of things, you might even consider the other an enemy and feel justified in killing him if he opposes your interests. (You might say, "Oh, but I would never kill anyone"—yet doesn't the government that acts on your behalf do just that?) By contrast, when you are in the process of overcoming *māyīya-mala*, you realize that another human being, even one whose actions you condemn, is no different from you, only with different pressures, programs, and life circumstances. You might have done exactly the same thing in his shoes, in his life's circumstances. Seeing this truth, condemnation gives way to compassion. When you begin to see through *māyīya-mala*, you see all beings as holding up a mirror to yourself. The initial awakening to your innate divinity described as *śaktipāta* above makes it far easier to break through the false me-versus-you, us-versus-them, self-versus-other dichotomy engendered by *māyīya-mala.*

If you are having a hard time seeing the other as yourself in another form, that simply means that you must expand your sense of self and take hold of the realization that the capacity to do both wonderful and terrible things exists within you and the other person in exactly the same degree. Overcoming *māyīya-mala* does not mean believing that all people are the same or that all are equally good. It means seeing the reality that all entities are *different forms of the same thing,* each subject to unique conditions, but each with the same fundamental capacities. You can stay grounded in the Real by grasping that though there is only one substance to reality, it can manifest in an infinite variety of different forms. Of course, though all beings are God, some are highly contracted forms of God, expressing the divine Power of self-concealment by perpetuating ignorance and suffering. Seeing all beings as equally Divine does not mean equally approving the actions and viewpoints of all beings, because some are expressing the divine capacity for concealment, and some are expressing the divine capacity for revelation. It is vital that this particular point be understood with crystal clarity.

Ultimately, releasing the ignorance of *māyīya-mala* means seeing that differentiation is not and never was a problem. For Tāntrikas, seeing difference in the context of a greater unity does not mean devaluing difference but rather celebrating it as the very source of beauty itself. The power of Māyā is finally experienced as the power by which divine Consciousness loves itself in the particular manifest form of you and I and each and every being.

The Impurity of Action

The Impurity of Action or *kārma-mala* refers to the bondage of karma. As long as the first two *malas* are active, you will see yourself as a limited, separate being who must strive to give yourself every advantage at any cost. This viewpoint naturally gives rise to volitional actions with repercussions that will further enmesh the actor in bondage. The cycle of action that is motivated by ignorance and corresponding reactions is called karma. Only those actions performed out of ignorance and grasping create karmic repercussions.

The primary forms of that ignorance in this context are attachment and aversion, *raga* and *dvesha*. Attachment is the conviction that we need something outside ourselves (success, a partner, the right job, approval, etc.) to be fulfilled. Aversion is the same vibration, only inverted: the conviction that we cannot be fulfilled until certain things are eliminated or avoided. When we are driven by attachment and aversion, we naturally commit divisive actions that can cause suffering for ourselves and others. The more overcome we are by a particular attachment or aversion, the more extreme our actions become (as in the case of someone who believes "I can't live without him!"). The more extreme the beliefs motivating our actions, the greater the karmic repercussions. Only actions that arise spontaneously as an expression of our essence-nature, without personal motive of gain or loss, have no binding karmic repercussion.

You can be free of karma: stop being the person to whom those karmas apply.

Karma can seem a very heavy doctrine: since we have committed so many karmic actions in the past and continue to do so in the present, how can we possibly overcome the burden of their consequences? The masters of Śaiva Tantra saw that worry about the enormous burden of past-life karmas was a real barrier in people's spiritual development. So, they devised an initiation ceremony (called *dīkṣā*) that was said to purify people of all their past-life karma destined to bear fruit in future lives, leaving only the karma of this life intact. Whatever the reality of this metaphysical claim might be, the psychological effect of this ceremony is undeniable: it made people feel that liberation within this very life is within reach—and, because Consciousness creates reality, it became so. The simple fact is that if you had to heal and process every karmic trace

See page 332

within your being in order to reach the goal, liberation would be impossibly distant. Therefore, there is only one viable solution in the Tantrik View: *stop being the person to whom those karmas apply.* Once you fully relinquish the identity of the one who generated the karmas and to whom they tenaciously stick, you are free. Such a solution is not a shortcut on the path, because from the spiritual point of view, you only need to go through as many karmas as *you* personally need to go through in order to reach the point of fully dedicating yourself to the process of dissolving your limited self back into God. That is to say, this is not a system in which you need to be punished for every "bad" thing you've done; for if you truly stop being the person who performed those sorts of actions, then the karmas no longer apply to you.

The best way to overcome *kārma-mala* is to address the root from which it arises: become thoroughly convinced that there is nothing outside yourself that need be added to make you complete nor is there anything that need be subtracted to make you pure. This state of profound love and respect for your own being will, if achieved even in part, make it easier for you to perform actions without any selfish grasping motive and thus you will increasingly be free of karma. It should be noted here that an action can make you feel good and still be without selfish motive; the question is whether it spontaneously wells up from your Heart as a natural expression of your authentic nature. It is the root, not the fruit, of an action that makes it selfish or not. So this is not a doctrine that you can't enjoy the results of your actions. Needless to say, if you are able to undermine and destabilize *māyīya-mala,* the belief in yourself as separate from other beings and objects, then *kārma-mala* will naturally start to fall away as well. Only if you see others as separate from you could you consider your own needs without considering theirs, or vice versa. So, the long and short of the Tantrik view on this is the following: Don't worry about karma. Focus on the more fundamental *malas*, and karma will take care of itself.

Finally, everything comes back to *āṇava-mala.* Only if you are experiencing yourself as cut off from the Divine—unworthy, incomplete, and imperfect—can the other two *malas* operate. If a being manages, through much effort, to remove *māyīya-* and *kārma-mala* without removing *āṇava-*, which is possible, then in the tradition he is called a *Vijñānākala*, one who is nearly liberated but remains stuck on the threshold of true liberation, unable to surrender his limited identity. *Vijñānākala* literally means "one who is free of the limitation of two *malas* by means of his own insight" but who, denying the grace of an even greater divine power than his individual soul, remains bound by the most fundamental Impurity. Such a one transcends Māyā but remains, as it were, forever at the gates of heaven, barred from the entry permitted for those who cast aside identification with their limited self, who realize that only one Being has ever existed, and who know their embodied form was merely a temporary part He played, a dance She danced.

VĀK: THE FOUR LEVELS OF THE WORD (& THE SIX-FOLD PATH)

The form in which the highest divinity is worshipped in one school of NŚT (the Trika) is the Goddess called *Parāvāk*, also known as Parāvāch, "the Supreme Word," or simply sometimes called Parā. Parā is the Tantrik equivalent of the mainstream Hindu deity Sarasvatī, except that She is revered in the Trika as the highest principle of reality rather than as one goddess among many. She is also called Anuttarā, "the feminine Absolute." In the Trika, the totality of existence is understood as an expression of the Supreme Word, and thus *all* beings are "the Word made flesh," as it were. This concept is parallel to Greek thought (found in the beginning of the Gospel of John) in the Christian tradition, where "the Word" is the English translation of *logos,* denoting the deep structure of reality, the harmonic animating principle of the universe. In this view, everything is a harmonic vibration of the one Word.

Parāvāk, then, is both the power of inspiration and the organizing intelligence of embodied consciousness: the subtle patterning in Awareness that shapes both the world of things and the corresponding world of ideation and representation. The Word manifests in two different ways, and these mirror each other: signifiers and that which they signify. That is, the Word becomes both the symbolic units of language and the objects of experience to which they refer. These are the internalized and externalized dimensions of one Consciousness, the Goddess Parā. When we do not see the common root of both external objects of experience and the internal ideas that reflect them, we fail to realize their interdependence. For example, we erroneously believe that "external" reality shapes our inner world but not the other way around; whereas in fact, both aspects are constantly shaping and reshaping each other in a two-way dialectical process.

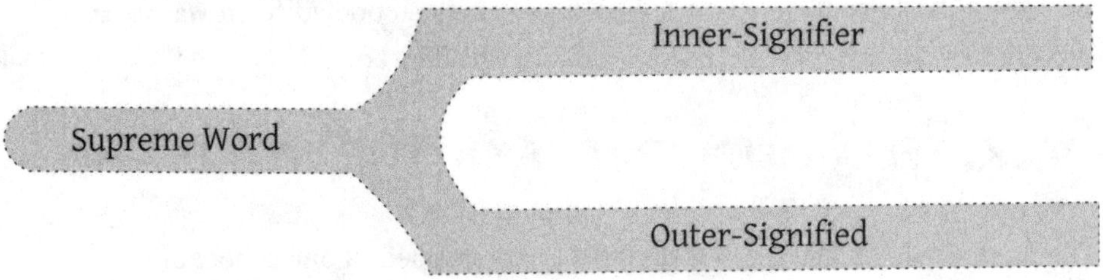

The two sides of this process are described in Śaiva Tantra as each having several aspects, thus giving us the so-called Sixfold Path of Reality (*ṣaḍ-adhvan*), presented below. (Note that the "outer Path" on the right is the *prakāśa* aspect, and the "inner Path" on the left is the *vimarśa* aspect in the Pratyabhijñā analysis; page 61.)

Signifier (vācaka),the inner Path	**Signified (vācya),the outer Path**
1. *varṇa* (phonemes, subtle pulsations)	4. *kalā* (5 major divisions of reality)
2. *mantra* (morphemes, thought-units)	5. *tattva* (36 principles of reality)
3. *pada* (words and phrases)	6. *bhuvana* (118 planes of reality)

This listing moves from the subtler at the top to the more tangible and concrete at the bottom (*sūkṣma -> sthūla*). This process is simply the densification of the singular energy of Consciousness. We should also note that the division into "internal" and "external" makes sense only from the perspective of the individuated conscious being. From the Absolute perspective, of course, nothing at all is external to Awareness.

This Sixfold Path is a pan-Śaiva doctrine, not just found in the Trika. However, it is the Trika that explores and builds a theology around the inner Path of the Signifier. It is this theology that I mean when I refer to the "linguistic mysticism" of the Trika.

Now, you may have already noticed an apparent problem with this picture of things, which is this: if the so-called inner Path of ideas and language and the outer Path of things and worlds have a common origin and mirror one another, why do they not correspond perfectly? Why do we as individuals often hold ideas that are not in alignment with the nature of our external reality? The answer lies in the fact that Consciousness, the ground of reality, is by its very nature absolutely free and autonomous—so free, in fact, that it is free to construct any picture it likes of reality, to build up any discourse about reality that it enjoys or is fascinated by, even one that is very much at odds with the deep structures and patterns of nature. In other words, Consciousness in its contracted form is subject to limited knowledge, and when, because of its contracted awareness, it takes its limited knowledge of reality as being complete, it builds up a picture of reality on that basis that is skewed and distorted, however many truths that picture may contain. And of course, this skewed picture of things does correspond to a reality: the reality of the limitation in our perception. So, all thought-forms do correspond to *some* aspect of reality—just not usually in the way that we think they do.

Sādhanā (spiritual practice) consists of careful observation and deep surrender.

From this point of view, the whole process of *sādhanā* spiritual practice is nothing but the process of carefully and slowly aligning our internal mental constructs of reality (*vikalpas*) with the actual patterns of reality itself, and of discarding those that cannot be so aligned. (Note that in the fully expanded mode of awareness, this process can happen effortlessly of its own accord.) Putting it another way, *sādhanā* consists of learning how to cast aside our presumptions, to carefully observe what is happening around and within us without labels, and then to surrender our various skewed stories about reality to Reality itself. (This is nondual language for what many religions call "submitting to the will of God.") At some point, the effort involved in this process gives way to an epiphany, a deep and profound insight into the deep structures of Consciousness, into "the mind of God," if you will, as a result of which the process of alignment unfolds more or less spontaneously.

The Trika articulates a doctrine of four levels of the Word in order to help us understand the inner Path, the process by which we each construct a particular experience of reality. Understanding all of this is crucial for those who wish to open themselves to the real nature of things and surrender all mind-created suffering. We will investigate the four levels here. We have already mentioned the highest level, Parā; now we will start from the lowest level and come full circle. We start, as usual, from the so-called "lowest" level because that is the most concrete and obvious, the most familiar to us. We always start from where we are on the spiritual path.

The chart below will make sense as you read through the discussion.

Name	**Translation**	**Predominant aspect of consciousness**	**Predominant Śakti**	**Sphere of perception**
4. *Vaikharī*	Corporeal	object	Action	duality
3. *Madhyamā*	Intermediate	process	Knowledge	synthesis
2. *Paśyantī*	Visionary	subject	Will	nonduality
1. *Parā*	Supreme	transcendental subject	Freedom	supreme nonduality

Vaikharī Vāk:
The Corporeal Level of the Word

If we start from the most concrete, the first of the four levels is *Vaikharī*, the level of ordinary everyday articulate speech. *Vaikharī* functions on the level of duality, and in it, object-awareness is predominant. Human language is inherently dualistic, for each word achieves a particular meaning only by negating all other possible meanings. Further, spoken language is oriented to the objects of consciousness, and it operates analytically—that is to say, it helps our minds divide reality into discrete chunks and then sort and categorize them. This creates a problem, for if we believe that language reflects reality accurately, we will necessarily see reality dualistically. That is, we will perceive a world carved up into different chunks of differing values, a world of separate entities acting on (and often against) one another, instead of a continuum of unity in dynamically balanced interrelationship.

Indian philosophy has long articulated a powerful critique of the (usually) unconscious process by which we take a linguistic concept, which is really just a convenient shorthand designation for a complex process or set of factors, and believe that that linguistic term denotes a given static reality. That is to say, we mistake a linguistic symbol for a fact, a thing in the world.[47] This may not seem a big deal—mere philosophizing, you might say—but the consequences of this cognitive act of "reifying" a linguistic symbol are serious. In the realm of religion, we call it fundamentalism (which basically means believing that your religious text is literally true rather than symbolically true), and as we know, this has been responsible for some of the most vitriolic hatred and horrific bloodshed of recent history. So, this is not "mere philosophy." There are serious real-world consequences to these subtle processes by which we build up our picture of reality. Therefore we must try to understand them.

To help us penetrate to a deeper level of reality than dualistic perception, the Trika doctrine shows us that the world of articulated human language is actually the most superficial and coarse level of the Word, and investigating its deeper, subtler layers helps us see reality more accurately. The top-level "corporeal" discourse in which we engage every day is, in this philosophy, like the surface of the ocean—it gives little indication of what's happening underwater. Your ordinary speech is constantly informed by deeper levels of discourse and can point you toward those deeper realities, should you care to look. In other words, ordinary speech (*Vaikharī*) is shaped by how you think (*Madhyamā*); how you think is shaped by your deep unconscious convictions about reality (*Paśyantī*); and those in turn are partial articulations of the singular divine Awareness (*Parā*) that freely chooses to express itself in a rhythm of contracted and expanded forms. In light of this, the way you speak expresses something of the underlying pattern of your consciousness. If change is desirable, then, on the Tantrik path we do *not* seek that transformation in terms of superficial programmatic adjustments of our words to conform more successfully to social sanction (even the sanction of a very spiritual community). Rather, we seek shifts on the deeper levels of our awareness that then express themselves naturally through the spontaneous play of our thoughts and words. So, words *do* matter, not in terms of themselves but in terms of what they signify, where they are arising from, what they point to or reveal about the way we are encountering and understanding our world. Additionally, words are important because they are forms of action, by which we affect (or inflict) change on the world around us. Our words are patterns of energy that powerfully shape other people's experience of reality and our own, and therefore must be used with care.

Madhyamā Vāk: The Intermediate Level of the Word

The second level of the Word is *Madhyamā*, the level of thought or "internal discourse." On this level, the process of knowing is more predominant than the things known (see the chart on page 166). Language on this level is not like that which we speak exactly; it is what some call "mentalese"—the language with which the mind thinks to itself in: a mixture of words, images, fragmented phrases, and half-formed ideas. The *Madhyamā* level is the substrate for the formation of persistent dualistic thought-structures called *vikalpas*; in other words, this is the arena in which the mind formulates its thought-constructs—the forms of verbal symbolization that it then superimposes on reality. *Vikalpas*, mental constructs are essentially the distorted and oversimplified stories that we tell ourselves about reality and that we then reify or take as fact. The ability to distinguish that a *vikalpa* is a representation of reality—and an inherently faulty one—rather than reality itself is a crucial skill for the Tantrik yogī; some say *the* crucial skill.

Yet this level of discourse is closer to the essential nature of Awareness than the previous one, for by its very nature, it operates not within the realm of duality (*bheda*) but within the sphere of synthesis or unity-in-diversity (*bhedābheda*). All the various concepts, contradictory though they may be, are unified by the field of one's individual consciousness.

The inner discourse of the *Madhyamā* level operates through the three aspects of the mental instrument (see pages 129–133). In the intellect (*buddhi*), it takes the form of deliberation, contemplation, judgment, and imagination; in the *manas,* it manifests as sensory images, and in the ego, as self-referentiality. Some of these, like contemplation and imagination, are expansive forms of inner discourse that can be tools in moving closer to our natural state of freedom and presence. For this reason, there are Tantrik practices that are performed on the *Madhyamā* level, purifying and aligning it, such as the practices of visualization (*dhyāna*), deity-yoga, meditation, and creative contemplation (*bhāvanā*). These are like *āsanas* (yogic postures) for the mind. The proverb that typifies Tantrik practice is "We rise by the support of the same ground that trips us." It is important to note that our thought-constructs, our *vikalpas*, limit the range of possibilities for how we experience any given reality, yet cultivating purified thought-constructs—those aligned with the organic patterning of awakened consciousness—can by the same token expand our range of possibilities. (This will be explored further.)

We rise by the support of the same ground that trips us.

Paśyantī Vāk: The Visionary Level of the Word

The cultivation of purified thought-constructs is very difficult to accomplish if we are not also working down into the third level, the *Paśyantī* or "visionary" level. This is a level beyond ordinary discourse, where the vibrations of thought and feeling seem entirely wordless. It is the level of precognitive Will (*icchā śakti*), the initial impulse of Consciousness toward expression. On this level of the Word there is no differentiation of space and time, and sound and light as well are synesthetically fused. The Word is very much active here, though in a compacted and concealed form. This is the plane of so-called *nirvikalpa* awareness: in this context that term does not mean "without thought," but rather that the *vikalpa*s (differential thought-constructs) have become converted into pure energy in very subtle forms. Because these are so deeply internalized, they have more power to influence us on this level—for good or ill.

On this level, subjective awareness is dominant; that is, the subject-object split of ordinary thought is scarcely operative for the various objects of experience have collapsed into the subject. We perceive the impressions of the various experiences as part of ourselves (and again, with good or ill results, depending on the impressions). So, this is the level of our precognitive,* deeply held beliefs about reality, woven into our sense of self, and all the stronger for being wordless. This level is called "visionary" because the pattern held here powerfully shapes our vision of reality, structuring our thoughts on the *Madhyamā* level and our words on the *Vaikharī* level. The subliminal impressions of past experiences (*saṃskāras*) held here constantly provide the template for our mental and physical engagement with reality. Hence, if our yoga does not reach to this level, lasting change is impossible. This is the level of deep healing, where our goal is to create a pattern in the deepest level of individual awareness that perfectly aligns with the cosmic divine pattern.

*That means prior to cognition, limiting the range of possible cognitions and shaping their character.

The model of the four levels of the Word helps us understand why it can be so hard to tell the difference between a "hunch" that expresses deep intuitive insight and one that expresses deep subconscious programming. We feel both viscerally, but while the former is completely reliable, the latter is only sporadically so. The difficulty in telling them apart is that both bear the mark of the *Paśyantī* level: the former rises from the fundamental level of the Word (see below) and passes through the *Paśyantī* level of the subconscious to simplify it and emerges into the mind, whereas the latter, the hunch that comes from subconscious programming arises from *saṃskāras* (subconscious impressions), which have been imprinted on the *Paśyantī* level.

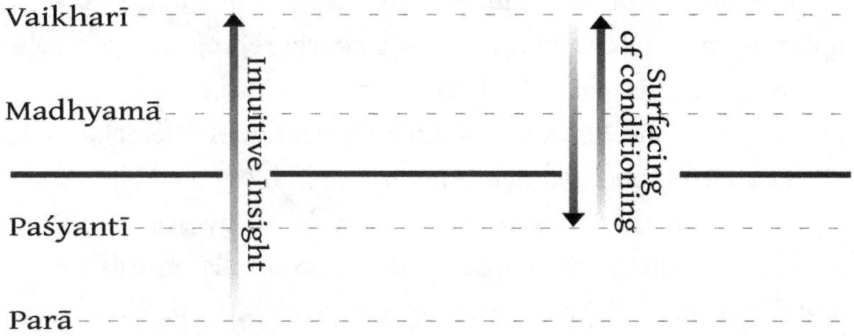

So in other words, the difficulty in telling deep intuition and deep programming apart is simply because the deep intuition arises from the *Parā* level through the *Paśyantī* and the *Madhyamā* levels, whereas the deep programming arises only from the *Paśyantī* level.

We must therefore be skeptical of our hunches and investigate their real nature. One way to tell the difference between the arising of true intuitive insight (from the *Parā* level) and the arising of deep conditioning (from the *Paśyantī* level) is this: when you question the hunch, if it comes from your *saṃskāras*, the mind will defend and justify it, arguing for its validity and pointing to the "evidence" that seems to corroborate it. By contrast, when you question a real intuition, it simply remains silent, a silent persistent pull or feeling about what's right in that situation. The insight does not justify or explain itself, just offers itself as a gift. It does take practice to listen to the voice that is quieter than the mind.

The more our yoga progresses, the more our intuition does become accurately aligned with the deeper pattern (the *Parā* level). To facilitate the deep healing and clearing that makes this possible, we must allow our spiritual work to penetrate to the *Paśyantī* level, where our subliminal impressions or *saṃskāras* are lodged.

There are three methods to penetrate to this level. The first is to repeatedly cultivate purified thought-constructs on the *Madhyamā* level of conscious thought, until that patterning of awareness becomes strong enough to spill over and shape the unconscious pattern on the Paśyantī level. For example, by marinating your mind in profound, uplifting spiritual teachings, you will slowly reprogram your subconscious mind. This method is beautifully explained by Abhinava Gupta in chapter 4 of his *Essence of the Tantras* (more on this later).

See pages 363–374

The second method is a type of mindfulness meditation, which is oriented to the *Paśyantī* or visionary level. By accessing the all-accepting Witness Consciousness that also dwells on this level, we create a healing space of awareness in which old *saṃskāras* are automatically released. To be clear, in this type of meditation, instead of focusing on a mantra or the breath for the whole time, you spend some time simply sitting in a space of quiet openness, with a willingness to see whatever needs to be seen, to feel whatever wants to be felt, neither seeking nor pushing away thoughts but simply watching nonjudgmentally whatever arises and subsides. This simple act of sitting and being is actually the most effective method of meditation for healing the *saṃskāras*. When you hold the space of non-judgmental loving-awareness, opening up to whatever needs to be seen, then the *saṃskāras* that are ready to be released will start to arise into that space and be felt and then dissolve.

The third method is mantra repetition. This practice begins on the *Vaikharī* level (simply speaking or singing a mantra such as *om nama shivaya*) and on the *Vaikharī* level, where not much benefit is experienced. If sufficiently practiced, however, the mantra becomes subtler and subtler until it purifies all three levels of speech, we are told. To work with this method, you recite your primary mantra with faith and loving, full-hearted awareness, both in meditation and many times throughout the day, and in time it will naturally transition from an articulate form to a kind of rhythmic pulsation in which the words are no longer distinct but their vibration is still present. When this pulsation starts to arise spontaneously (that is, with no conscious volition) and blissfully, the mantra has successfully penetrated to the *Paśyantī* level. When the *Paśyantī* level is purified, whether by the method of purifying thought-constructs, mindfulness meditation, or subtle mantra repetition, then the unobstructed light of divine Will Power directs you to awakening—to the realization of your ultimate nature.

Parā Vāk: The Supreme Level of the Word

That ultimate nature is the Supreme Word. It is totally beyond the distinction of the three planes described above and yet constitutes the deepest identity of each of them, the vibration from which they all arise. It is the realm of higher nonduality. That means it is a reality that coincides with no single plane, yet is that from which the various planes derive the capacity of performing their respective functions. Unlike the other three levels, it cannot be measured in terms of greater or lesser degrees of contraction for it embodies the very divine Freedom that presides over the appearance of contraction in its various forms and degrees. It is called the Supreme Word because, though beyond all verbalization, it constitutes the power of verbalization and symbolization. That is, it is the very essence of self-reflective awareness (vimarśa), the power by which Consciousness represents itself to itself in various forms, that it may know itself fully.[48]

The fundamental vibratory essence from which all language, thought, feeling, and perception arise, Parā is a divine mystery, for despite being the highest principle of reality, we all experience Her every day in the form of our own self-awareness. She is not some mystical state stowed away in a void, but rather the singular all-encompassing vibration by which all things move and sing. Abhinava Gupta describes his goddess, Parā Vāk, in this way:

An Exposition of the Thirty Verses of Parā

> *She is the primordial, uncreated Word, the very essence of the highest reality, pervading all things and eternally in creative motion: She is simply luminous pure Consciousness, vibrating with the greatest subtlety (as the ground of all Being).*

Everything is a harmonic vibration of the one supreme Word.

He goes on to say that everything—stones, trees, birds, human beings, gods, and demons—is a harmonic vibration of that one supreme Word. Her dominant powers are *svātantrya-śakti,* the Power of absolute Freedom, and *vimarśa-śakti,* the Power of Self-awareness, self-reflection and self-representation. She is most fully expressed in human experience in the state of *chamatkāra,* the state of fully self-aware expansive wonder, where Consciousness is suffused with the sudden rapture of great beauty, vibrating with awestruck joy. This state, beyond words, transcendent yet completely engaged with the reality present in awareness, reveals to us how the Goddess Parā can be simultaneously the transcendent source of all things yet completely immanent in all things. She suggests to us, then, that ultimately we can experience exquisite beauty in each aspect of human existence: in stillness and change, in death and birth, in growth and decay, in pain and joy.

THE FIVE STATES OF AWARENESS

As you might imagine in a spiritual culture so preoccupied with the nature of consciousness, attention is given to the various states of awareness that each of us moves through every day: waking, dreaming, deep sleep, and so on. Of course, as usual, the Tantra has an argument to make about how many states of awareness there actually are. Many people not familiar with spiritual practice would say there are three. Meditators who have experienced *samādhi* (deep meditation) might think there are four. Nondual Śaiva Tantra argues that there are five primary phases or states of awareness.

As the great American philosopher William James wrote at the turn of the 20th century,

> *Our normal waking consciousness is but one special type of consciousness, while all about it parted from it by the filmiest of screens there lie potential forms of consciousness entirely different. We may go through life without suspecting their existence, but apply the requisite stimulus and at a touch they are there in all their completeness. No account of the universe in its totality can be final which leaves these other forms of consciousness quite disregarded.*
>
> William James

The five basic states or phases of awareness are presented in tabular form on the next page, followed by a discussion of each and how they interpenetrate each other.

State	Body	Associated Breath	Predominant aspect of Consciousness	Predominant sphere of perception
Waking	Physical	Out-breath	Object	Duality
Dreaming	Subtle	In-breath	Object-impressions	Unity-in-diversity
Deep Sleep	Causal	Samāna	Subject	Nonduality (unaware)
The Fourth	Supracausal	Udāna	Subject	Nonduality (aware)
Beyond the Fourth	All/none	Vyāna	Transindividual subjectivity	Supreme nonduality

JĀGRAT: THE WAKING STATE

The ordinary waking state is one in which we tend to perceive ourselves primarily in terms of the physical body. In this state we are focused on (even lost in) the objects of perception, perceiving them in terms of their mutual differentiation and our resultant preferences. Though we call this "the waking state" to differentiate it from sleep and dreams, from the spiritual perspective it is the most unawake of all the states. As scholar Mark Dyczkowski has written, "[In this state, a person is] completely unconscious of his own subjective nature, [and] he never asks himself who he is. Whenever he sees an object, he immediately identifies with it and totally forgets about himself as the perceiver."[49] This is why Abhinava Gupta calls this state "the unawakened." Most people move through their waking life as if in a dream. Thus the *Bhagavad-gītā* says (I paraphrase), "What is day to most people is night to the person of wisdom, and vice versa."

Within the waking state, we also experience the other states, for according to Tantric philosophy, the first four states all interpenetrate each other. Dreaming-in-waking is the state we call daydream, reverie, or fantasy, in which we are lost in our mental impressions and almost unaware of our physical surroundings. This state of deep sleep-in-waking is a moment of completely blanking out, a spontaneously thought-free state in which one stares off blankly into space. It is rare in adults but often observed in children or teens, who unfortunately are discouraged from it. It is a natural state of unity-consciousness, but we are not aware of it as such. The fourth state-in-waking is a moment of spontaneous meditation, a thought-free state in which self-awareness is primary, even while perceiving the "external" world. This is called "true wakefulness" by Abhinava Gupta. So unlike in the deep sleep-in-waking state, in the fourth in-waking state, there isn't a self-forgetting or total abstraction.

Svapna: the Dream State

In the second of the five states, the dream state, we occupy our subtle body (sometimes called the "energy body" because it is composed of the *prāṇa*, subtle elements, and mental faculties),[50] and we roam in the world of the impressions of our various experiences, exercising our capacity for imaginative mental representation. In this state there is unity-in-diversity (*bhedābheda*), as opposed to the seemingly strict diversity of the waking state, for all the various elements of the dream state are unified by being aspects of a single mind. The dream world is not a creation of random firings in the brain, as some suppose, but can tell us about our subconscious life. Therefore, there is the possibility of doing "dream yoga," a topic addressed by Abhinava Gupta in chapter 10 of his *Light on the Tantra.* As he says there, "Wise ones experience dream as a form of inner knowing, which operates on known entities in whatever way it wants, independently of their external existence." In other words, through dream yoga we can make inner shifts, rewrite our past, and have new insights.

The state of waking-in-dream, commonly called lucid dreaming, is an important part of dream yoga; for to make conscious choices in the dream world, you must learn how to wake up in it and realize you are dreaming. Otherwise lucidity in the dream state will come and go at random. Some people never experience this; but if you have, you can cultivate it. A state called dreaming-in-dream is the ordinary kind of dreaming, in which awareness is scattered and self-reflection is difficult. Deep sleep-in-dreaming is said to be a state in which one has greater self-awareness in the dream (because deep sleep is associated with subjectivity; see the chart on page 176). Finally, the most important is the state of the Fourth-in-dream, *turiya* in-dreaming, that is to say, fully focused awareness, meditative awareness, while dreaming. This is very rare. It is said that if you can learn to practice meditation in the dream state, it bears fruit more rapidly than in the waking state.

Sushupti: The Deep Sleep State

In deep sleep, the third of the five states, we are immersed in pure subjectivity but without self-awareness. Entering this state every night is necessary for mental and physical health. In this state, we are temporarily free of our waking thoughts and our subconscious impressions, both of which can be taxing on our systems. From the yogic point of view, it is precisely because the deep sleep state is so close to pure subjectivity, the innermost Self, that it is refreshing and rejuvenating. The human being cannot survive long without deep sleep or meditation, one or the other, or both.

Waking-in-deep sleep is a state where some trace of awareness emerges, by virtue of which, when you wake up, you are able to say, "I slept well," or, "I slept a long time." How do you know, if there isn't a trace of awareness in deep sleep? Dreaming-in-deep sleep is an expansive state in which one is unconscious but still receiving impressions: for example, some people in comas are in this state, and though unconscious, when they come out of the coma, they have some sense of who was with them during that time. By contrast, in the peaceful state of deep sleep-in-deep sleep, one is aware of nothing whatsoever, and upon waking, has no notion of how much time has passed, but wakes feeling deeply refreshed. Finally, the Fourth-in-deep sleep is an extremely rare state of becoming conscious of the absolute void of pure subjectivity during one's sleep period, and meditating there spontaneously. In his book, *I Am That*, Nisargadatta mentions that he has this experience.

Turya: The Fourth, or Transcendental State

The transcendental state of meditation, commonly known as *samādhi*, consists of accessing the state of total subjectivity, the void of pure consciousness—with the usual objects of awareness (including thoughts) absent, the senses quieted, and even the subliminal impressions temporarily quelled. Simply, it is a state in which one accesses the level of deep sleep while completely awake and aware. Put another way, it is nondual awareness of pure subjectivity or "I-ness," on the level of the individual Self (*puruṣa*, *ātman*), not yet the all-encompassing universal Self.

Samādhi literally means "absorption," because in classical yoga the most common method of achieving this state was to quiet the mind by focusing it one-pointedly on any object (a candle flame, the breath, the point between the eyebrows, etc.,) until the mind merged with the object of meditation and thus dissolved. In this state, the object alone shines forth, suffused with consciousness, yet free of any associations, interpretations, or cognitions. One skilled in this technique eventually learns to attain it even without an object of meditation (*nirbīja samādhi* in Patañjali's *yoga sutra*).

For many Indian (and indeed Asian) spiritual traditions, this is the highest state. They regard it as the only state untainted by the messy and limited manifestations of nature. Such schools of thought are "transcendentalist" in that they seek transcendence as their goal. But in the tradition of Śaiva Tantra called "Supreme Nondualism" (*paramādvaya*), which was discussed briefly before, it is taught that we can exist in the stainless clear Light of Consciousness even in the midst of worldly activity. This is the condition known as *turyātīta*, "beyond the Fourth."

We can exist in the stainless clear Light of Consciousness even in the midst of worldly activity.

Turyātīta: Beyond the Fourth

As you might expect if you are starting to understand the pattern of reality according to this philosophy, this state is not called "the Fifth" because it does not top a hierarchy; it is not comprehensible in hierarchical terms. Referred to as that state "beyond the Fourth," literally, Turyātīta is best described as the complete permeation of the first three states by the Fourth state, that is to say *samadhi* in waking, dreaming, and deep sleep. It expresses the fundamental movement of the self-liberating autonomous consciousness: *transcendence followed by pervasion of the mundane by the transcendent.* Thus it is final liberation and full awakening, as the Tāntrikas conceive it, under another name.

See page 287

In other words, the nondual Tāntrikas assert that it is possible to experience the supreme Light of the Divine in the midst of any and all worldly activities, and even in the midst of any and all moods or states of mind. To be more accurate, in this state we do not experience the Light *in spite of* our mood or condition or activity but *as the very substance* of those. The successful abiding within this state is Turyātīta, the liberation beyond that of the transcendentalists, the liberation that realizes the transcendent in the immanent and therefore embraces total intimacy with reality. As it is taught in the *Īśvara-pratyabhijñā-kārikā, Stanzas on the Recognition of the Divine:*

Stanzas on the Recognition of the Lord

> *One whose self is the universe, knowing fully that "All this is my own expansion," experiences the divine state even in the flow of differential cognitions. So says the great master Utpaladeva.*

Once again, then, the ultimate Reality is simultaneously transcendent and immanent, constituting the very substance of your moment-to-moment experience yet inexpressibly more than that: the timeless ground upon which it all unfolds.

The Innate Structure of Reality

The Trika-Krama Synthesis of Abhinava Gupta

We have explored many of the basic concepts and principles of nondual Tantrik thought. It is important to realize that much of the cohesiveness and organization of classical Tantrik philosophy is due largely to the work of two geniuses, two masterful scholar-sages of 10th-century Kashmīr: Utpala Deva and Abhinava Gupta. The first, Utpala, was an accomplished intellectual philosopher, one of the finest India ever produced; he was also a great-hearted passionate poet and lover of God, so he serves as a perfect example of the total integration and expansion of all the levels of one's being that the Tantrik path promises. The second, Abhinava, was also a great philosopher and theologian, and he was an accomplished yogī as well, expert in a wide range of spiritual practices found in the Tantrik scriptures, as well as being quite an advanced aesthetic philosopher and a critic of dance and poetry. You will learn more about both of these *siddha gurus* in the history section of the book.

See pages 289 & 292

In this section we will briefly explore Abhinava's theological vision and why it was so important to the Tantrik tradition. First we must realize that by the year 950 CE, hundreds of Tantrik scriptures had already been produced. Each was followed by a different lineage: some scriptures were fairly obscure productions of small marginal groups, others vast and detailed works commanding many followers in multiple lineages. In this body of scripture there are shared themes, practices, and vocabulary, but not much doctrinal agreement, coherence, or systematic thinking can be found. Near the end of the 10th century, Abhinava Gupta wrote his magnum opus, *Light on the Tantras* (*Tantrāloka*), and in this and other associated works he created the theological structure that makes sense out of the vast and diverse

See page 296

scriptural corpus of the Tantrik tradition. Through extensive quoting of more than a hundred scriptural sources and careful explanation and creative exegesis of these same sources, he demonstrated that there is a single, coherent View of reality that can be derived from them. To articulate it from Abhinava's perspective, this is the View that Lord Śiva intended us to realize through His scriptural revelation. Thus we may compare the place of Abhinava Gupta in the Tantrik tradition to that of Thomas Aquinas in the Christian tradition, whose *Summa Theologica* forms an interesting parallel to the *Tantrāloka*, not in content of course but in form, function, and influence.[51]

Not only did Abhinava organize and make sense out of a vast and diverse body of materials, he also innovated by creating a philosophical structure for the teachings that was designed to lead the practitioner, inevitably, to the highest and most complete, all-encompassing realization. Though his writing is extremely sophisticated and detailed, we can summarize his unique contribution through the organizing principle of the "3 + 1" model. Almost everything of importance to Abhinava can be understood in light of this model. And this is not surprising, for the model is provided by the very name of the school of Tantra with which Abhinava is most associated: the Trika or "Trinity," whose central teaching is that the triad of the individual soul, Śakti, and Śiva are, in reality, three expressions of an undifferentiated unity, the timeless ground of all reality, known as the Heart of Being, as the +1 to the 3, as it were.

This is what Abhinava means when he states that the Trika is the one revelation within which the entire tradition is grounded. He quotes a beautiful scriptural passage that states,

Tantrāloka 35.30–34

> *[This truth] resides within [all] the scriptures like the scent in a flower, the oil in a sesame seed, the soul in the body, or nectar in water.*

The analogies given point to the notion that the innate truth of the 3 + 1 teaching constitutes the very essence of the scriptures. Like the scent of a flower or the consciousness that animates the body, this essence is ever-present and obvious, but so subtle it is hard to grasp and certainly not graspable as an object.

Let us investigate the forms in which the supreme truth of the 3 + 1 pattern of reality manifests in the Tantrik teaching of Abhinava Gupta.

In every experience that you've ever had, there are three factors: the thing known or perceived, the means by which it is known, and the knower or perceiver. These three are expressed in every sentence that articulates conscious experience, even the most basic sentence, such as "I see a pot." Perceiver, perception, perceived. But the three factors of experience are, upon deeper investigation, realized as three aspects of a single dynamic process by which Consciousness reflects on itself in the form of the apparently differentiated and distinct objects of awareness. They are three flowering buds of a single root, as it were, and it is only language that fools us into thinking that there are really three separate things: perceiver, perception, perceived. This is why spiritual practice *must* go beyond the realm of language and the mind, since that realm conditions us to experience dualistically. This is what I mean by the 3+1 model: not that there is actually a +1, but that the +1 is the underlying unity of the three.

Similarly, the three primary powers of Consciousness-in-form, those of Willing (*icchā*), Knowing (*jñāna*), and Acting (*kriyā*), are to be understood as the expressions of the fundamental ground in which they inhere, which is—to only approximate it in words—formless, autonomous Consciousness, blissful through reposing in itself (*cidānanda*). This ultimate ground is your ever-present true nature, the Deity-Self revealed by the scriptures, whose primary purpose is to point you to its realization. Abhinava's powerful articulation of this ultimate truth was stunningly captured by Professor Sanderson (the foremost expert in Abhinava's work), when he wrote that the Deity-Self is defined as,

See page 107 and following

Alexis Sanderson

The absolute autonomy of a nonindividual consciousness which alone exists, containing the whole of reality within the bliss of a dynamic "I"-nature, projecting space, time, and the interrelating fluxes of subjective and objective phenomena as its content and form, manifesting itself in this spontaneous extroversion through precognitive impulse (icchā), cognition (jñāna), and action (kriyā) as the three radical modes of an infinite power.[52]

See page 346 and following

We again see the same pattern in the presentation of the three Means to Liberation, the *upāyas*, which form the subject of the last part of this book. These three different means—focused on body, heart-mind, and spirit respectively—bring one to the realization of precisely the same ultimate reality because they derive from and are rooted in that very reality, the nameless Fourth, which simultaneously transcends them and yet is present in them, constituting their essence. By the way, in case you haven't realized it, in every example of the 3 + 1 pattern the +1 is the same: it is the One that gives rise to all the triads.

In the same way, Abhinava notes that Śaiva Tantra consists of three (+1) basic orders or lineage groupings (*santānas*), founded by three ancient sages plus the daughter of one of the three. Since describing these here would be confusing (until you have read the history section), they are described in this endnote.[53]

See page 286

The 3 + 1 pattern is also seen in Abhinava's interpretation of the Spanda doctrine. The Spanda is a lineage of teachings (described in part 2), which are so profound and powerful they merit a whole other book.* Suffice to say here that the term *spanda* refers to the innate dynamism or vibrancy of Consciousness. It is the dynamic core of the Light of Consciousness, which creates the pulsating appearance of movement in the ultimately motionless. By meditating on the spanda, one penetrates through the Śakti state to the nondual ground (+1) in which the triad of Nara (individuated consciousness), Śakti, and Śiva coincide in undifferentiated unity.[54] Abhinava alludes to three phases of spanda experience in chapter

* In fact two such books have been written by Mark Dyczkowski, *The Doctrine of Vibration* and *Stanzas on Vibration,* which while excellent are difficult for the nonscholar.

5 of his *Light on the Tantras.* In the first phase, individuality is predominant and the vibration of consciousness is focused on the objects of its experience. In the second, the śakti level of unity-consciousness, one has the awareness, "Whatever exists is nothing but myself." In the third, there is only the One, the universal "I." All three of these modes, though, are expressions of the nondual ground, the nameless Fourth.

Finally, and most importantly for the development of the theology of the tradition, we see the same 3 + 1 pattern in Abhinava's doctrine of the ultimate nature of reality. Some see reality as inherently dualistic, in other words that distinction is ultimately real. This is called the *bheda* view. They do good works and worship a separate almighty God that they hope will bless them with his grace. Others see distinctions that are subsumed within a greater unity, with distinction and unity having equal weight in experience (the *bhedābheda* view). They cultivate spiritual knowledge and relish beautiful things as a vibration of consciousness. Still others see completely nondualistically, that is, seeing difference as unreal or only very superficially real, with unity absolutely dominant in experience (the *abheda* or *advaita* view). They reject all practice, subtle and gross, and dwell in the immediate intuitive insight of the transcendent "I"-nature. So, where does the +1 come in, in this model of things? This is the key to understanding the ultimate consummation of Tantrik philosophy. You see, the nondual view just mentioned *excludes* the dualistic view, seeing it as simply wrong. It is not an all-inclusive nonduality, and therefore it lends itself to transcendentalism, a spiritual by-passing, a major pitfall on the path. Therefore Abhinava Gupta presented a View he called *paramādvaya,* "the supreme nonduality," which we have already mentioned a couple of times. This View includes both duality and nonduality as valid experiences and levels of perception. Nonduality transcends duality, but the "supreme nonduality" transcends the transcendent. So how do we understand this seeming paradox? Because again, the supremely nondual nameless Fourth is simultaneously transcendent and immanent: it englobes, includes, *emanates as* all these different views. It is

See page 149

the all-inclusive Heart of reality, the dynamic power of Consciousness (*cidānanda*), which articulates every possibility, becomes everything, *and yet is no-thing*. We have stressed, over and over, this higher Tantrik view that that divine is simultaneously transcendent and immanent precisely because masters of the tradition tell us that understanding.

The supremely nondual nameless Fourth is simultaneously transcendent and immanent.

From this perspective, then, Lord Śiva has compassionately revealed dualistic scriptures for the benefit of those who see reality that way; and even in these texts, He has concealed hints and clues that point toward nondual awareness so that those in the dualist path may, when they are ready, "graduate" to a more inclusive nondual awareness. And lest they then become stuck in nondual rejection of dualistic modes, there is the teaching about the "higher nonduality" that includes all possible modes as the levels of emanation of the One.

Now, since all this might be seen by some as rarefied philosophizing, let us examine the real-world implications of this 3 + 1 vision of reality. Abhinava Gupta discusses this in chapter 4 of *Light on the Tantras*, showing how the doctrine of supreme nonduality resolves the disputes between the dualists and the nondualists. He writes,

Light on the Tantras

> *In the dualistic Orthodoxy [of the Siddhānta sect], worship of the liṅga [the stone idol representing Śiva] is taught, with the intention of coming to see it as embodying the whole universe; but in the Kula and similar systems, liṅga-worship is forbidden, so that one may come to see the universe in one's own body. But here in the all-inclusive [way of supreme nonduality] what reason could there be either for requiring the ritual or forbidding it?*[55]

He goes on to discuss other practices: mimetic rites of impersonating the deity (with one's dress, behavior, and so on) in order to acquire Her power, rites rejected by nondualists who seek to realize Her as formless and all-embodying; pilgrimage to sacred sites is discussed, denigrated by nondualists who seek to realize that the Self is found everywhere and is all-encompassing; and the wearing of sectarian marks and the following of lineage rules is mentioned, forbidden by nondualists who seek to see Reality as undivided.[56] Then he says:

Tantrāloka 4.271–2

In our way, none of this is enjoined or prohibited. No practice is specifically enjoined, because it is not a guaranteed means of access to Śiva [for a given individual], and no practice [even a dualistic one] is specifically prohibited, because it can do nothing to divide or diminish that [divine] Reality. For the Lord is all-encompassing, so injunction and prohibition are merely differential constructs within his nature. They cannot compromise that nature itself.

This is not a doctrine of "anything goes," as it might appear to a Westerner. It is rather arguing that no single practice can be universally enjoined or prohibited for all practitioners. Each person must have a committed practice, but each practice must be carefully tailored to that person's constitution, psychology, and desired goal. Here Abhinava is following a rather extraordinary passage found in his primary source scripture (*The Final Triumph of the Goddess Garlanded by the Letters* or *Mālinīvijayottara-tantra*). This passage is, in the context of any body of premodern religious literature, unusual for its radical openness of mind. It reads:

Mālinīvijayottara-tantra
Chapter 18

Here there is no purity and no impurity, no dualism nor nondualism, no ritual nor its rejection, no renunciation and no possession...all the observances, rules and regulations [found in other Tantras] are neither enjoined nor prohibited in this way. Or, everything is enjoined, and everything forbidden here! In fact, there is but one commandment on this [higher path], O Queen of the Gods: the yogī is to make every effort to steady his awareness on reality. He must practice whatever makes that possible for him.[57]

The truly radical nature of this passage is mostly lost on 21st-century individuals who take its message for granted. But in the context of a highly rule-bound tradition, it is an astonishing example of liberated awareness. But even in the modern world, there are so many who could benefit from this teaching. On the other hand, it is not a teaching usually given to beginners on the path, because the basic foundational practices are largely the same for everyone, and this teaching can be used by the deluded or self-important as a pretext for skipping those basic practices.

We have seen how the 3 + 1 pattern applies to the phenomenology of experience, to the primary powers of Consciousness, the methodology of practice, the primary lineages, the teachings of the Spanda, the nature of reality, and we've gotten a hint of how it plays out in real-world application. If we closely study Abhinava's theology, we discover that he has a powerful motivation for articulating this pattern: it is, in essence, the fruit of synthesizing the two primary traditions that he inherited, the Trika and the Krama. Initiated into the radically nondual Krama as a young man but attaining the final goal through the grace of a master of the Trika, he was obviously compelled to integrate the teachings of both in a greater harmony. He was not the first to do so, however, and there are even scriptures that teach this uniquely powerful synthesis of those two lineages.

See pages 235 & 248

We can conclude this section with a consideration of the theology of the Trika/Krama synthesis as an instantiation of the 3 + 1 pattern. There are three goddesses of the Trika (as we will discuss in the next chapter of this book) that embody the three aspects of experience, Knower, Knowing, and Known. These three are seen, in the Trika/Krama synthesis, as emanations of the Supreme Goddess, sometimes known as Mātṛsadbhāva, which means both "the essence of all mothers" and "the essence of all knowers," sometimes known as Parāvāc (the Supreme Word) and is also identified by Abhinava as Kālī Sankarṣaṇī, Kali as the devourer of time, and this is the name of the

See page 237

See page 248

high Goddess of the Krama tradition. She is considered the Nameless, the timeless ground, the ultimate all-consuming Power of Awareness into which dissolution itself dissolves. She is called the Fourth, for She is the ground of the threefold process of Creation, Stasis, and Dissolution that applies to all things. She is the ultimate emptiness, the no-thing-ness that is simultaneously complete fullness. Integrating Her, whether she goes by the name Kali, Parāvāc, or Mātṛsadbhāva, into the theology of the three Trika goddesses provides the +1 of the 3 + 1 pattern and is the key to Abhinava Gupta's theology.

Abhinava goes further, however. Central to the Krama is the worship of the phases of Awareness in the form of the twelve Kālikās or emanations of Kālī. Abhinava argues that these twelve goddesses arise through the confluence of the three aspects of experience (Knowing, Knower, Known) with the four phases of the Krama, i.e., Creation, Stasis, Re-Absorption, and the Nameless ground (3 x 4 = 12). As he puts it, "*These Powers spontaneously tremble in emission, persistence and re-absorption, and so become the twelve.*" The twelve Kālīs are thus the nodal points and troughs of the complex interference pattern set up by the confluence of the energies of the Trika goddesses with the Krama's Kālī Sankarṣaṇī in her four aspects.[58]

To put it in simpler terms, we are multiplying the three aspects of experience by the four sequential phases of cognition. For example, the first of the twelve Kālīs is Sṛṣṭikālī, and her essence expresses the creation (or rather emission) of the object of experience. The second is Raktakālī, the persistence of the object of experience. And so it goes, all the way to the twelfth Kālī, who is the Nameless ground into which the Knower of the object experienced dissolves. Thus the series of twelve also constitutes a map for the involution of consciousness to its final resting place, the mind's faculties having been withdrawn into the individual subject, the individual subject having been withdrawn into the transcendental Subject, and that having been withdrawn into non-subjective indescribable pure Awareness (= the twelfth Kālī).

The names for the twelve Kālīs preexisted Abhinava's analysis; since for the most part they fit well the map he provides, it lends weight to his argument that he is not making this up, but rather illuminating the hidden pattern of ultimate reality that is the self-revelation of the Absolute in the form of the body of scripture, which is thus seen as a kind of encoded energy, a cipher of the deep structure of reality. Thus Abhinava actually considers the twelve Kālīs to be the primary circuit of power in the analysis of Awareness' innate capacity for self-expression. All other circuits of deities (*śakti-cakra*) are to be seen as condensations or amplifications of this primary circuit, this basic *śakti-cakra* of the twelve Kālīs.[59]

Scripture is encoded energy, a self-revelation of the Absolute.

The reader who finds this teaching difficult will probably wish for greater explanation or at least a chart of the twelve Kālīs. But this teaching is considered highly secret by the tradition, and is not to be given out casually. Following Abhinava's cue in his *Essence of the Tantras* chapter 4, I am here alluding to this key teaching without presenting it in full. Those who truly wish to learn it will find a way to do so.

Abhinava's teaching on the Trika/Krama synthesis was so successful that it influenced much of the later tradition. His disciple Kṣemarāja produced the most condensed transmission of this combined Trika/Krama view in his seminal text in twenty sūtras and commentary, *The Heart of the Doctrine of Recognition*, aka *The Recognition Sutras*, which I have translated and will soon publish.

2
The History of Śaiva Tantra

In Part 1 we explored the spiritual philosophy of nondual Tantra, which constitutes just a part of the total Tantrik literature. In Part 2 I will present a condensed history and overview of the entire tradition of Śaiva Tantra, in all its various permutations. I say condensed, because to write the complete history of this tradition would run to many volumes. A start has been made in that direction by the world's foremost scholar of Shaivism, and of Tantra, Professor Alexis Sanderson of Oxford University, who has published over 1,700 pages of rigorous academic articles largely focused on the history of Śaiva Tantra, which will serve as a foundation for the next hundred years of research on the subject. This section could not have been written without his work and that of his foremost students.

EARLY HISTORY

FRAMING THE TRADITION IN TIME AND SPACE

Tantra originated as a distinctly Indian religious phenomenon, though in time it diffused through many Asian cultures. Our first certain evidence of it dates from a little over 1,500 years ago in North India. This was a turbulent time in Indian history, for the great Gupta empire had crumbled, leaving numerous petty warring kingdoms. The uncertainty of life was at an all-time peak: there was no sure security of home, livelihood, or even one's life. At such times people crave modes of empowerment, and it was to fill this need that the Tantra arose, offering new, more effective technologies for the transformation of mind, body, and environment. Though the Tantra did promise worldly advantages to some, what it ultimately had to offer was the greatest empowerment of all: the power to determine your own inner state, regardless of changing external circumstance.

Tantra was a spiritual movement that originally arose entirely within the religion of Shaivism.

Scholars have been debating for some time now about the precise origins of Tantra as a spiritual movement, as a religious aesthetic, and as a new way of performing yogic and ritual practice. Some say its beginnings are irrevocably lost in the mists of time. Some believe it derived from tribal or shamanistic practices far outside the brāhminical heartland of India.* It is difficult to be sure about the beginnings of Tantra, because the only early evidence we have consists of a couple of manuscripts and inscriptions carved on temple walls. However, through the mammoth efforts of Professor Sanderson, we now can draw some firm conclusions about Tantra's origins. He has recently shown (with several hundred pages of evidence and close argumentation) that Tantra was a spiritual movement that originally arose entirely within the religion of Shaivism and from there passed into Buddhism and Vaishnavism, propagating throughout the Indian subcontinent and into East Asia, Southeast Asia, and Indonesia.[60]

* Called Āryāvarta, this is the area of north-central India where mainstream Indian religion prevailed, a religion largely controlled by the priestly caste of the brāhmins. They included some brilliant thinkers but were usually paid ritual functionaries whose outlook was deeply conservative.

TANTRA TIMELINE

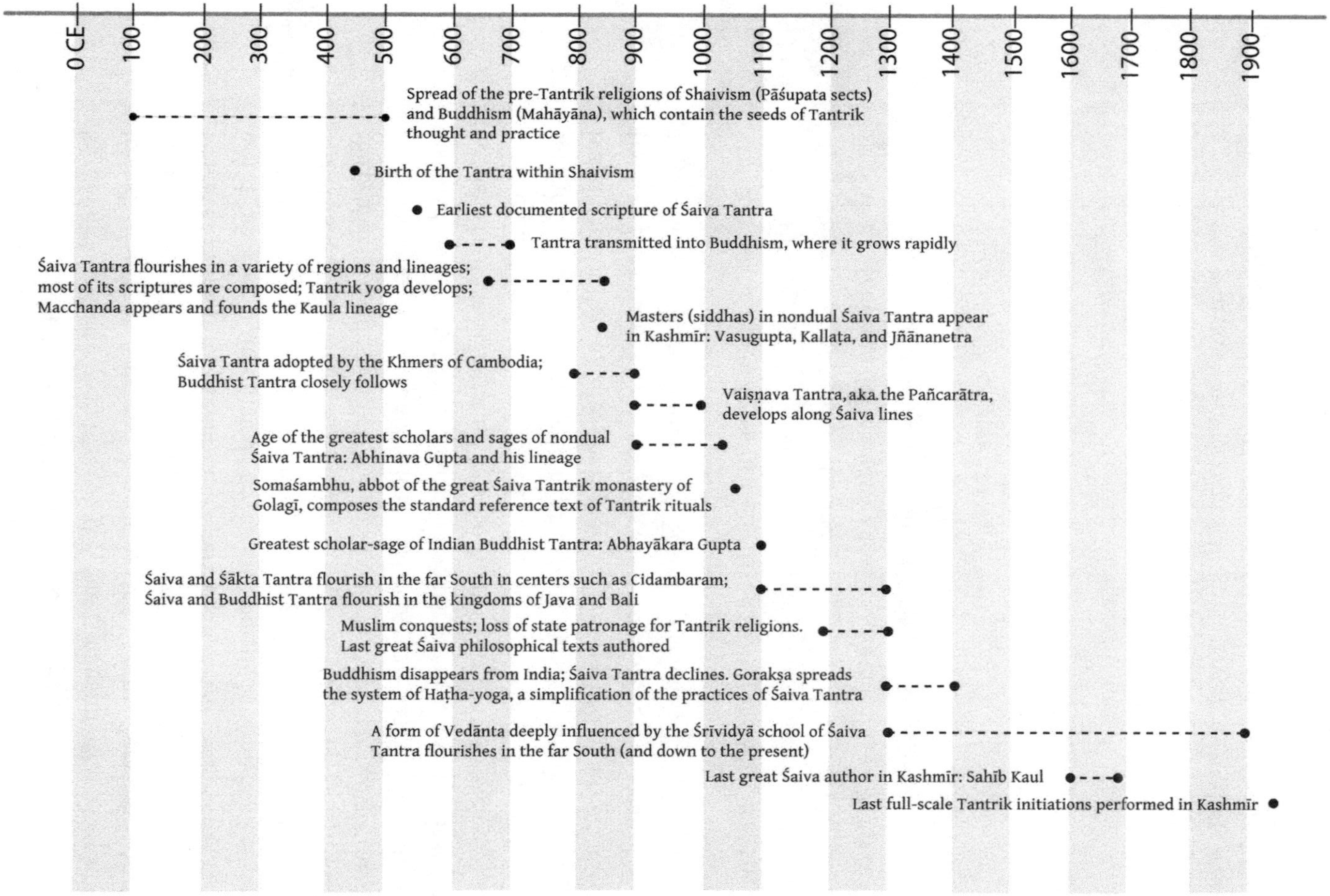
0 CE
100
200
300
400
500
600
700
800
900
1000
1100
1200
1300
1400
1500
1600
1700
1800
1900
Spread of the pre-Tantrik religions of Shaivism (Pāśupata sects) and Buddhism (Mahāyāna), which contain the seeds of Tantrik thought and practice
Birth of the Tantra within Shaivism
Earliest documented scripture of Śaiva Tantra
Tantra transmitted into Buddhism, where it grows rapidly
Śaiva Tantra flourishes in a variety of regions and lineages; most of its scriptures are composed; Tantrik yoga develops; Macchanda appears and founds the Kaula lineage
Masters (siddhas) in nondual Śaiva Tantra appear in Kashmīr: Vasugupta, Kallaṭa, and Jñānanetra
Śaiva Tantra adopted by the Khmers of Cambodia; Buddhist Tantra closely follows
Vaiṣṇava Tantra, a.k.a. the Pañcarātra, develops along Śaiva lines
Age of the greatest scholars and sages of nondual Śaiva Tantra: Abhinava Gupta and his lineage
Somaśambhu, abbot of the great Śaiva Tantrik monastery of Golagī, composes the standard reference text of Tantrik rituals
Greatest scholar-sage of Indian Buddhist Tantra: Abhayākara Gupta
Śaiva and Śākta Tantra flourish in the far South in centers such as Cidambaram; Śaiva and Buddhist Tantra flourish in the kingdoms of Java and Bali
Muslim conquests; loss of state patronage for Tantrik religions. Last great Śaiva philosophical texts authored
Buddhism disappears from India; Śaiva Tantra declines. Gorakṣa spreads the system of Haṭha-yoga, a simplification of the practices of Śaiva Tantra
A form of Vedānta deeply influenced by the Śrīvidyā school of Śaiva Tantra flourishes in the far South (and down to the present)
Last great Śaiva author in Kashmīr: Sahīb Kaul
Last full-scale Tantrik initiations performed in Kashmīr

THE SOCIAL CONTEXT OF SHAIVISM

By definition, those members of the Śaiva religion who were not formally initiated were not practicing the Tantra. Remember that Tantra constitutes the mystical, initiatory, and *esoteric* dimension of whatever religion it is found in. Nevertheless, briefly examining the world of these uninitiated devotees—known as *Śiva-bhaktas* or *upāsakas**—gives us a much richer picture of the social context of Shaivism, as well as its social conscience. These devotees also constituted the primary base from which initiates would be drawn; for any of these devotees who was favored with a Descent of Power (*śaktipāta*)—a spiritual awakening that could come to a person of any caste, class, or gender—could seek initiation into the Tantrik form of the religion.

* The same word is used for Buddhist lay devotees.

Uninitiated devotees focused primarily on the discipline of devotion (*bhakti-yoga*), as opposed to the ritual-, yogic-, and knowledge-based path of the initiate. Their practice is described in a text called the *Śiva-dharma,* which means "the religion of Śiva" or "the way of life aligned with Śiva's teachings." The *Śiva-dharma* teaches:

Śiva-dharma

Unswerving devotion to God is the essence of the religion of Śiva. He has said that its eight aspects are to be practiced diligently and incessantly. The Lord said:

1. *Show affection towards My devotees, like that of a cow for her calf;*
2. *Practice your worship with devotion;*
3. *Rejoice in others' worship;*
4. *Offer selfless service to Me;*
5. *Be devoted to listening to My tales;*
6. *Cultivate a devotion so strong that you are affected in voice, eye, and limb;*
7. *Remember Me; and*
8. *Do not live off My revenues.*

One who practices this eight-fold devotion, even a foreigner, is [as good as] a foremost brāhmin, a venerable sage, an ascetic, or a scholar.

These "eight commandments" give us a picture of the religious life of the majority of people at this time, which was about 12 or 13 hundred years ago, and perhaps illustrate the type of practice that might have been considered a prerequisite for Tantrik initiation, though we know initiates could theoretically come from any background.[61]

Lay devotees would also participate in grand and beautiful devotional festivals, called *utsavas* or *mahās*. These, the *Śiva-dharma* tells us, involved an all-night celebration or "night vigil," which featured singing of devotional songs, sacred dancing, telling stories of Śiva and Pārvatī, chanting (Kirtan), theatrical performances, and even swings and games for the children. The next day, after this all-night celebration, a sacred scripture of Shaivism, usually the *Śiva-dharma,* would be paraded through the city on a three-tiered shrine atop an elephant, with scented water, flowers, and rice scattered wherever it went. The citizenry wore white and flew colored banners from their rooftops, also throwing flower petals and rice. The king forbade all violence for the duration of the festival (even toward plants!), and granted amnesty to prisoners who might have been imprisoned unfairly.[62]

This sort of celebration would take place only in a town with a consecrated temple of Śiva. The temple complex was an important part of life not only for devotees but all the citizenry, for it owned large tracts of land, employed large numbers of people, and was the center of civic and cultural life (other than that of the king's court), commissioning architects, sculptors, painters, dancers, musicians, and scholars. One such Śaiva temple in South India, built at the peak of the Tantrik period, boasted more than two thousand resident dancers, with one thousand servants devoted to their care.* The temple complex always centered on a shrine of Śiva in the form of a *liṅga* (see the image on page 196), in which Śiva's presence had been invoked and installed in the form of his living mantras. The deity was treated as a living presence, even a legal entity: it was Śiva who was the owner of the lands and employer of the temple staff.

* This is the Bṛhadīśvara temple in Thanjavur, completed in the 11th century; a lengthy inscription on its base tells about temple life one thousand years ago.

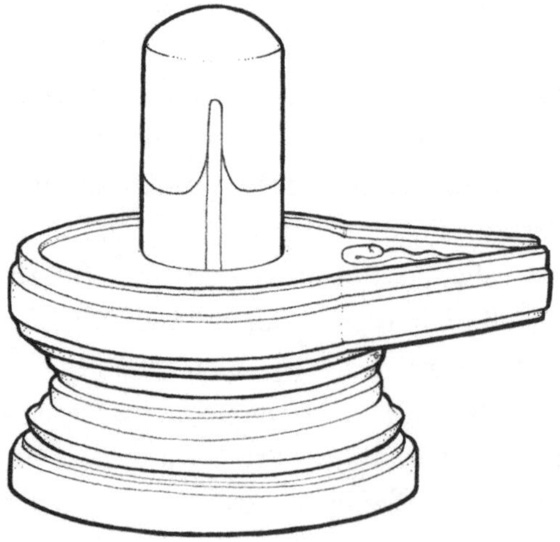

Śiva-liṅga

The temple complex increased its social significance through its various ancillary institutions, which often included welfare facilities such as an Āyurvedic medical clinic, a maternity ward, and a food dispensary. The temple complex nearly always included a *maṭha* or *āśrama*, a monastery where full-time initiated practitioners would live with a guru or *ācārya* (which is sort of like someone with a Ph.D. in the Tantra, requiring many years of study and practice). The āśrama environment was ideal for those who wished to dedicate some years of their life to the full-time study and practice of the path. It was sometimes connected to something like a full-fledged spiritual university, as at the once-famous Śaiva Tantrik sites of Mattamayūra and Golagī. These were major centers of learning, literary production, debate, and practice, housing large numbers of scholar-practitioners, comparable to the Buddhist university at Nālandā. (These institutions were generally managed by authorities of the right-current of Tantra, called Siddhānta, which was more institutionalized than the left-current. More about these distinctions later.) Unfortunately, all of these university complexes were, like Nālandā, destroyed in the Muslim invasions.

The world of public worship and celebration centered on the temple contrasts strongly with the initiate's world of private worship and meditation, which centered on his home and that of his teacher. The initiate's practice was largely interiorized and needed few external elements, most commonly a small portable *liṅga*, or platform for worship, and an *akṣa-sūtra* or rosary. In terms of lifestyle, in their probationary period the younger initiates (*samayins*) would actually live with the guru in his home and receive frequent instruction. Full initiates (*putrikas*) would generally be married and have their own homes but would attend periodic gatherings with their teacher. These gatherings or *satsang*s, for initiates only, would usually include a ritual (*pūjā*), teaching (*upadeśa*), and a communal feast (*mandara*). The *kula* gatherings of the Kaulas of the far left would sometimes have a very sensual, even orgiastic quality. These gatherings were called *melāpas*, and in them ordinary cultural and psychological boundaries would be temporarily dissolved in an attempt to throw off mental constructs and cultural conditioning and trigger a raw, immediate, intense experience of consciousness, saturated with the blissful perception of beauty in all things. Though many Westerners imagine that this kind of orgiastic gathering is what Tantra was all about, in fact these sorts of gatherings were not common and were considered well outside the mainstream of the Tantrik religion. We will discuss this briefly later on.

See page 427

THE ORIGINS OF THE TANTRA

The earliest texts and inscriptions that we may call Tantrik date from the 5th to the 7th centuries CE. They appeared roughly around the same time within Shaivism and Buddhism, the two religions that subsequently became the dominant Tantrik traditions of the Middle Ages. Therefore, there has been much controversy about which of these two religions originated the Tantra. This controversy can now be dispelled. Let's briefly and simply review the evidence. Around 600 CE, we see the great Buddhist philosopher Dharmakīrti (who was not a Tāntrika) criticizing an early form of Śaiva Tantra. Given Dharmakīrti's status, he would not have bothered to articulate this critique had

The first Shaiva Tantrik text to present a complete and detailed system of practice is a full century earlier than the first Buddhist Tantrik text to do so.

Śaiva Tantra not already achieved considerable success. But he does not mention any Tantrik practices within Buddhism, which he would have been likely to criticize had he been aware of them.

There is also much broader evidence of the priority of the Śaiva form of Tantra. The first Śaiva Tantrik text to present a complete and detailed system of practice (granting both spiritual liberation and worldly powers) is, by current dating, a full century earlier than the first Buddhist Tantrik text to do so (early 6th and early 7th century respectively, if not a few decades before that).[63] Earlier texts that some might wish to assign to the Buddhist Tantra are essentially minor manuals of practical magic that present neither a complete system of spiritual practice nor any doctrinal View or cosmology. By contrast the earliest Śaiva Tantrik text (which we will discuss later) is large, complex, sophisticated, and demonstrates by its content the existence of a new and distinct esoteric Tantrik religion, within Shaivism with its own unique doctrines, clearly related to and yet different from the earlier non-tantrik Shaivism.

Furthermore, the early Buddhist tantras defend themselves against accusations of taking rituals and mantras from Shaivism. One text does so by proclaiming that in fact it was the Buddhist *bodhisattva* named Mañjuśrī who taught "everything that the inhabitants of earth without exception refer to as the teaching of Śiva."[64] There are several other Buddhist examples of this, including texts that teach explicitly Śaiva mantras, but there are no counterexamples of Śaiva texts presenting Buddhist material (at least not until 500 years later). Recent scholarship in this area has sealed the deal on the origin of Tantra within Shaivism, though this is not yet general knowledge.

CONNECTIONS WITH PRE-TANTRIK SHAIVISM

The case that the Tantra as a movement began within Shaivism is strengthened by the fact that it has many defining features in common with pre-Tantrik Shaivism that are not shared with any other documented tradition. This earlier, non-Tantrik form of Shaivism was called the *Atimārga*, or "the Higher Path" (because it saw itself as transcending ordinary religion and society). It existed for at least four centuries before Tantrik Shaivism burst onto the scene. Unlike the Tantra, it was limited to male brāhmin renunciates, did not embrace worldly aims, and did not emphasize spiritual community (among other differences). Nonetheless, it also had much in common with the later Tantra. For example, in the Atimārga, practitioners sought to transcend the ego, attachment to the body, and fear of death. They did this through solitary meditation near cremation grounds, using the five *brahma-mantra*s that also appear later in the Tantra.* Some of these ascetics—worshippers of Bhairava, the fierce form of Śiva—sought this same transcendence by enacting the so-called "Great Vow" (*mahā-vrata*) in which one imitated Bhairava by wandering naked, smeared with ash, begging one's food in a bowl made from a human skull, meditating in the cremation ground, and sometimes pretending to be insane. Amazingly, these ascetics voluntarily adopted the behavior and markings of the most rejected members of society.[65] This was all part of a carefully designed strategy to throw off social programming, inflated pride, and bad karma while simultaneously overcoming fear of death and ultimately attaining a divine state. Their religious life, including its sometimes unconventional behavior, was detailed in a thoroughly laid out path to transcendence described in a scripture called the *Pāśupata-sūtra*, from whence they took their name (the Pāśupatas). This text is at least several centuries earlier than Patañjali's *yoga sutra*.

Bhairava is the name under which the divine Absolute is most frequently evoked in nondual Saiva Tantra.

We see similar antinomian or purposefully socially deviant behavior in some of the more radical branches of nondual Tantra, though since the practitioners of the latter were usually house-holders rather than ascetics, it generally took place in private rituals, rather than public settings. We may also note that Bhairava is the name under which the divine Absolute is most frequently evoked in nondual Śaiva Tantra. So there are a number of points of continuity between (pre-Tantrik)

* These five mantras constitute one of the very few links between the Vedic and Tantrik traditions. They correspond to the five faces of Śiva. The most well-known of the five today is the Rudra *gāyatrī* mantra, *OM TATPURUṢĀYA VIDMAHE | MAHĀDEVĀYA DHĪMAHI | TANNO RUDRAḤ PRACHODAYĀT*, corresponding to the Eastern face of Lord Śiva.

Shaivism and the Tantra that cannot be found in other Indian religions.

Additionally, there are similar points of doctrine. Śaivas of the Atimārga were complete monotheists, some of the earliest monotheists in Indian religion. Like the later Śaiva Tāntrikas, they believed in one supreme Deity, whom they called Śiva (hence the name of the religion, Shaivism). Some of them also believed that Śiva had many lower emanations, called the Rudras, divine beings that ruled the various dimensions of reality. Their cosmological vision of a hierarchy of other planes of existence was important for their practice, because they believed that attaining knowledge of each of these planes of existence, they would be able to ascend to the highest level of reality, that of Śiva himself, when they left the body. This was very influential on early Tantrik View.

So the Atimārga influenced the development of the Tantra in at least three ways:

- the practice of yoga (= meditation) as a means to liberation,
- the doctrine of liberation through rising through the planes of reality to become identical with the deity, and
- the transcending of karma through certain antinomian or transgressive forms of behavior it advocated as spiritual practice.

Additionally, the Atimārgins worked with mantras that would be used in later Tantrik practice (the brahma-mantras already mentioned) and they had nascent ideas about the internalization of sacred geography that were developed into the pan-Tantrik teaching of the body as microcosm of the sacred universe.

Anyone who cares to investigate in an unbiased manner will discover more doctrinal, cultural, and aesthetic similarities between Tantra and earlier Atimārgic Shaivism than with any other contemporaneous Indian religion; therefore, the most likely conclusion is that the one grew organically out of the other.

EARLY ŚAIVA TANTRA: BEFORE SECTARIAN DEVELOPMENTS

We know very little about the early history of the Tantra. Śaiva Tantra proper, with nearly all the characteristics we listed in the introduction, probably began around the mid-5th century (this estimation is based on the textual evidence; the oral tradition would like to date the beginning of Tantra far earlier). But by definition, we have no actual evidence of that. Around year 500 CE, we get the first indisputably Tantrik text, the *Niśvāsa-tattva-saṃhitā,* which means something like "the collection of principles exhaled by God." This voluminous text is so lengthy and detailed in its cosmology that it suggests the existence of an earlier tradition of at least a century or two. In its hierarchy of worlds it clearly draws on the Atimārga teachings of Shaivism, again implying that the Tantra probably evolved from that religion. The *Niśvāsa* was composed somewhere in North India, and the only surviving manuscript of it is in Nepāl. Finally, after many years of study, the first English translation of this seminal text was released in 2015.

This scripture nominally belongs to the first of the nine sects of the Tantra detailed later (i.e., the Siddhānta); in fact it is sometimes considered the root-text of that school, and yet it also exhibits some features that would later be associated with very different (transgressive goddess-worshipping) groups. This suggests that in the earliest phase of the Tantra, the tradition had not yet differentiated into the two primary currents discussed below (that is, the Siddhānta and the Kaula, currents of right and left, respectively).

The *Niśvāsa* contains the earliest chapter available to us on Tantrik Yoga (defined as spiritual practice with features unique to the Tantrik scriptural corpus). This chapter is found in the portion of the text called "Aphorisms on the Way" (*Naya-sūtra*). I offer here a brief but fascinating quote from this chapter:[66]

Nayasūtra 4.11–13

> *The Goddess said: "How does union [yoga] with the Independent Deity [Nirālamba Śiva] come about? Having experienced the 'One Taste' (eka-rāsa), how further is the state of [abiding in] Divinity obtained?"*
>
> *The Lord said: "That which may be seen by the eye, that which is within the realm of speech, those things which the mind thinks and which the imagination imagines, are made aspects of 'I' [i.e., appropriated by ego], as is whatever has a specific form; [therefore] one should search for the place in one's own body where there is no such form.*

So this fascinating passage implies that all that can be named in words can be appropriated by the ego, and all that has a specific form, and therefore look within to the formless within yourself. So I give this passage just to demonstrate some of the subtlety of the earliest text, which also has a variety of other types of material. This passage shouldn't be thought to represent the entire work.

Scholarship in this area is still in its early days, but the above passage shows us an apparent overlap with Buddhist ideas, this instruction to find a place within ourselves that is formless and that cannot be appropriated by the ego, is, one might say, somewhat Buddhist in character. But actually, as later scriptures show, the idea of an innate ground of being that is formless and indescribable is just as much a part of Śaiva Tantra as Buddhism.

See pages 251 and following

EARLY ŚAIVA TANTRA: TWO STREAMS

Let's take a step back now and sketch the most general features of the emerging landscape of Śaiva Tantra in its first few centuries (especially 700–1000 CE). It is a tradition of two primary streams. On one side, sometimes called the "right current," we have a dualistic tradition that

- emphasized worship of Śiva without Śakti,
- believed that liberation was solely the result of a powerful

ritual initiation and subsequent ritual practice, and

- ❖ did not wish to challenge the social norms prescribed by the brāhmin priests of Vedic society but rather sought their acceptance.

This current is called the Śaiva Siddhānta (*siddhānta* means "the established doctrine" or "the orthodoxy"). Its adherents were called Saiddhāntikas. The Śaiva Siddhānta was the first of the Tantrik groups to come out with a coherent body of scriptural texts and commentary, and this group also held sway over the organized religious institutions of Shaivism, like temples and monasteries.

I noted above that the Saiddhāntikas were dualistic. This means they held the doctrine that there are three eternally separate principles of reality: God, the manifest universe, and the individual soul. Here, the universe is seen as the source of bondage. God frees your soul—whose Godlike quality is concealed by its embodiment—from bondage by bestowing His grace on you, causing you to seek a guru for initiation. The mantras of that initiation ritual, revealed by God for that purpose, destroy most of your karma and guarantee that you will be liberated from *saṃsāra* (the cycle of suffering and repeated death) when you leave your current body and you will dwell with Śiva in heavenly reality. That means your innate divinity will fully manifest, and you will be completely equal to God, but still separate. Now, you may be thinking, "These Saiddhāntika guys don't sound very Tantrik to me." That is because you are influenced by the common misconception that the *other* primary stream of Tantra, the "left current," is the whole instead of just a part. But whether you like the Siddhānta or not, it is part of the Tantra, because the Saiddhāntikas drew on explicitly Tantrik scriptures, they used Tantrik mantras, and they created forms of Tantrik Yoga that were influential across the entire tradition. Even the nondualists of the left current acknowledged that the Saiddhāntikas were part of the same tradition as them—though they argued heavily against their dualistic interpretations of that tradition. By analogy, the fact that the nondual teachings of the Christian mystics are so different from the mainstream

Christian thought wouldn't lead you to argue that they weren't part of the same religious tradition.

The left current of Śaiva Tantra—whose philosophy we referred to as "NŚT" throughout the first half of the book—was a primarily nondualistic group of lineages that are harder to pin down because they were less homogenized and institutionalized.[67] In general, the left current

- emphasized worship of female divinities and fierce deities,
- taught that liberation could be attained in this life (not merely at its end) as the result of powerful spiritual experiences attained through the cultivation of insight and yoga, and
- chose to challenge the traditional social order in various ways, such as by empowering women and performing rituals with transgressive elements (more on this later).

These left-current groups went by a variety of different names, but eventually tended to designate themselves with the term "Kaula," which means "from the family (*kula*)," meaning the family of esoteric Tantrik goddesses. Though it is something of an anachronistic over-simplification, we may designate the whole left current as Kaula.[68]

It is interesting to note here that the Kaulas generally did not call themselves; they reserved that term for the non-Kaula followers of the Tantrik scriptures. So we find ourselves in a state of some terminological confusion: the part of the tradition that Westerners refer to when they say "Tantric" is the Kaula tradition, ironically the very ones that did not prefer to use that term. This was partially because "Tāntrika" can mean a ritualist, and while the Kaulas also performed ritual ceremonies, they saw themselves as transcending the necessity for ritual. However, we will continue to follow current usage and use "Tantrik" as a general overarching term referring to all that derives from the scriptures known as tantras as well as *āgamas*.

Lastly, we should note that there were some schools in between these two main streams that advocated a kind of middle path, incorporating elements from both. This was not really a middle path of

See page 227

reasonable moderation between two extreme views, but rather a philosophically vague compromise between transgressive and non-transgressive practice alternatives. While culturally and aesthetically rich, the middle ground was philosophically noncommittal and thus did not articulate a vigorous theology. Though the middle ground was popular in its own time, it is less important in a history of ideas.*

* Having said that, the primary text of this "middle ground" tradition, the *Svacchanda-tantra,* is incredibly rich in cosmology and yogic practices, and very much deserves to be mined for its many hidden gems. It was sufficiently influential that sections of it were incorporated by a later text of the Trika. See page 227.

THE COMMON CORE DOCTRINES OF ŚAIVA TANTRA

So what did the two streams have in common? They both adhered to the most basic doctrines of Śaiva Tantra, which we will summarize here. The individual soul is innately divine, that is, of the same nature as God, but exists in a veiled state, so that it is ignorant of its own true nature. Therefore, it suffers. Out of His compassion, the Lord has revealed scriptures that explain how the soul can be liberated from this bound state. These scriptures teach a ceremony of initiation called *dīkṣā,* in which powerful mantras (that are in fact aspects of Śiva's own consciousness) burn away all the karma that would otherwise destine you to take birth many more times, thereby granting you the capacity to attain spiritual perfection and freedom during, or at the conclusion of, this very life.

Anyone who was fit could be initiated, including women and lower-class or even outcast people. (Nor were you required to become a renunciate after initiation, as in some traditions.) You were considered fit if you had received something called "the Descent of Grace" or *śakti-pāta.* This was considered a private, interior spiritual event in which God awakens your longing for liberation by infusing you with His spiritual energy (*śakti*). This awakening causes you to seek out a guru for initiation. The guru then examines you for the "signs" by which he may infer that the Descent of Grace has taken place. That is the sole qualification for initiation (along with your *dakṣiṇā* or financial offering). Once approved, you undergo the *dīkṣā* ceremony, either alone or with several other people. The guru performs the *dīkṣā* as a vehicle of the Lord, who is the true initiator.

See pages 153 & 321

Śaktipāta, the descent of grace, is the sole qualification for initiation.

See page 331

See page 151

The ceremony lasted at least two days and often had a powerful impact on initiates. Initiation was thought to remove some of the *mala* or impurity that clouds one's perception and limits one's scope of activity. Initiation also empowers one to undertake a daily practice aimed at bringing about both spiritual liberation and success in worldly goals.

THE KEY DIFFERENCES

The above account of the common doctrinal core obscures how different the two streams actually were. The right-current Saiddhāntikas believed that *mala* or impurity was an actual psychic substance that mars the soul and that only ritual action can cleanse the soul. They compared mala to a cataract on the eye that obscures your vision and that can only be removed by skilled surgical intervention, in the metaphor the surgery representing the ritual of initiation. By contrast, those of the left current, the Kaulas or Nondual Saiva Tantrikas (= NŚT), argued that *mala* is actually nothing but ignorance, and that ignorance (of our ever-existent true nature) is the only cause of bondage and suffering, and that therefore only insight into the true nature of things can liberate us. This difference between the two streams is the necessary result of their respective dualist and nondualist doctrines. The nondualists taught that the soul has in fact never been separate from God, for the Divine is all that exists. Therefore liberation is merely having a complete and permanent realization of how things really are and have always been. There is no problem, and there has never been any problem— other than fact that you think there's a problem: the flawed human understanding from which all suffering springs.

These contrasting views resulted also in different forms of practice, with the dualists' emphasizing ritual and the nondualists' emphasizing the acquisition of experiential knowledge, whether through contemplation, meditation, or other practices. For the nondualists, even ritual could be a vehicle for this wisdom and, indeed, was only valuable to the extent that it was such.

See page 409

These views also corresponded to differing views regarding the role of the guru. The Saiddhāntikas viewed the guru as primarily a ritual officiant, and neither required nor expected him to be an enlightened master. The Kaulas preferred the liberated, charismatic type of guru, because only that type could transmit the power and experiential wisdom that was the central element of their practice. (To be clear, the mystic transmission from the guru was not the only way to attain liberating insight in the left current, but it is a way not available to those in the right current.)

Differences in the social sphere

There were also social differences between the right and left streams. The right-current Saiddhāntikas initiated low-caste people, but as part of their conformist stance regarding the norms of Indian society, they continued to acknowledge caste divisions in their initiation names and by requiring separation by caste at their gatherings. By contrast, the Kaulas declared that *all* initiates formed a single "caste," that of the lovers of God, within which all were equal. While they allowed initiates to observe caste in their daily lives, there was to be no acknowledgment of caste in gatherings of the *kula* (initiated community). Such acknowledgment was in fact grounds for removal from the group. Some of the Kaulas went further, initiating even the lowest-status outcastes or "untouchables," who were considered almost like another species, absolutely beyond the pale of proper Indian society. These extreme followers of the Kaula left current argued that the whole notion of caste was merely a cultural construct, not a fact of nature, and therefore must be wholly transcended.

The Kaulas both initiated women and encouraged them to practice.

See page 430

While Saiddhāntikas did initiate women, they did not in general allow them to undertake a daily practice. As you might have guessed, the Kaulas both initiated women and encouraged them to practice. The most extreme Kaula group, known as the Krama or Mahānaya (the Great Way), even consecrated women as full-status gurus. These attitudes to human women were paralleled in each group's ritual relations with goddesses. Saiddhāntikas barely acknowledged Śiva's female counterpart, Śakti, in their worship. The Kaula groups worshipped pantheons of goddesses, which were pictured as increasingly dominant over the male deities the further "left" the group was (see the chart on page 211). Indeed, the word "Kaula" can sometimes be used as a synonym for "goddess worshipper." The Krama was the only group to worship the Goddess exclusively.

Early Shamanistic Roots and Their Kaula Reinterpretation

While the right-current Siddhānta modeled their religion on the Vedic prototype that had been dominant in earlier elite Indian religion (especially 1000 BCE–400 CE), the left-current Kaula path emerged out of an equally old but more "populist" stratum of Indian religion, a fascinating and strange shamanistic visionary world of propitiation of nature goddesses and animal-headed yoginīs. This is an area of Indian religion that is not well documented because it was largely illiterate, though we may see many signs of its influence on literate religion. This shamanistic world, which was the older cultural background of the Kaula stream and thus provided its aesthetic template, involved rituals and power-seeking rites that might seem disturbing, unbelievable, or even abhorrent to us. The *sādhaka* or ascetic practitioner performed these rites in frightening places such as cremation grounds, using mortuary elements like human skulls and ash from the funeral pyre. The rites invoked groups of wild and fierce goddesses, often envisioned as nature spirits (sometimes called *ḍākinīs* or yoginīs), led by a chief Goddess or by the fierce form of Śiva called Bhairava. If the *sādhaka*'s practice was successful, the deities appeared to him, at which point he would make a blood offering, usually of his own blood. If he successfully resisted the pull into fear and confusion, staying steady in his devotion, he would be accepted by the goddesses and would rise into the sky with them, becoming the leader of their wild band—in other words becoming exactly like Bhairava. Or so the narrative goes.[69]

Now, before you get too scared, let me be clear—this picture of things does *not* describe the type of practice undertaken by the Kaulas of the nondual Tantra in the era with which we are concerned. Rather, it forms a part of their ancient cultural background, the wild and weird popular religion that was inherited by the Kaula tradition. By the late 9th century the Kaulas often were highly educated* people and refined aesthetes (lovers of art and beauty) and sometimes were connected to the royal court. Still, they had to deal with an earlier scriptural tradition that at times emphasized these otherworldly magical rites, some of which were offensive to educated society. You see, ancient India was a deeply traditional society in which there was no possibility of simply rejecting an earlier layer of one's own tradition. If the earlier tradition did not fit the current paradigm, it had to be reinterpreted. This is precisely what the more sophisticated Kaulas of classical Tantra did. They did not take the shamanistic rite described above literally; rather, they argued (and no doubt believed) that the wild goddesses were expressions of the various energies of the human mind and body. The mortuary symbols were taken to represent transcendence of the ego, fear of death, and attachment to body-based identity. When the ego is suspended, they taught, external objects lose their otherness and shine within consciousness as the flavors of pure aesthetic experience. The goddesses of the sense-energies are gratified by this offering of "nectar" and thereby converge, fusing with the practitioner's radiant and expansive awareness. He thereby experiences himself as a single mass of blissful consciousness. Finally then, flying through the air as Bhairava himself in the narrative was taken to indicate an awe-inspiring divine state in which the liberated practitioner flies free in the sky of pure consciousness, unbound by ordinary limiting cognitions but still embodied, i.e., still possessed of his senses and faculties, represented by the band of goddesses in the narrative.[70]

* By "educated" I mean literate individuals who underwent a systemic training in the traditional culture and literature of India and its language, Sanskrit.

For the Kaulas, the "wild goddesses" were expressions of the various energies of the human mind and body.

This process of reinterpretation is central to all religions. The important thing to understand is that from inside the religion, it has no quality of artificiality. Rather, the interpreters believe that they are simply drawing out the real, deeper meaning of the early scriptures, the meaning that God had always intended, as it were. (This is not to say that the sophisticated Kaula interpreters totally rejected those ascetics who chose to pursue cremation-ground ritual and power-seeking; such ascetics, who had become the minority, were benignly tolerated as something like an eccentric and socially inappropriate cousin, embarrassing at times but still part of the family.)

We should take a moment here to distinguish between the words "ascetic" and "aesthetic," since these are commonly confused. "Ascetic" is a noun referring to a renunciate who practices some type of self-mortification or intense spiritual practice that involves the renunciation of job, family, sexuality, or possessions. "Aesthetic" is an adjective referring to art and beauty. So, aesthetic philosophy, for example, refers to the philosophy that focuses on art and beauty and what makes things beautiful. So, these are entirely different words with very close pronunciations.

So the sophisticated and literate expression of left-current nondual Śaiva Tantra "purified" the shocking or repellent elements of early goddess worship, not by rejecting them but by reinterpreting them as the elements of interior spiritual experience. These Kaulas were great aesthetes, especially in Kashmīr, where the left current flourished. For them, the highest state of consciousness was that of *camatkāra,* that is, wonder or aesthetic rapture, the experience of amazement at the raw and vivid beauty of embodied existence. Their "aestheticization" of earlier tradition fit in well with their nondualist beliefs, for now they could confront even the apparently horrific states of death and so-called impurity as aspects of their own divine inner being, aspects of the total beauty of existence. You may see this perspective in certain varieties of Tantrik art that still survive, depicting fierce yet benevolent deities, such as seen in the art tradition of the Newars of the Kāthmāndu Valley, the art styles that inspired the illustrations in this book.[71] Fierce deities are an exclusive characteristic of the nondual type of Tantra.

THE NINE MAIN SECTS OF ŚAIVA TANTRA

Above we have examined Śaiva Tantra in terms of two streams. The truth is there was a spectrum of groups, as the diagram below indicates. The further left on the spectrum a group is, the more it emphasizes the following features: nondualism, worship of the feminine, inclusion of women, transgression of social norms, occasional mortuary symbolism, and charismatic gurus.[72] As we've just discussed, there is a near-total absence of these on the far right of the spectrum, and in the middle there are some groups that have some of these features and not others.[73]

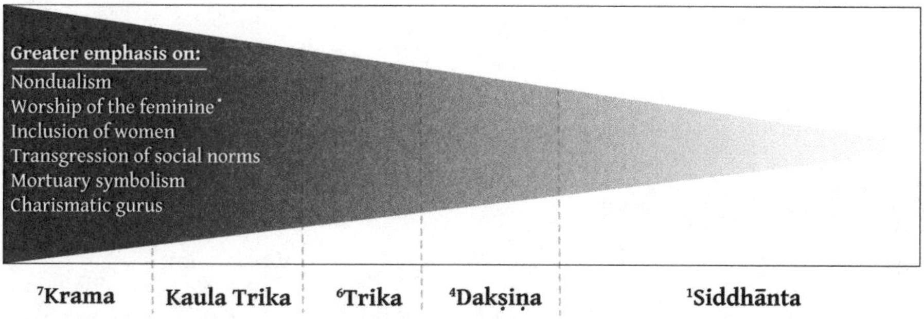

Now we will look at the nine main sects of Śaiva Tantra that populate the spectrum, in more or less chronological order. The development of these groups spans about five hundred years (600–1100 CE), with their literature slowly increasing in sophistication over this period. We also see gradual shifts toward a householder rather than ascetic audience, more teachings on liberation rather than worldly attainments, and increasing attention to the goddess-centered nondualist groups over this time period. The geographical reach of the Tantra in this period is the entire Indian subcontinent, comprising modern India, Pakistān, Nepāl, Bhutan, Tibet, and Bangladesh, as well as parts

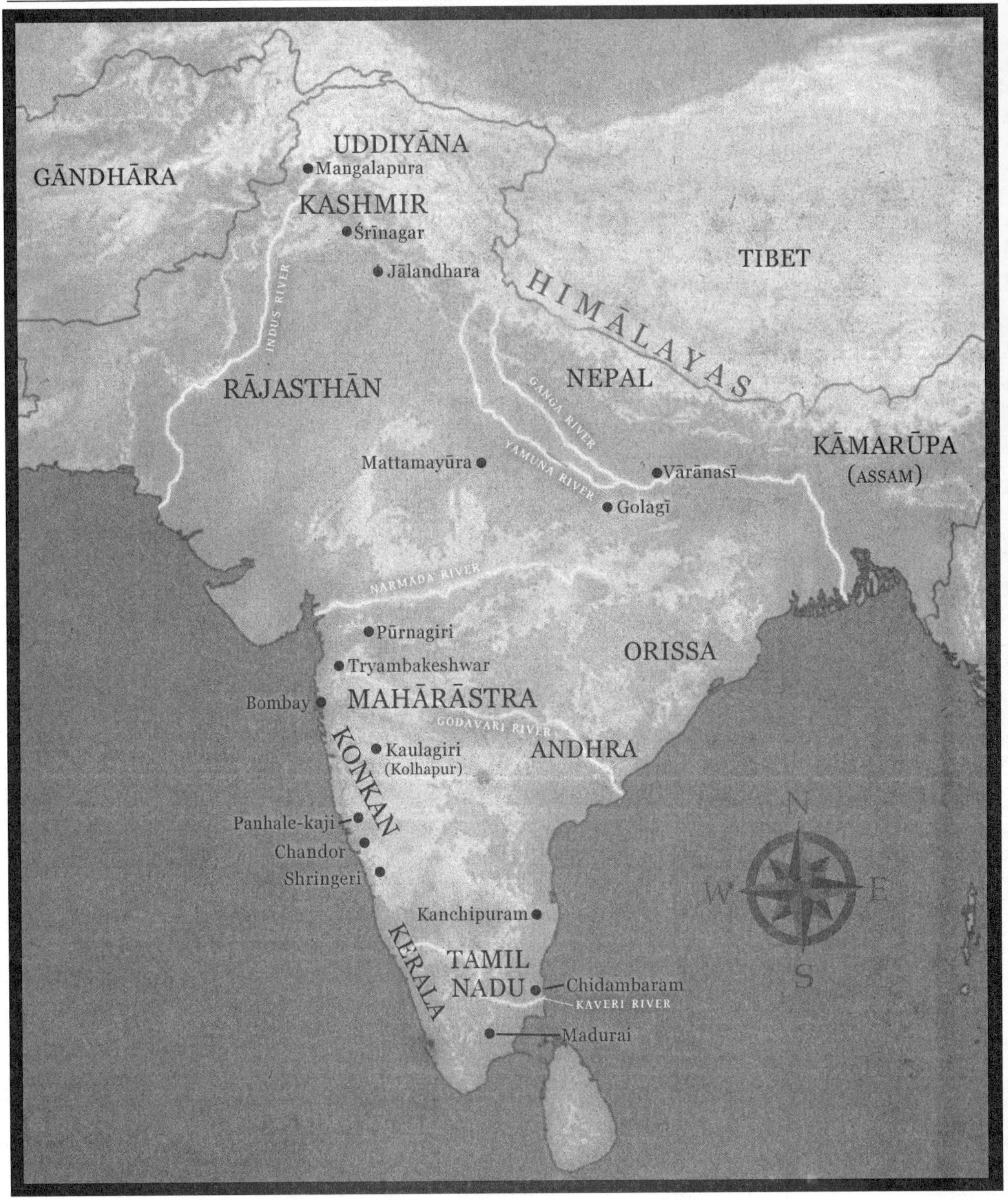
UDDIYĀNA
Mangalapura
GĀNDHĀRA
KASHMIR
Śrīnagar
Jālandhara
TIBET
HIMĀLAYAS
INDUS RIVER
RĀJASTHĀN
NEPAL
GANGA RIVER
YAMUNA RIVER
Mattamayūra
Vārānasī
KĀMARŪPA
(ASSAM)
Golagī
NARMADA RIVER
Pūrnagiri
ORISSA
Tryambakeshwar
Bombay
MAHĀRĀSTRA
GODAVARI RIVER
KONKAN
Kaulagiri
(Kolhapur)
ANDHRA
N
Panhale-kaji
Chandor
Shringeri
W
E
Kanchipuram
KERALA
TAMIL
NADU
Chidambaram
KAVERI RIVER
S
Madurai

of Cambodia, Vietnam, and Indonesia. (On page 212 you can see a map of the Indian subcontinent indicating some of the key Tantrik sites.)

For each of the nine original Tantrik sects, I will list the form of the Deity worshipped, the principal mantra, and give a quote from its principal scripture. (For a more comprehensive list of the key texts associated with each sect, see appendix 3.) These are the three features that most clearly distinguish one Tantrik group from another, for in traditional India practice was more definitive than doctrine. For example, people of different religious groups would ask each other not "What do you believe?" but rather "What do you practice?" or "Whom do you worship?"

Images are symbols that point toward the essence, and they are never confused with the essence itself.

A note on correct terminology: the word "sect" is associated in the minds of many with the sectarian history of religion in Europe, which consists of schisms, hatred, and violent struggle. This is not the case here; though there is evidence of competition and debate, there is in fact no evidence whatsoever of violence or open animosity amongst these groups. There was rather a considerable amount of sharing; so rather than the word "sect," we can use a much nicer Sanskrit word, *sampradāya,* which means something like "lineage group, specific tradition, practice tradition," and "school of thought," or all of these combined. Let us now turn to sample the flavor of the nine Śaiva Tantrik *sampradāyas*.

THE NINE SAMPRADĀYAS OF ORIGINAL ŚIVA-ŚAKTI TANTRA

- ***Śaiva Siddhānta*** – the Orthodox Doctrine
- ***Vāma*** – the Feminine
- ***Yāmala*** – the Couple
- ***Mantrapīṭha*** – the Throne of Mantras
- ***Amṛteśvara*** – the Lord of Nectar
- ***Trika*** – the Trinity
- ***Kālīkula*** – the Family of Kālī
- ***Kaubjika*** – Kubjikā's Tradition
- ***Śrīvidyā*** – the Goddess of Auspicious Wisdom

Tatra siṃhāsane devaṃ śuddha-sphaṭika-nirmalam |
pañcāsyaṃ daśadordaṇḍaṃ prativaktraṃ trilocanam ||
jaṭā-mukuṭa-śobhāḍhyaṃ sphuraccandrārdha-śekharam |
Sadāśivaṃ nyasen mūrtiṃ śivaśaktyantagocarām ||

SAMPRADĀYA 1:

Śaiva Siddhānta

Deity: Sadāśiva

Visualization: white-bodied, five-faced, three-eyed, and ten-armed, in the posture of a meditating yogī.

Mantra: HAUṂ

हौं

Principal Texts: *Kiraṇa-tantra, Parākhya-tantra, Kālottara**

The first *sampradāya* is that of the Siddhānta, which we have already discussed above. We will not spend much more time on it, for it is not the focus of this book, despite its crucial historical significance. Before moving on, however, it is important to stress the relationship between the Saiddhāntika and Kaula scriptures.

See page 203

* Since there are so many Saiddhāntika texts, and no main one, I list the ones available in English, translated by Dominic Goodall and Christopher Tompkins respectively.

The Siddhānta was considered by most initiated Śaivas as the broad base of the tradition, the general revelation, while the Kaula texts were considered (by their adherents, at least) the specialized revelation. Thus, the Kaula texts assumed knowledge of much that was contained in the Siddhānta-tantras, inflecting or refining or transcending that knowledge in various ways. After describing all the differences between the two, this relationship may seem surprising. But remember that there are many commonalities between them, such as belief in the innate divinity of the soul, its obscuration, the importance of initiation, and so on. Furthermore, we should note that practice was, on the whole, much more important than doctrine in Śaiva Tantra, and between the right and left currents there were even more commonalities in practice than in doctrine. So you see, the Kaula scriptures were "specialized" in the sense that they needed only to include information on what differentiated them from the broad base of the orthodox Siddhānta.

The other important distinction to mention in this regard is how the two groups saw each other. The Siddhānta regarded the Kaula teachings critically, seeing them either as invalid or as specialized techniques for the attainment of particular powers. Of course, the Saiddhāntikas did not believe that the Kaula teachings gave any special advantage in the attainment of liberation, and they denied that the nondualist interpretation of the scriptures was correct. By contrast, while the nondualist Kaula Śaivas saw their teachings as transcending the Siddhānta, they did not deny the truth of many of the Saiddhāntika doctrines. This may seem surprising. But recall that NŚT had an inclusivist view, in which it posited a "hierarchy of revelation." According to this view, if we move from the exoteric to the esoteric, everything in scripture A is true except what conflicts with scripture B, which overrides the former and is itself overridden by the more esoteric and more specialized scripture C, and so on. So from the perspective of the nondual Kaulas, the Siddhānta simply constituted a lower revelation, revealed by Śiva for the benefit of those who were not yet ready to embrace nondualism. As you can see, the argument for a hierarchy of revelation corresponds to an argument for a hierarchy of truth as well. Lower truths are valid in their own domain but can be superseded by a higher truth when the practitioner attains perception of a higher, more encompassing level of reality. The nondualists practiced what they preached by trying to avoid any exclusion. While some might see the hierarchical structure as condescending to those ranked low, it really is the only way to have a coherent nonrelativist yet nonexclusivist system.[75]

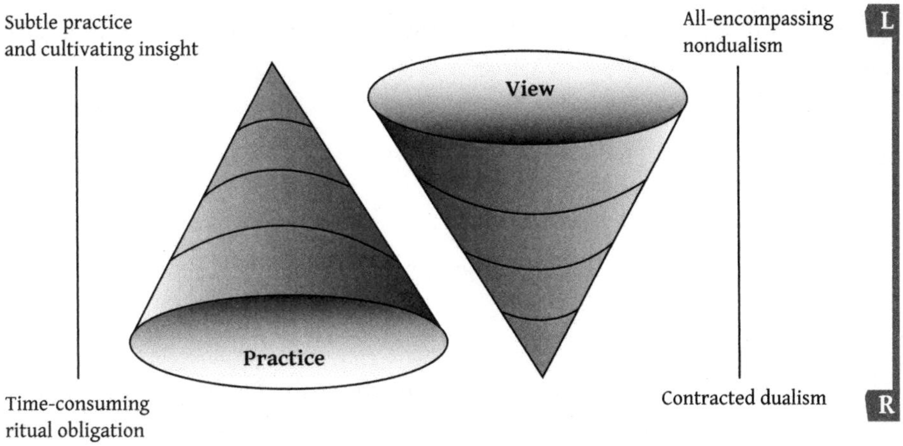

As the diagram above shows, the way in which the Kaulas saw themselves as transcending the exoteric Śaiva Siddhānta differed in the domain of practice versus doctrine. In the latter domain, the higher (increasingly nondual) views were also more all-encompassing and all-inclusive (right cone in the diagram). By contrast, at least in terms of a visual metaphor, the higher forms of practice added to the broad base of the tradition while also entailing the option of dropping the lower forms, since the higher forms—though simpler and more gnostic than ritualistic—were thought to incorporate the lower in compressed form by virtue of that very gnostic power of all-encompassing insight (left cone in the diagram).

It is important to note that much of the powerful yogic technology developed within the Tantra had its origins in the Siddhānta. Other groups borrowed extensively from the large Saiddhāntika repertoire of yogic practices (i.e., meditation techniques, *prāṇāyāmas*, subtle body practices linked with mantras, and so on). The Kaulas often came up with simpler, easier, and more direct techniques of awareness cultivation, but these were often modifications of the standard Saiddhāntika forms. Furthermore, the Siddhānta tantras contained some quite beautiful and thought-provoking passages on the nature and practice of *yoga,* such as:

Matanga-pārameśvara

> *Yoga is the means of revealing the infinitely radiant light of the divine soul.*[76]

So we would be foolish indeed to discount the Siddhānta's crucial contribution simply because their theologians adhered to a dualistic view.

All of the Saiva Tantrik traditions were originally pan-Indian.

The last point to be made here about the Siddhānta concerns its later development into an important tradition that survives in South India to the present day. Like all of the Śaiva Tantrik traditions, the Siddhānta was originally pan-Indian. As time went on, it became particularly successful in the South, especially the Tamiḷ region, supported by and connected to the strong Śaiva devotional movement there, the bhakti movement. Under the influence of the growing success of another Indian philosophy called Advaita Vedānta, the Siddhānta made a fundamental shift in its philosophical position in the period after the 12th century: it became nondualist. Eventually, the Siddhānta survived only in Tamiḷ Nāḍu, where it shaped the pattern of ritual in the temple culture, still seen today. Today, most practitioners and even many scholars of the Tamiḷ Śaiva Siddhānta do not realize that it is a *direct* descendent of the earlier dualistic Tantrik tradition that we have been discussing. This is not surprising, because it has changed a lot doctrinally over the centuries (to the extent that its philosophy can no longer be called Tantrik, though its practice in some ways still is). That the later southern nondualistic Siddhānta is a direct descendent of the earlier pan-Indian dualistic Siddhānta has been indisputably proven by Alexis Sanderson and one of his foremost students Dominic Goodall, who specializes in this area.

We will conclude this section on the Śaiva Siddhānta with a brief sample passage from its literature. This will serve the important function of demonstrating that the yoga taught in the Saiddhāntika texts is integral to the Tantra as a whole. You may be surprised to recognize terms in this passage; this is because, as we will see, Śaiva Tantrik Yoga went on to influence if not give rise to the *haṭha-yoga* tradition.

See page 311

Since this is the History section of the book, we will not explain each sample passage fully. But note that in the quite early (c. 7th century) passage below, Kuṇḍalinī is visualized in the region of the heart, after being summoned there from her home in the crown of the head, where she dwells eternally with Śiva.[77] The Goddess-energy, here called the Primordial Power, is summoned to the heart center and fixed there by a fusion of the vital energies, breath, mantric resonance, and concentration of mind. This yogic practice activates her potential as Kuṇḍalinī, so that she can surge upward toward the highest spiritual center, bringing the soul that is (contracted individuated consciousness) with her.

Sārdha-triśati-kālottara: 350 Verses on the Transcendence of Time

A lotus with eight petals dwells within the center of the space of the heart. Inside its pericarp, there are four Powers, shining with the radiance of the sun, the moon, fire, and gold. The primordial Power of God moves above these four. The soul [individuated consciousness] is concealed there, like a bee, in the heart-lotus with its fourfold power.

The Primordial Power is Kuṇḍalinī [when] fused with the sun [piṅgalā channel], moon [iḍā channel], and fire [suṣumnā channel]. She is to be visualized and experienced in the region of the heart, abiding there in the form of a tongue of flame.[78]

SAMPRADĀYA 2:

Vāma

Deities: the four sister-goddesses Jayā, Vijayā, Jayantī, and Aparājitā, with their brother Tumburu-bhairava

Principal text: *Vīṇāśikhā* (only surviving text)

This tradition was widespread in the early period (it was mentioned even by the Buddhist scholar Dharmakīrti in 600 CE, and one of its scriptures was discovered far from India, in the Dunhuang caves in China); it had all but died out well before the peak of Tantrikculture. It does not concern us much, as its influence was minimal, but it must be mentioned as one of the nine original *sampradāyas*. Though we know little about the Vāma *sampradāya*, we can see that it was significant as one of the earliest goddess-worshipping traditions to emerge in the previously highly masculine-oriented religious culture of India. It is also one of the earliest transgressive traditions, where power accrues to the worshipper in part through the breaking of social norms and their associated thought-structures. Its system was adopted by one of the earliest Buddhist tantras, the *Mañjuśriya-mūla-kalpa.*

The only surviving text of the Vāma tradition, the *Vīṇāśikhā-tantra* tells us that the four goddesses, whose names indicate that they were probably originally worshipped in order to secure victory in battle, are visualized as white, red, golden, and black respectively. Their vehicles are, respectively, a corpse, an owl, a horse, and a flying car. Their four-faced brother Tumburu (the name indicates a non-Sanskritic, perhaps even tribal, derivation) is visualized as a composite of his four sisters. The five deities of this cult are sometimes depicted as arrayed in a sailing ship, with Tumburu the Trader as their helmsman. This too seems to suggest an origin on the margins of Indian civilization.

SAMPRADĀYA 3:
Yāmala

हूं
चण्डे
कापालिनि
स्वाहा

Deities: Aghoreśvarī (a.k.a. Caṇḍā Kāpālinī) with her consort Kapālīśa-bhairava

Visualization: pale yellow and white respectively, naked and wearing ornaments of human bone.

Mantra: [OṂ] HŪṂ CAṆḌE KĀPĀLINI SVĀHĀ

Principal text: *Brahma-yāmala* a.k.a. *Picu-mata*

The Yāmala tradition is attested early on (for it is mentioned in a 6th-century mythological text, the *Skanda-purāṇa*), though as far as we can tell, it did not survive much into the classical period (after about the year 900). It is positioned on the spectrum just to the left of the Mantrapīṭha tradition, which we will discuss next (see page 227), and thus the female deity is slightly emphasized over the male there. The Yāmala does not fit neatly into the spectrum, however, for it features some of the most intense mortuary imagery and transgressive cremation ground practices of any of the sects.

In the ancient Yāmala tradition, which is aimed primarily at the power-seeking ascetic, we are deep in the shamanistic roots of Tantra described earlier (page 208): a world of magical powers and arcane rituals performed in the cremation ground on a new moon night, using human skulls and summoning spirit powers. The primary text of this tradition that has come down to us, the *Brahma-yāmala*, is primarily concerned with ritual, and contains a huge amount of material on the magical technologies wielded by Tāntrikas: mantric incantations, special hand gestures (*mudrā*), mystic diagrams (*yantras*), and so on.[79] Now, the fact that the *Brahma-yāmala* is quoted a number of times by the later sophisticated Kaula writer and spiritual genius Abhinava Gupta in his *Light on the Tantras* shows us something important about the development of the classical tradition. Though Abhinava Gupta was not at all in accord with the type of Tantra presented in much of the *Brahma-yāmala*—for example, he preached against grasping after magical powers, seeing them as antithetical to spiritual liberation—he still could (and did) cite the text in support of his teachings on spiritual nondualism (*paramādvaya*). This is possible because of an important doctrine found in the nondual tradition: that in His mysterious wisdom, Śiva has hidden nuggets of the Truth even in the dualistic and power-obsessed scriptures, nuggets that reveal themselves when the given text is "bathed in nondual awareness" by the reader, to use Abhinava Gupta's phrase. Thus an author like Abhinava can cite a text like the *Brahma-yāmala* without condoning everything that is found in it. This is important because it is a theology of scripture that is quite different from the one most Westerners are used to (in which all of the passages in a book like the Bible or Qur'ān are equally authoritative and divine). The guru is (as Douglas Brooks has argued) a kind of "living canon." This means that if Abhinava were your guru, the parts of the *Brahma-yāmala* that he cites would be scripture for you, and *not any other parts*.

See page 296

See pages 149, 185, 297

The following sample passage from the *Brahma-yāmala* might be an example of one of these "truth-nuggets." I should note that selecting this passage reflects my own preferences, for it is not at all representative of the text, which contains very little in the way of theology or philosophy. Indeed (from what I've seen), this passage is the sole View teaching (*darśana*) given in the text. Given its original context, the beauty of the passage is, however, especially remarkable.[80]

Brahmayāmala
1.122–26

The One described as "beyond conception" is Śiva, the supreme cause, yet without name and unchanging, all-pervasive and quiescent. He is without an inherent nature [for he becomes everything], O great Goddess; He is devoid of action and cause, undifferentiated, un-graspable through mental constructs, formless, free from the three Guṇas, beyond notions of "I" and "mine," and situated in the state of non-duality. Yogīs [alone] may approach Him through meditation, for his nature is wisdom. Abiding in the state beyond normative action, that Highest Lord is nothing but Consciousness. He, the bestower of grace for all, has the form of unparalleled Light, and is pervasive, unmanifest, beyond mind, and great.

His Śakti arises by Her own nature, not produced [from him]. Her nature is like that of the refreshing and delightful moonlight, with crystalline rays. She is his Will Power, emerging in the form of pure insight yet transcending the mind, and without semblance: she is called Avadhūtā. She, the Infinite One, awakens the supreme Point* (bindu) *and the supreme Sound* (nāda) *instantaneously. Shaped like a coil, she exists in the sounds of the alphabet, beginning with the vowels . . . . Thus, the Kuṇḍalinī Śakti exists with the sixteen vowels in a circle of power.*

* She who has cast off all form and limitation. I think it is probably not a coincidence that in Buddhist Tantra, the central channel is called *Avadhūtī*.

Svacchanda-bhairavaṃ devaṃ sarva-kāma-phala-pradam |
dhyāyate yas tu yuktātmā kṣipraṃ sidhyati mānavaḥ ||

SAMPRADĀYA 4:
Mantrapīṭha

Deities: Svacchanda-Bhairava, a.k.a. Svacchanda-lalita-Bhairava (Independent Bhairava or Bhairava of autonomous play) with consort Aghoreśvarī

Visualization: white, five-faced and three-eyed, eighteen-armed, wearing dreadlocks and a garland of human skulls

Mantra: HŪṂ

Principal text: *Svacchanda-tantra*

This *sampradāya,* which is as the *Mantra-pīṭha* or Throne of Mantras, is important because of its great popularity for many centuries in Kashmīr valley, where Tantrik culture especially flourished. Its practice was also known in the Kathmandu valley of Nepal. Its central text, a vast work called the *Svacchanda-tantra,* tells us much about Tantrik practice and cosmology but little about philosophy. The Mantrapīṭha tradition occupied a kind of middle ground between the Siddhānta and Kaula traditions we have discussed at some length; that is, it had some goddess-worship and some mildly transgressive elements (for example, wine or rice-beer would be offered to the deity but not consumed by the practitioner). The Mantrapīṭha did not have a clearly defined philosophy or View, thus, in a probable attempt to win adherents from this very popular school, both the Saiddhāntikas and the Kaulas produced commentaries on the *Svacchanda-tantra*, interpreting it in light of their own doctrines. We may infer that the nondualists won this debate, as their commentary is preserved down to the present day while that from the Siddhānta is not. I am referring to the Kaula commentary called the *Svacchanda-tantra-uddyota* (*Illumination of the Tantra of the Independent Bhairava*) written by the great scholar-sage Kṣemarāja of the Trika school (see *sampradāya* #6). We can only hope that someone translates this important text soon, though at least there exists a major dissertation in English on it.[81]

The Mantrapīṭha's success can also be measured by the fact that Svacchanda-Bhairava received worship in Kashmīr and Nepāl all the way down to the 20th century. The deity provides an interesting balance of the playful and the intensely powerful, as can be seen by the illustration. Both qualities relate to His essence-nature of radical autonomy.

The following sample passage emphasizes the egalitarian nature of the *kula* (spiritual community) that prevailed in the Bhairava- and Goddess-focused groups. It stresses that cultivating equal vision is part of the path to freedom.

Svacchanda-tantra

> *All those who have been initiated are of equal nature, whether they be brāhmins . . . or outcastes. They have been brought into a state of fusion with the nature of the divine. [In assembly] they may not sit according to the divisions of their former castes; [for] they are said to form but a single caste of Bhairava, auspicious and eternal. Once a person has taken up this Tantrik system, he may never mention his former caste. . . . O Empress of the Gods, it is through [this] freedom from discrimination that one will certainly attain both siddhi and liberation.*[82]

In Abhinava Gupta's esoteric writings, *sampradāyas* #2 and 4, the Vāma and the Mantrapīṭha, which he calls the Left and Right schools, are correlated to two aspects of the Tantra that we have discussed: on the one hand, those of preoccupation with sensual beauty and, on the other, mortuary imagery aimed at the transcendence of death. They are also correlated with the two lateral channels of the subtle body. To spell out his correlations:

See page 388

Vāma	**Mantrapīṭha**
Feminine	Masculine
Sensual	Mortuary
Creation	Dissolution
Knowing	Acting
Left channel	Right channel
Inhale	Exhale

The purpose of making these correlations, which he justifies with reference to the scriptures, is to argue for the Kaula Trika (*sampradāya* #6) as the middle path into which these streams feed and which constitutes the balance point of the two extremes. Thus the Kaula tradition, which harmoniously fuses elements from both columns above, corresponds to the central channel, the *suṣumnā nāḍī,* and the power of pure will (*icchā*). And the Kaula Trika is pictured as the summit and fusion point of these channels, the undifferentiated Bliss of Consciousness, which through its dynamic oscillations creates these three polarities.[83] This, at least, is the teaching of Abhinava Gupta. For more on the Trika, see the discussion beginning on page 235.

Note that the correlations in the above columns are commonly found throughout the tradition; Abhinava's innovation here is to connect them with the Vāma and Mantrapīṭha sects.

māmānandayase deva prasannenaiva cakṣuṣā |
amṛtākāravac chubhraṃ jagadāpyāyakārakam ||

SAMPRADĀYA 5:

Amṛteśvara

ॐ जुं सः

Deity: Amṛteśvara (Lord of Nectar), also know as Mṛtyuñjaya-Śiva, Śiva as the conqueror of death, still venerated today

Visualization: white, one-faced, and four-armed, with his consort Lakṣhmī

Mantra: OṂ JUṂ SAḤ

Principal text: *Netra-tantra* (The Scripture of the Eye)

This tradition did not command the exclusive devotion of a substantial group of followers like the others named here, but was influential nevertheless, especially in Kashmīr. This influence was possibly due to its unusually broad-minded and nonsectarian attitude: its central text, the *Netra-tantra* teaches that the Amṛteśvara mantra may be used in the worship of *any* form of the deity without distinction, whether Viṣṇu, Gaṇesh, etc., and including even the Buddha (this is most unusual in the given cultural context). In other words, whatever form of the Divine you want to honor, you can preface your obeisance or reverence with the Amṛteśvara mantra, *Oṃ juṃ saḥ*. In so doing, you are acknowledging that all deities are emanations of the one Divine, the Lord of Nectar, whose nature is to bestow nectarean blessings on all His devotees, who worship him in any form. For example, if you were bowing to the Buddha, you would say *Oṃ juṃ saḥ buddhāya namaḥ,* thus honoring the Buddha as an emanation of Amṛteśvara, the Lord of Nectar. (Of course, many Buddhists would likely disagree with the notion that the Buddha is an emanation of Śiva.) In its eighth chapter the *Netra-tantra* says:

Netra-tantra 8.56–7

> *Though One, He can be meditated upon in many forms, all of which will bestow their fruit. He can be worshipped alone or with His consort, as expressing duality, nonduality, or both, using any of the methods described in the scriptures; all will bear their fruit (when combined with Amṛteśvara's mantra).*

Furthermore, the scripture suggests that the Amṛteśvara mantra can be used to enliven old mantras from lineages no longer extant, and that have therefore lost their potency.

Kṣemarāja, the primary disciple of Abhinava Gupta, wrote a full commentary on this text as well. Following the lead of his teacher, Kṣemarāja uses his commentary to introduce nondual teachings, as in his analysis of the visualization of Amṛteśvara. Amṛteśvara is to be visualized, we are told in chapter 3, as brilliant white, one-faced, three-eyed, wide-eyed, and four-armed, sitting on the lunar disc in the center of a white lotus. In two of His four hands He holds a jar of nectar and a full moon. The other two display the gestures of boon-granting (*varada-mudrā*) and protection (*abhaya-mudrā*). Kṣemarāja comments on this as follows:

Commentary on Netra-tantra 3.17–22

See page 291

> *When the scripture says "one should visualize the Lord of gods in His own form" or essential nature, it means you should contemplate your own form as white and translucent, as the pure, joyful light of unlimited consciousness, delightful because it manifests the entire universe on its own canvas through the power of its autonomy. The deity is described as "one-faced" because He is one with the extraordinary Power of Freedom; and He is "three-eyed" because He is united with the three Powers of*

Willing, Knowing, and Acting, which are manifested through the greatness of that freedom. He is "wide-eyed" to express the fact that the universe manifests from these three powers. His four hands display the gestures of boon-granting and protection and hold the jar of nectar and the full moon to indicate respectively that the Divine bestows worldly success, uproots all fear, and unfolds the true nature of the Self as consisting of the divine powers of Knowing and Acting.[84]

In this beautiful commentary on the visualization given in the third chapter of the Netra-Tantra, Kṣemarāja translates the visualized features of the deity to the various powers and capacities of the individual, who is an embodiment of that deity. This is an example of nondualist commentary. We see this strategy of micro-macro-cosmic correlation again and again on the part of the nondualist commentators. In other words, whatever features are present in the nature of the Divine are also present in each individual, for each individual is an instantiation of the divine, and the Tāntrikas are interested in mapping those features in detail and realizing each of them internally.

Take note that since it is the deity that is primary in these systematic correlations, we are not seeing a deification of the human personality so much as an *overwriting* of the latter with the Divine personality that is its true nature and ground. That is to say, the central Tantrik teaching "you are God" should not be taken to indicate a kind of anthropocentric narcissism but something close to its opposite: that your real self is not what you think, is not your socially and psychologically constructed persona at all, but rather is the infinite Light of Consciousness, in which your whole personality and life history constitute a kind of fleeting thought, a moment of self-reflection.

Within the infinite Light of Consciousness, your whole personality and life history is a moment of self-reflection.

naumi cit-pratibhāṃ devīṃ parāṃ bhairava-yoginīm |
mātṛ-māna-prameyāṃśa-śūlāmbuja-kṛtāspadām ||

SAMPRADĀYA 6:

Trika

Deities: the three goddesses Parā, Parāparā, and Aparā

Visualization (of Parā): white, radiant, two- or four-armed, displaying cin-mudrā, holding a manuscript, a mālā, and a trident

Mantra: SAUḤ; in other contexts also HRĪṂ

Principal text: *Mālinī-vijaya-uttara-tantra; Vijñāna-bhairava-tantra*

सौः

If you hear the term "Kashmīr Shaivism," it is generally referring to the philosophy of the Trika school of Śaiva Tantra. The Trika school is often associated with Kashmīr because its greatest exponent, Abhinava Gupta, was from Śrīnagar in the Kashmīr Valley. In fact, though, the Trika was pan-Indian, like most of the Śaiva groups. We have evidence of this from an early period in both Orissa and Mahārāṣṭra, and it seems that the latter may have been its homeland. It is certainly the case that Abhinava Gupta's guru's guru came from Mahārāṣṭra (in west-central India). The founder of the Trika is said to be a sage named Tryambaka, who might have been associated with Tryambakeshwar, a beautiful power-site in rural Mahārāṣṭra where there is a temple still in operation today.

The Trika (Trinity) was an unusual *sampradāya* because, in its later phase, its doctrine encompassed duality, nonduality, and the inexpressible teaching beyond both. This is why the great master

Parā (top), Parāparā (left), and Aparā (right)

Abhinava Gupta made the Trika the fulcrum of his summation and explanation of the whole tradition of Śaiva Tantra.

See page 182 & 292

Abhinava embraced the more strongly nondualist version of the Trika known as the "Kaula Trika," which is said to have been founded by Tryambaka's daughter, making it the only major lineage to have been founded by a woman, though there are some lineages that have female gurus.* Briefly, the Kaula Trika is an essentialized, interiorized, and aestheticized version of the Trika, and is thus considered a higher, more esoteric expression.

* Unless we take the Krama's originator Mangalā to be a human woman instead of a form of the Goddess.

Adherents of the Trika worshipped three goddesses: the sweet and gentle Parā-devī (Supreme Goddess), flanked by Her two lower, fierce Kālī-like emanations, called Parāparā and Aparā (see the illustration). These three are understood as the embodiments of the following principles:

Parā	**Parāparā**	**Aparā**
Knower	Knowledge	Known
Willing	Knowing	Acting
Unity	Unity-in-diversity	Diversity
Emission	Stasis	Reabsorption

Aparā, the third goddess, is described as utterly terrifying because the world of duality and karmically-charged action *is* indeed terrifying. However, through the spiritual practices of the Trika, you are supposed to realize that this ferocious and frightening goddess is nothing but an emanation of the nectar-sweet, beautiful, and soothing Parā-devī, the Goddess of unity and creative impulse (*icchā-śakti*). With

this realization, Aparā becomes unterrifying (*aghorī*) and her fierceness is seen as your own heroic power in the sphere of action, now properly grounded in its source, the transcendental Goddess. Finally, then, the second goddess Parāparā is depicted as midway between the other two, sharing both their qualities.[85]

These three Goddesses are to be visualized on lotus-thrones positioned on the tips of a trident (a symbol of Śiva), the staff of which is visualized as coextensive with the meditator's central channel (see the illustration).

With this image, an icon of essence which visually depicts the Deity-Self revealed by the scriptural transmission, we are invited to contemplate the entire map of sacred reality within our own bodies. All thirty-six *tattva*s are contained in this map. The swelling at the base of the staff represents the five fundamental elements, the staff constitutes the tattvas up to Māyā, the knot of the banner at the level of the palate is Māyā-*tattva*, the plinth at the level of the third eye is Śuddhavidyā-*tattva*, the lotus above that is Īśvara-*tattva*, and lying on the lotus in *śavāsana* is Sadāśiva, gazing upward to the higher light of the Trika above him. The trident itself emerges from the practitioner's fontanelle, the top of the meditator's head (which is coterminous with Sadāśiva's navel) and expresses Śiva-Śakti in three aspects: the All-pervasive Power (*vyāpinī*), the Equalizing Power (*samanā*), and the Transmental Power (*unmanā*). With this last Power, the level of the three white lotuses on the tips of the trident (and above), we have left the universe behind; that is, we are "outside" time and space. The Transmental is what remains after the whole of manifest reality dissolves: the ultimate "ground of being." On this level, the meditator is to see the three Powers of willing, knowing, and acting represented by the three goddesses, who then abandon their differences and fuse into the Heart of his own consciousness. This Heart, the invisible Fourth Power, is the secret doctrine of the Trika (*trika-rahasya*). It is the point of repose within the pure autonomy of the Self, the point

See page 125

that finally reabsorbs the distinction between Power and "I" as the holder of Power (*śakti* and *śhiva*), between the worshipped and the worshipper.[86]

See page 148

So the three goddesses of the Trika are actually expressions of one Great Goddess, Mātṛsadbhāva, yet another name for *tattva* #0. She is the transcendent yet all-encompassing Power of *cidānanda,* blissfully self-aware Consciousness (or we could translate, "Consciousness in love with itself"). It is from this *cidānanda,* the fundamental, ever-existent, essential nature of reality, that the three Powers mentioned above arise. So the secret principle, Mātṛsadbhāva, is understood to be the higher or inner nature of Parā, so I will continue to use the latter name for Her.[87]

See page 163

Sarasvatī is the non-Tantrik, popular expression of Parā.

Parā is also short for Parā-vāk, "the Supreme Word." She is the deep structure of reality, the organic patterning of Consciousness. She is characterized with the word *pratibhā,* a word with no English equivalent: it simultaneously means "intuitive insight," "creative inspiration," and "natural instinct." This identity, plus her iconography, indicates that she is none other than the Tantrik manifestation of the popular deity Sarasvatī, goddess of speech, knowledge, art, learning, and creative inspiration. Actually, to put it more accurately, Sarasvatī is the exoteric, non-Tantrik, popular expression of Parā. Unlike Sarasvatī, Parā is venerated as the Supreme Divinity, not as a member of a pantheon of gods.

This points us toward the most unique feature of the Trika's doctrine and practice: a complex and beautiful system of *linguistic mysticism*, whereby the phonemes of human speech (especially Sanskrit, the paradigmatic language) are thought to be concretizations of patterned vibrations of divine energy that are the foundation for all human thought and, simultaneously, the building blocks of the entire manifest universe. That is to say, on this view, the apparently dualistic division of words and objects (signifier versus signified) is ultimately grounded in a single nondual matrix of subtle vibration.

Sarasvatī

SAUḤ in the sacred Śāradā script

That is called Parā-vak, the Supreme Word, embodied as the Goddess Parā.

Parā has two main mantras, one of creation and one of dissolution. The first is the seed-syllable (*bīja-mantra*) SAUḤ, which sounds very much like a contented sigh; we might say it expresses the Goddess breathing forth Her revelation. The other mantra is highly secret; it is a seed-syllable central to the Kālīkula (see *sampradāya* #7), one of many indications of a special connection between the Trika and Kālīkula.

The Trika is the first group we have encountered in our survey that initiated women as full practitioners. We are now getting into the sects that practiced various forms of social transgression from within society; empowering women to pursue their own spiritual liberation (instead of simply accruing merit by proxy from their husband's practice) was extremely transgressive in traditional Indian society. Indeed, the earliest text of the Trika* even specifies that its most powerful mantra (called the yoginī's heart mantra) is specially intended for women, having been handed down orally from woman to woman.[88]

* The *Siddha-yogeśvarī-mata*, "Doctrine of the Perfected Yoginīs," c. 7th century.

The Vijñāna-bhairava Tantra

Another scripture of the Trika, probably the most unusual of all the Śaiva Tantra scriptures of the early period, is called the *Vijñāna-bhairava-tantra* or "Scripture of the Wisdom-Bhairava."[89] This text teaches an esoteric form of the Trika in which a practitioner of high *adhikāra* (aptitude and qualification**) cultivates deceptively simple methods for directly accessing luminous expanded Consciousness—in other words, methods for becoming perfectly centered in the absolute fullness of the natural state of awareness that results from dissolving all thought-constructs into their ground. Like nearly all Tantrik scriptures, the text takes the form of a dialogue between Śiva and Śakti. It begins with the Goddess asking Bhairava the Big Question:

**Higher degrees of *adhikāra* can be attained only through the process of refinement and "polishing" engendered by regular spiritual practice and contemplation. Your guru determines what your level of *adhikāra* is.

O Lord, I have heard the entire teaching of the Trika that has arisen from our union, in scriptures of ever-greater essentiality, but my doubts have not yet dissolved. What is the true nature of Reality, O Lord? Is it . . .

Vijñāna-bhairava-tantra verses 1–2

The goddess proceeds to name a variety of esoteric technical terms from the higher yogas taught in the scriptures (verses 2–4). Śakti argues that if Parā is to be visualized with a particular color and form, as we mentioned before, then She cannot really be Absolute (*para*) and entreats Bhairava to clear up the confusion (verses 5–7a). I should mention here that in the literary device of the tantras, the Goddess pretends confusion or lack of knowledge for our sake, knowing that we are overhearing Her dialogue with Her Beloved. (In the Krama texts, their position is reversed, with Śiva asking the questions.)

Bhairava replies,

Bravo! Bravo, my dear one. You have asked about the very essence of the Tantra. Know that the forms of the Divine I have taught in the scriptures are not the real essence, O Goddess. They are like magical dreams, or palaces in the sky, taught only to help focus the meditation of those men who are debilitated by dualistic thought, their minds confused, entangled in the details of ritual action. In reality God is not. . .

Vijñāna-bhairava-tantra verses 7–11

and he reiterates the various technical terms the goddess has already introduced. He goes on:

These were taught to help unenlightened people make progress on the path, like a mother uses sweets and threats to tempt her children. Know that in reality, the one pure universe-filling "form" of Bhairava is that absolutely full state called [Goddess] Bhairavī: beyond reckoning in space or time, without direction or

Vijñāna-bhairava-tantra verses 13–17

> *locality, impossible to indicate, ultimately indescribable, a field free of mental constructs, blissful with the experience of the innermost Self. When this is the ultimate Reality [para-tattva], who is to be worshipped, who gratified? This experience of the awe-inspiring Absolute is supreme; it is Parā Devī in Her ultimate nature.*

It is important to situate this teaching in its proper context. It was not intended as an excuse to shortcut the process of real spiritual work. Rather, being given to an intermediate or advanced practitioner who had already made efforts in disciplining the mind and attaining clarity of heart through meditation and ritual, this teaching would come as a profound revelation, empowering her to begin to focus on what triggers that *Bhairavī* state in life apart from the spiritual practices with which she was already familiar. For that is the topic of much of the text: though it imparts a number of specific yogic exercises of breath, visualization, and subtle-body awareness*, it also focuses on unconventional techniques for entering into expanded states of consciousness. These include:

*None of which have yet been adequately explained by the published translations.

- gazing at a blank wall, a vast open space, or the clear blue sky,
- spinning around and around and falling down,
- becoming aware of the space between thoughts or between breaths,
- gazing at the pattern of sunlight on the floor,
- meditating on the liminal state between waking and sleeping,
- accessing intensified awareness through pain of a piercing,
- contemplating that the sky is in your head,
- just repeating the vowel "a", and simply sitting and doing "nothing" (nonconceptual meditation).

Additionally, there are meditations on pure thoughts, such as simply repeating (and feeling into the vibration of) phrases like "All this is Her play," "Everything I think I know is a fabrication," "I am the same as the Highest Divinity," and "What is inside, is outside; what is outside, is inside." This is called contemplating suddha vikalpas, purified thought forms, and we'll discuss it quite a bit later on. Some of the teachings of this peculiar scripture cannot even truly be called techniques; rather, the text invites us to notice daily-life opportunities for accessing that expanded state of awareness that we might otherwise let slip by:

- contemplating the feeling of wonder that arises from watching a magic show,
- meditating on becoming absorbed in the aftermath of an orgasm,
- the practice of following desire back to its source,
- listening to the vibration of live instrumental music or becoming one with the joyous feeling of a song,
- the arising of inner delight when savoring fine food and drink, or the feeling of satiation immediately after a good meal,
- the repetitive gentle motion of a swing or a carriage, and
- the energy of sharpened and heightened consciousness in any intense experience.

These are some of the opportunities that the text gives us.

Actually, there is a subtle technique here, for in all of these experiences, we are to turn our awareness within toward the vibration of a specific feeling that's arising, not so much focus on an external object as we usually do. You can begin to see how the text presupposes a strong meditation practice. Coming to these techniques with no prior experience of meditation, they are not going to be very effective.

The text seems to exhibit a strong Buddhist influence, for one of the most common themes is meditating on the "voidness" (*śūnya*) of things: the inside of the body as empty space; the space of the heart; the senses as voids; the whole universe as a pure, open, spacious, expansive void. Yet this is not a case of Buddhist-Śaiva syncretism, for the scripture maintains throughout a theology of Śiva-Śakti, where Śiva is unbounded spaciousness and Śakti is energy. Either one can be the means of accessing the other, we are told, for they are inseparable, like fire and its heat (verses 18–19). The Śiva practices clarify the energy work, giving it definition and direction; the Śakti practices vitalize the spacious states of Śiva consciousness. But it is easier for most to access the nonconceptual space of Śiva through the energy of Śakti than to go the other way around. The *Vijñāna-bhairava* frequently stresses that the state it describes is wide-open and free of any mental constructs, even if a mental construct was used to get there.

We have dwelt on this text at some length because, though it is atypical, it is also seminal, for it laid the groundwork for a "gnostic" version of the Trika, specifically the Kaula Trika, in which traditional ritual could be infused with profound inner meaning, or dispensed with altogether by those (and only by those) who were ready to make all of life a spiritual practice. (See the concluding verses of the text, translated on page 381.)

Now, despite its aesthetic appeal and fascination for us, the Trika was not a dominant school of the Tantra in its time. Yet Abhinava Gupta made it famous as the foundation of his Tantrik encyclopedia, *Light on the Tantras,* such that teachings from the Trika continued to be cited centuries after the active worship of its three goddesses had died out, indeed, all the way down to the 20th century.*

*The 20th century Kashmīrī guru Lakṣman Jū was a teacher of the Trika's philosophy, but not its rituals or yoga.

Our final sample passage for the Trika comes from its root-text, the *Mālinī-vijaya-uttara-tantra* or "Latter Scripture on the Triumph of the Alphabet Goddess." It describes the fully liberated and awakened guru who can transmit direct awareness of one's essence-nature, listing five signs by which one may know such an extraordinary master.

Mālinī-vijaya-uttara-tantra verses 2.10–16

The Lord said: One who knows all the Principles of Reality [tattvas] exactly as they are, is said to be a Guru, equal to Me, revealing the potency of a mantra. Those people whom he sees, converses with, or touches, [if he is] pleased with them, are released from [the karma of] evil deeds of the past seven births.

Yet greater are those living beings who, impelled by Śiva to seek out such a Guru, are initiated by him. Having obtained whatever [they] desire, they then go to the highest state. The state of being infused with divine Power is always present in him [the Guru].

When that state [of Rudraśakti-samāveśa] being infused by Divine power is present, the following are the signs that one may observe. This then is the first sign: steady devotion to God. The second is successful attainment through mantra, giving immediate evidence of its efficacy. It is said that the third mark is awareness of all the levels of reality (the tattvas). The fourth sign is the accomplishment of whatever tasks that are begun. The fifth is the ability to spontaneously compose enchanting poetry, and knowing the essential matters taught in all the scriptures (even without reading them).

खफ्रें महाचण्ड- योगेश्वरः

SAMPRADĀYA 7:

Kālī-kula, esp. Krama

Deity: Kālī Kāla-saṅkarṣiṇī (the beautiful Dark Goddess, as the Devourer of Time itself)

Visualization: no anthropomorphic form

Mantra: KHPHREṂ MAHĀCAṆḌA-YOGEŚVARḤ

Principal texts: *Jayadratha-yāmala; Kālīkula-pañca-śataka*

The *Kālī-kula* or "Family of Kālī" denoted several interrelated groups whose primary deity was Kālī, the beautiful Dark Goddess. To be clear, we are not speaking of the later Bengālī version of Kālī, the so-called "goddess of destruction" whose image is well known today. The Kālī worshipped by the Kālīkula was the all-encompassing Highest Divinity, the ground of being itself, ultimate Consciousness.

One of the groups of the Kālīkula rose to prominence and eclipsed all the others: it was called the Krama, which means "the Process," "the Cycle," or "the Sequence."[90] It was so named because its initiates worshipped the phases of the cognitive process (whether analyzed as having five, twelve, or seventeen components) as forms of the Goddess. The followers of the Krama viewed Kālī as the Supreme Divinity whose ultimate nature is formless—the insatiable void in the Heart of Consciousness, which the limited self cannot enter and survive.[91] The Krama was unequivocally the most radical, transgressive, feminine-oriented, and nondualistic of all the Śaiva Tantrik groups. It was the Kaula path *par excellence*, for unlike the other *sampradāyas* it had no non-Kaula variant. The Krama was also (in its post-scriptural phase) the most sophisticated and subtle of them all in terms of its thinking, especially in the careful way it assimilated philosophical ideas with ritual practice, and in its determined attempt to make the latter truly meaningful. Thus, the Krama includes some of the most refined spiritual thinking in the same sphere as some of the most transgressive practice, a seeming paradox that fits well in a system that thinks of the Divine as precisely that which can meaningfully subsume all paradoxes within itself.

The Krama, despite its serious challenges to the social order, rose to a place of prominence in Kashmīr, counting many highly placed people (such as royal ministers) amongst its initiates. It influenced the Trika school, which adopted some Krama doctrines, and the two schools finally became fused in the theology of Abhinava Gupta, who essentially propagated an esoteric Kaula Trika with a Krama core.

See page 181

Having said all this about the significance of the Krama, it may come as a surprise to hear that there are no translations into English of Krama texts and very little published work on the subject. Virtually no one realized the Krama's historical significance, or the stunning power of its ideas and its poetry, before Alexis Sanderson's pioneering 2007 study, "The Śaiva Exegesis of Kashmir," which I quote frequently in this section. Even Buddhist scholars will (it is hoped) take note, for the Krama's teachings are strikingly similar to the most refined forms of Tantrik Buddhism.

The documented history of the Krama begins with the story of a devoted spiritual practitioner and seeker of the Truth, probably from Kashmīr, who in the mid-9th century made a pilgrimage to the small kingdom of Uḍḍiyāna, in the far northwest of the Indian cultural region, a site later considered one of the four most important Tantrik centers.* (Note that this is also said to be the homeland of Padmasambhava, who brought Tantrik Buddhism to Tibet around this same time—probably not a coincidence!) There this spiritual practitioner of whom we speak journeyed to a town called Mangalapura,** in the

* Uḍḍiyāna was located in the extremely beautiful Swāt Valley, now in the sadly war-torn northwest province of Pakhtunkhwa, Pakistān.

**Modern Mingora, 34°46'34" N, 72°21'40" E

heart of Uḍḍiyāna, where it is said nearly everyone at that time was a practicing Tāntrika. Situated next to the town was a sacred power-center (*śakti-pīṭha*), the great cremation ground called Karavīra. This cremation ground is said to be the dwelling place of the Goddess Maṅgalā (Goodness, Auspiciousness), a benevolent form of Kālī, together with the sixty-four Yoginīs or Tantrik goddesses that made up her retinue.

There this pilgrim took up residence, propitiating and meditating on the Goddess until She revealed Herself to him in an awesome epiphany, granting him divine insight. Thereafter this *siddha* ("perfected master"), now called Jñānanetra Nātha (the Lord of the Eye of Wisdom) became the first guru of the Krama lineage and the transmitter of the principal Krama scriptures. An account in Old Kashmīrī says:

Old Kashmīrī
Mahānaya-prakāśa

> *The Nātha, after being taught in the sacred site where Oṃ resonates [Uḍḍiyāna], was filled with compassion for living beings, and as the Promulgator [he] emitted the internal and external silence of ultimate Reality as the corpus of the Krama.*[92]

The tradition records that Jñānanetra was a fully awakened master. A later text called *Hymn to the Five Voids* lauds his greatness; it purports to have been an oral transmission from all the yoginīs of Uḍḍiyāna. The yoginīs, in a great assembly, sang the praises of Jñānanetra with these words:

Hymn to the Five Voids

> *Lord Jñānanetra has merged with the level where all experience is one!* * *He is the solitary Hero of that beyond essence, in whom all phenomena have been brought to silence, radiant with the vision of his gnosis, who has realized the ultimate Reality, who has attained the bliss of understanding, and who has relished the highest awakening.*[93]

* *Samarasa:* everything is imbued with the flavor of the one divine Consciousness.

Aside from the Krama scriptures, which like all scriptures have no authorial voice, we have only one work by Jñānanetra, the *Kālikā-stotra* or "Hymn to the Divine Mother," a beautiful text that subtly alludes to the phases of Krama worship. Here we will quote the first three verses and the last two, which have some autobiographical hints. Jñānanetra exultantly sings his experience of the Divine in these words:

Kālikā-stotra: Hymn to the Divine Mother

O Goddess! Supreme is Your nature, which is formless yet has the form of all three worlds. It is prior to all limitations, impossible to grasp through dualistic categories such as "existent" versus "nonexistent," and attainable through the purest Consciousness. || 1 ||

Supreme is Your completely pure nondual form: One, yet existing in many guises, pervading the universe that is flowing forth within You entirely free from change—it is known as the integral nature of Awareness. || 2 ||

Supreme too is Your extraordinary act of taking on embodiment—surging up within through Your own pure Will, and expressing the Light of Consciousness in its unsurpassable and spontaneous essentiality. || 3 ||

Through Your grace, O Mother, may the whole world abide as the essence of the Goddess within the transcendent Śiva, just as She was experienced by myself in the Great Cremation Ground. || 19 ||

Thus, this hymn of essence-nature is sung by myself, Śiva, through the force of the state of complete immersion [samāveśa]. O Goddess named Maṅgalā (Beneficent), may it be a blessing [śiva] to the whole world that is itself myself. || 20 ||*

* Jñānanetra's other name is Śivānanda.

The full poem and many others by Krama masters will be published (in collaboration with other scholars) under the title *Tantric Hymns of Enlightenment.*

Jñānanetra began a lineage which successfully preserved the transmission of full awakening through at least nine generations, a rare feat in the history of religion. We can see the success of the transmission in the consistently high level of insight, joy, and gratitude in the poems of the Krama masters, which are positively aflame with awakened consciousness. Jñānanetra directly initiated seventeen disciples. His three primary disciples were women, including his successor, the *siddhā yoginī* named Keyūravatī ("she who wears a bracelet"), informally yet respectfully known simply as "the Goddess K."* Unfortunately, we have no works from Keyūravatī, though some of the oral teachings of the Krama tradition recorded in Old Kashmīrī called Chummās may be hers.

* The Krama is the only pre-modern Indian tradition to grant women the full status of Guruhood.

Her foremost disciple was a fascinating figure named Hrasva Nātha, a.k.a. Vāmana, a.k.a. Vīranātha. Two of his three names indicate that he might have been extremely short of stature, though his charisma apparently more than made up for that. He was the minister of war and peace under King Yaśaskara in mid-10th-century Kashmīr. He wrote a work that has come down to us called *The Efflorescence [of Techniques] for the Arising of One's Innate Awakening* (*Svabodhodaya-mañjarī*).[94] This exquisite meditation manual was certainly influenced by the *Vijñāna-bhairava,* and it taught a "new and easy method" (a phrase that characterizes the Krama) for attaining the Bliss of Consciousness. Hrasva Nātha clarifies his project while explicitly setting himself against the earlier yoga of Patañjali, writing:

Svabodhodaya-mañjarī

> *The nature of the mind is unsteady, being inundated by the subliminal impressions arising from false mental constructs; realizing this, one sets out to dissolve the mind. This process of dissolution [nirodha] was taught by the ancients as being due to*

the yoga of renunciation and hard repetitive practice. Here I will teach dissolution of the ordinary mind through the release of effort.

Sanderson writes with his usual precision about Vīra Nātha's method as follows: "[The text offers subtle] practices to bring about liberation-in-life through the dissolution of contracted awareness by means of insight into the emptiness* of [all] objective and mental phenomena and reversion into the uncontracted inner ground [of Consciousness] by observing the process of the arising and dying away of cognition, especially where the latter is particularly intense, as in the perception of the beautiful [or] meditation on the sensation of orgasm or any other sensation that slowly dies away."[95] To put it simply, like all yogīs, Vīra Nātha acknowledged the need to dissolve the contracted mind in order to be in Presence, but instead of doing so through cultivating distaste for worldly experiences that the mind becomes attached to, his uniquely Tantrik "new and easy method" was to allow yourself to become totally absorbed in a beautiful sensual object that naturally dissolves or fades away. The more complete your absorption in the object, the more complete the dissolution of mind you would achieve. These verses of the Svabodhodaya-mañjarī may serve as clarifying examples:

* "Emptiness" here means "lack of separate objective reality."

Whatever captivating sound that comes into one's hearing [such as a gong or rumbling thunder], one should become one-pointed on it, until, dissolving, the mind dissolves with it. . . . One should not think on what has dissolved, [but remain] full of the intensified sense of one's own immediate being. || 15–16 ||

Svabodhodaya-mañjarī

One should cast one's mind into the point between the navel and the sex organ [i.e., the kanda] at end of good lovemaking;[96] as the bliss of lovemaking dies away, one may become waveless [i.e., the mind becomes still] in a moment. || 38 ||

> *Keep a delicious confection on the tip of your tongue; when the pleasure of the flavor fades away, liberation arises. || 42 ||*

The text also includes other methods, from hovering on the edge of sleep to trying to find the location of the mind to asking gently and repeatedly, "Who (or what) am I?" For the practitioner who is ready for these methods, they do indeed constitute a far easier path to successful centering in one's awakened nature. Like the *Vijñāna-bhairava,* the *Svabodhodaya* also contains some teachings on esoteric yoga that require extensive training to interpret correctly. I'm please to say I have completed a translation of the *Svabodhodaya-mañjarī* that will be published in the near future.

Vīra Nātha's primary disciple and successor was his nephew Cakrabhānu, a dreadlocked Kāpālika ascetic who bore the five transgressive marks of the cremation ground, such as wearing ornaments of human bone and eating out of a bowl made from the top of a human skull. Such practitioners were deliberately provocative, challenging the norms of appearance and conduct in mainstream society. (For this reason, some of the "reform" Kaulas forbade the Kāpālika observance of wearing these bone ornaments and other sect-marks.) An interesting story about Cakrabhānu is found in the old historical records of Kashmīr. It seems that he regularly presided at events called *cakra-melāpas* or "circle gatherings." These were lengthy group Krama rituals of an orgiastic character that began with great ritual solemnity and meditative cultivation and became. . . well, pretty wild. As the presiding guru, Cakrabhānu would receive a *dakṣiṇā* or donation from each of the participants. It seems that the king of Kashmir at that time disapproved strongly of respectable members of society spending their money on this sort of event, for he punished Cakrabhānu harshly by branding him on the forehead with the mark of a dog's foot, a punishment reserved for grand theft.[97] We know that the kind was not punishing him for sexual transgressions because the traditional

See pages 427–429

punishment of that at this time was the brand of a vulva. Prevented from participating in his favorite practice, he wrote, "When may I [again] follow the path of the Devī-kula in the company of proud Heroes at the onset of night, my mind made blissful through dissolution [of contracted thought-forms]?"[98]

Before we judge Cakrabhānu as nothing more than a debauched libertine, we should know that he became a highly regarded guru in his own right, initiating eight key disciples, three of whom became renowned gurus themselves: Īśānī (a female Kāpālika); Prabodha the Ascetic, who headed a lineage of some wonderful writers and poets; and Bhūtirāja, who became the Krama guru of Abhinava Gupta (see the chart below).

The Krama Guru Lineage

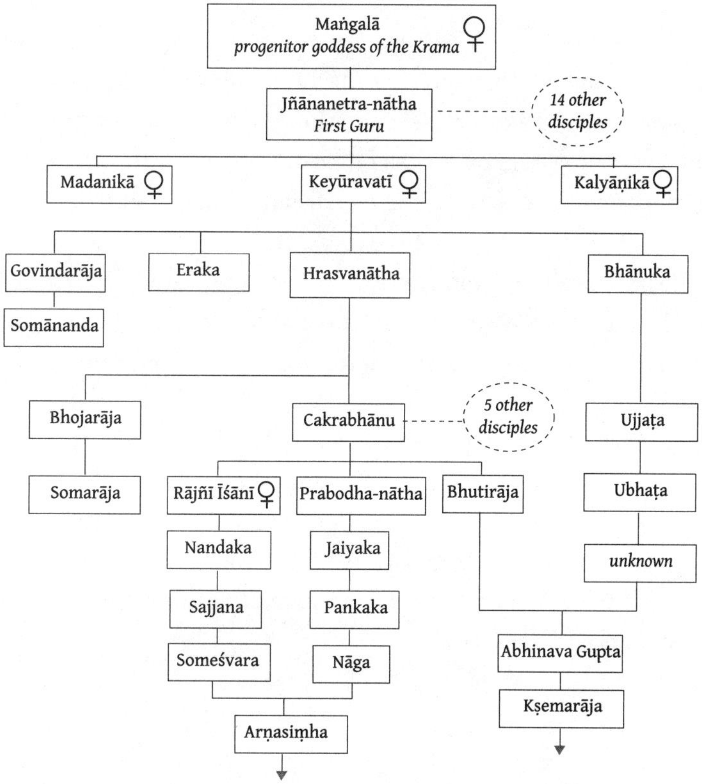

All these earlier Krama masters eventually became so revered that in the later tradition, the teachers of this lineage (up to and including Cakrabhānu's eight disciples) were worshipped as the *paramparā* or succession of masters embodying a single awakened consciousness. We see this teaching, for example, in the *Kaula-sūtra*'s first three aphorisms:

Kaula-sūtra

1. *There is but one Guru, the unbroken transmission of the rays [of awakened consciousness] passed on to us through the initiatory lineage.*
2. *There is but one God: the Reality that they have perceived.*
3. *The singular power of [its] Consciousness is identical with the state of their innate self-awareness.*[99]

This teaching that the Guru is not a series of personalities but a power transmitted through a properly maintained lineage is central to the Krama, and we can feel something of its truth, for the writings of the Krama masters over the course of nine generations are imbued with the same flavor—the same nectarean ecstasy wedded to piercing insight.

We have one text from Cakrabhānu's disciple Bhūtirāja, the Attainment of One's Own Awareness (Svabodha-siddhi), a sophisticated and well-written philosophical poem, from which we here quote:

Svabodha-siddhi

I venerate the supreme Śiva located in the self, who can be known only in self-experience, who is devoid of the mental torment of fixation on any specific doctrine. I bow to the Benevolent One, the destroyer of the flood of conceptual constructs, free of the snare of the mind's imaginings, transcending [even] the level of the highest bliss. || 2–3 ||

The method of attaining the goal is to be constantly awake to one's own awareness. By this means the sage achieves the state free of differentiation. There is no method other than staying with [awareness of] one's own being. Closely maintaining awareness of this alone, the yogī will become joyful, resting in the self.[100] *|| 9–10 ||*

These teachings are clearly influenced by Bhūtirāja's guru's guru, Vīra Nātha. However, Bhūtirāja's primary historical importance, as we will see later, rests on the fact that he initiated Abhinava Gupta into the Krama.

Cakrabhānu began three different productive lineages, as the lineage chart on page 255 shows. Bhūtirāja's coinitiate, Prabodha the Ascetic, was (to judge from his writing) a profoundly realized master. I love these sayings of his:

Prabodha the Ascetic

[O Divine Mother,] Whatever form I conceive, however transcendent, is lower than You! Yet nor can I conceive of anything, however low, in which You are not completely present!

The verse is clever in that though he does not name Her, we know he is thinking of Goddess Kālī because of the uncommon verb he uses for "conceive," √*kal,* which is also the root for Kālī's name.

Speaking of the power that remembering the divine has to get us out of our egoic and limited self, Prabodha wrote:

By mere remembrance of You, we make into a humble servant this demon called "I", that thirsts for the blood that is the fortitude and sense of men, ripping them apart with its treacherous fangs called "mine."[101]

Two of Prabodha's verses are particularly special because they have survived the demise of Śaiva Tantra in Kashmīr and have been reverently recited all the way down to the present day. They are probably the only two verses from the entire Krama tradition still preserved amongst a substantial segment of people, though their author and the Krama itself is long forgotten. They now form the conclusion of the *Bahurūpa-garbha-stotra* or "Hymn to the Multiform Womb [of Reality]," recited by many Kashmīrī brāhmins even today.

Bahurūpa-garbha-stotra: Hymn to the Multiform Womb

> *You, I praise, the unborn beloved of Śiva in the lotus of my heart, seated in deepest consciousness [on your throne that is] full of the radiance created by all the Causes.*
>
> *You, I praise, who are ever eager to drink the honey-wine exuded by the lotus-maṇḍala in the innermost awareness of all living creatures, hidden within the pervasive power that is the variety of phonemes, rending the snare of bound existence.*[102]

The next major author from whom we have writings is Nāga, three generations later, at which point the lineage's enthusiasm and enlightenment remain undimmed. Nāga is indeed one of the finest Krama poet-sages; for sample verses, see pages 267 and 415. Nāga's main disciple was Arṇasiṃha, which leads us into the discussion of the last phase of the Krama.

The Mahārtha: The Final Phase of the Krama

After the 10th century, the teachings of the Krama were primarily transmitted under the name of Mahārtha or Mahānaya, "the Great Teaching" or "the Great Way."[103] In the 11th and 12th centuries, three texts were composed by three different authors on the teachings of the Mahārtha, all with the same title: *Illumination of the Great Way (Mahānaya-prakāśa).* All three are masterpieces of spiritual philosophy. None of them, unfortunately, exists in an English translation as of yet.* The first *Illumination of the Great Way* was by a sage called Arṇasiṃha (active c. 1050–1075), who was fortunate to receive transmission from two Krama gurus in Cakrabhānu's lineage, one of whom was the poet Nāga. His text explains how the structure of Krama worship reflects and embodies the core structures of Consciousness itself (see Appendix 2).

* Though scholar-practitioner Carlos Pomeda has worked on the second Illumination extensively, and I hope to translate the third one at some point.

The second *Illumination* is in two parts: the root-text and the commentary. The root-text is remarkable because it was not written in Sanskrit but in the common language of the Kashmīrī people at that time; a Sanskrit commentary by a man named Śitikaṇṭha, of unknown lineage, was appended to explain it. The text contains some unique features, such as detailed instructions on a nine-day intensive course of training in Krama worship. It also innovates by reading the structures of worship not only in terms of the natural flow of cognition, but also mapping them onto the flow of energy within the human body. Here is a brief sample of the text:

> *The body—termed kula, the sacred site, the holy field, the first letter (a), the Five-cluster mantra, and the Praṇava (Oṃ)—is the temple of the Self, being the support of the awareness, identified with the [pure] I-sense, whose nature is that it manifests all [that appears to it].*[104]

Old Kashmīrī *Illumination of the Great Way*

So, if it wasn't clear, the key teaching in the paragraph is simply that the body is the temple of the divine self, a teaching popular in today's yoga scene, but not found in pre-Tantrik yoga.

The third *Illumination of the Great Way* was anonymously authored. It must have been influential, for though it was written in Kashmīr, the one surviving manuscript we have of the text was found in Trivandrum, Kerala, near the southern tip of India. Of all three, this is the most sophisticated *Illumination*, and the one that most clearly shows the influence of Abhinava Gupta, as well as earlier gurus like Utpala Deva and Vīra Nātha. The text presents an extremely subtle and sophisticated explanation of Krama worship, presenting it as "embodying a process of the unfolding of sudden enlightenment in which Consciousness devours its own content and subjectivity to burst forth into the mind and senses as a transfigured mundane experience in which the polarity of liberation and bondage itself is obliterated."[105] In other words, in this process of spontaneous realization, Consciousness, as it were, takes hold of its own inner strength, realizing that all the concrete elements of experience are in fact expressions of the One energy that is itself, and thus what before seemed ordinary appears as an extraordinary revelation, and mundane life becomes a source of endless wonder, unveiling its ever-present radiant freedom.

The anonymous *Illumination* also analyzes the process of each and every cognitive act (whether of an awakened or unawakened person) in terms of the veneration of its phases as the five Flow Goddesses of the Krama. Finally, it also presents an innovative take on the relationship between God and Goddess (Śiva and Śakti), whereby the latter is defined as the central core of the former, the absolute center-point within Śiva (i.e., Consciousness) that He Himself cannot make an object of perception, for it is the point of ultimate groundedness from which all seeing is done. Here is that passage, which I think you'll agree is quite extraordinary:

See Appendix 2

Anonymous
Illumination of the Great Way

> *The Great Lord's repose within himself is the highest state of self-awareness. But by the finest of distinctions there shines a state even higher than that. This is the Goddess-ground [devī-dhāma], in which even the Lord cannot see his way.*

Being and non-being reach their ground in the Light of Consciousness [prakāśa], and that [reaches its ground] in the aesthetic rapture of awareness [camatkāra] free of all need and requirement, which in turns comes to rest spontaneously in the limit of the supreme [state of] repose [para-viśrānti], far from the wounds of the impressions made [on the psyche] by judgements of "higher" and "lower."

What we mean by "the Goddess" is that unsurpassable Ground [viśrāntir anuttarā] that remains when it has devoured even the subtlest traces [saṃskāras] of the wounds of these impressions, positive, negative, and both, which can persist even in the state of repose in the supreme Light of Consciousness.

The nature of the Supreme Lord is the self-groundedness [viśrānti] that devours time [and all forms of limited awareness]. We define the nature of the Goddess to be the point in which That itself comes to rest. Thus though the two Supreme Lords [Śiva and Śakti] are one and the same, a subtle experiential difference between them has been [here] revealed. || 3.104–111 ||

Clearly this passage begs for explanation and exploration. This is, however, the history section in which tastes of all the branches of the Tantrik revelation are given and where there is not room to explore any one of them in detail. However, just such an exploration is perfect for live teaching environments, where we can also discuss how these seemingly esoteric teachings are immediately relevant to the unfolding of our spiritual growth. I hope to see you in one of those live teaching environments such as a retreat or online class sometime soon.

The Mahārtha moves South

In the centuries after the peak of Tantrik thought in Kashmīr, the heart of the tradition transferred to the far South of India, Tamiḷ and Keralan country. Nondualist authors there, while not as productive of original thought as the Kashmīrīs, became very learned in the literature of the Krama and Trika, as well as the Kaubjika and Śrīvidyā traditions that we have yet to discuss. We have seen that one of the *Illumination* texts was preserved only in Kerala. But the preservation of the Krama in the deep South can best be seen in the figure of Maheśvarānanda, a great guru who lived and wrote around 1300 in Chidambaram (the name means "the Sky of Consciousness"), the sacred site that houses the original temple to Śiva Naṭarāja, the Lord of the Cosmic Dance. Maheśvarānanda was initiated into both the Krama and the Śrīvidyā (as well as probably the Kaubjika lineage), receiving instruction from a guru whose lineage contained some extremely accomplished masters.

See page 110

One night, after performing his worship of the Goddess, Maheśvarānanda was dozing in a state of contented intoxication when he had a powerful vision of the Goddess as a mighty yoginī. Maheśvarānanda fumbled to make her an offering, and she waved her hand dismissively and signaled the number seven with her fingers. By turns gentle and stern, she spoke the ultimate Truth to him in the beautiful literary language of Māhārāṣṭrī. Upon awakening, we are told, he visited his teacher, who told Maheśvarānanda to write down her transmission as seventy verses in the Māhārāṣṭrī language. He also composed a Sanskrit commentary on the verses. The verses he called *The Efflorescence of the Great Teaching (Mahārtha-mañjarī)*, and his lengthy commentary *The Fragrance of. . . (-parimala)*.

The verses of the *Efflorescence* itself are presented as poetic scripture, obliquely attributed to the Goddess. The *Fragrance* commentary is more philosophical and argumentative. In it, he shows a wide command of many dozens of Tantrik sources, and he cites the Kashmīrī masters frequently and reverently. Thus he preserved the tradition, but was not afraid to innovate as well, showing it was still in his time a living tradition. We may consider the *Efflorescence*, a vigorous and profound work, as the final flowering of the tradition of the Mahārtha, formerly known as the Krama, and one of the last pieces of truly original writing of nondual Śaiva Tantra. Though it is not yet published in English, scholars are beginning to do some good work on the text.[106] Here are a couple of sample verses:

Mahārtha-mañjarī: The Efflorescence of the Great Teaching

Within the range of Paramaśivaand Earth—which is all ultimately the one Light of Consciousness [prakāśa]—mutual distinction is nothing other than the heart's unfolding of its infinite capacity for Self-reflection [vimarśa]. || 12 ||

The single fusion of thousands of Powers that can be seen in different ways is called Śiva, supremely free, the upsurge of one's own Heart. || 13 ||

Mahārtha-mañjarī: The Efflorescence of the Great Teaching

It is not really surprising that the Krama did not survive, for its liberated ethos represented a tremendous challenge to the conservative, patriarchal, xenophobic, and deeply inhibited mainstream brāhminical culture.[107] More than any other religious sect in premodern Indian history, the Krama repudiated hierarchies based on caste, class, or gender. Furthermore, its frank acceptance of sexuality and inclusion of that and other sensual elements in spiritual practice was at odds with the values of both the brāhmins *and* their Muslim conquerors, who brought North India under their sway in the 13th century. An additional factor undermining the survival of the

Krama and related Kaula groups was the existence of plentiful false gurus, who used the teachings of transgressive nondual Tantra as an excuse for sexual exploitation and alcoholic overindulgence. We have evidence that the Krama responded to this behavior with sarcastic criticism, showing that teachers of this tradition were aware that its teachings could be quoted accurately by those with no real understanding of them:

One Hundred Verses on the Unity of Teaching and Practice

> *Adopting misconduct they make love to others' wives, declaring constantly that it is wrong to impede the inclination of the powers [of consciousness]. They are deluded in their constant relish of the objects of the senses, saying that the goddesses of their faculties are [thus] filling the Lord that is consciousness with the objects of their enjoyment.*

This passage seems significant to me, for it shows us clearly that understanding the teachings on a mental level does not in any way require a person to understand the real inner state that they point to. This difference is precisely what makes the Krama an esoteric tradition—it embodies an understanding that, while it can be pointed to, cannot in fact ever be properly conveyed in words. There will always be those who are unable to grasp its real purport, and who even doubt there is such a level to be grasped, though they may be able to articulate well the ideas that point to it.

THE TEACHINGS OF THE KRAMA LINEAGE

Since there are not yet any publications for the nonscholar that convey the teachings of the Krama, we will explore them in a brief way here. The explicit goal of Krama practice was liberation in this life through a radical and abiding awakening of blissfully free, expansively open autonomous awareness. This awakening was brought about through one of three methods:

- direct transmission (*saṅkramaṇam*),
- oral instruction (*kathanam*), and
- ritual worship with nondual awareness (*pūjanam*).

Direct transmission was thought to consist of an encounter with a fully awakened Master in which the disciple's awareness, ripe for expansion, spontaneously fuses with that of the Guru in a moment of revelation that triggers a deep opening, a permanent shift. The Guru's glance is the most commonly cited example of this mystical transmission, though there are other forms as well. This method of realization was, of course, considered the rarest and quickest of the three.

Second is the method of oral instruction (*kathanam*), which in the Krama is also a kind of transmission of transformative power, in the form of condensed statements on the nature of ultimate reality called *chummās*, thought to have been revealed by the divine Yoginīs of Uḍḍiyāna and passed down by the women of the tradition in the vernacular Kashmīrī language. The way to approach these esoteric teachings is through intuition rather than intellection, holding their vibration in awareness until an inner meaning spontaneously unfolds in a wordless state of realization. The first four of the *chummās* are:[108]

See page 371

Chummā-saṅketa-prakāśa

> *LINGU ABHIJÑĀNU: The point of fusion is the means of recognition.*
> *ARAṆI-SAMUDĀYU: It arises from the [two] kindling sticks.*
> *CAKREŚĪ-MELAKU: The goddesses of the circle merge.*
> *KĀLA-GRĀSU: Time is devoured.*

But most *chummās* are so cryptic that they yield no meaning without some explanation. When the *chummās* came to be written down, they received a Sanskrit commentary that explained them. I will give two examples of *chummās* with commentary.

> *RAMI EKĀYANU: The One Ground plays.*

The Sanskrit commentary explains the meaning thus:

> *He who is the One Ground, complete and all-pervading, plays without falling from his nature as he performs every action of every kind throughout the universe.*[109]

We know from context that the One "plays" by taking on every kind of embodiment and subjecting itself to every kind of experience; that is, He enacts the total range of possibilities within his being as a divine play. The second *chummā* reads:

> *MACCĪ UMACCĪ: Wild, then tamed [or: Mad, then free of madness].*

The commentary explains:

> *Because Consciousness surges up with innate autonomy she becomes reckless, taking on ever-new forms and [then] dissolving them all. She gives no thought to what is proper or improper, being constantly in motion. But when this same [Goddess Consciousness] is sated, she completely transcends this madness. When she catches sight of the*

highest Śiva [i.e., the quiescent ground of consciousness], he tames her recklessness. For this reason Consciousness, who never deviates from Her [inner] nature for those blessed [to know Her], has been called "mad, then free of madness"[110]

We have an example of a master who attained his realization through contemplating these oral teachings: the figure of Śrī Nāga, the disciple of the disciple of Prabodha the Ascetic, mentioned above. Nāga, from whom we have two texts of staggering power and beauty, writes with exultant gratitude about what he received from his guru:

By great good fortune I stand today overflowing with the blissful relish [camatkāra] of the nectar of the non-local Consciousness that surges up from its unbound stainless ground. I am astonished by the fruition of the instruction in the inexpressible practice that I obtained from the heart of my sadguru's oral teaching.[111]

Nāga's *Thirty Verses on Contentment of Mind*

As we will see when we come to the section on practice (part 3), this method of *kathanam,* relying exclusively on accessing the vibrational essence of powerful spiritual teachings, corresponds to Abhinava Gupta's category of the *śākta-upāya* or the Empowered Means.

See page 357

The third category of Krama practice, then, is *pūjanam* or worship. The Krama carefully set itself apart from other Tantrik systems by creating a system of ritual worship that expressed its philosophical and metaphysical stance on the nature of Consciousness. Thus the worshipper makes offerings to goddesses that embody the powers of his or her own body, senses, mind, and awareness. The practitioner is required to understand the inner significance of ritual action that it may blossom into full nondual awareness—a requirement not found in the other Tantrik schools. In this way, the nature of Consciousness is unveiled through a meditation-in-action on the cyclical flow of cognition.

The structure of Krama ritual worship is complex, but for those who want to know the details of how the sequence of worship of circuits of arcane goddesses—on the subtle level, vortex wheels of pulsating energies—map the flow of the arising and subsiding of every cognitive event whatsoever, appendix 2 provides a summary of that map.

The Teaching of the Manuscript

The final Krama teaching that we will examine is the Teaching of the Manuscript. We find in the Krama an interesting tension regarding the role of knowledge and learning in the spiritual life. On the one hand, the Krama is a very textually productive lineage, with many scriptures, hymns, poems, and commentaries; on the other hand, its masters warn us repeatedly about the "snare of learning" and the danger of getting lost in mere intellectual understanding of the doctrine. The symbol of the manuscript is a central one, yet the recurrent theme is one of "breaking open the boards" of the manuscript to reveal the transmental experiential reality that exists between the polarities that the two boards represent. (Sanskrit manuscripts consist of sheaves of palm leaf or birch bark protected by two wooden boards and bound by two cords.)

We see this theme in the frame story of the text of the aphoristic *chummās* mentioned earlier. The author of the commentary on the *chummās*, Niṣkriyānanda Nātha, claims to have received them in a visionary transmission from one Siddhanātha. The impactful glance of this guru gives Niṣkriya an overwhelming experience of essence-nature beyond the mind, beyond time and space, even beyond Bliss. When Niṣkriya recovers, he asks how this awakening may become an abiding one, and Siddhanātha (who never speaks) casts a glance into the depths of the sky. Through its power, the Supreme Word (*parā vāk*) that is one with Śiva, Bhairavī Herself, emerges from the highest space. She is said to be the embodiment of fusion with the lights of extraordinary Consciousness. She says to Niṣkriya,

Why are you so proud? What is [the value of] this snare of learning? Still you have not shaken off your delusion. Behold this manuscript in the hand of Siddhanātha. O you who have mastered the Krama, know that its tightly bound five-hood [knot] is the power embodied in the five sense-faculties and that its two encircling rings are waking and dreaming. Learn in brief the nature of these its two boards. (Translation Sanderson)

Chummā-saṅketa-prakāśa

She then gives the teaching of the two boards, which represent two apparently opposite aspects of the Goddess:

Upper board	**Lower board**
outgoing breath	ingoing breath
immanence	transcendence
immersion into extroversive expansion	immersion into introversive expansion
all-encompassing Fullness	all-devouring Emptiness
full-figured sweet Goddess (Parā)	emaciated fierce Goddess (Kālī)

She then commands Niṣkriya: "Break open the two boards and behold the great spaciousness beyond the void!" This spaciousness is the convergence of all the above polarities, the paradoxical superposition of both aspects of divinity. It is said to be unlocatable, free of both the transient and the eternal, unmanifest yet always present in everything, the devourer of Time and its processes: and it has as its sphere one's very own Self. It is your essence-nature (*svasvarūpa*).

As a result of this teaching, Niṣkriya experienced directly the ultimate Reality and went forever beyond the snare of knowledge. Siddhanātha, filled with loving compassion, then bestowed on him the teaching of the *chummās*, that is "hard to understand for even the greatest of yogīs." As a result, Niṣkriyānanda Nātha became a fully Awakened One (*suprabuddha*).[112]

See page 266

Kubjikā with Navātma-bhairava

SAMPRADĀYA 8:

Kaubjika

ऐं ह्रीं श्रीं फ्रें ह्सौं

Deity: Kubjikā (the Crooked Goddess)

Visualization: dark blue, twelve-armed, and six-faced, including the faces of Parā, Kālī, and Tripurā

Mantra: AIṂ HRĪṂ ŚRĪṂ PHREṂ HSAUṂ

Principal texts: *Kubjikā-mata-tantra*; *Manthāna-bhairava-tantra*

The Kaubjika tradition is named for the Goddess Kubjikā, a complex figure who incorporates features of earlier Tantrik deities. Like Svacchanda-bhairava, she is simultaneously fiercely intense and sweetly benevolent.[113] She is sometimes viewed as an emanation of Parā, connecting her with the Trika *sampradāya*, and indeed much of the root-text of the Kaubjika is adapted from the scriptures of the Trika. On the other hand, one of Kubjikā's emanations is that of Tripurā or Lālita, connecting her closely with the Śrīvidyā *sampradāya* discussed next. For modern practitioners the primary significance of Kubjikā's tradition lies in the fact that her scriptures are the main source for the theory and practice of *kuṇḍalinī-yoga*[114] (including its six-*cakra* system) which later appeared in the texts of *haṭha-yoga* as well as through oral transmission all the way down to the present day. More on this soon.

Kubjikā's myth of origin is sufficiently interesting to be summarized here, drawing on the *Kubjikā-mata-tantra.* Once upon a time (in the Time before Time), Bhairava, the awe-inspiring form of Śiva, visited the residence of the god of the Himālaya mountains, where he meets the Daughter of the Mountain, usually called Pārvatī but here named as Kālikā (Little Kālī). Quite taken with her, Bhairava gives her a vision of the universe blazing with the bliss of the Empowering Transmission (*ājñā,* a key term of this sect), a vision that profoundly awakens her. He tells her she must attain her essence-nature beyond all qualities, and then he disappears. She is confused and disoriented and in a state of wonder asks, "Who are you, and what am I doing?"

After deliberation, she travels to the Mountain of the Moon in the West to look for Bhairava. Here, in a paradise filled with all manner of exquisitely beautiful birds, bees, and flowering plants, where the power of passionate love resides, she comes upon a magical stone. She mounts the stone and enters a yogic trance, having received the energy of the Empowering Transmission. She becomes the "female *liṅga,*" a fusion of masculine and feminine principles. In this form she is independently blissful and is thus sometimes depicted as doubled over and licking her own vulva, which is one reason she is called "the Hunchback" (*kubjikā*). This is symbolic not of erotic narcissism but of the introversive self-savoring of the divine Absolute when it experiences the fullness of its own innate being, inclusive of all polarities. Bhairava appears and praises her in this androgynous form of the female *liṅga*, thereby arousing the goddess from her introverted contemplation, and she bursts forth into the form in which she is worshipped (illustrated on page 270), said to be "beautiful and ugly and multifaceted." Bhairava asks her for the Empowering Transmission (signalling that she is now in the dominant role), and she bends over with embarrassment, for she knows it must be given through conjugal union: that she must actualize in the external world her internal realization. This posture of bending over in embarrassment is another mythological explanation for her name. Ultimately, though, the explanation of *kubjikā* that would become dominant is that she is a personification of *kuṇḍalinī*, the "coiled power," the liberative and integrative goddess-power that exists, usually in a partly dormant state, in all embodied sentient beings.[115]

The union of Śiva and Śakti (in their sexual embodied essence) gives rise to the immortal Point of Ultimacy, a singularity "blazing with the light of ten million suns."[116] The explosion of this Point, this *bindu*, through the Goddess's empowering command (*ājñā*) generates the universe in a series of emanations. But we should note that in the Kaubjika tradition, there is a higher Divinity than the sexually conjoined pair of Śiva and Śakti, and this is the point of their absolute fusion: Anada-sakti, the Power of Bliss called the Neuter, which is the potential, unmanifest state, the timeless Void of Consciousness, which is what exists "before" the manifestation of the bindu Point, and "after" it, and pervades the universe that manifests out of it.

In the final stage of the emanation of the Point (the first micro-second of time), it expands out into the triangular generative *yoni*, its three points the powers of Willing, Knowing, and Acting. (This is the same cosmological narrative seen in the Śrīvidyā as well: see the next *sampradāya*.) We do not have space in this overview to explore the successive stages of this emanation.

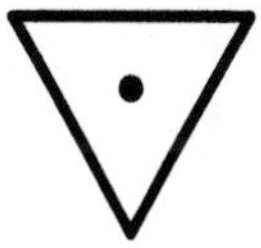

In the following sample passage, we have a clear example of the influence of the Krama on the Kaubjika, since we see specific Krama technical terms being used. Here Kubjikā is, like Kālī, the seemingly terrifying radiant Void underlying all things that awakens the aspirant to reality, after which he sees all form as an expression of the imperishable formlessness. This Void is paradoxically experienced as *flowing* even as it is the place of supreme stillness and rest.

Manthāna-bhairava-tantra

In the Center is the ground of perfect repose [viśrānti]; *it is the experience of flowing Presence, the realization of which constitutes one's own spiritual authority* [adhikāra].

The power of bliss is melted between the exhale and the inhale; in the center of the staff of space [i.e., the central channel], She pervades the energy of consciousness of the individual soul. The limbs of her slender [i.e., transcendent] body are variegated by time and tide; dissolved in the level beyond bliss, imperishable and terrifying, She awakens one to reality.

We will close this section with an important historical note based on new research. There is some evidence that Kubjikā's tradition arose in the western Himālayas in the late 10th century, but if so, its base soon became the city of Candrapura (modern Chandor) in the kingdom of Konkana (modern Goa), from which locale it was transmitted to the far South. In the South, an alternate form of the Kaubjika flourished, called the Śāmbhavānanda lineage, in which worship of Kubjikā's partner Navātma-śiva (or the worship of them as a couple) prevailed. The Śāmbhavānanda lineage was syncretistic in that it incorporated the Śrīvidyā worship of Tripurā as well (see the discussion that follows). The Śāmbhavānanda is of crucial significance for the history of yoga because it is a probable source for the *haṭha-yoga* system that came after the decline of classical Tantra. Recent scholarship has been done on a scripture that is transitional between Tantra and *haṭha-yoga*, a 13th-century text called the *Compendium of Matsyendra* that is associated with the Śāmbhavānanda lineage that combined the Kaubjika and Srīvidya.[117]

We see evidence for the connection of the Śāmbhavānanda with early *haṭha-yoga* in the archaeological site of the caves of Panhāle-Kājī (originally Praṇālaka), found in the Sindhudurg district of Mahārāṣṭra, just south of Goa. In these caves, also dated to the 13th century, we find a wealth of images of the Nāthas, a lineage that, as we shall see, was the primary holder of the *haṭha-yoga* tradition in its first few centuries. Cave 29 contains images of eighty-four Nātha *siddhas.* The caves, which also contain images of Tripurā, are located near the heartland of the Kaubjika sect in Goa. These caves may be the site described in the *Compendium of Matsyendra* as the place where Gorakṣa, after wandering around India in search of his teacher Matsyendra Nātha[118] (whom he had briefly met previously in the Tamil country), finally found him and received his initiation. This last point is, of course, speculative.

See page 309

Scholar Mark Dyczkowski has recently published a twelve-volume study and translation of the *Manthāna-bhairava-tantra,* an 11th-century scripture of the Kaubjika *sampradāya.* Increasing availability of English-language studies of this branch of the tradition will allow more and more people to realize that many of the elements of modern yoga (e.g., the teachings on energy centers called *cakras*) have their roots in this *sampradāya.*

Lalitā Tripurasundarī

SAMPRADĀYA 9: *Śrīvidyā a.k.a. Traipura*

ऐं ह्रीं सौः

Deity: Tripurasundarī, a.k.a. Lalitā

Visualization: young and beautiful, red, four-armed, with goad, noose, sugarcane bow, and flower-arrows

Mantra: OṂ KA E Ī LA HRĪṂ HA KA HA LA HRĪṂ HA SA KA LA HRĪṂ; also AIṂ HRĪṂ SAUḤ

Principal text: *Nityāṣoḍaśikārṇava; Yoginī-hṛdaya*

We have seen that the theology of Kubjikā includes a divinization of passion and sexual desire, since the coupling of the Goddess and Śiva is responsible for the creation of reality. This theme comes to its fruition in the ninth and last *sampradāya* of classical Śaiva Tantra, known as the Traipura and better known as Śrīvidyā, which means both "Auspicious Wisdom" and "the Sacred Goddess Mantra." The Goddess is here pictured as the young and beautiful Lalitā (the Coquette, the Playful One) or Kāmeśvarī (the Goddess of Erotic Desire), Her skin the red color of passion. She is pictured seated atop the meditating Śiva prostrate in *śavāsana,* signalling that in this sect the embodied experience of passionate desire trumps the quiescent introversive meditative state, though that is still present as the ultimate ground of "pure" desire (that is, desire that arises as a spontaneous expression of embodied Consciousness instead of from appetitive conditioning). From the perspective of the Śrī-vidyā, desire (*icchā*) is the motive force of the universe, since without it nothing would arise and divine Consciousness would remain static. The work of the spiritual practitioner, then, is to first release her judgments concerning her own desires, judgments that cause a contraction of Consciousness, and secondly to merge her limited desire into the greater pattern of divine Will. This does not mean giving up desire but rather learning to want passionately what life wants, what the Goddess wants, which necessitates becoming one with Her. What the Goddess wants is simply to flow in relational patterns of ever-greater harmony, and we naturally fall into that dance when our conditioned desires that arise from a false sense of lack have fallen away. But this *cannot* happen as long as we are judging or condemning them instead of seeing that they are the same energy as divine Will constrained by our ignorance from expressing themselves in maximum harmony.

The Śrīvidyā arose out of an older cult of love-magic (called the *Nityā* cult), which sought to develop rituals to secure the affections of a prospective sexual partner.[119] Under the influence of the Tantrik movement, this rapidly developed into a full-blown path to liberation through worshipping the beautiful feminine radiance (Śrī) that embodies the very nectar of human life. It is Śrī that brings beauty and good fortune to any home, vivifying the otherwise static patterns of inertia that the masculine otherwise falls into. In time, the Śrīvidyā developed rituals of worshipping Śrī as a young girl (*kumārī*) and as a fertile married woman (*strī*), the source of auspiciousness. The last to develop, the Śrīvidyā is also the only sect of original Śaiva Tantra to survive intact to the present day, though the cost of doing so was the loss of its independence, it being assimilated and "sanitized" by the conservative brāhmins of the Tamiḷ South and practiced today exclusively by them. It nonetheless kept some of its doctrines and many of its rituals intact (though the transgressive elements were carefully excised). The Śrīvidyā entered into the non-Tantrik Vedānta tradition and "tantricized" it to the extent that the highest authorities of Vedānta in the South began practicing the worship of the Śrī Yantra, and still do so today.[120]

The most salient feature of the Śrīvidyā is the threefold form of its central goddess, Tripurā or Tripura-sundarī (Beautiful in the Form of the Three Citadels). The first of the three "citadels" is her coarse (*sthūla*) form, that is, her iconographic depiction as a sixteen-year-old woman just come into her sexual power, bare-breasted or (in the later tradition) wearing a red sārī, symbolic of passion. Tripurā's second, subtle (*sūkṣma*) form is that of the *Śrī Cakra* or *Śrī Yantra*, the most popularly known mystic diagram of the Tantrik tradition and one of the most popular forms of sacred geometry in the world (see the illustration below).

This *yantra* (= diagram for working with and chanelling the energies of life) is also a *cakra* (= circuit of deities) depicting the sequences of the emanation of reality from a central Point of Ultimacy (*bindu*), which contains all of those energies in unmanifest form. In other words, when you look at the *Śrī Cakra*, you are seeing the energies of creation pulsing out from the singularity at the center. This map also enables us to trace our way back to the source, finding the point of maximum centeredness from which all the energies of creation (and resorption) are experienced as pulsing out from (and returning to) one's own Self, the radiant Heart of Consciousness. Thus the *Śrī Cakra* is simultaneously a dynamic map of reality, a substrate for ritual, and a focal point for meditation.

The third and most subtle (*ati-sūkṣma*) form of this Goddess is Her mantra, given above. Because it has sixteen syllables, She is also known as Ṣoḍaśī, which means "sixteen." Tripurā's mantra itself subdivides into three parts, which each express one of three goddesses, whose combined essences make up Tripurā (note the strong structural parallel with the Trika). Not counting Oṃ, the first five syllables are said to express the Power of Insight (*jñāna-śakti*), are associated with Vāgīśvarī (= Parā-vāk), and bring about liberation; the second five express the Power of Action (*kriyā-śakti*), are associated with Kāmeśvarī, and bring about the attainment of one's romantic and sexual desires; and the third set of five express the Power of the Will or Creative Upsurge (*icchā-śakti*), are also associated with Parā, and are said to remove obstacles. It is the second of these three aspects that is most prominent in the root-text of this sect.

See page 163

The Śrīvidyā became very successful and widespread throughout India, from Kāshmīr to Tamiḷ Nāḍu, though it survives today only in the latter region. It was more attractive to some royal patrons than other Tantrik sects, partially because it focused on enhancing the pleasures of life, not the cremation ground imagery focused on conquering death. The Śrīvidyā came to eclipse the traditions that nurtured its development, the Trika and the Kubjikā sects. The Trika flourished for a time in the South side by side with the Śrīvidyā, and when it eventually disappeared, it nonetheless survived there through the incorporation of the principle mantra of Parā-devī (sauḥ) into the core of the Śrīvidyā liturgy. The Trika Goddess Parā was preserved as the heart-mantra of Tripurā. This is appropriate, given the profound influence of the Trika's doctrine, practice, and philosophy on the Śrīvidyā.

In the following brief sample passage from *The Heart of the Yoginī* (*Yoginī-hṛdaya*), we see in play some of the ideas I've just hinted at. Here, the *Cakra* refers both to the mystic diagram and the manifest universe that it represents. As in the Kaubjika teaching given in the previous discussion (remember the strong connection between these two schools in some areas), the universe is born when the infinite Void of Consciousness manifests as the Point, the all-containing singularity from which everything flows forth. This Void is not of course a void of empty space, but rather is analogized to an ocean of light or potential energy (Śiva), through which undulate waves of pulsation (Śakti). When this Consciousness recognizes itself (using metaphor to point to something beyond words), the Point bursts forth in waves of emanation, beginning with the threefold Goddess who is *icchā*, *jñāna*, and *kriyā* as well as knower, knowing, and known.

The Heart of the Yoginī
verses 9–13

When one perceives the Supreme Power—who assumes the form of the whole of reality by Her own free will—as the pulsating radiance of one's own Self, then the Cakra arises from the Point of Ultimacy, the vibrating Consciousness, the state of Absolute Potential in the form of the Void. Because that ultimate reality is the Light of Consciousness, and because it is wedded to the waves of pulsation, the foundation of the waves of manifest reality flows forth: the Triad of Mothers [i.e., the tripartite Śrīvidyā mantra and the three main Powers]. . . . This great bindu-born Cakra of nine yonis and many mantras is utterly replete with the Bliss of Consciousness.

The Structure of the Śaiva Canon

Having examined the nine *sampradāyas*, we may consider briefly their relationship to one another. For, though they were presented as nine separate traditions, they are in fact all part of one whole. There is plenty of evidence to suggest that the adherents of Śaiva Tantra saw the tradition in this way. The primary such evidence is the teaching that the entire body of Tantrik scriptures is to be seen as a single complex utterance, a vast interrelated patterning of Consciousness flowing forth from the five faces of the one Śiva.

The canon is gradated into a kind of hierarchy of revelation. The following diagram, adapted from Sanderson's pioneering 1988 study, illustrates this hierarchy. It preserves the left/right distinction we have addressed earlier while also presenting a vertical axis.

See page 211

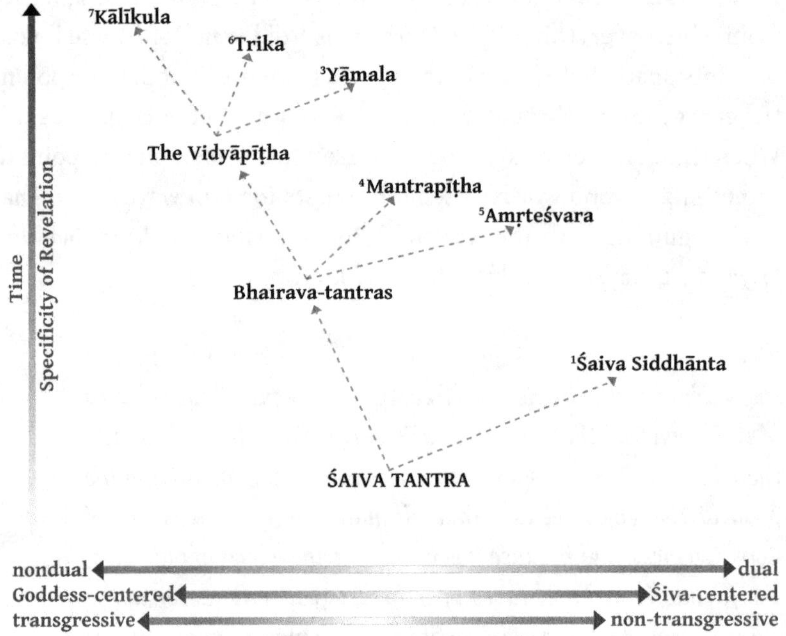

To reiterate, the further to the left, the more transgressive, goddess-oriented, and nondualist a group tends to be. On the vertical axis, whatever is lower down is a more general revelation, whose scriptures are considered universally valid except where superseded by the instructions of a group higher up. (Thus, as noted above, the Siddhānta is seen as the lowest in the sense of being the base, for it is the most universal in its prescriptions, at least in the domain of practice.)

Here we see that the most basic division of the tradition (at the bottom) is between the Siddhānta-tantras and the Bhairava-tantras. The latter subdivides again, one of its three divisions being the *Vidyā-pīṭha* (Throne of Wisdom-goddess-mantras), a designation for the branch of the tradition in which the divine feminine is predominant. This subdivides into three of the groups described above. The Kaub-jika and Traipura *sampradāyas* are not included here, because they are later, because they don't fit neatly into these axes, and because we are presenting the hierarchy from Abhinava Gupta's point of view, for more than anyone he articulated the theology of scripture for the Tantrik tradition. Quite beautiful and complex mystical teachings on the Śaiva hierarchy of revelation as the natural embodiment of God's self-awareness are given in his *Mālinīvijaya-vārttika,* published as *Abhinavagupta's Philosophy of Revelation.*

KASHMIR SHAIVISM

The Refinement of the Tradition in its Post-Scriptural Phase

We have already alluded to the fact that while Śaiva Tantra was pan-Indian, it particularly flourished in the valley of Kashmīr to the far north. Kashmīr is on the border of the geographical regions of Central Asia and South Asia, and was close to the routes of the Silk Road, and thus enjoyed a kind of cosmopolitan multiculturalism not seen in the Indian subcontinent at that time. The Kashmīr Valley is protected by mountains on three sides, creating a perfect site for the capital of the little kingdom. This ancient city, situated by a large lake, was (and still is) named Śrīnagar (the Blessed City, the Goddess' City). This exquisitely beautiful site was called the *tilak* (sacred forehead mark) of Mother India. All the Indian religions flourished there, especially the Śaiva, Śākta, Bauddha, Vaiṣṇava, and Saura traditions—that is, those devoted to the teachings of Śiva, Śakti, the Buddha, Viṣṇu, and Sūrya (the Sun-god) respectively. Furthermore, the kings of Kashmīr in the early Middle Ages were patrons of philosophy and the arts, allowing for the development of sophisticated philosophical schools side by side with a flourishing literary tradition of plays, ornate poetry, witty social satire, and carefully thought-out aesthetic theories.

It was in this environment that a crucially important post-scriptural or *exegetical* phase of Śaiva Tantra developed, a phase that would eventually make its influence felt all the way down to the tip of the subcontinent. "Exegesis" means explanation and interpretation of scriptural materials. So here we are broadly contrasting two chronologically successive and distinct phases of the Śaiva Tantrik tradition. The first is that of the nine *sampradāyas* detailed above, as revealed in anonymously written scriptures that claimed to be spoken by Śiva Himself (or, in the case of the Krama, Śakti Herself). These texts were often mysterious, elliptically worded, and focused on practice rather than philosophy. The second phase, then, consists of texts authored by named individuals, often highly educated people, who composed in a very different style of Sanskrit. Though their works were intended to explain the scriptures, either they are highly philosophical or they present a sophisticated theology. These authors show knowledge of the prevalent pan-Indian theories of knowledge and logic. Their arguments concerning the nature of reality are built on three levels: through reason, through appeal to the scriptures, and through appeal to personal experience. These three methods of discourse corresponded to the three traditional means of knowledge: direct experience, inference, and trusted authority. The method of appeal to reason could be used in debate with Buddhists and other non-Śaivas, the method of appeal to the scriptures or trusted authority in debate with Śaivas of other schools, and the method of appeal to personal experience along with the other two methods could be used in instruction of the author's own disciples.

We are now concerned with this second phase, the exegetical writings of the Śaiva Tantrik masters from Kashmīr. It is this body of literature that has been called "Kashmīr Shaivism" since the early 20th century and taught in the West under that name but entirely disassociated from the full context of Śaiva Tantra and its scriptures, which have just been outlined in detail. This happened because, though much of the Tantrik tradition had been forgotten, in the early 20th century some scholars started reading the philosophical texts in isolation from their context and published on them in English, coining the phrase Kashmīr Shaivism in the process. These publications, which continued sporadically through the rest of the 20th century, showed little to no knowledge of the powerful practices of the tradition. Even today, there are still no accurate translations of the original Sanskrit sources on *kuṇḍalinī* and the subtle-body practices so crucial to the classical tradition. Furthermore, 20th century writings on Śaiva philosophy often present it as rarefied and esoteric speculation on the ultimate nature of Reality little connected to "real life." And yet the primary concern of the original Tantrik authors was to give an accounting of how Consciousness creates the reality of our moment-to-moment experience of life.

The primary concern of the original Tantrik authors was to give an accounting of how Consciousness creates the reality of our moment-to-moment experience.

To return to our main topic: the ancient exegetical writers of Kashmīr, inspired by the scriptures, created coherent and elegant systems of thought not found in the earlier period. This spiritual thinking, it should be emphasized, was never divorced from practice, even at its most esoteric. We will now briefly review the key lineages of the exegetical period (900–1050 or 1100 CE; see the timeline on page 193).

In the 9th century, the Trika and the Krama rose to prominence in Kashmīr, not among the masses, but in a circle of individuals with connections to the royal court. These two *sampradāyas* counted amongst their initiates extremely learned individuals, even geniuses. They composed works that gave these two groups much greater philosophical sophistication and respectability. More important, several of these authors were, according to the tradition, fully liberated and awakened spiritual masters, whose words vibrate with the full power of their attainment, giving us the most direct insight into the nature of reality possible through words, at least in this author's opinion. Therefore, their writings came in time to be revered as equivalent to scripture.[121]

See pages 289 & 292

The Spanda Lineage

The masters of the Spanda (Vibration) lineage drew on both the Trika and the Krama in the composition of their works, furthering a synthesis that had begun in the scriptures themselves. The first and most original of these master philosophers was Vasugupta (c. 825–875 CE). He revealed the text known as *The Aphorisms of Śiva* (*Śiva-sūtra*). The unusual innovation of this text, which cannot be easily tied to any known school of Śaiva Tantra, was explained through a story related several generations later by Kṣemarāja:

Śiva-sūtra-vimarśinī: Reflection on the Aphorisms of Śiva

> *Once the Supreme Lord, desiring to benefit mankind by preventing the esoteric tradition [of nonduality] from dying out in a society that was almost completely permeated by the dualistic doctrine, graced Vasugupta in a dream and revealed to him that there was an esoteric teaching [written] on a huge rock on that mountain [Mt. Mahādeva] and that he was to learn it and reveal it to those capable of receiving grace. When he awoke, he looked for that great stone and, turning it over by a mere touch of his hand, saw*

that it confirmed his dream. He then acquired from it these Aphorisms of Śiva, which are the epitome of the secret teachings of Śiva.[122]

This story was intended to elevate the *Śiva-sūtra* to the status of scripture. It is also reported by multiple sources that the *Śiva-sūtra* is based on otherwise unrecorded oral teachings from numerous male and female adepts of the Tantra (*siddhas* and *yoginīs*) from whom Vasugupta received transmission.

Much of the *Śiva-sūtra* is very difficult to understand, and the commentaries we have are from six generations later, though their value is enhanced by the fact that the lineage was unbroken throughout that time. Here is a small sample from the text, sūtras 6–11 out of 77 total:

6. *When one absorbs the circle of Powers, the universe is withdrawn.*
7. *[Then] arises the expansion of the Fourth state into the divisions of the waking state, dream, and deep sleep.*
8. *The "waking state" refers to cognitive activity.*
9. *"Dream" means mental constructs.*
10. *"Deep sleep" means non-discernment, concealment.*
11. *One who experiences these three [as the Fourth state] is the Lord of Heroes, [the embodied form of the Divine].*

Śiva-sūtra: the Aphorisms of Śiva

The *Śiva-sūtra* received two important commentaries, by Bhāskaraand Kṣemarāja, six and seven generations after Vasugupta respectively.[123]

Vasugupta's disciple was named Kallaṭa (c. 850–900 CE). His great work is the *Stanzas on Vibration* (*Spanda-kārikās*). In it, he expanded on his Guru's teachings and added to them, drawing more on texts of the Kālīkula, though the *Stanzas* also maintained a sect-neutral—but clearly nondualistic—philosophical stance. The central concept of this work of great beauty and spiritual power is that God is nothing but the vibrant pulsation of Consciousness, moving through successive phases of expansion and contraction. The *Stanzas* received no fewer than seven commentaries, one by the author himself and two others of note by Kṣemarāja and Rājānaka Rāma, a disciple of Utpala Deva (of whom more will be said).

The Pratyabhijñā Lineage

Approximately two generations after Kallaṭa, another lineage was born, this one consisting of masters initiated into the Trika but again writing in a language that transcended sectarian boundaries. Its first guru was Somānanda (c. 900–950), who wrote *The Vision of Śiva* (*Śiva-dṛṣṭi*). In the first verse of this work, he implies that his ability to author it arose from a state of oneness with the Divine. Usually the author of a spiritual treatise begins with an homage to God, to invoke divine blessings and remove obstacles to the completion of the work. But since Somānanda felt no separation between himself and God, he prayed rather that the Divine should simply honor itself through him (after warding off any obstacles, that as a nondualist, he also saw as being nothing but God):

The Vision of Śiva

> *asmad-rūpa-samāviṣṭaḥ svātmanātma-nivāraṇe śivaḥ karotu nijayā namaḥ śaktyā tatātmane || 1.1 ||*
>
> *May Śiva, who has completely permeated my embodied form, himself ward off [the obstacles which are] himself, and by his own Power [śakti] bow to his greater Self.*

Lest we regard this unusual invocation as a sign of the author's delusions of grandeur, Somānanda goes on in the second verse to teach that the Divine constitutes the essential identity of *all* beings, and that all forms of manifestation and dynamic change are expressions of His powers:

> *The Lord Śiva of contented awareness is the very Self vibrating in all things, His will flowing freely and His knowledge and action expanding everywhere. || 1.2 ||*

Somānanda here alludes to the six principal Powers of the Divine: Awareness (*cit-śakti*), Bliss (*ānanda-śakti*) Freedom (*svātantrya-śakti*), Willing (*icchā-śakti*), Knowing (*jñāna-śakti*), and Acting (*kriyā-śakti*), which are the principal powers of the embodied being as well.

See page 102

Somānanda's disciple was the great *siddha* master Utpala Deva (c. 925–975), who simultaneously possessed one of the greatest intellects and one of the most passionately devotional hearts in the whole documented history of nondual Śaiva Tantra. Utpala wrote many works, but is best known and remembered for two remarkable books. The first of these is the *Stanzas on the Recognition of the Divine* or *Īśvara-pratyabhijñā-kārikās*.

It is from this work that the Pratyabhijñā or "Recognition" school gets its name. It is a dense, intellectually challenging, richly philosophical work that also includes some remarkable mystical passages in its last quarter. One such verse shows Utpala's indebtedness to the teaching of his Guru:

> *There is only one Great Divinity, and it is the very inner Self of all creatures. It embodies itself as all things, full of unbroken awareness of three kinds: "I", "this", and "I am this."*

The Recognition of the Lord

A number of commentaries on the *Stanzas on Recognition* have survived, attesting to its importance.

Utpala also authored a great number of devotional hymns and verses, which were later collected as the *Garland of Hymns to Śiva* (*Śiva-stotrāvalī*). These extraordinary verses show that awakened beings like Utpala are multifaceted and cannot be easily pigeonholed. For while the *Stanzas on Recognition* shows us a towering intellect with a profound grasp of the most subtle and complex philosophical and logical issues of his time, the *Garland* shows us a heart overflowing with love, longing, and devotion. Without becoming overly autobiographical, the hymns depict Utpala's feelings and experiences with an intimacy unusual for a Sanskrit writer. We see Utpala in a variety of modes in the hymns: anguished and self-doubting, full of sweet longing, exultant with the ecstatic experience of the Divine, confused as to how to recapture it, and blissfully awakened to the presence of his Lord in himself and all the situations of his everyday life. Let us quote a few verses here to capture something of the flavor of the work, verses that beautifully express the Tantra's unique vision of spirituality in the world:

Śiva-stotrāvalī:
Garland of Hymns to Śiva

> *O Lord, May I aspire to liberation by worshipping You, without withdrawing from experience and the world, and without even seeking dominion or power, but becoming intoxicated with the abundant liquor of devotion. || 15.4 ||*
>
> *Dwelling in the midst of the sea of supreme nectar, with my heart-mind immersed solely in the worship of You, may I attend to all the common occupations of man, savoring the ineffable in every thing. || 18.13 ||*
>
> *Making Yourself radiantly manifest, You make all things unfold; contemplating Your own form, You contemplate the universe. As You whirl in intoxication with the juice of the aesthetic rapture of Your own nature, the entire circle of existent things dances and radiates forth into manifestation. || 13.15 ||*

Utpala's disciple was Lakṣmaṇa Gupta, whose writings, if any, have not survived. The latter's disciple was the great Abhinava Gupta, the most prolific author of the lineage. We will return to him in detail, for he was the inheritor of several lineages; here we will just note that he highlighted the importance of Utpala's *Stanzas on Recognition* by writing not one but two major commentaries on that work. His second and longer commentary, running to several volumes in the original Sanskrit, was probably his last work (completed, he tells us, on a dark December night in the year 1015). It is a masterwork, and the only book of his that can rival his *Tantrāloka.*

Abhinava Gupta's disciple Kṣemarāja was nearly as prolific as his teacher, writing commentaries from a nondual perspective on the major Śaiva scriptures of the time as well as a number of independent works. While not quite as brilliant or charismatic as his teacher, Kṣemarāja did great service to the Pratyabhijñā lineage by writing a short work—twenty *sūtras* plus his own commentary—that clearly and beautifully summarized the Recognition teachings, as he put it, for readers who are spiritually inclined but not trained in the rigorous discipline of logical philosophy. This work is the *Pratyabhijñā-hṛdayam* or *The Heart of the Doctrine of Recognition.* It accomplished its goal admirably, for this text continued to be taught by Kashmīrī Śaiva masters nearly down to the present day.[124] Here are just a few *sūtras* to get a taste of the teachings of this sublime work:

Awareness, free and independent, is the cause of the performance of everything. || 1 ||

She unfolds the universe through Her own will and on Her own canvas. || 2 ||

It becomes diverse by its division into mutually adapted subjects and objects. || 3 ||

Pratyabhijñā-hṛdayam: The Heart of the Doctrine of Recognition

The individual conscious being, as a condensation of universal Awareness, embodies the entire universe in a microcosmic form. || 4 ||

Abhinava Gupta: Polymath, Scholar, Aesthete, Poet, and Mahāsiddha

When studying the writings of the nondual Śaiva Tāntrikas of Kashmīr, there is one figure who appears as the lynchpin of this branch of the tradition, the convergence point of much that had come before and the source of much that was to come after: the unparalleled master Abhinava Gupta (c. 975–1025 CE). Abhinava's parents were advanced Tantrik practitioners who conceived him in Kaula ritual. He was thus said to be *yoginī-bhū,* "born of a yoginī," and thereby possessing a special capacity for liberation. Abhinava alludes to his parentage and conception in his signature verse, found at the beginning of five of his major works. This verse has *double entendre,* a double meaning, for its primary meaning is praise of God and Goddess (Śiva and Śakti) and celebration of the pulsing energy of their unified nature that is the source and ground of the universe and the very Heart of all beings; the secondary meaning is the autobiographical one, alluding to Abhinava's own parents and their conception of him.

Tantrāloka:
Light on the Tantras

vimala-kalāśrayābhinava-sṛṣṭi-mahā jananī
bharita-tanuś ca pañca-mukha-gupta-rucir janakaḥ |
tad-ubhaya-yāmala-sphurita-bhāva-visarga-mayaṃ
hṛdayam anuttarāmṛta-kulaṃ mama saṃsphuratāt || 1 ||

Meaning 1: *The Mother is She who is the ground of pure power, radiant with ever-new genesis. The Father is He who is filled [with all the śaktis], maintaining His Light through His five faces. May my Heart, one with the diverse creation flowing forth from the fusion of these two, embodying the nectar of the Absolute, shine forth!*

Meaning 2: *My mother Vimalā is she for whom the birth of Abhinava was a festival of joy; my father is renowned as Siṃhagupta, full [of the state of Śiva]. May my heart, formed from the emissions of the ecstatic state of their union, embodying the nectar of the Absolute, shine forth!*

This extraordinary verse is analyzed at length in Sanderson's brilliant article "Commentary on the Opening Verses of the Tantrasāra of Abhinavagupta," probably his finest article on Abhinavaguptan theology. I will therefore make just a few observations here. The verse serves as a kind of nexus point for the whole of Abhinava's teaching as well as his personal history, and in this, it perfectly expresses an idea that is central to his theology: that the Divine is the transcendent source of all things and, simultaneously, completely immanent *as* all things—most especially as self-aware embodied beings. These two modes interpenetrate in balanced dynamism, eternally unified yet arising fresh in every moment of experience. Thus every procreative sexual act of two humans in dynamic balance recapitulates the divine act of the creation (and eternally arising re-creation) of the universe. The difference in the case of Abhinava's parents is that they were fully aware of this truth and fully embodying it at the moment of his conception (or so he tells us). Thus the two different meanings of the verse are actually expressing one truth in expanded and contracted modes that are reflexes of each other. This alludes to the Spanda and Pratyabhijñā doctrines.

The other central and key teachings that are embedded in the verse are these five:

- All that exists expresses the nature of the Goddess, who is the stainless ground of absolute Power from which all specific forms of power and energy emanate and into which they return.

- All things and states are aspects of the one Light of Consciousness that continually arises in a dynamic play which expresses the creative intuition of that Light in its self-aware mode.
- God is that which gives unity and cohesion to all the diverse powers (śaktis), providing structure for the free-flowing dynamism of the Goddess.
- The ultimate Deity, the ultimate Reality, is the fusion of these two as the paradoxical two-in-one (yāmala), the reality known as the Heart (hṛdaya) or the Essence (*sara*), for all creation flows forth from it.
- This Heart, when penetrating and pervading every level of our embodiment, is experienced as unsurpassed nectar-sweet joy and eternal life.

Thus we see that Abhinava Gupta has managed to impregnate much of what he will teach in many thousands of verses of writing into this one verse, which thereby serves as a seed to the five major works that it begins. That he has done so while simultaneously honoring the specific circumstances of his own embodiment, bowing to the *siddha* and *yoginī* who conceived him, makes this verse one of the most extraordinary literary achievements of the tradition.

The death of Abhinava's mother, Vimalā, at a relatively young age may have contributed to his passion for spirituality. He learned Sanskrit from his father, Narasiṃha Gupta (commonly known as Cukhulaka), and received initiation into the Krama lineage at an early age from his father's Krama Guru, Bhūtirāja, who had been a direct disciple of the famous Cakrabhānu. In his early twenties, Abhinava wrote his first work, a hymn to the goddess powers of the Krama, which is now unfortunately lost. Then he wrote a commentary on the *Bhagavad-Gītā,* which we do have, a work that shows the

See page 255

young Abhinava as learned but still callow, his words lacking the power, precision, and mature wisdom of his later works. In this commentary, he alludes to his knowledge of esoteric Krama teachings but does not reveal them; so those readers looking to this commentary for a Tantrik interpretation of the *Gītā* will mostly be disappointed.

In time, Abhinava studied with many gurus—around seventeen in total—and received direct transmission in the Trika, Pratyabhijñā, Krama, and Saiddhāntika lineages, lacking only a direct transmission of the Spanda, the works of which he nevertheless studied carefully. He described himself as a bee, going from flower to flower, collecting the nectar of each of these branches of the tradition in order to make them all into the sweetest honey. But it was not until he met his true master (*sadguru*) that he had an experiential realization of all that he had studied. This meeting was like that of Rumi and Shams in the Sufi tradition, for Abhinava was already an expert scholar of the scriptures and not lacking in spiritual experience. Yet something was missing: the final descent of grace (*śaktipāta*), triggering the complete and permanent expansion into all-encompassing blissful nondual awareness, expressed and grounded in embodiment. It was said in the Kaula tradition that this state could only be granted by a guru who had attained it fully. This guru, for Abhinava, was a man named Śambhu Nātha. He came to Kashmīr from the great *śakti-pīṭha* or holy place of Jālandhara, in the Puñjab. Śambhu was a master of both forms of the Trika (Kaula and non-Kaula), having been taught by a guru from Mahārāṣṭra, the probable birthplace of the Trika lineage. It was to this master that Abhinava attributed his Self-realization, and thus he praised him before all his other teachers. For example, introducing both his two major works on Tantrik philosophy and practice (*Tantrāloka* 1.21 and *Tantrasāra* 1.3), he invites the reader to study the text by saying:

Tantrāloka

As an act of divine worship, may all contemplate the lotus of the heart of Abhinava Gupta, < its blossom opened by the light falling from the rays of the sun, || that is to say its contraction forever banished by the wisdom descending from the feet of the illuminator, > [my master] Śambhu Nātha.

There is a kind of *double entendre* in this verse, too, though here it is not two separate meanings conveyed but rather a single meaning conveyed through the rules of metaphor. Thus I have translated one phrase twice, the metaphor and what he means by it, separated by the symbol ||.

Having come fully into his attainment, Abhinava then wrote his mature works. All of these are written from the perspective of the Trika, which was his primary reference point due to the influence of his *sadguru* Śambhu Nātha. However, Abhinava maintained his commitment to the teachings of the Krama, incorporating these as the esoteric core of his theology. His primary works include his *Commentary on the Mālinīvijaya,* notable for its mystical explanation of the origin and nature of the Śaiva Tantrik canon; his commentary called *Unfolding the Thirty Verses of Parā* (*Parātriṃśika-vivaraṇa*);[125] and most notable of all, his magnum opus, to which the next section is dedicated.

See page 181

Light on the Tantras

The *Tantrāloka* is a monumental explication of Tantrik practice and philosophy in over 5,800 verses. It is encyclopedic in its scope though not organized like an encyclopedia, for instead of just enumerating theories and practices, it brings them all into a coherent framework in which everything has its place and everything makes sense in relation to the whole. It is, then, an awesome work of synthesis, which presents to the reader a vision of Śaiva Tantra as a unified system: far-reaching in its scope, powerful in its cohesion, and complex yet clear in its interrelations. To accomplish this synthesis, of course, he has to explain apparent contradictions amongst the scriptures, which were originally addressed to differing audiences in varying periods. He does so by creating a hierarchy of understanding. For example, he explains that dualism is a valid view of reality at one level of understanding and development and that, therefore, God compassionately revealed the dualistic scriptures for those who could not yet comprehend or relate to nondualism. Nondualism, then, is both a higher understanding and a higher experience that one can progress to. Beyond it there an even higher teaching: *paramādvaya,* or "supreme nondualism," which we discussed in part 1. This is the view that simultaneously encompasses and subsumes both dualism and nondualism, the view that goes completely beyond the notion of "levels of understanding." It is the inexpressible experience of the totality of reality in which no perspective is excluded, for each is seen as fitting into the pattern of a greater whole. However, it is very clear that in Abhinava's viewpoint, one must carefully ascend through ever more refined levels of understanding in order to reach that all-inclusive state of no-levels. One cannot attempt to leap straight to that realm, lest all understanding decay into incoherent relativism.

See pages 148 & 185

Abhinava lived in the cosmopolitan capital city of Śrīnagar. When his disciples and friends entreated him to write *Tantrāloka,* he agreed and decided to move out of the capital to a quieter village in the valley, a village where all the inhabitants were faithful devotees of Shaivism. In this unnamed location, in a house provided by a former government minister who had retired to devote himself to religion, Abhinava composed his great work. Because of its profound significance to the tradition and widespread curiosity about it, we will outline some of its contents here briefly.

Contents of the Tantrāloka

Chapter 1 sets out the fundamentals: the nature of bondage and liberation, the role of insight, and the four means to liberation (which we will later discuss at length). A translation of this chapter is available on my blog, tantrikstudies.org.

Chapter 2 explains the first of the four means, that of *anupāya* or sudden realization based on a single teaching-transmission from a realized master.

Chapter 3 covers the second means, the method of nondiscursive, direct intuition called *śāmbhava-upāya* or "the Divine Means," together with a lengthy meditation on the metaphysical basis of the Sanskrit alphabet.

See page 350

Chapter 4 is on liberation through knowledge, i.e., cultivating thought-patterns in alignment with the nature of reality; this is the third means, which is called *śākta-upāya* or "the Empowered Means." The chapter also includes an excursus on the gradations of guru-hood.

See page 357

Chapter 5 expounds the methods of meditation, visualization, and breath practice collectively called *āṇava-upāya* or "the Embodied Means," which is the fourth and final means to liberation.

See page 383

Almost everything in the text after chapter 5 can be understood as a continuation of the explanation of the "Embodied Means," for methods emphasizing the use of the body, mind, and subtle body constitute the great majority of all spiritual practices. This large corpus of techniques can be roughly divided into two basic interrelated categories: yoga and *kriyā* (ritual). Chapters 6 and 7 cover the yoga of time:

- Chapter 6 explains how the cycles of time correlate to the flow of the vital energy or Prana in the body, how to meditate on those cycles, and how to transcend time altogether.
- Chapter 7 shows how the sequences of various mantras are to be mastered by contemplative repetition within the cyclical flow of the breath.

Chapters 8 through 11 address the dimensions of space, all of which have both cosmic and microcosmic aspects (the latter being within the subtle body of the practitioner).

- In chapter 8 the hierarchy of "worlds" or dimensions of existence (*bhuvanas*) are detailed.
- Chapter 9 treats the hierarchy of the *tattvas* or 36 Principles of Reality, along with an excursus on causality. See page 124
- In chapter 10 the seven layers of consciousness or types of conscious beings are discussed, along with an excursus on objectivity.
- In chapter 11 we learn about the five cosmic divisions/ primordial creative powers (*kalā*), which are also the five constituents of the subtle body.

Chapter 12 culminates and summarizes these discussions by treating the six distinct paths to liberation (the *sad-adhvans*), three of which he has already treated in detail (*kalā*, *tattva*, and *bhuvana*). See page 164

Chapter 13 discusses the Descent of Power (*śaktipāta*) or grace by which embodied Consciousness liberates itself, either directly or (more commonly) through initiation. Portions of the chapter are translated in my doctoral dissertation. See pages 152 & 321

Chapter 14 covers the opposite force, the power of occlusion by which Consciousness binds itself.

So these last two chapters cover the fourth and fifth of the five acts that we discussed in part 1 of this book.

Chapters 15 through 33 cover ritual and its various elements.

- Chapter 15: the longest, covers the nondualist understanding of ritual, the basic type of ritual initiation, and the rules of discipline for initiates[138] See page 409
- Chapters 16 and 17: The full form of liberating initiation (*nirvāṇa-dīkṣā*) See page 332
- Chapter 18: Abbreviated initiation
- Chapter 19: Initiation for those close to death

- Chapter 20: The ritual called scales initiation
- Chapter 21: Initiation for those who have just left the body
- Chapter 22: Initiation after conversion from another faith
- Chapter 23: Ritual consecration of gurus
- Chapter 24: Cremation rites
- Chapter 25: The ritual of making offerings to the ancestors
- Chapter 26: The daily Tantrik ritual of worship
- Chapter 27: Consecration of substrates of personal worship (statues, etc.)
- Chapter 28: Miscellaneous rites, including worship of Yoginīs (in human form), rites preceding the teaching of scripture, and worship of the person of the guru, plus an excursus on the nature of death and the pathways of the soul after death
- Chapter 29: Rites of the Kaula Trika, including Kaula initiation and the Kaula sexual ritual (ādi-yāga or "primal worship")

See page 427

- Chapter 30: Mantras
- Chapter 31: Maṇḍalas
- Chapter 32: Mudrās or "seals," configurations of body, prāṇa, and awareness to achieve particular states
- Chapter 33: Ancillary deities of the Trika
- Chapter 34: The relationship among the three means to liberation described in chapters 1–5
- Chapter 35: The canon of scripture and hierarchy of revelation
- Chapter 36: The transmission of the key Trika scriptures, The Doctrine of the Perfected Yoginīs (Siddha-yogeśvarī-mata) and The Latter Triumph of the Alphabet Goddess (Mālinī-vijaya-uttara)
- Chapter 37: Why the study of Tantrāloka is valuable; and an account of Abhinava's family line, his gurus and spiritual history (in brief), and acknowledgment of his close disciples

This table of contents shows us that by Abhinava's time, the Tantra had extended its reach into the domain of exoteric religion. Yet ever faithful to his esoteric goals, Abhinava works to prevent the decay into routine and mindless adherence to rule that such involvement usually implies. He teaches that the mantras, meditations, and rituals of the Tantra are living embodiments of the Divine, and that they have no real use if separated from the energy that is full and complete Awareness. Once they have lost their power through the practitioner's lack of understanding, faith, or awareness, they become like dead bodies that can only be brought back to life through contact with an awakened master for whom they are still vibrating with life-energy, imbued with *śakti.* Thus Abhinava allows the Tantra to encompass the domain of religion as well as spirituality, but ever labors to infuse the potency of the esoteric realm of the latter into the exoteric realm of the former. This, after all, is the real goal of the Tantra: to experience the Divine not just in rarefied "spiritual" environments but in every aspect of mundane life.

The mantras, meditations, and rituals of the Tantra are living embodiments of the Divine.

The *Tantrāloka* is such a significant work that Abhinava chose to rewrite it twice, for the benefit of those who were less highly educated in the complexities of Indian philosophy. The first rewrite was *Essence of the Tantras (Tantrasāra),* a work mostly in prose with key summary verses at the end of each chapter. The main purpose of the *Tantrasāra* is to summarize the *Tantrāloka,* but the ever-fresh Abhinava also adds some new material. I would argue that the *Tantrasāra* is a more important work for those with a practical interest in the Tantra, for by mostly leaving aside the discourse of intellectual/logical debate that we see in the *Tantrāloka,* Abhinava was able to write in a more tightly focused and powerful manner, with every phrase resonating with Truth. The tone of the work is precisely what one would expect if, having discovered that the *Tantrāloka* was too difficult for most people, Abhinava thought to himself, "Okay, let's get serious and get down to the real essence (*sāra*) of what really matters." The result feels more like a transmission than a dissertation.*

*The first third of the *Tantrasāra* will be published in my own translation in the near future.

Following the *Tantrasāra,* Abhinava composed the shortest recension of this material by taking just the summary verses of the *Tantrasāra* and giving a short commentary on each. This work is called the *Tantroccaya.* None of these works is available yet in English, but the first five chapters of the *Tantrāloka* are published in French and the whole work in Italian, albeit in a flawed translation. The first chapter of *Tantrāloka*, we are told, is about to be released in English by Mark Dyczkowski.

Abhinava's final major works of Tantrik philosophy were his commentaries on Utpala Deva's *Stanzas on the Recognition of the Divine* mentioned earlier. Abhinava also composed a number of exquisite devotional-cum-philosophical poems, such as the *Hymn to Bhairava* and *Fifteen Verses on Awakening.* Finally, we should note that Abhinava was quite a renowned philosopher of aesthetic philosophy, writing a number of works on what makes art beautiful and affecting, works that were (for the most part) separate from his spiritual writings. He specialized in the study of poetry, and his most important work in that area was his commentary on *Light on the Theory of Suggestion (Dhvanyāloka),* an earlier work of profound significance in the study of aesthetics. In Abhinava's erudite and thoughtful commentary, he analyzes the nature of aesthetic experience in terms of how it comes about, what it signifies, and what are its various dimensions. His exposition of the nine *rasas* or "flavors of aesthetic experience" has become quite famous. Indeed, his work in this area is better known amongst academic Sanskritists than is his spiritual material.

See page 289

One of my teachers, the masterful scholar Somadeva Vasudeva, explained *rasa* theory perfectly when he wrote,

Rasa is the experience one has viewing artwork; it refers to the experience itself. Therefore what we call rasa is not located in the work but in the viewer. Rasa does not refer to the everyday, worldly emotions of love, sorrow, humor etc., but to their transformation into aesthetic sentiment. The transformation of worldly emotion into aesthetic sentiment occurs when we become keenly aware of the worldly emotion in our own hearts. This very act of awareness, in which we witness the arising of one basic emotion (love, sorrow, laughter, etc.), entails its transformation into aesthetic sentiment. This act of awareness and synchronous transformation is rasa.

Somadeva Vasudeva

This is, of course, a technical use of the word *rasa*. In common, everyday usage it simply means "juice" or "flavor."

This is thought to be an experience that (people who are not spiritual practitioners) can obtain only through experiencing art, because it is only with art that we allow ourselves to become detached enough to become witnesses to our emotional states, savoring them without getting caught up in them.

The nine *rasas* are: the erotic (*śṛṅgāra*), the comic (*hāsya*), the wrathful (*raudra*), the compassionate (*kāruṇya*), the disgusting (*bībhatsa*), the terrifying (*bhayānaka*), the heroic or inspiring (*vīrya*), the astonishing (*adbhuta*), and the peaceful (*śānta*). What is so interesting about this list is that all of these are experiences brought about by art, and therefore they are all to be understood as experiences of beauty. We can easily find examples of all of these in (say) contemporary film, though whether any given example constitutes "art" is open to debate; and in the context of *rasa* theory, that debate would center on whether the film was successful in transforming emotion into beauty, into real aesthetic sentiment.

The nine *rasas* are 'flavors' of aesthetic experience.

In *rasa* theory we can find spiritual principles: The first is that the function of art is to center us in ourselves, savoring the vibration of awareness flavored by the particular *rasa* that the art has evoked. The second is the fact that art allows for the transformation of unpleasant emotions into the experience of beauty, for example lust is transformed into the erotic *rasa,* sadness into the compassionate *rasa,* anger into the wrathful *rasa,* and world-weariness into the peaceful *rasa.*

The influence of Abhinava Gupta, while not widespread, went deep. The Kaula Trika/Krama synthesis he presented was compelling enough to have been adopted by a number of other lineages. Not only that, other Śaiva schools, like that of the Śrī-vidyā, formulated their thought along the lines of Abhinava and his disciples. This influence was felt even in other religions: the Tantrik Vaiṣṇava scripture called the *Lakṣmī Tantra* clearly borrowed ideas from *The Heart of the Teachings of Recognition* by Abhinava's disciple Kṣemarāja.

See page 181

The teachings of Abhinava's lineage continued to be transmitted for centuries in two primary locations: in their native Kashmīr (where the lineages preserving these teachings became increasingly diminished after Muslim conquest in 1300), and in the far south of the subcontinent, another place that was a spiritual heartland for many centuries. It seems that a native of Madurai, an ancient city of the Tamiḷ country, came 2,000 miles to receive initiation from Abhinava. This man, named Madhurāja, wrote a beautiful description of Abhinava as part of a set of verses he composed for meditation on his guru. The stylized nature of this "pen-portrait" has led scholars to question whether or not Madhurāja really met Abhinava; but I would argue that following standard literary forms in his paean to Abhinava hardly disproves that an actual meeting took place. And we do know for certain that Abhinava's teachings were known in the Tamiḷ region shortly after his passing. Madhurāja's description of Abhinava follows, in Paul Muller-Ortega's translation:

Gurunātha-parāmarśa of Madhurāja

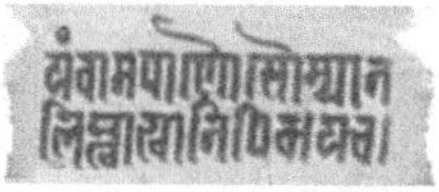

Out of his deep compassion, [Śiva] has taken a new bodily form as Abhinava Gupta and come to Kashmīr. He sits in the middle of a garden of grapes, inside a pavilion [adorned with] crystal and filled with beautiful paintings [of nature]. The room smells wonderful because of flower garlands, incense sticks, and oil lamps. It is constantly resounding with musical instruments, with songs, and with dancing. There are crowds of yogīs and yoginīs, realized beings, and siddhas. . . . In the center of the room there is a golden seat from which pearls are hanging. It has a soft awning stretched over it as a canopy. Here sits Abhinava Gupta attended by all his numerous students, with Kṣemarāja at their head, who are writing down everything he says. . . . Abhinava Gupta's [half-closed] eyes are trembling in ecstasy. In the middle of his forehead is a conspicuous tilaka made of sacred ashes. He has a rudrākṣa bead hanging from his ear. His long hair is held by a garland of flowers. He has a long beard and reddish-brown skin. His neck is dark and glistening with musk and sandalwood paste. Two dūtīs or consorts stand at his side holding refreshments [wine etc.]. . . . He wears a silken cloth as a dhoti, white as moonbeams, andhesits in the yogic posture known as vīrāsana. One hand is held on his knee holding a japa-mālā and his fingers make the mudrā that signifies his knowledge of the highest Śiva. He plays on a resonating lute [ektār] with the tips of his quivering fingers of his lotus-like left hand.

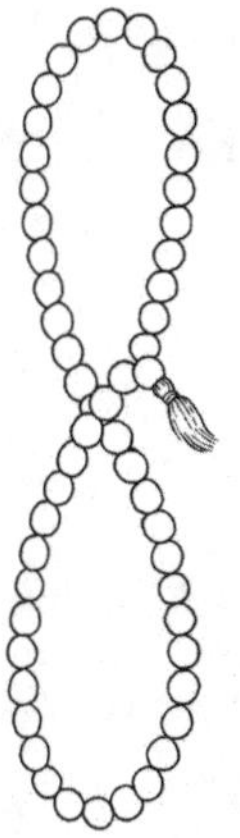

Again, we can't be sure whether Madhurāja actually met Abhinava, but even if it is not a factual historical description, this pen-portrait tells us how near-contemporaries of Abhinava thought about him. What we notice most of all about it is its strong emphasis on refined sensual beauty, as befits a description of a Tantrik master.

THE KAULA LINEAGES

To close our history of the classical Tantrik tradition, I will offer the briefest of glimpses into the formation of the Kaula lineage. Earlier I referred to the whole left side of Śaiva Tantra, the nondual Goddess-worshipping side, as "Kaula." But within that general rubric, there was also a specific lineage grouping called "Kula" or "Kaula," the lineage that was the original source of the more general term. It is headed by the semi-historical, semi-legendary figure of Macchanda Nātha (a.k.a. Matsyendra), "Lord Fisherman," who possibly live in the 8th century. Macchanda is one of the most highly revered masters of the Tantra, considered a *mahāsiddha* in both Śaiva and Buddhist camps and has even been made into a deity in Nepāl's Kāthmāndu valley, which still celebrates an annual festival in his honor, though they have long since forgotten his teachings. In the original sources, he is revered as the *avatār* or revealer of the Truth in the fourth and current age.* He was from Kāmarūpa (modern Assam) in the far east, but must have traveled widely, for we know that his partner and consort was named Konkanāmbā, "the Mother from Konkan," a place on the western coast, in the region of Goa, in southern Maharashtra. (See the map on page 212.) Unfortunately, her name is not as well-remembered as her partner's, even though the two were originally praised as a pair of awakened masters. Unsurprisingly, they worshipped Śiva and Śakti as a conjugal pair, under the names Kuleśvara and Kuleśvarī (Lord and Lady of the Family). Later practitioners influenced by Kaulism often used these names for whatever specific forms of Śiva and Śakti they worshipped.

* I.e., the *kali-yuga*, the "age of discord." The term has no relation to the Goddess Kālī.

Macchanda and Konkanāmbā are said to have had twelve sons. Six became celibate ascetics, and six became married householders. It was the latter six whom Macchanda and Konkanāmbā initiated, transmitting to them their wisdom-teachings, which they withheld from their celibate sons. Interestingly, the names of these six sons are not Sanskrit, but rather are associated with tribes beyond the pale of normal Indian society, thus possibly alluding to the early shamanic origins of the Kaula teachings. These six sons became (together with their consorts) the heads of six lineages, called *ovallis*. The lineages developed into specific clans, which maintained networks of lodges near sacred sites around the subcontinent and had special hand-signals so members could recognize each other. The names of these six Kaula clans were Ānanda, Bodhi, Āvali, Prabhu, Pāda, and Yogī, and their members, accordingly, had names ending in one of the six clan-names.

This Kaula lineage group originated by Macchanda and Konkanāmbā was not included amongst the nine main schools we discussed earlier because it was not a separate school in the same sense, with its own sectarian doctrines and specific cult of worship. It was rather a particular way of practicing the Tantra (i.e., with greater emphasis on the sensual and embodied aspects), and its real significance lay in the profound influence it exerted on some of the left-current schools, so that in time two variants of some sects were acknowledged, for example the regular Trika and the Kaula Trika. One group, the Krama, only had a Kaula form, arising as it did under strong Kaula influence. This influence served to counter the transcendentalist emphasis seen in other parts of the tradition, for what characterized the Kaula above all was its emphasis on the primacy of the body and on the immanent aspect of the Divine. A totally practice-based lineage, it taught the use of sensual experience as a springboard into divine Presence. Therefore it is solely within the Kaula-influenced lineages that sexual rites were practiced and that transgressive substances were both offered to God and consumed by the offerer (as is considered necessary in a nondual view that "walks the talk"). The only source we have for the details of Tantrik sexual ritual (*kula-yāga*), chapter 29 of Abhinava's *Tantrāloka*, presents the rite in the context of

See page 428

Kaula initiation. One the primary purposes of the rite as described there is to produce the sacramental substances to be used in that type of initiation, which may further imply that in Abhinava's view the *kula-yāga* ought only to be practiced by qualified gurus.

POST-CLASSICAL TANTRA AND THE ADVENT OF HAṬHA-YOGA

In these final parts of the history section, I will give a brief overview of the history of the tradition's ramifications in the centuries after its classical period (800–1200 CE). After the dissolution of the institutional base for Śaiva Tantra with the coming of Islam, it was the Kaula-influenced lineages, with their grassroots noninstitutionalized structure, that survived best after the Muslim conquests. At the same time, the word "Kaula" increased in ambiguity as it became a kind of free-floating signifier associated with a wide variety of transgressive and bodily practices that proliferated in this post-classical period of late Tantrism (roughly 1300 onward). One of the results of the loss of the institutional base for the Tantra (both Śaiva and Buddhist) in this period, and the evaporation of huge amounts of funding that base formerly attracted, is that the householder tradition which had been dominant in the classical period began to contract and disappear, slowly making the wandering renunciate ascetic Tantrik yogīs the main holders of the tradition. This was problematic in that, though these yogīs were supported by the general public (with food and sometimes shelter), they were also feared and regarded with suspicion, since so many of them were known to pursue supernatural powers. It was also a problem because these often illiterate or partially literate wandering *sādhus* did not systematically document their yogic discoveries. Furthermore, some of these Tantrik yogīs made a living by performing magical rituals on behalf of clients who wanted wealth, or sex, or to hurt an enemy.

This, then, was the beginning of the process by which the Tantra acquired a bad name during the late medieval and early modern period. In my opinion, the substantial decline in the number of female practitioners during this shift from a householder base to a wandering ascetic base partially accounts for the loss of balance that allowed seeking of worldly power to come back to the forefront of the tradition, as it had been more than five hundred years previously.[126] Of course, there were still many practitioners pursuing liberation in a sober and dedicated manner, but these households were not the visible face of the tradition anymore, so the more prominent power-seeking ascetics were the ones who gave the tradition a bad name over time.

We will briefly chart the development (some would say decline) of the Tantra into what, in the post-classical period, came to be called *haṭha-yoga*. Much more research is called for into this subject, but very recent work done by European scholars has shed some much-needed light. In the 12th to 13th centuries, the South Indian Śāmbhavānanda lineage of Śaiva Tantra (see *sampradāyas* #8 and 9) featured a yogic practice centered on the ascent of *kuṇḍalinī* energy through six subtle centers called *cakras*. This is precisely the system we find in some later *haṭha-yoga* texts. The bridge text between this Śāmbhavānanda lineage of Śaiva Tantra and the later *haṭha-yoga* is *Matsyendra's Compendium* recently translated by European scholar Csaba Kiss. It tells the story of Matsyendra and his chief disciple, the man credited with founding the practice tradition of haṭha-yoga.

According to the account in *Matsyendra's Compendium* in the 13th century a man from the royal family of the Chola kingdom (present-day Tamiḷ Nāḍu) who would later be called Gorakṣa Nātha met a master named Matsyendra (clearly named after the founder of Kaulism from five centuries earlier). This meeting so impressed Gorakṣa that he wandered India for two years looking for Matsyendra, finally finding him in the Western country, the Konkan. Matsyendra was cavorting with wine and women, and when Gorakṣa humbly

See page 275

Goraksha is now considered by many to be the founder of the haṭha-yoga system.

approached him with no indication of a judgment of such conduct, he passed the test and received initiation from the master.

Gorakṣa is now considered by many to be the founder of the *haṭha-yoga* system, and though he did not use that exact term in the works attributed to him, there is probably some truth to this. It seems that Gorakṣa travelled widely, teaching practices such as bodily purification; postures called *bandhas*, *karaṇas*, *āsanas*, and *mudrās*; subtle body visualizations; and meditations—all designed to awaken the inner meditation energy called *kuṇḍalinī*, leading to a state of union with the Divine. He is the probable author of some of the earliest texts associated with *haṭha-yoga,* such as *The Sun of Discernment (Viveka-mārtaṇḍa)* and *The Hundred Verses of Gorakṣa.* These texts, along with the *Attainment of Nectar* by Virūpākṣa Nātha,[127] would be adopted by a lineage group that became known as the Nāth Yogīs, who looked back to Gorakṣa Nātha (a.k.a. Gorakh Nāth) as their founder and Matsyendra Nātha (a.k.a. Macchendra Nāth) as their patron saint.

The most important text of the Nath Yogi lineage group is the 15th-century Hatha Yoga-Pradipika.

The Nāths were quasi-Tantrik ascetic yogīs who propagated non-brāhminical practices enshrined in texts with a nondual view but lacking a substantial philosophical component. They venerated nine *nāthas* or masters, beginning with Matsyendra and Gorakṣa Nātha. The most important text (probably) produced by the Nāth Yogī lineage group is the 15th-century *Haṭha-[yoga]-pradīpikā.* This text, the first *haṭha-yoga* text to include a wide range of postures that it called *āsanas*, was hugely important for it became the most-cited text on *haṭha-yoga* after the 15th century. The *Haṭha-pradīpikā* is not original but rather a compilation of earlier works, citing more than twenty of the scriptures that came before it. Curiously, after the production of this text and around 1500, the Nāth Yogīs stopped practicing yoga, but their practices were preserved by other lineages, notably the Rāmānandīs Dasnāmī Sannyāsins, who are still active today as the most high-profile yogic lineage group of modern India.[128] For more information about the development of early *haṭha-yoga*, please see the work of James Mallinson, who might not agree exactly with some of the things I've said here, and I defer to his extensive knowledge in this area.

But before we come to modern yoga, let's clarify a little more the relationship between *haṭha-yoga*, the forerunner of modern yoga, and Śaiva Tantra. Compared to the latter, the *haṭha-yoga* texts have a marked lack of View teachings ("philosophy"), probably due to the loss of the patronage that made such profound learning possible in the period of classical Tantra. They also jettison the complex mantra system that largely defined classical Tantrik practice. Yet many of the practices found in the *haṭha-yoga* texts are simplified from those of classical Tantra. Thus these texts can be seen as an attempt to capture the most essential Tantrik practices, especially those of the subtle body, in the face of the dissolution of the classical tradition. This explains why the language of these texts is relatively simple: they wanted to be understood by people who could not undertake the years of education required by the classical Tantrik systems.

EVIDENCE OF THE TANTRIK ROOTS OF HAṬHA-YOGA

Since there is a widespread misunderstanding today that *haṭha-yoga* derives from or relates to the yoga of Patañjali, it will be useful to briefly present some evidence from the primary *haṭha-yoga* sources that demonstrate that they were (and saw themselves as) inheritors of the Tantrik tradition. Yoga scholar Christopher Tompkins has done a study in which he documents dozens of passages in *The Hundred Verses of Gorakṣa* and other texts that are drawn from a much earlier scriptures of Tantrik Yoga (specifically, various recensions of the influential text The Kalotra, *Transcendence of Time*).[129] Material currently thought by some scholars (and the general public) to originate in *haṭha-yoga* that in fact comes from Tantrik yoga includes the following:

Teachings in the *haṭha-yoga* texts that are sourced directly from Tantrik scriptures

- the subtle body physiology of 72,000 channels (*nāḍīs*) with 10 primary channels, of which three are most important;
- the analogizing of those three primary channels to the three mystic radiances of sun, moon, and fire;
- explanation of the functions of the ten vital energies (*prāṇa-vāyus*);
- installation and activation of mantras in the subtle centers of the body;
- the mantra of the "recitation of the Self" (*haṃsa, so'ham*) occurring naturally 21,600 times per day;
- the opening of the heart center analogized to a blossoming lotus;
- ascension of the soul through the central channel (*suṣumnā nāḍī*) by means of *prāṇāyāma*, *dhāraṇā*, and *dhyāna*;
- description of the primal Goddess who effects this process as the "coiled power" (*kuṇḍalinī*); and
- the fructification of *yoga-sādhanā* known as the experience of "nectar pervasion."

All of these concepts that appear in the Guraksha and other *haṭha-yoga* sources appear to be taken directly from *The Transcendence of Time* or from an intermediate source that faithfully transmitted them. This, according to Tompkins' work and, I think, the work of other scholars points in the same direction. As we have seen, the Kubjikā tantras are clearly another source that the *haṭha-yoga* tradition used.

To put it as plainly as possible, then, there is no direct connection between Patañjali's pre-Tantrik yoga and the discipline of *haṭha-yoga*, whose respective periods of ascendency are separated by many centuries. In fact, many of the texts of the *haṭha-yoga* tradition explicitly see themselves as inheriting practices from the Tantrik tradition. The Tantra itself had absorbed Patañjali's practice teachings early on (while rejecting his philosophical dualism). Though quotes from the *Yoga-sūtra* are very rare in Tantrik literature, none of the techniques the *Yoga-sūtra* taught were forgotten by the Tantrik tradition. The part of the *Yoga-sūtra* that appears again and again in the middle ages in India is its formulation of the eight primary practices of yoga (*aṣṭānga-yoga*). All eight were absorbed by the Tantra and passed on to *haṭha-yoga*.[130]

In an early modern Sanskrit source called the *Haṃsa-vilāsa*, we see clearly that authorities of that time did not think of *aṣṭānga-yoga* ("the yoga of eight components") as something different from *haṭha-yoga*. In fact, they saw *haṭha-yoga* as a Tantrik amplification of *aṣṭānga-yoga*. We see this in the *Haṃsa-vilāsa*'s 18th-century presentation of a yoga of fifteen components in which nearly all the additional components (*aṅgas*) come from Tantrik sources.[131] And, indeed, the commentator in this particular system uses the terms *haṭha-yoga* and Patañjali yoga interchangeably, showing that, in his understanding at least, the authority of Patañjali did not survive as as separate stream from the Tantrik tradition. The bolded items on the list below constitute the *aṣṭānga-yoga* of Patañjali. Explanations of the practices given in brackets are particular to this early modern text, which understands many of these practices differently from Patañjali.

Haṭha-yoga is a Tantrik amplification of *aṣṭānga-yoga*.

1. **the five yamas** *[= those of Patañjali]*
2. **the five niyamas** *[= those of Patañjali]*
    2a. The ten niyamas of the *Haṭha-pradīpikā*
3. *tyāga,* renunciation [the nonattachment of mind and body to worldly things]
4. *mauna,* silence [speaking only the truth if one has to speak at all]
5. *deśa,* the place for practice
6. *kāla,* time [auspicious astrological moment]
7. *mūlabandha,* the root lock [presented in conjunction with āsana]

8. **āsana, posture**
9. **prāṇāyāma, breath control** [understood as purification of the *nāḍī-cakra*]
10. *deha-sāmya,* equanimity of the body
11. *dṛk-sthiti,* fixed gaze

    Additional aṅgas [optional]:
    - *ṣaṭkarma,* the six purifications
    - *aṣṭa-kumbhaka,* eight subtypes of breath retention
    - *nāḍī-śuddhi,* purification of bodily channels
    - *Kuṇḍalinī*
    - *Khecarī mudrā* [here = raising the energy to the third eye and dissolving it in meditation]
12. **pratyāhāra, sense-withdrawal**
13. **dhāraṇā, fixation** *of attention*
    - *13a.* dissolving the mind in the *turya-pada,* the state of the fourth
14. **dhyāna,** *visualization of Paramaśiva or the Self*
15. **samādhi, absorption**
    - *15a.* *nāda,* sonic experiences in *samādhi*
    - *15b.* *unmanī,* transmental state
    - *15c.* *mukti,* liberation

Nearly all of the terms in this list that are not found in Patañjali's text originate in Tantrik sources. Examining this evidence and that presented below forces us to the conclusion that to present the *Yoga-sūtra* separately from its adoption by Tantra is to engage in an artificial revivalism divorced from the organic history of the yoga tradition. Yet somehow, with more than a hundred English translations of the *Yoga-sūtra* published over the last century and a segment on the *Yoga-sūtra* required in nearly every modern yoga teacher training, the realization is still not widespread that the yoga that text describes bears little resemblance to our modern practice of the same name. For example, there are only two sentences on posture and another couple on breath in the entire *Yoga-sūtra*. (I should note, however, that the intrinsic value of the text is quite high for anyone intensively practicing and studying meditation.) This is the overlooked elephant in the room of modern yoga curricula.[132]

By contrast, when we turn to the primary sources of *haṭha-yoga* in Sanskrit, there we find many of the practices given in modern yoga. And as already noted, these very texts link themselves to the Tantrik tradition from which they draw many of their teachings. For example, the *Śiva-saṃhitā* (c. 1500 CE) calls itself a tantra and presents itself as a dialogue between Śiva and Śakti, the classical form for a Tantrik scripture. The *Gheraṇḍa-saṃhitā* (c. 1700 CE), while not claiming scriptural authority, presents itself as the teachings of a *haṭha*-yogī named Gheraṇḍa to his student Chaṇḍa Kāpāli, "the Fierce Skull-bearer," an explicitly Tantrik name. Furthermore, it describes its key teachings as secrets previously concealed in the Tantrik scriptures. For example, the practice of inversion (*viparīta-karaṇī*), commonly practiced in yoga today, is said in verse 3.30 to have been "concealed in all the Tantras." Indeed, this phrase is almost a cliché in these texts.

Haṭha yoga focuses on the rise of Kundalini Shakti.

One general organizing principle in the classic (i.e., most influential) haṭha-yoga texts is the concept of the rise of the innate Goddess Power, latent within all human beings, called *kuṇḍalinī-śakti*. This term, and the subtle body physiology that it implies, is quintessentially Tantrik. It is found described in the Tantrik scriptures under that and alternate names, such as *kula-kuṇḍalī* and *kaulikī-śakti*, terms that allude to the definition of *kuṇḍalinī* as the fundamental organizing intelligence of embodied Consciousness. We see a prototypical example of *haṭha-yoga*'s appropriation of these teachings in the *Gheraṇḍa-saṃhitā*, as translated by one of the finest current scholars of *haṭha-yoga*, Sir James Mallinson:

Gheraṇḍa-saṃhitā

> *Sitting in siddhāsana, having drawn in Prāṇa with repeated applications of kākī-mudrā, he should then join it with apāna and meditate on the six cakras in succession. Using the mantras* HUṂ *and* HAṂSA*, the wise yogī should bring the sleeping serpent Goddess to consciousness and raise her, together with the jīva [= soul], to the highest lotus. Having himself now become made of Śakti, he should visualize supreme union with Śiva, as well as various pleasures, enjoyments, and ultimate bliss. As a result of the union of Śiva and Śakti, he will experience the ultimate goal [while] on earth.*

I hardly need point out that this passage is entirely Tantrik in its language, tone, and tenor. However, having said all this, I should also mention that the scholar James Mallinson has shown that Śaiva Tantra is not the only source for the *haṭha-yoga* tradition. In fact, it's best understood as a combination of two originally separate streams of Indian spiritual practice. One, Tantrik, which we've been discussing, and two, the very ancient stream of practices of bodily discipline and self-mortification that date back to the very beginnings of documented Indian culture. These practices of intense self-mortification are still seem amongst Sadhus or renunciate yoga practitioners today and formed no part of the Tantrik tradition per se, so indeed those and the practices of seminal retention and some other practices came not from Tantra, but from this other, in fact earlier, stream of yogic practice.

Other elements of post-classical Tantrism

The *haṭha-yoga* tradition was not the only late medieval tradition to preserve some of the teachings of classical Tantra. In fact, there were many such, each preserving a different piece of the original whole. Tantrik ritual was practiced and studied in the South, especially in the form of the Śrīvidyā, which came in time to be incorporated into the practice of followers of the increasingly successful Vedānta philosophy. (Note that the *Śiva-saṃhitā* mentioned earlier shows both Śrīvidyā and Vedānta influence.) The Śrīvidyā's influence was so extensive that its practice was taken up even by the most orthodox representatives of the Vedānta, the Śaṅkarācāryas of the major South Indian monasteries at Śringeri and Kāncīpuram— figures equivalent to an archbishop or even a pope in Christianity. One of these wrote a famous text called the *Saundarya-laharī* (*Billows of Beauty*), which again combines Vedānta with Śrīvidyā, though the view and aesthetic of the latter is dominant.

Manuscript evidence attests to the post-classical study and practice of Tantra in Kerala, in Andhra Pradesh, in Orissa, and in Nepāl, where it especially flourished throughout the entire second millennium. There were Śaiva Tantrik āshrams in Rājasthān (where *haṭha-yoga* also flourished) almost up to the present day. We know that in the 19th century, for example, a king of Rājasthān was initiated into the Tantra; and it was there, some accounts attest, that Swāmī Satyānanda—probably the most knowledgeable 20th-century exponent of the practices of Śaiva Tantra—learned at least some of what he knew about the subject. This is important because a series of books published under Satyananda's name include a wealth of information on Tatrik practice.

Post-classical Tantra certainly flourished in Bengal, where goddess worship was especially strong. It was in this eastern region that the tradition of the *daśa-mahā-vidyās* or "Ten Mantra Goddesses" developed.

The Ten *Mahāvidyās*

- ❖ Kālī (The Dark Goddess)
- ❖ Tārā (She Who Saves)
- ❖ Tripurasundarī (Beautiful in the Three Worlds)
- ❖ Bhuvaneśvarī (She Whose Body Is the Earth)

- Chinnamastā (the Self-Decapitated Goddess)
- Bhairavī (the Intense Goddess)
- Dhūmāvatī (the Smoke-Colored Widow)
- Bagalamukhī (the Paralyzer of Demons)
- Mātangī (the Outcaste Goddess)
- Kamalā/Lakshmi (the Lotus Goddess)

All ten of these goddesses are found beautifully illustrated and described in the book *The Shakti Coloring Book*, by my friend Ekabhūmi Ellik. This is much more than a coloring book, but an incredible resource for the study of goddess imagery.

This set of ten, still popular today, represents a synthesis of originally separate Tantrik schools, as some of their names indicate: Kālī (from the Kālīkula traditions); Tārā and Chinnamastā (from Buddhist Tantra); Tripura-sundarī, a.k.a. Ṣoḍaśī (from the Śrīvidyā); and Bhairavī (probably from the Trika). Note that the usage of the word *vidyā* to mean "a goddess embodied in a mantra" is exclusively Tantrik. For more on this set of ten, see David Kinsley's fine book on the subject.*

* Tantric Visions of the Divine Feminine: The Ten Mahāvidyās from University of California Press.

A variety of texts from the far south and also from the far east of India document this syncretistic and largely philosophy-free phase of late Tantra (1400–1800), which almost exclusively emphasized undertaking the *sādhanā* (meaning practice with mantra, yantra, and visualization) of a particular deity in order to come to embody that deity and activate her powers within oneself (something also found in the classical tradition, but here the deity is often *not* understood as the one overarching Divinity, since s/he is invoked for the attainment of specific worldly goals in late Tantra). A number of these later Tantrik texts have been studied by scholar Gudrun Bühnemann, whose published works may be consulted for a reliable accounting of them.

Finally we may consider the case of Kashmīr. There, though the tradition contracted considerably under Muslim rule, and sometimes persecution, a body of teachings continued to be transmitted concerning the attainment of liberation through three primary means: ritual, meditation, and mystical knowledge (*karma*, *yoga*, *jñāna*). Abundant textual evidence from the early modern period (16th–18th centuries) in Kashmīr shows that the form of yogic meditation then preferred was a variety of *kuṇḍalinī-yoga* directly taken over from the Śaiva Tantrik sources. In this practice, one is said to attain identity with Śiva by withdrawing the vital energy into the central channel through breath regulation (*prāṇāyāma*) while mentally repeating Oṃ, thereby raising *kuṇḍalinī* to the crown of the head, penetrating the six *cakras* along the way.[133] Furthermore, the liberating mystical knowledge (*jñāna*) taught here is based on that of Abhinava Gupta. Thus 20th-century Kashmīrī gurus of Śaiva Tantra, such as Swāmī Lakṣhman Jū, could claim a continuous transmission back to the classical period, though by the nature of Indian guruhood, they were not able to acknowledge how much was lost over that period. Lakṣman Jū, frequently cited as the last living master of the Trika lineage in Kashmir, is discussed in the conclusion.

See page 433

MODERN POSTURAL YOGA

The person mostly responsible for the creation of what scholars call "modern postural yoga," as practiced in some form today by about 20 million people in the West, drew heavily on *haṭha-yoga* teachings. His name was Kriṣhṇamācārya, and his school of yoga founded in Mysore, South India, in the 1930s was the arena for the constitution of the modern discipline. As commonly practiced today, modern postural yoga (MPY) is a form of exercise that often bears only a slight resemblance to the *haṭha-yoga* tradition that inspired it. Though most of its postures are of a 20th-century provenance, about eighty or one hundred of them can be documented as deriving from premodern *haṭha-yoga*, in addition to a variety of non-postural elements, which all

About 100 asanas of modern postural yoga derive from premodern haṭha-yoga.

derive from that source. Scholar Mark Singleton's work has shown us that despite claims to the contrary, MPY is a product of modern globalization, having early 20th-century European and American exercise forms (such as "harmonial gymnastics") as its other influences.[134]

Krishṇamācārya wished to emphasize the traditional roots of MPY and thus claimed to have received a direct transmission of sacred knowledge from a disembodied *siddha* he called Nāthamuni (note the connection to the Nāths mentioned above). He documented this transmission in a Sanskrit text he called *The Secret of Yoga (Yoga-rahasya),* which he evidently intended to be the scriptural authority for the modern instantiation of yoga. This is of course a perfectly valid claim within the tradition, which possesses an "open canon" that can theoretically be added to at any time—and transmission from disembodied beings in dreams and visions is well-attested, as we have seen.

See page 310

See page 286

So speaking in the broadest possible terms, we may say that if Krishṇamācārya is the father of modern postural yoga, its grandfather was Gorakṣa, a Nāth in a Kaula-influenced lineage, which makes Matsyendra, the originator of that lineage, its great-grandfather.* This of course is an oversimplification. Since Matsyendra/Macchanda was a guru of Śaiva Tantra, I think it is legitimate to argue that when modern yoga teachers seek to re-embed postural yoga practice in a spiritual context and further seek to align themselves with the ancient system of thought that fits most harmoniously with that practice—thereby empowering and enhancing it—then the system that makes most sense to align with is the very one that modern yoga can ultimately be traced back to: that of classical Śaiva Tantra.[135]

*Remember that Gorakṣa's guru was named after the original Matsyendra and may even have been a literary invention based on him with the purpose of strengthening the ties between the new discipline of *haṭha-yoga* and the Śaiva Tantra from which it in part derived.

This brings to an end our survey of the history of Śaiva Tantra and its key figures. Next we turn to a survey of the classical teachings on Tantrik practice, which we have thus far only touched on.

3
An Introduction to the Practice of Śaiva Tantra

This portion of the book will be devoted to a relatively brief examination of the various practices that were performed in the context of classical Śaiva Tantra, nearly all of which have survived in some form down to the present day, though they are not commonly known. We will also give some substantial attention to the theory of practice found in NŚT as well as the prerequisites for it.

THE CONTEXT OF PRACTICE: ŚAKTIPĀTA AND DĪKṢĀ

As mentioned in the history section, to practice the Tantra, to have access to its scriptures, and to have access to a guru, the prospective student must undergo initiation. Historically, initiation was open to anyone who really wanted it and whose sincere longing was demonstrated through reverent and loyal devotion to the tradition (*bhakti*), offerings of selfless service (*sevā*), and financial offerings proportionate to one's income (*dāna, dakṣinā*[136]). The longing for initiation was thought to be a direct result of a spiritual awakening called *śakti-pāta,* the "Descent of Grace" or "Influx of God's Power."

See page 152

The Descent of Grace might be called a conversion experience because it is an awakening that brings a person to the spiritual path, regardless of whether that person previously had any spiritual inclinations whatsoever. Such an awakening is a part of every spiritual tradition, but it is given especial prominence in Śaiva Tantra, for a person could not be initiated unless the initiating guru had good reason to believe that the applicant had experienced the *śaktipāta* awakening. That is to say, from the perspective of the dualist branch of the tradition, a guru had to believe that Śiva wanted that person to be initiated and therefore would look for signs that s/he had received *śaktipāta,* signs we will examine below. (The issue is more subtle on the nondualist side, as we will see.)

The doctrine of *śaktipāta* survives into the present day, in lineages such as that of Swāmī Viṣhṇu Tīrth and Swāmī Muktānanda (who was very much influenced by the former). These 20th-century gurus take *śaktipāta* to be synonymous with the awakening of *kuṇḍalinī-śakti,* arguing that the latter is brought about by the agency of a realized master. By contrast, classical Tantra typically pictures *śaktipāta* as occurring spontaneously; it is said to impel the recipient to begin searching for such a guru.

Inspired by my comparative study of religion, I take *śaktipāta* to be one name for a real, universal, cross-cultural human experience, a shift in consciousness that is a biological potentiality in all humans. If we strip away the cultural and religious ideas that are usually immediately attached to this experience, we find remarkably similar features of the experience cross-culturally. *Śaktipāta,* whatever we call it, is a transformative direct experience of what some call "God," others call "the inner Self," and still others call "Buddha-nature"; an experience that consecrates one to the spiritual path. Some people experience two such transmissions of grace: one, usually milder, that initiates their seeking for a path or a teacher, and another, more powerful one, when they have found that path or teacher.

Whether one's *śaktipāta* is subjectively weak or strong, it has the same effect: it is a life-changing experience, forever altering how one sees reality, though such alteration is immediate in the case of a strong *śaktipāta* and gradual in the case of a weak one. It is such a profound "game-changer" that those who have not had this awakening often find it hard to believe such a thing could be real and suppose it to be the product of wishful thinking, an overactive imagination, or a diseased mind. But those who have had it never doubt that they have been given a glimpse of the hidden order of things, of something much more real and meaningful than that which most people call reality.

My experience of *śaktipāta*

My own experience of *śaktipāta* occurred at the age of sixteen through meeting a powerful and loving meditation master. It was not the product of wishful thinking because I didn't even want to be there, at least not on the level of the conscious mind. My mother had persuaded me to take a two-day meditation retreat and I had acceded because I wanted the reward she was offering me; she essentially bribed me to attend, and I had neither expectation nor hope that anything particularly magical would happen. And indeed, the whole thing was fairly boring, though in the final meditation of the weekend, I did make a grudging effort to be fully present in the warm, dark stillness of the meditation room. It was nice, but nothing special, until I opened my eyes and walked outside. I was astonished to discover that the whole world had apparently changed. Everything was more vivid and real, and almost sparkling. Not only that, I was feeling an indescribable, incredible energy in my heart, and it was flowing palpably between my heart and the hearts of everyone else I could see. I call it "energy" for lack of a better word; it was a tangible power or force, not a passive feeling, and it had the nature of exquisitely pure love. It was not only more love than I had ever felt, but more love than I ever would have dreamed was possible. It was connecting the hearts of all the people around me, coursing freely in a kind of web or grid of power, entirely independent of whether these people liked each other or not, or whether I liked them. Then I noticed it was really everywhere; the very air around me seemed thick with it; it was undoubtedly the most "real" thing in reality, though not perceptible with any of my five senses! It was astonishing, and I was never the same, now that I knew this power, this love beyond anything I had ever imagined, was a real possibility in human life. I continue to cultivate and deepen that experience, hold that perspective, and try to live from that place. The experience initiated the unfolding of a process that I have in turn facilitated and resisted, but since then there has never been a serious possibility of playing any other game in life.

Śaktipāta, an act of Grace, is not earned by being a 'good person' and can come to anyone at any time.

Śaktipāta is referred to with the word "grace" because this awakening is not earned by being a "good person" and can come to anyone at any time. It is spontaneous and totally true. As Abhinava Gupta says, "*Śaktipāta* and devotion to the Divine are independent of family, caste, body, actions (karma), age, religious practices, and wealth." This powerful infusion of grace is commonly experienced by those who come into contact with a fully awakened being, such as a meditation master. However, we should note here that the modern notion that *śaktipāta* is something given by a guru is not what we find in the ancient tradition, where the understanding is that *śaktipāta* always comes from God, or the universe if you will, and the guru is simply one possible conduit for it. The confusion on this issue is due to the conflation of the two terms *śaktipāta* and *dīkṣā* (initiation): while *śaktipāta* is spontaneous and can flow through virtually any conduit, initiation is always given by a guru. (Though *śaktipāta* can of course spontaneously occur *during* an initiation, which is probably the original reason for the conflation.) More on this to come.

Since it transcends individual will, there is nothing that can be done to trigger *śaktipāta*, other than ardently praying for it and trying to be as open as possible toward it. As you might have intuited by now, to reserve initiation only for those who had had this awakening experience was an attempt to create authentic spiritual community, groups of people for whom religion was not civic or cultural or political but a deeply felt experiential reality. Of course, how often this ideal was actually fulfilled in practice, we have no way of knowing. Still, it is clear that the idea was widespread in the tradition that all initiates should have received this infusion of divine grace. Let's look at some of the signs of *śaktipāta* described in the scriptures.

Mṛgendra-tantra

Those embodied souls on whom Śakti descends, for the cessation of their bondage, show these signs: eagerness for liberation; aversion to remaining in the mundane world of delusion and suffering [saṃsāra]; devotion toward the devotees of God; faith in their teacher and rites.

Svayambhuva-sūtrasangraha

The Descent of Grace erodes the impurity (of one's separate individuality), which is the cause of the cycle of suffering. When that has waned, the desire to go to the highest, unsurpassed beatitude arises. Having obtained a guide [= guru], who cuts his bonds by initiation, he attains identity with God, free from impurity and affliction.

These passages represent the tradition's mainstream view of *śaktipāta*, in which it is more or less conceived of as "getting religion." The nondualist texts describe *śaktipāta* more in terms of a powerful mystical experience: waves of bliss, a feeling of oneness, spontaneous tears, trembling of the body, and so on. That is, the nondualists looked for more substantial signs of a real infusion of divine energy, a greater inner shift than might be connoted by merely becoming interested in the spiritual life.

In his two masterworks, *Light on the Tantras* and *Essence of the Tantras,* Abhinava Gupta makes a sustained argument for understanding *śaktipāta* nondualistically. In the latter he writes:

Tantrasāra: ch. 11

> *In our tradition that holds to the View of the nonduality of the autonomous Highest Divinity, it occurs in this way: the Highest Divinity, as a play of hiding His true nature, becomes an apparently bound soul, an individual, a contracted being, and yet there is no contradiction of His true nature in manifesting within the circumscribed divisions of space, time, and a particular form. As another complementary expression of the same play, when bringing to an end the concealment of his true nature, and experiencing a return to that true nature instantly or gradually, He is called an individual soul that is a fit vessel for śaktipāta. And He is Supreme Śiva throughout this whole process, whose essence is simply His total autonomy: the one who causes Power to descend.*

In this beautiful passage, Abhinava argues that "the Highest Divinity" and "the contracted individual soul" are just different names for one Consciousness in two different states or phases, much as we have two different names for water in two different states: ice and vapor. Thus, though *śaktipāta* remains here an act of grace, it is in fact an act of gracing yourself because in your ultimate nature you are that grace-bestowing power of God. *Śaktipāta* is a profound moment of turning a corner at the deepest level of your being: a choice made by your divine-self to begin to bring the contracted phase of existence to an end by initiating the process of expanding back into the fullness of your true nature.

In a parallel passage in *Light on the Tantras* Abhinava writes, in reference to a statement from the dualists that God "waits for the right time" to bestow his grace on someone who is "fit":

Tantrāloka: 13.204–7

The "particular time" [kāla] that is referred to is that of a particular activity [kalanā], consisting of awareness, directed toward one's own nature. The "fitness" is in our philosophy said to be the quality of being finally ready for the spiritual process [yoga] of identification with the Divine. Thus the question "Why did it happen only then, why not before?" is not appropriate. For there is no occasion whatsoever for the manifestation of the Descent of Grace aside from this. But when his Power does shine forth in this way, due to his autonomy, the power of time cannot contradict this expansion, it being simply a form of his majesty, arising within God.

The dualists suggest that one may earn *śaktipāta* through religious actions and good works, an idea to which Abhinava is fiercely opposed. *Śaktipāta* cannot, for him, be an issue of merit, because otherwise we relegate it to the world of karma, not of divine grace. He writes:

Tantrāloka: 13.259–62

But surely," an objectioner might say, "those who attain the state of liberation do so through worship [pūjā], mantra repetition [japa], meditation, zealous service of God [sevā], and so on. How then can their attainment be independent of actions?" It is not like this, we [nondualists] say. Let us begin first by investigating why in the first place such people engage in things such as mantra repetition, meditation on the transcendent Divine, and so on. . . . If you say the cause is the Lord's Will, then the one and only form of that cause is the Descent of Power [śaktipāta].

Thus Abhinava makes the interesting argument that rather than "good works" drawing God's grace, it is only through grace in the form of *śaktipāta* that one can have any real capacity for, or sustained interest in, such spiritual practices. This accords with his view that *śaktipāta* marks the beginning of the true spiritual path, not some point of merit reached along the way. Further, all activities on that path are an expression of divine Power, and thus are not part of the normal karmic set-up. This is because their purpose is, according to him, to bring about identification with one's true nature and not to produce change within the matrix of ordinary reality as normal actions are intended to do. He explains,

Tantrāloka: 13.262–3

> *Mantra repetition and the other practices are expressions of the divine Power of Action [*kriyā-śakti*], not karma. For "karma" in general usage is that which grants lower forms of experience and obscures the true nature of the experiencer.*

In both works we have been quoting, Abhinava outlines nine types of *śaktipāta,* from the most to the least intense. We will briefly review these here, paraphrasing the account in *Essence of the Tantras.* Lest there be any misunderstanding, I should perhaps note here that *śaktipāta* is not a general term to be used for *any* infusion of divine power (the general term would be *samāveśa*) but something that happens once or twice in one's life. This, by the way, is the subject of my doctoral dissertation, so if you'd like more information on *śaktipāta* and *samāveśa*, please consult that work.

The strongest grade of *śaktipāta* is so powerful it brings about immediate liberation, a fierce and total awakening, with the unfortunate side effect that the intensity of the experience causes the body to drop (i.e., physical death). Needless to say, this is extremely rare. The second grade, also very rare, causes a spontaneous arising of intuitive insight, naturally leading to full awakening, without any other assistance necessary. When this intuitive knowledge arises, if it rapidly grows to completion of its own accord, the recipient is said to be a "Self-revealed guru," a giver of both enjoyment and liberation, displaying the six signs of completion. On the other hand, if the intuitive insight is unsteady or incomplete, then s/he will need the scriptures and a teacher to confirm and strengthen it. This is much more common. Depending on the steadiness or shakiness of one's intuition, Abhinava says, one must perform self-refinement through the sacred vow of disciplined yoga practice, either by himself or as directed by a guru. Please note, by the way, that the word "guru" simply means "teacher," any qualified teacher.

See page 246

The third grade is much more common and is the weakest grade of *śaktipāta* that still permits one to attain liberation in the same lifetime. One who has received it experiences a strong desire to approach a true guru and has the intuition necessary to recognize such a teacher. In the recipient of the third grade, the burning questions, "What is the Truth? Who knows that Truth?" lead one, through intuition or the company of spiritual friends, to develop the longing to meet a master (*Tantrāloka* 13.222). If this desire is strong enough, says Abhinava, the longing will inevitably be fulfilled. Having met such a master, attainment of insight into things as they are follows rapidly, culminating in living liberation in the same lifetime.

A true Guru (sadguru) is an awakened being of perfect integrity who can give transmission by any one of a number of means.

Abhinava notes that this is also the type of *śaktipāta* that helps one to leave a false guru and approach a true teacher, one of total integrity. He writes, "One thing alone marks a Guru: wisdom that is expertly put into practice" (*Tantrāloka* 13.333). A true guru (*sadguru*) is an awakened being of great integrity who can give transmission by any one of a number of means. Though a physically embodied guru is by far the most effective, if such is not to be found, then one can invoke a meeting with a guru in the dream-world or become a disciple of a master who has left his body, but only if that master is actually alive for you in some sense. That is to say, a fondness for the inspiring words of a deceased guru is insufficient— that guru must come to you as a living force in dreams and visions, giving transmissions and challenging you in your practice. In other words, the only way a relationship with a disembodied guru can be effective, according to the Tantra, is if that person is almost as palpably present to you as a an embodied guru would be.

Is a guru absolutely necessary? (Again, defining "guru" as an effective teacher.) According to the Tantra, if you have not received the strongest grades of *śaktipāta* (#1 or #2), yes, a teacher is necessary, for at least part of your journey. Even though the guru ultimately empowers you to a be a guru unto yourself, and that inner guru is your final refuge, most of us are way too confused and disoriented to find that refuge on our own. According to the Kaula tradition, we all need the clarifying empowerment of the guru's transmission, some of us just once, others perhaps many times. The means of this transmission are hearing the guru's words, being in his/ her company, receiving his compassionate glance, studying the teachings, practicing with him, receiving a mantra from him, seeing him perform a ritual or daily task, or direct transmission of energy; or some other, secret, means (*Tantrāloka* 13.227-28). Note that these means of initiation can only be given by a self-realized guru and need not be given through the guru's conscious intent. If your karma has ripened and thus your "kindling" is dry, it will catch fire by mere proximity to an awakened being. Nor is it true that such a guru needs to know who you are on the surface level (your history, psychology, etc.). However, we should note that *your* mental image of what a guru is can sometimes be a problem. We are not talking about someone who is ostentatiously spiritual or adored by many. In fact, a true teacher has a heart of compassion and humility—abiding in Presence doesn't require any ostentatious outward show.

The fourth grade of *śaktipāta* leads a person to take initiation, though his perception of the divinity of his real Self is not as firm as a third-grade recipient, because it is difficult for him to break through his conditioned convictions and mental constructs of reality. Nonetheless, through the gradual ripening of his insight through practice, the fourth-grade recipient merges with the Divine upon leaving the body. This and the following grades account for the majority of people on the path. (By "the path" I do mean to imply that there is really only one path of spiritual transformation, regardless of what name it is given or which religion or culture it is articulated within.) The fifth and sixth grades are received by those who are ready for the spiritual life but who also have a strong desire for worldly enjoyment and prosperity. They thus seek, and find, a teacher who can support them in both endeavors. They practice a yoga that leads them to enjoyment and then to liberation, at the time of leaving the body or shortly thereafter.

The three lowest grades of *śaktipāta* are received by one whose desire for enjoyments is stronger than for liberation. These grades of awakening grant one access to the path to enjoyment through yoga, culminating in liberation in a future life. These grades are not given much attention in the texts, but it is important to note here that what grade of *śaktipāta* you receive is not due to how "worthy" you are but to how intense your longing for awakening is in relation to your longing to enjoy "the good life." Though the latter is described as the slower path, it is not denigrated by the Tantrik tradition. In fact, integrating your desire for abundance with your spiritual practice instead of keeping it separate helps ensure that, in time, you will indeed attain the final goal. Abhinava writes:

What grade of *Śaktipāta* you receive is not due to how "worthy" you are.

Because a yogī's desire for enjoyment is fulfilled by means of the mantras and yoga of Śiva, that desire necessarily eventually culminates in liberation. Thus we can still say such a one receives śaktipāta. So drawing divine grace in the form of the Descent of Power is most important even for those who desire enjoyments.

Tantrasāra: ch. 11

We turn now to examine the second, and closely related, prerequisite for the practice of the Tantra: that of *dīkṣā*, or initiation.

DĪKSHĀ:
THE RITE OF INITIATION AND ITS EFFECTS

Initiation was the central rite of all forms of Tantra throughout most of its history. It served a crucial role in the psychology of the religion, for it addressed the deep-seated cultural belief in karma, or the repercussion of actions performed in past lives. Since the number of previous incarnations was held to be incalculable, one's storehouse of karma was vast, far more than could be resolved in a single life. This oppressive belief made the goal of radical freedom (*mokṣa*), the power to determine one's own inner state, seem unreachably remote. One of the most significant features of the new Tantrik teaching, then, was that the ceremony of initiation (*dīkṣā*)—or rather the divinely revealed mantras employed during that ceremony—liberated one from all karma destined to bear fruit in future lives, thereby bringing the goal of the path within the reach of a single lifetime. We need not concern ourselves with the metaphysical question of whether this doctrine was "true," since the empowering psychological effect of the ceremony is clear enough— recipients of initiation believed that it worked, and thus they opened to the possibility of liberation in this life (*jīvanmukti*). The historical record attests that many did indeed attain that goal.

In traditional Indian society, rites of passage were only given to those with the proper *adhikāra,* which means something like "entitlement" or "qualification." *Adhikāra* for initiation into Vedic study was determined entirely by the caste and gender of one's birth, so the Tantrik teaching that candidates for initiation were accepted on the basis of the evidence of their *śaktipāta* alone (as adjudged by a qualified guru or *ācārya*), without reference to other factors such as caste, class, gender, or ethnicity, was a radical departure from the norm. (Initiates were expected to offer a substantial percentage of their income as an acknowledgment of the inestimable value of initiation; if this rule of percentage-based offering was applied properly, however, it did not necessarily bar those of low income from initiation.) Receipt of initiation granted *adhikāra* in a slightly different sense: the privilege and the obligation to study the scriptures.

There were two levels of initiation: the *samaya-dīkṣā,* or probationary initiation for novices, and the full *nirvāṇa-dīkṣā,* or initiation that placed one on the irrevocable path to liberation (*nirvāṇa*). This elaborate two-day ceremony was sometimes dispensed with in the more radical Kaula branches of the tradition, in which (as we have seen) initiation could be granted by a fully awakened master with a word, a glance, a touch, or a thought. The nondualists believed that initiation, to be effective, must trigger a second *śaktipāta,* observable in the degree to which the initiate was affected by the ceremony.

Initiation can be granted by a fully awakened master with a word, a glance, a touch, or a thought.

The first form of initiation, the *samaya-dīkṣā,* granted the initiate the right and obligation to study the scriptures and begin a daily practice. Samayins, as they were called, were required to take a vow that they would follow a strict code of conduct (or *samaya*), a code set out in endnote 137. Unmarried samayins would usually live in the home of the guru to receive instruction, and also to be observed during their probationary period. After some time (probably one to five years), if they felt ready and were judged to be ready, they would take the full initiation.

The *nirvāṇa-dīkṣā* was the central rite of Śaiva Tantra in all its forms, across India and Southeast Asia. It was adopted with little change by the Tantrik Buddhists, and we can see some elements of it preserved today in Tibetan Buddhism. If the performance of *nirvāṇa-dīkṣā* is our primary measure of the survival of the Śaiva Tantrik tradition, then we must say that the tradition finally died out in the early 20th century, when the last real *nirvāṇa-dīkṣā*s were performed. And here I'm not counting the *dīkṣās* that are still performed for the priests at Chidambaram temple in Tamil Nadu. However, since Shaivism by that time existed also in purely gnostic forms (insight-based instead of ritual-based), this rite need not be our primary measure of the tradition's survival. (See the conclusion for discussion on this.) Because the ceremonial *dīkṣā* was so central to the tradition for so long, and because it is very beautiful, we will describe it briefly here. The first of the two days of the ritual was performed for all students, whether they were taking either the basic *samaya-dīkṣā* or the full *nirvāṇa-dīkṣā;* the second day is only for those taking the full initiation.

See page 431

In preparation, the guru and his or her assistants created a sacred space centered on the initiatory *maṇḍala* (or sacred diagram) of that lineage. The *maṇḍala*, anywhere from 12 to 35 feet in length, or on a side for a square *maṇḍala* was carefully drawn with chalk and filled in with various colored powders, much like Tibetan Buddhist *maṇḍala*s still seen today (which were originally derived from Shaivism in their basic design).

A white canopy was suspended over the *maṇḍala*, with curtains of multicolored cloth hanging from it on all four sides, concealing the *maṇḍala* from view and creating a container for the energy to be generated. The inner side of the curtain-walls was decorated with flags, pennants, and mirrors as well as garlands of flowers, strings of little bells, and protective threads in five colors. Ghee-burning lamps were arranged around the perimeter of the space, the dozens of flames casting a warm glow. Also placed at various points around the *maṇḍala* were parasols, yak-tail whisks, and sacred bronze vases; the latter contained a gold coin, were filled with water and flowers, and were decorated with a cloth belt and a flower garland.[138] And those kinds of kallasas or bronze vases are still used today in Indian ritual.

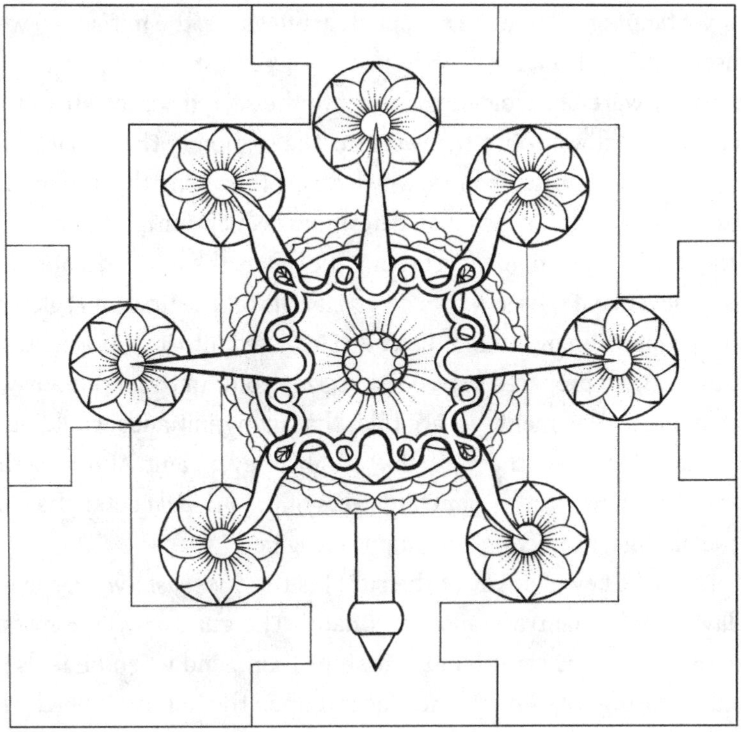

At the appropriate points on the *maṇḍala* the guru installed the energies of the deities (considered as aspects of the one Deity by the nondualists), in the form of their mantras, thus enlivening the sacred diagram. These sonic or "mantric" forms of the Divine are, paradoxically, both the primary instruments of worship and that which receives the worship being offered. This worship takes the form of recitation of the mantras, concentration on their visualized forms, and elemental offerings of flowers, fire, incense, bell, and water. The guru performing the rite first meditates on his identity with Deity, who will perform the initiation through him.

Traditionally, between one and five initiands gathered for the ceremony. Standing outside the canopied sacred space, the initiand(s) were consecrated with mantras, holy water, sacred ash, and *darbha* grass. Then they were blindfolded and led into the sacred space, where they each threw a flower onto the *maṇḍala*. The section of the *maṇḍala* that the flower lands on determines which form of the Deity the initiand will subsequently worship and also determines which initiation-name the initiand will be given. After receiving the name, the initiand's blindfold was removed and s/he saw the secret *maṇḍala* for the first time, glowing with the mantra-powers that had been installed into it, at the center of the exquisitely prepared sacred space. This point in the ceremony was such a magical moment, we are told, that many initiands would burst into tears of joy and others tremble, laugh, or even faint. Abhinava says that at this moment the mantra-powers of the *maṇḍala* enter the body of the disciple, protecting and empowering her.[139]

The next key element of the ritual is the *Śiva-hasta-vidhi,* the rite of laying on a mantra-empowered hand. The guru or *ācārya* installs the mantras in his right hand, worships them, and when he feels his hand vibrating with energy, he places it upon the initiand's head. This powerful moment begins the process of the student's becoming one with the mantric powers of her divine identity. Next, offerings were made to the initiand as an embodiment of the Divine and to a consecrated sacred fire; these included offerings that removed the caste of the initiand (a radical idea, since many in Indian culture believed that caste was a permanent inherited trait) and granted him a status equal to that of the highest caste, regardless of his background. Of course, Indian society in general would not acknowledge this change, but it must have had a strong psychological impact on the initiate, creating a sense of an inner, truer, secret identity within the socially constructed persona.

The guru then performed an elaborate meditative visualization in which he fused the central channel (*suṣumnā*) of his subtle body with the central channel of the initiand. Then, through meditative visualization and special *mudrās*, the guru fused his own consciousness—his soul if you will—with that of the initiand and raised it through his own central channel, passing through the stations of the deities (*cakras*), thus elevating it to a higher state before infusing this purified and elevated consciousness back into the initiand's body. This yogic process concluded the first day; those undergoing the full *nirvāna-dīkṣā* lay down to sleep and dream in the sacred space.

The next morning, after discussion with the guru about the dreams the initiand had, the primary fire-ritual began. This consisted of a ritual process that incinerated all the disciple's karmas, or effects of past actions, destined to bear fruit in future incarnations. This was done so that the disciple would be able to attain liberation in the current lifetime, as we've said. Of course, karma destined to bear fruit in the current lifetime is left untouched. How are the other karmas burned? Through a complex process of visualization, mantra, fire-offerings, and (for lack of a better phrase) the manipulation of consciousness. To give an example of the technicalia of this ritual, at one point the guru vividly imagines the endless wombs in which this soul is destined to be incarnated, then summons the Goddess of the Supreme Word (*Vāgīśī, Parāvāk*), visualizing Her as pervading those wombs, then enters the initiand's body through his (the guru's) outbreath, separates the initiand's consciousness from his/her heart, draws it out through the top of his/her head with the *ankuśa-mudrā,* breathes it down into his own heart with the *saṃhāra-mudrā*, holds *kumbhaka* breath while meditating on the principal mantra, and then raises it to the *dvādaśānta* point above his head, takes hold of it and with the gesture of throwing forward from the upturned fist (*bhava-mudrā*), incarnates it simultaneously in all those wombs. Then, with fire-offerings, he rapidly fast-forwards through the lives of all those incarnations simultaneously, performing their life-cycle rituals, causing their karmas to fructify and then dissolve harmlessly.[140] This is, in fact, a greatly simplified and abbreviated description.

The guru then separated the soul of the initiand from the bonds of *āṇava-mala*, *māyīya-mala*, and *kārma-mala*, and offered up the eight elements of his/her subtle body to the five Cause-deities.[141] Finally, the culmination of the ritual arrived (and believe me, a lot of detail is being left out here), the rite of fusing the initiand's consciousness with the Divine Absolute (*śiva-yojanikā*). No details of this will be given here; suffice to say that on one level it centers on successfully raising the soul (i.e., the locus of individual awareness) up the central channel to the *dvādaśānta,* the level of the Absolute at the upper limit of one's subtle body. The resultant experience, if it is perceptible to the initiand (now an initiate), is merely a taste of the final liberation s/he will experience. Whether the experience is perceptible is dependent on the strength of the *śaktipāta* or the *samāveśa* triggered by this climactic act of fusion with the Divine,[142] but the effect in any case is thought to be the same, which is that the initiate is now a potential locus for the full manifestation of divinity; or to put it another way, the barriers to liberation in this life have been removed.

See page 150

Since the two key elements of the *nirvāṇa-dīkṣā* are destruction of the three primary bonds and (momentary) fusion of the soul with the Divine, when the Kaula-influenced lineages claim that a powerful and charismatic guru can initiate with simply a look, a word, or a touch, they are claiming that those acts can transmit sufficient spiritual power to accomplish both these fundamental aspects of initiation, severing the bonds and grating an experience of union with the divine. Of course such union is, from the highest view, always already accomplished. You are never separate from the Divine, but we are talking here phenomenologically, meaning to say in terms of your experience of union or lack thereof.

In an intriguing passage of the remarkable essay that appears at the end of his commentary on chapter 5 of the *Svacchanda-tantra,*

Rājānaka[143] Kṣemarāja addresses criticisms of the Śaiva doctrine of liberating initiation. The opponent argues, "Even after initiation, we see that character faults, together with the *saṃskāras* [subtle karmic impressions] that give rise to them, are unaffected in the initiate. So what have the mantras (of initiation) really done for him?" Kṣemarāja responds,

Svacchanda-tantra-uddyota

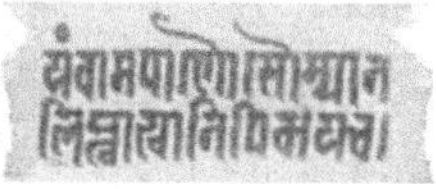

Just as manipulative mantras can bring a heavenly beauty under the control of an ugly man without getting rid of his ugliness, similarly the liberating mantras [of initiation] undo the power of the three bonds, but they do not necessarily quell attachment, aversion, and their products.

For that, he implies, spiritual practice is necessary. He goes on to say,

And also, we have seen, on hundreds of occasions, that there is a quelling of attachment and aversion immediately after initiation for those who have been purified by an intense śaktipāta.

Kṣemarāja here testifies that in his lineage, real transformation often *is* observed after initiation, and he links that shift to the strength of the *śaktipāta*, awakening not to the initiation ritual itself. Kṣemarāja answers the objection that some initiations are given in which the initiate feels nothing. He writes,

If the objection is, "Why does this manifestation of divinity due to initiation not take place at that very time?" Then we reply: In fact, we do see that manifestation occurring, countless times, in the case of those initiations performed by those Gurus possessed of the highest insight.

The only factor that can influence the effectiveness of initiation apart from the initiand's ripeness is the guru's degree of access to the energy of true insight. Perhaps this is why the Kaula lineages emphasize the transmission of power from the perfected guru that triggers *śaktipāta* as the "true initiation."[144] A final quote from Kṣemarāja, from the same source, aptly sums up our discussion of the related concepts of *śaktipāta* and *dīkṣā*:

> *Therefore, purification of the self—destroying the bonds of āṇava and so on and bestowing capability for the manifestation of Divinity—is achieved through initiation, which is accomplished following the Descent of Power [*śaktipāta*], which is inferred by observing the disciple's devotion, their spontaneous desire to approach a guru, and so on. This is taught in the sacred tradition with this verse:*
>
> *"The essence of insight [into one's true nature] is given; the saṃskāras of being a bound soul are destroyed. Therefore, [because] it involves giving [*dī*] and destroying [*kṣi*], it is known in our system as* dīkṣā."

See page 423 and following

The question of whether someone today could take up a Tantrik practice, or the practice of yoga in a Tantrik mode, without *śaktipāta* or *dīkṣā* is addressed in the conclusion of this book. Here I will only mention that the practices are said to be markedly less effective without *śaktipāta* (for example, mantras have little to no potency). If you have had some success in *sādhanā* and then receive *śaktipāta,* it's like getting an injection of rocket fuel. If you have not yet experienced this profound awakening, this powerful infusion of divine grace (*rudra-śakti*), though there is nothing you can do to *make* it happen, you can greatly increase its likelihood by ardently praying for it, stoking the fire of your longing, and practicing being as open to it as possible. If the spiritual path is the dominant feature of your life and you can palpably feel the effects of the yogic practices and mantras, then you have received *śaktipāta* and just didn't have the name for it. Recall that in part 1 we give some of the signs of *śaktipāta*, so you can check whether they match your own experience.

In the case of *dīkṣā*, however, the issue is more complex; some type of initiation, or a ceremony that has a similar effect, would seem to be required for authentic Tantra. And that ceremony cannot be an exact replication of the original *nirvāṇa-dīkṣā,* for reasons that will be addressed in the conclusion.

THE ROLE OF THE GURU

Western sentiments about the figure of the guru are often highly charged and polarized, with strong feelings for and against. Though the Indian tradition has also expressed a wide range of opinions over the centuries, the centrality of the guru in every kind of Tantra cannot be denied. As far as the original tradition is concerned, you must have a living guru to be a Tāntrika, though the extent of the direct involvement of that guru in your spiritual life might vary. One model that was probably followed quite a lot was that of taking *samaya-dīkṣā* at a relatively young age, and living for a period in the guru's home (*guru-kula*) with other *samayins*. This allowed the initiate to receive a thorough grounding in the system while being observed in this probationary period as to suitability for the full *nirvāṇa-dīkṣā*. Usually, after receiving the latter, the initiate would become an independent householder. As a householder, s/he would take turns with other disciples of the guru in sponsoring regular gatherings at the guru's home for ritual, *satsang,* eating together, and receiving the guru's teachings. As mentioned, this is one model of how a community of co-initiates (*guru-kula*) would function. There were probably others.

Right-handed Tantra sees the guru as a teacher of the doctrine, left-handed Kaula Tantra sees the guru as a liberated master who can transmit the actual experience of one's essence-nature.

We have alluded to the difference between the right-current's picture of the guru as priest and teacher of the doctrine (= *ācārya*) and the Kaula left-current's picture of the guru as liberated master who can transmit the actual experience of one's essence-nature. Practitioners undoubtedly had very different relationships with these two different types of gurus, and of course there are other types that we are not detailing here. For example, Abhinava Gupta tells us that he had a number of different gurus and studied in various lineage traditions, but it was not until he found his *sadguru* that he finally attained the highest state, through opening his heart totally to the embodied wisdom of his Master. In *Tantrāloka* 1.16 he describes his own state as *bodha-ujjvala,* "aflame with awakened Consciousness," a state he says is due to devotion both to his guru Śambhunātha and the latter's consort, a devotion which "removed the poison of the bonds that [cause the perception that] anything is other than Divine Consciousness." He further praises the guru-disciple relationship in a beautiful verse we have already cited:

Tantrāloka 1.21

May all contemplate the lotus of the heart of Abhinava Gupta, <
its blossom opened by the light falling from the rays of the sun, ||
its contraction forever banished by the wisdom descending from
the feet of the illuminator, > [my teacher] Śambhunātha.

There was in principle nothing stopping a person from taking initiation from more than one guru, provided that each subsequent initiation was a higher one (i.e., you could not go to another guru for the same kind of initiation you had already received due to some doubt about its efficacy). As Abhinava describes, some people thus progressed through a series of initiations, each one higher, more specialized, and more secret than the last.

In time, the disciple could progress to the role of guru himself, though this was never a self-appointed role. In order to take up the office of guru or teacher, you must have received a consecration (called *abhiṣeka*) from your own guru. Contrary to what Westerners might expect, there was not a particular level of spiritual attainment that qualified you for this role. You would be consecrated based solely on whether your guru thought you capable of initiating and instructing others. Thus, the title of "guru" was no guarantee of a particular spiritual attainment—which seems to me a very intelligent system, since it requires devotees to exercise their own discernment in assessing a teacher.

GURU-YOGA

As we see in the rules for *samayins* (see endnote 137), the figure of the guru was treated with special reverence. You were to practice seeing your teacher as Lord Śiva made flesh,[145] either when s/he was engaged in ritual practice and formal teaching, or even all the time in some lineages. This was of course done for the benefit of the devotee, not the guru. In time a practice of guru-yoga developed in the Tantrik tradition, in which one's guru is contemplated in inner meditation as identical with Supreme Śiva. This sort of thing makes the Western mind, attached as it is to the value of independent self-determination, quite nervous. Many I've talked to criticize the practice of guru-yoga, and all paths that recommend it, because of the various abuses perpetuated by fraudulent gurus over the years. But this only indicates a misunderstanding of this particular practice. One does not in fact need to relinquish one's self-determination, or at any rate not to another human being. There is simply nothing in the practice of guru-yoga that indicates the disciple ought to give up her capacity for independent critical thinking. Though this might seem very strange, the practice of *seeing* one's guru as Lord Śiva does not require one to actually believe he *is* Śiva, at least not any more than anyone else. That is, in this practice, one is not engaging with the guru as human being

There is nothing in the practice of Guru-yoga that indicates the disciple ought to give up her capacity for critical thinking.

at all but as a touchstone for divine Essence. One does not, therefore, need to "divinize" his personality, believe he is free of defects, or convince oneself that his humanity fits an abstract ideal of perfect conduct that in fact no one can ever achieve. Indians seem to understand this principle instinctively and at least some of them can practice guru-yoga assiduously without necessarily paying attention to anything their guru says that is not coming from a very deep place. Not understanding this has been responsible for some tragic self-brainwashing on the part of modern Western and Indian disciples of gurus, and some of these gurus have, unfortunately, been happy to go along with it (though it might be the case that some of them did not even realize the delusive psychological state their devotees were in). In the end, according to this tradition, it is up to individuals to keep their wits about them and exercise discernment; and if they fail to do so, and are taken by a fraudulent guru, they have no one to blame but themselves, since the onus is on each individual to choose his teacher, his path, and his practices.

Having said this, a few more words on the practice of guru-yoga. Though it may be attended by all kinds of visualization exercises and inner or outer rituals, what is at root is the simple practice of using your teacher as an "icon of essence,"[146] projecting onto him and seeing in him the Absolute light of divine Consciousness. This light exists in everyone; but it is only through a resolute practice that one can come to really see and feel it in anyone. The principle here is "Love one person completely and you fall in love with the whole universe."[147] This practice does not entail debasing oneself in any way; paradoxically, you must have great self-respect to undertake guru-yoga, for it is a means of actualizing the guru's own state in yourself. Thus the sense the disciple has is one of equality between his guru and himself, although the two sides of the equation are expressed potential and unexpressed potential respectively, an understanding that keeps the

Guru-yoga is a means of actualizing the guru's own state in yourself.

disciple humble. And of course earlier, when I said "love one person completely," the use of the word "love" here does not mean "like an awful lot." Rather, it means "let go of the conditionality of regard and allow yourself to experience Divinity in another human being."

Now, I have implied that this practice has everything to do with the disciple's own efforts and nothing to do with the guru. However, the more perfectly integrated the guru actually is, the less difficult it is for the devotee to practice guru-yoga. That is, it is easier to follow the *sādhanā* of seeing your teacher as divine if his state of union with the Divine is more or less complete and his conduct is, therefore, not much of a bar to this practice.[147] Thus, we are met with the (to the Western mind) bizarre paradox that the less accomplished the guru is, the more perfect must be one's devotion to him if you're practicing guru yoga. And if you have the karmic misfortune to be working with a false guru, your devotion must be absolutely sublimely perfect for the guru-yoga to work (of course, if you actually realize that the person in question is a false guru, you will probably choose to move on and do guru yoga with someone else). This might sound dangerous to you, unless you remember that guru-yoga is not necessarily about doing everything your guru tells you—discernment must always be operative in that dimension, for you cannot shortcut your individual process of realization. The practice of seeing the guru as divine in spite of his human flaws—in other words, of having unconditional love for him—is preparatory to extending that sentiment to all other beings. So you see that this practice is actually all about you, not about your teacher. It's not necessary for your teacher to even know that you're doing guru yoga if you're doing it, and it's not necessary to do it at all. It's not a required part of a Tantrik sādhanā, though for those who are suited to it, it can be a very powerful practice. There is further discussion of this in this endnote[148] and in the conclusion.

Love one person completely — love the whole universe.

We turn now to the specific practices of Śaiva Tantra.

UPĀYA: THE THREE SKILLFUL MEANS TO LIBERATION

In the domain of practice we always start from the highest.

One of the key teachings of the great master Abhinava Gupta, which influenced much of the rest of the Tantrik tradition, was that of the three *upāyas*, or Skillful Means to Liberation. These are three different modes of cultivating liberating spiritual insight; though they are distinct, they all lead to the same goal, that of *samāveśa,* or continuous immersion into divine Reality. The goal can be reached, says Abhinava, through *śāmbhava-upāya,* the method of accessing Consciousness through direct intuition; through *śākta-upāya,* the method that emphasizes working with the energy of thought-constructs and the feelings they produce; through *āṇava-upāya,* the method that emphasizes the physical body, breath, and imagination; or through all three, simultaneously or sequentially. On the following page, the three *upāyas* are shown in tabular form.

See page 91

In our presentation of the categories of Tantrik philosophy, we nearly always have proceeded through the given map of reality from the "bottom up" (e.g., from Earth to Śiva in the map of *tattvas*). In the presentation of the *upāyas*, however, we proceed from the "top down," because in the domain of practice we start from the highest view. In part this is because it is possible that some aspirants will simply "get it" right away through the most direct means of intuitive insight, and therefore we want to offer them that opportunity. The vast majority of students, however, will need to resort to the various body-based practices to create the opening that makes such insight possible. Indeed, it is almost always the case that those for whom the most direct method (*śāmbhava-upāya*) succeeds immediately have already worked to create a clear, aligned, and open body-mind.

Method (*upāya*)	**Operative Power**	**Level of Experience**	**Center**	**Process**
The Divine Means *śāmbhava-upāya*	Willing *icchā-śakti*	Unity *abheda*	spirit/ intuition	nonsequential *akrama*
The Empowered Means *śākta-upāya*	Knowing *jñāna-śakti*	Unity-in-Diversity *bhedābheda*	heart-mind/ energy	sequential-cum-nonsequential *kramākrama*
The Individual Means *āṇava-upāya*	Acting *kriyā-śakti*	Plurality *bheda*	body	*krama*

Since Tantrik practice seeks nothing less than a total integration of our being, the realization of ourselves as an undivided, unitary mass of awakened consciousness, it makes sense that Abhinava discusses Tantrik *sādhanā* as something that must function on all three levels of body, heart-mind, and spirit.[149] Even if we primarily pursue one of the three modalities, it must necessarily come to entail the other two in order to achieve its full expression. Thus, as we progress in practice, these three distinct parts of ourselves (body-mind-spirit) start to seem less and less distinct, until, as Abhinava says, the nectar of blissful self-awareness floods and overflows the internal dams that divide us, dissolving all distinctions. Then we experience ourselves as one united whole, a mass of blissfully self-aware Consciousness (*cidānanda-ghana*), spontaneously responding with the whole of our being to each moment of experience.

AN-UPĀYA: THE "NON-MEANS"

Before we discuss the three *upāyas* proper, let us look first to what Abhinava Gupta calls the "non-means." This applies only in the very rarest of cases; it consists of a *śaktipāta* awakening so intense that one single teaching from a true guru is enough to stabilize that awakening permanently. For such a one, there is no need for practice at all, unless we count the brief period in which s/he ponders on the teaching of the guru, absorbing it successfully into every level of her being.

Teaching this *an-upāya* level can be dangerous, for often someone who has had a very powerful awakening mistakes it for final liberation and believes themselves above and beyond any need for spiritual practice. Such a mistake is tragic, for if believed for too long, it cannot be rectified in the same lifetime, in which case the great *śaktipāta* that person received, which could have been for the benefit of all beings, is wasted, at least temporarily. Though it may be surprising to hear, even very powerful and very pure awakenings can turn into delusions if misunderstood. Worse, if such an individual appoints themselves a guru, they incur extremely serious karmic repercussions by deluding others as well. Be warned: such a person may have the powers and charisma of a minor god and still be deluded and dangerous. How can you tell? By a careful and sober assessment of the real spiritual attainment of his community of followers. Note that the anecdotal evidence of one or two followers of a guru whom you know is insufficient; to have an adequate sample size for evaluation, you must spend a little time in that teacher's community.

Having said that, there are upon very rare occasions, beings that attain everything in a very short time without any formal spiritual practice. A 20th-century example is that of Bhagavān Nityānanda, who was established in the highest state by age eighteen without doing much formal *sādhanā.* Such beings are said to have done extremely dedicated *sādhanā* in previous lives.

Abhinava Gupta gives an example of the sort of teaching that, when pondered and assimilated by such a one, is all that is necessary to take him or her to the highest state: I translate it below. This is an example of a complete teaching—if only you truly understand and thoroughly feel it, if only you could allow its implications to ramify through every level of your being, it would in fact liberate you forever. However, if you are like 99.9% of human beings, it will have no such effect, in which case you must do spiritual practice, removing the various veils of ignorance until the same Truth you've heard a hundred or a thousand times before finally bursts fully into vibrant life in every cell of your being. However, it is still worthwhile to hear such a teaching to get just a small taste of the perspective of radically liberated awareness even if the teaching cannot generate that awareness upon first hearing it.

Take a deep breath now, center yourself, and see if you can feel just a little bit of the power of a pure Truth-statement (*śuddha-vikalpa*). Abhinava here describes the spontaneous unfolding of wisdom in one who has heard and understood his teacher's declaration of *Tat-tvam-asi*, "You are that very Reality."

Tantrasāra: ch. 2

This very Highest Divinity, the self-manifest Light of Consciousness, is always already my very own Being—when that is the case, what could any method of practice achieve? Not the attainment of my true nature, because that is eternally present; not making that nature apparent, because it is constantly illuminating itself; not the removal of veils, because no "veil" whatsoever exists; not the penetration into That, because nothing other than It exists to enter It. What method can there be here, when there is an impossibility of anything separate from That?

Therefore, this whole existence is One reality: Consciousness alone—unbroken by time, uncircumscribed by space, unclouded by attributes, unconfined by forms, unexpressed by words, and unaccounted for by the ordinary means of knowledge. For it is the cause, through its own Will alone, by which all these sources of limitation—from time to the ordinary means of knowledge—attain their own natures. ***This Reality is free and independent, a mass of bliss, and That alone am I; thus the entire universe is held as a reflection within me.***

Though represented here in words, this *an-upāya* experience is in reality entirely wordless; it could unfold in a few seconds or over the course of several days or weeks. There is no need for one who has had it to self-identify as one who has had it (indeed, that would probably be proof that one hasn't had it), for confirmation will come in time from one's teacher or one's deepest innate intuition and from the evidence that the revelation of the nature of Reality has indeed taken root and is abiding, affecting every aspect of your life and benefiting all beings.

ŚĀMBHAVA-UPĀYA: THE DIVINE MEANS

A small warning: most people find the following section very abstruse or difficult to understand because it is very subtle. If that's you, I advise you to simply skip to the next section because there are some very juicy and powerfully applicable spiritual teachings to be found there.

The subtlest—that is, the most refined, direct, and difficult to grasp— of the three *upāyas* is that called *śāmbhava.* Though it is a method, there are no practices as such at this level, at least none that are easily explained in ordinary words, for this level transcends all conceptual thought. I will summarize the salient features of this "Divine Means," then we will unpack them. As you can see in the chart on page 346, *śāmbhava* works with and requires only the Power of pure Will (*icchā-śakti*), the spontaneous creative upsurge of Consciousness, as well as the metapower of Freedom or Autonomy (*svātantrya-śakti*). In this means, we work with direct intuition we can have of pure Being by bringing attention to the upsurge of the dynamic flow of Consciousness' will to perceive (totally independent of what is perceived). Such intuition (*pratibhā*) results in wordless insights into some facet of the truth that blossom spontaneously.

This means emphasizes subjective awareness, not objective, especially the transcendental unity of the subject with all she perceives. It accesses the spacious and expansive sky of pure Consciousness (*cidākāśa*). This level of awareness functions "within the undivided realm of Śiva's pure Consciousness, which, free of all thought-constructs, [constitutes] the universal subject who contains within himself all objectivity."[150] In other words, the *śāmbhava* level is the level of total unity-consciousness into which all apparent duality is subsumed. But it reaches beyond unity-consciousness as well, for ultimately it accesses the infinitely vast stainless void of the Mind of Śiva that transcends both existence and non-existence—containing within it all that is and all that is not.

Open to grace in every moment.

In teaching the "practice" of *śāmbhava-upāya,* we can emphasize three primary aspects. The first is that this *upāya* is a way of grace. The practice of it consists primarily of opening to grace in every moment. One who is truly ready to practice on this level sees no distinction between the spiritual and the mundane and moves through the world expecting (and therefore finding) divine teachings and learnings around every corner. She sees the guru not just in her teacher but in all beings. She realizes and feels that grace is being offered constantly and, therefore, ceaselessly opens to receive it. She sees the divine Light in all people and situations. Though not yet constant, that is her baseline. (As you might have noticed, on the *śāmbhava* level path and goal are not sharply distinguished.) Working the *śāmbhava-upāya* involves the way you move through the world; it touches all the moments of life in which you are not doing formal spiritual practices. If you are always just "going about your business," believing you know who you are and what you are doing, you will miss many of the subtle unexpected moments of grace that are constantly being offered to you. Hence you cultivate a kind of divine unknowing here, for *not knowing* can be a state of openness and aliveness. This *upāya* invites you to explore the delicate and expansive joy of hovering on the knife-edge of divine uncertainty.

The second aspect of the practice of *śāmbhava* is the Spanda teaching of "catching hold of the first moment of perception," as it's called, or rather "bringing attention to the initial arising of an energy state" (different ways of translating *unmeṣa-daśā-niṣevaṇa*). In this practice, you tune in to the will to perceive the arising of each new experience, before the analytical and labeling mind gets involved. You can learn, through moment-to-moment nonanalytical awareness of your energy state, to become sensitive to the arising throughout the day of any mood, state, or feeling. Rather than leap to the thought, "This is hunger," or "This is sadness," or "This is contentment," you simply notice the initial subtle shift into a new energy state and rest in what that particular vibration feels like. If your interpretations of experience follow too closely upon the arising of experience, as they do for most people, you may not be ready yet to practice this subtle *upāya*. But for those whose minds have slowed down sufficiently (usually through meditation) to parse the phases of cognition, there is the possibility of "catching hold" of the initial burgeoning of a perception and dwelling in the simple flowing of awareness itself, prior to any application of mental understanding. As Abhinava writes in *Light on the Tantras*,

Tantrāloka 1.146–7

> *That which shines forth and is directly grasped in the first moment of self-aware perception, the single ground free of differential thought-constructs, is said to be the pure Will [to directly perceive]. Just as an object appears directly to one whose eyes are open without the intervention of any determinate cognition, so for some does Śiva's nature.*[151]

Such a practice is virtually impossible in the lifestyle of the average modern person, bombarded as it is with stimuli of all kinds.

The "noise floor" is simply too high. But if you have created sufficient space and silence in your life to simply be aware of the subtle movement of energy as each new state of the body-mind arises, many times each day, it becomes a fantastic opportunity to fall into easeful harmony with what is. There is of course no question here of trying to change what arises, for such a desire comes into being only after the mind has labelled what is arising as bad or undesirable; and this practice is about the movement into *vikalpa*-free perception, that is perception free of such differential mental constructs.

For help in understanding the *śāmbhava-upāya* (although, of course, the only purpose to an intellectual understanding of it is to get the mind on board with the process of its own negation), we may turn again to the *Vijñāna-bhairava-tantra*. Though in general *śāmbhava-upāya* cannot be explained, and there are therefore few attempts to do so in the literature, this atypical scripture includes a number of Zen-like techniques that are labelled as *śāmbhava-upāya* by Abhinava's disciple Kṣemarāja.[152] These techniques entail directly accessing the space of pure consciousness with no support other than one's immediate perception of an object or state. For example, in *Vijñāna-bhairava* verse 59, one simply allows one's awareness to be absorbed in the space within a jar or pot; in verse 60, one gazes at a vast open space or a blank wall; in verse 84, one looks up at the sky and allows one's mind to become like it; in verse 89, one uses sensory deprivation to perceive the inner void; in verse 101, one focuses one-pointedly on the burgeoning of any intense emotion. No instructions are given in the text: simply perceive and become absorbed, allow the mind to dissolve, and entry into Śiva-consciousness spontaneously occurs.

See page 242

Now, if you think this is easy, then you are probably mistaking a trance state for this Śiva-state. Entering into trance states of abstraction is *not* what is meant here, but something much more difficult for most people to attain: clear wakeful presence, effortlessly free of all thought-constructs. By contrast, a trance state is relatively dull, numb, or sometimes pleasantly luminous but hazy, without sharp wakeful clarity. Even dwelling in the real Śiva-state for a few moments is a successful beginning to *śāmbhava-upāya* practice. However, if effort is involved, other than the subtle act of simply giving yourself into flowing presence, then you are not at *śāmbhava-upāya* level but rather *āṇava-upāya*, since that is the level of meditation practice. *Śāmbhava* feels more like surrendering and opening than focusing. Finally, the practitioner of *śāmbhava* must do regular contemplative inquiry into whether s/he is accessing truly *nirvikalpa* states when practicing non-conceptual meditation or rather dwelling in a subtle *vikalpa* of meditation. (It's okay if that doesn't make sense yet.) If the latter is the case, more work at *śākta* and *āṇava* levels is needed, and a discussion of those levels is coming up next.

See page 383

The third and final aspect of *śāmbhava* practice, an aspect that is very important in the Trika, is working with mantras on nonconceptual levels. Nonconceptual mantras are ones that have no semantic value, no specific meaning, but are considered to be vibrations of the Divine (like OṂ, AIṂ, and HRĪṂ). In this practice, the subtle (i.e., inaudible) phonetic units of the mantra are experienced within oneself, taking on their essential nature as modes of Divine awareness. The practitioner directly accesses these modes of expanded consciousness, which express fundamental potencies of the Divine, by means of the Sanskrit syllables that embody them. If engaged as a technique (e.g., *mantra-uccāra*), this is in fact *āṇava-upāya*, and if engaged as a contemplation, it is *śākta-upāya*. However, there is a way to engage mantra practice as pure *śāmbhava-upāya*, in a little-understood technique by which you access *icchā-śakti*, pure will power, by focusing on a given phoneme without its vowel component—an unpronounceable letter like a "vowelless k." This is a kind of hovering on the edge of the impulse to articulate. It's like the feeling you have when you are about to do something, but you've forgotten what—except that instead of

See page 394

trying hard to remember, you simply remain on the leading edge of that "about to do" state.

Since there is no way to explain *śāmbhava* in purely *śāmbhava* terms, it being beyond the mind, Abhinava resorts to a rather arcane presentation of the Trika doctrine of linguistic mysticism in the chapter of the *Tantrāloka* that is meant to be devoted to *śāmbhava-upāya* (#3), a strategy that has confused many modern readers of his text. One of the few scholars in the world who has worked successfully to comprehend the material on linguistic mysticism is Paul Muller-Ortega, a scholar-practitioner and specialist in Abhinava Gupta. I offer here a sample of Paul's writing where he is mirroring Abhinava's method (and drawing also on the language of quantum mechanics) by providing a refined *śākta-upāya* contemplation of a *śāmbhava-upāya* process.

The process of parāmarśa, of setting up separate cognitions that will give rise to the phenomenal universe of everyday experience, is spelled out [by Abhinava] in terms of the coagulation or thickening of realities around interference patterns set up in the fundamentally unbroken and waveless Shiva. The vocalic order of phonemes represents this order of powers that arise as two masses or currents of consciousness collide. In this way disturbances in the perfect synchrony of the undivided self-referential consciousness arise and interference patterns occur. These disturbances are areas of patterned vibratory activity that result from the merging of the śaktis. They could be understood to constitute the generative matrices that give rise to finite objects and may be seen as discrete event areas.

Paul Muller-Ortega

Reading the third chapter of *Tantrāloka* (or the corresponding account in the *Tantrasāra*), which most people find extremely intellectual and difficult, gives a clue to the subtlety of access to the *śāmbhava-upāya* of linguistic mysticism. For in actuality, it is not a subject of intellectual philosophy but rather one of direct nonconceptual experience of the phonemic energies of pure Śiva-consciousness. Thus, I argue, Abhinava's account is meant to be understood intuitively and through meditative insight, not at all intellectually.

Śāmbhava-upāya is, to sum up, the immediate intuitive apprehension of the total flow of reality as it is, free of thought-constructs, dawning within awareness already whole and complete (*pūrṇa*), even if momentary. The key concepts for understanding this *upāya* are 1) *icchā*, the precognitive impulse of consciousness toward self-awareness within a given perception, prior to any language, excepting that on the level of 2) *paśyantī*, the visionary stage of language, where phonemes vibrate in their pure essences as the building blocks of both language and manifest reality; 3) *abheda*, the unity of subjective awareness, enveloping all object-awareness; and 4) *pratyakṣa*, the direct perception of the ground of Being as manifest in every moment of awareness, even the awareness of nothing.

See page 166

In his summary verse for *Essence of the Tantras*, chapter 3, Abhinava Gupta sings:

Tantrasāra

> *The entire universe shines here within the Self, just as a complex creation appears in a single mirror. However, awake Awareness consciously articulates the universe as an expression of the nectarean sweetness of its own self-awareness—no mirror can do that.*[153]

This verse suggests that Abhinava's focus on linguistic mysticism in his discussion of *śāmbhava-upāya* is due to the fact that he sees articulation as the natural result of the recursive quality within Consciousness by which it becomes aware of itself. Indeed, he uses the same word—*parāmarśa*—for both "phoneme" and "self-awareness." Since the phonemes represent the building blocks of reality, we are to see the entire universe as consisting of varied expressions of the loving self-awareness of the Absolute.

ŚĀKTA-UPĀYA

THE EMPOWERED MEANS

The Empowered Means focuses on shedding mental constructs that are not in alignment with reality (*aśuddha-vikalpas*) and the cultivation of wisdom, that is, modes of understanding that are in alignment with reality (*śuddha-vikalpas*). The process of the cultivation of wisdom is precisely analogous to the practice of yoga *āsanas*, for it challenges us to stretch our understanding by adopting postures of awareness. In adopting these postures, we seek to discover the alignments that create both greater strength and stability and greater ease and flow. We allow these postures to supplant old ways of holding ourselves and our world, ways that are not in alignment and thus create dis-ease. We will explore this profoundly empowering process in depth.

See page 108

In *śākta-upāya*, it is the Power of Knowing (*jñāna-śakti*) that is predominant. Since this *upāya* does not utilize external supports, but rather emphasizes the process of cognition over objects cognized, it is appropriate for those who wish to work directly with the heart-mind. In Abhinava's formulation, *śākta-upāya* primarily consists of refining, purifying, polishing, and perfecting our mental representations of reality (*vikalpas*) until they are fully aligned with the divine order, the true nature of things. In simpler terms, we replace our "negative" or misaligned stories with "positive" or aligned stories. When our mental representations become fully aligned with reality, they fall away, for we don't need them anymore. We can experience the beauty of reality without any story at all. Thus *śākta-upāya* naturally terminates in

Śākta-upāya consists of purifying our mind to replace our misaligned stories with aligned ones.

śāmbhava-upāya, wherein there is immediate intuitive apprehension of Reality without the intervention of the thinking mind.

This means is related to the Goddess (*śakti*), for it focuses on energy (*śakti*)—primarily the energy that inheres in thoughts and the emotions that are inextricably linked to them. Now, one of the most fascinating critiques of popular Western notions of self that Indian philosophy can offer is this: "mind" and "heart" are two different names for one and the same thing; they merely emphasize different aspects of that entity. That is to say, the Indian tradition holds that the locus of emotion and the locus of thought are one and the same, and therefore subconscious thoughts frequently manifest as emotions, and subconscious emotions as thoughts.

See page 95

It takes a few minutes (or years) to fully assimilate the implications of this. For one thing, it thoroughly undermines the American tendency to privilege feeling over thought or vice versa. A couple generations ago, people were taught to trust their reason over and against their wayward, irrational emotions. Emotion was seen as an unreliable guide to action. Nowadays, by contrast, we are told, "Listen to your heart," which unfortunately often really means, "Get in touch with your deeper programming." We are told, "Follow your heart," which unfortunately often is taken to mean, "Do what you want, putting aside reason, regardless of the consequences." If you watch television interviews as a sample, it seems that no one asks for reasoned opinions anymore: "What's your feeling on that?" "I really feel that..." which is usually just a way of giving an unthinking opinion that the person won't be obliged to defend because, after all, it is his feeling. I am critiquing this side of things more sharply because it is the current trend, but of course the other side is just as dangerous. We all know someone who is extremely rational and intelligent, and whose failure to be in touch with his human feelings enables him to perform actions that seem inhumanly insensitive.

By contrast, a yogī seeking to make a wise decision will carefully and soberly consult all aspects of his being—thought, feeling, intuition, instinct—and balance them all with the input of his teacher(s) and trusted friends. He privileges no one source over the others. To do so on a consistent basis, he knows, is to move ever further into disintegration.

Background to This View

Let us investigate a bit further the implications of the fact that the Sanskrit language does not have two separate words for "mind" and "heart." Both are used to translate the word *citta.* (Of course, the essence or core of our being is also sometimes called Heart [*hṛdaya*], but this is not at all the emotional heart that is the realm of psychology and valentines.) Nor does Sanskrit have distinct terms for "thought" and "emotion." Both are *citta-vṛtti*s, "vibrations of the mind-stuff" or "movements in the heart." A little investigation will show that the ancient sages were absolutely right, and it is only through lack of reflection that we picture ourselves as having two separate centers, one of which can be privileged over the other. The implications of this are crucial on the yogic path.

See page 95

First, it means that emotional states are often linked to a subconscious thought or thought-pattern. Whenever we are pulled from our natural state into a contracted state, we are almost always engaged in thinking about reality in a way that gives rise to that particular mood. Disliking the mood, or disliking yourself for having the mood—even if it is black depression, horrendous jealousy, or what have you—is missing the mark, for the mood expresses our natural embodied intelligence and signals that self-reflection is needed. Nature never acts without reason, and therefore every form of disease invites reflection. (This should not of course be taken to mean that whatever terrible state you find yourself in is "deserved." That kind of thinking is nothing more than a subtle form of self-hatred. Nor does it mean, "The universe is trying to show me something." That is often just the Judeo-Christian god of judgment under another name.) When we investigate, being ruthlessly honest and radically sincere with ourselves, we usually find that our "bad day" (or week, or month) was sparked by a negative thought-pattern, perhaps barely noticed at the time, which we believed and spun into a story, a picture of how reality is, one that is untrue and is disempowering to us. Nothing can drain us of our life-force energy (*prāṇa-śakti*) faster and more effectively than a well-spun story (*vikalpa*) that is not in alignment with reality. The problem is, we are often not even aware of our stories. Specifically the more the current story fits in with our generalized picture of reality (our *fears* about how reality "really is"), the less it stands out in our awareness. It must be ferreted out with self-reflection. Most of the time, the stories that rob us of our natural state are variations on the fundamental story that keeps us from Presence. For example, let's say that early in the day you make a minor mistake that creates a problem for someone. They get annoyed, but then see that the problem is not so major, and they forgive you. As far as they are concerned, it's done. Initially you feel better, but then you go on to have a rotten day in which nothing seems to go very well, and you are in a mild-to-severe bad mood until you get home and have a beer or watch TV, buffering your current state rather than enquiring into it. What has happened is simple but perhaps not obvious: the incident early in the day reignited your persistent subconscious story that you "just aren't good enough," or "always screw things up," or whatever. Since you believe that *vikalpa* at a fairly deep level, giving it just a little energy can make it simmer away beneath your threshold of consciousness, shaping your experience of reality all day long. Once this negative or cynical thought has been activated, you find more evidence to confirm it because now you are seeing reality from that perspective. This keeps the *vikalpa* stewing, and thus your day seems to go poorly (which is really just a pointer to the fact that something *inside* is being projected outward). We often feel we need some counter to this simmering negative story, like a critical mass of praise from our Facebook friends, to temporarily douse it. But until we finally digest and dissolve that *vikalpa*, something else will always heat it up again . . . and again . . . . Does this sound at all familiar? It is the nature of the cyclical stew we call *saṃsāra.* In fact, it's often called the ocean of *saṃsāra,* which means it's a very big stew.

After a lot of work in the *śākta-upāya* realm (which I will describe further below), I thought I was mostly free of *vikalpas*, those stories about reality that remove us from natural flowing Presence. But, still, I had bad days. If you are really free of *vikalpas*, you will never have a "bad day" again. Painful moments, sure, maybe even a whole bunch of them in a row, but a whole day (or week, or month) can only be "bad" with the help of stories. Knowing that, I had to reflect. And I realized that I still had this subtle story going on: if a few things in a row went well, if things were just clicking into place, it triggered the *vikalpa* "I am blessed, I am specially favored, everything's coming together, my life keeps getting better." Well, what's wrong with that, you might say. The problem is that a *vikalpa* exists in necessary relationship with its opposite. As long as we are caught in any pair of opposites, we move between the poles. We can't ever just stay on one side. So, if a few things in a row went poorly for me, especially early in the day, the opposite *vikalpa* would get triggered: "Nothing's going right, my life isn't really going anywhere, nothing really comes together for me," and I would get depressed, *even though I wasn't consciously aware of the story*. Though I'm able to state this plainly now, at the time it was quite subtle. I wouldn't really know why I was depressed until I did self-enquiry, a self-enquiry whose ability to pierce through to reality was greatly aided by radical honesty—the kind of honesty that comes only when I drop any sense of shame to be thinking anything so absurd as what I had been thinking.

This is a good illustration of why we must eventually become free of *vikalpas* altogether. For then we discover that having the wordless experience of "I am blessed" as the base reference point for our existence is *very* different from merely having the *vikalpa* of it; a state of being need not give way to its opposite, for it is not a construct. It has become reality.

A popular misunderstanding, one that must be corrected here, is that if you are experiencing a "negative" emotion, this is evidence that something is "wrong" or that you are out of alignment with reality. While it *is* often true that holding a view of things that is not in alignment will give rise to emotional states or moods that we (or others) find unpleasant, if we articulate it as the previous sentence did, we are in danger of saddling ourselves with a sin/guilt paradigm in disguise. A Tāntrika strives to see every state of mind, every mood and feeling, as a gift of the Goddess. The Tāntrika has two modes of learning about her true nature: learning from states of expansion, and learning from states of contraction. It is an absolutely false view to think that one mode is better than the other, or to measure your worth as a human being or competence as a yogī on the basis of how much time you spend in an expanded state and how much in a contracted one. True expansion into the fullness of your divine nature begins when you radically relinquish all such dualistic judgments. Such true expansion takes little or no effort to maintain, for it means entering into our true nature, whereas the dualistic type of expanded state takes effort to maintain, for we are still caught in the pairs of opposites—and every pole must eventually give way to its opposite. It is the natural law.

All states of mind, all emotions, are vibrations of the Shakti, manifestations of the one Goddess power.

All states of mind, all emotions or moods, are vibrations of the *śakti*, manifestations of the one Goddess/power. Therefore, the Tāntrika experiencing anger, or fear, or desire, acknowledges that this is a vibration of energy, that all energy is a manifestation of the Goddess, and therefore bows to her own emotion (whatever it is) with heartfelt gratitude, saying "O Goddess, thank you for coming in this form. What do you have to teach me?" Note how very different this posture is from the anxiety-ridden self-censorship of the so-called yogī who believes he has fallen from grace or is out of touch with God because he is experiencing a "negative" emotion. Such a person will not learn what that emotion has to teach if his only goal is to get back to feeling good as soon as possible. For such a person, the emotion will visit again and again, since he has failed to open to it as a teacher and, thus, has failed to integrate its energy. There is an enormous amount of energy locked in "negative" emotions that we cannot avail ourselves of without this basic self-acceptance. When we rise above self-condemnation and accept ourselves and what we are feeling, that energy naturally reveals its beneficial quality by pointing us to a deeper experience of our authentic nature. So let us drop this term "negative emotions" altogether, since it usually means "emotions we should not be having." On this path, there is no such thing. Practicing on the *śākta-upāya* level means casting aside forever the notion that one state of mind is "better" than another, and that you "should" be feeling this way or that. We accept what is. We work with what comes; we do our *sādhanā* on the basis of reality. Tāntrikas *must not fear pain or intense feeling of any kind or think it ungodly, or they cut themselves off from a huge source of life-energy*. Tāntrikas are sometimes called *vīras*, "heroes" or "adepts," because it takes heroic courage to look clearly at our pain and not push it away, saying, "That's not me," but rather embrace its power. All emotions are energy, and all energy (*śakti*) can empower us.

All emotions are energy; energy is power to transform.

We should also note the flip side of the above paradigm: that thoughts are often linked to hidden emotions. I was trained as an academic, and in the world of academia, we are taught to be "objective." So academics and other intellectuals tend to express their intellectual interests as though those interests exist in a vacuum, divorced from their feelings and humanity. But nothing exists in a vacuum, and once you get to know an academic (especially in my field of religious and cultural studies), you discover that their specific intellectual projects are in fact closely linked to their life history, psychology, and emotional landscape. By not acknowledging these forces that affect what point of view we argue for, we are actually making ourselves less objective by virtue of our lack of transparency. This hypocrisy or pretense in the academic world has been painful for me as a scholar-practitioner who has, until now, been "in the closet." This book, which seeks to integrate my academic and spiritual life, is in part my own personal "cry in the wilderness" against the compartmentalization of my humanity demanded by the culture of modern academia.

If you are a "heady" person, not fully in touch with your feelings, you have a tool in your hands now that you understand the link between thoughts and emotions that we have discussed. Note which opinions and views you hold strongly, if seemingly dispassionately, and trace them to a place in your being where they exist as pure emotion. For example, you may have strong opinions about what constitutes "justice" or "fairness." I'll wager that if you trace these abstract views to your emotions, you might discover suppressed anger about the time(s) when *you* were wronged. Seek it out and unlock its power.[154]

And when you do this, you are not so much moving from one center to another (such as from intellectual "mind" to emotional "heart") as much as uncovering the hidden threads of energetic structures that are larger than you realized. Once again, thoughts and feelings exist as a continuum, where the "thought" end is defined by its wordiness, its rationalization, and partial suppression of the full charge of the *bhāva* ("feeling, state of heart-mind") in question, and the "feeling" end is defined by its lack of wordiness and appearance of the full charge of energy in the given *bhāva*. When we discover the feeling component of a thought, or the thought hidden behind a feeling, we are bringing into full awareness the totality of the condensed energetic structure, which helps reveal its real nature and its effect on our reality.

ŚĀKTA-UPĀYA IN PRACTICE

Oriented in this way, let us then investigate the method of *śākta-upāya* that the Tantrik master Abhinava Gupta offers us in chapter 4 of his *Tantrāloka* and *Tantrasāra*. As indicated above, he distinguishes between *śuddha-vikalpa,* thought-constructs (or "stories") that are in alignment with the nature of reality, and *aśuddha-vikalpa,* those that are not in alignment. Of course, no *vikalpa* can express reality directly (i.e., nothing that can be articulated in words is completely or permanently true), so we are freed from needless debate about which propositions are "true" and which "false" and instead can focus on which are *effective* in bringing about direct experience of reality and which are not. This, then, is the key difference between the two types of *vikalpa:* the nonaligned ones generate an endless series of further thought-constructs, a sterile snake biting its own tail, whereas the aligned ones naturally lead you to (and then dissolve in) the wordless, storyless direct experience of reality: totally open, sharply real, and absolutely free. Have you ever had an argument with a loved one that went round and round in circles, until you got tired and finally just forgave each other, without arriving anywhere or reaching any real understanding? When, by luck or discernment or help from your teacher, you light upon a *śuddha-vikalpa,* it brings you to a point of profound touching-down in the experience of reality as it is. Speaking such a truth brings about that moment when the heart begins to soften and melt, when your eyes start with tears, when you drop into deep connection with the other person in the conversation, regardless of who articulated the truth.

The characteristic of ordinary *vikalpas* is that they create artificial mental divisions in the fullness of the one Consciousness that manifests as both self and world. By contrast, purified and refined *vikalpas* that are highly distilled, carefully contemplated, lucid, precise, and that conform to the true nature of reality help to bring about a liberative realization of that reality in its fullness. In other words, these purified *vikalpas* have the unique feature of pointing us beyond themselves to the raw, unmediated, nonconceptual experience of the real. (*aśuddha-vikalpa -> śuddha-vikalpa -> nirvikalpa.*[155]) How does this happen?

Vikalpas are, for the most part, like programs downloaded from the Internet that affect how your computer operates. We download programs from parents, teachers, television, and so on, from before the moment we can understand language onward. Some we are aware of; others manage to download themselves under our radar. All these programs get installed on the "hard drives" of our brains, and can even rewrite the code of our operating systems. If we download and install a "virus", it can take over completely, forming a limited view that seems impossible to escape. We start to work with *śākta-upāya* when we become aware that the way we see and experience reality is largely (in some cases, entirely) dictated by the network of programs that have been installed and that there are yet entirely different ways of experiencing reality unavailable to us until we do some reprogramming. Studying and internalizing spiritual philosophy is indeed "brain-washing" ourselves in the literal sense; we're cleansing ourselves of programs not in alignment with ultimate Reality. Such a process is express of your *svātantriya-śakti* or power of autonomy, for now you are consciously directing the writing of the code instead of automatically installing whatever is presented to you, as you did as a child. You are reprogramming yourself with the truth, for you know the result is freedom, connection, appropriate response to your situation, and self-determination. Sometimes, though, we encounter serious resistance in this process of challenging everything we thought we knew as the old programs violently reassert themselves. You might go through a phase of seeing your teacher as a self-righteous, self-satisfied manipulator; the teachings as bullshit; and your spiritual community as full of fakes. It is natural for episodes of cognitive dissonance to arise in this process. When you connect to your Core, you know you are in the right place, doing the necessary work, so you can ride out such episodes.

Having explained things in this way, an objection may arise, especially in the minds of those familiar with some postmodern thinking. How do we know that the new program we are calling "truth" really bears a more intimate and accurate relation to reality than the old one? Haven't we merely replaced a program that made us miserable with one that makes us happier in life? That in itself is hardly a guarantee that it is more aligned with the nature of reality. And if we present the counter-argument that these *śuddha-vikalpa*s take us past words and dissolve in wordless experience, the objectioner will reply that may be true of any *vikalpa* sufficiently deeply rooted. That is, any program installed on the "root drive" (the *paśyantī* level) shapes our experience of reality in fundamental ways without our conscious awareness. In reply to this objection, we may first say that even if the objection is correct, we could do worse than to impose upon the so-called formless, meaningless chaos of reality a view that makes us joyous and fills us with love for all living beings. From that perspective, we need hardly bother with the refutation. But, out of compassion for the objectioner's intellect-identified and suffering soul, Abhinava refutes it anyway. See page 170

He argues that the experience of reality grounded in differential mental constructs can be undermined, destabilized, and eventually obliterated through the cultivation of thought-forms that are purified, refined, and aligned—but not the other way around. That is, the true experience of the world, made possible by spiritual practice integrated in body, mind, and spirit and empowered by right View, *cannot* be undermined or destabilized by any dualistic thought-construct. That is because the experience of Reality-as-it-is is not contingent upon thought-constructs; in fact, no thought-construct can help it manifest *or* undermine it any way. "What?" the objectioner responds. "I thought you just said that these purified thought-forms can help it manifest?" No, Abhinava replies; what actually happens is that the *śuddha-vikalpa*s serve to destroy the *aśuddha-vikalpa*s that are the substratum of the false experience of duality as the ultimately real. When these are destroyed, the purified thought-forms naturally dissolve, their work done, and we simply see things as they truly are. Such true seeing can never be supplanted. Without the impositions of the programmed mind, we see that which is always right in front of our faces, because Reality *is* eternally self-manifest and needs no *vikalpa* to manifest it. The source of all light does not need to be illumined; it is self-luminous.

Are you experiencing Reality or a mental construct of reality?

This teaching gives you a great test to determine whether you are experiencing Reality or just a mental construct of reality (for if the construct is sufficiently refined, it can be *very* difficult to discern its presence). If someone else's opinion or argument or words in any form can rob you of the feeling or power or integrity of your spiritual experience, even a little bit, then your so-called "experience" either is or has become a *vikalpa,* not (yet) rooted all the way into Reality (which is not to say it has no benefit). This is why gurus with wisdom will send their disciples back home to their families at a certain point or tell them to get a job. Living in the bubble of spiritual community, or around others who all more or less agree with your values, you may think you have attained a high level. Around those who think you are a freak or weirdo for practicing this path at all, let alone agree with its principles, you will see your real attainment and come into your real situation. As my teachers say, when the rubber meets the road, you will find out what you really have. Humbled, you may have to begin again, but this time the beginning will be a real beginning. You have seen that living in a *vikalpa* (mental construct) of the spiritual life is not the goal. The goal is direct experience of reality, unmediated by *vikalpas*. With clear seeing, you can get real results in your practice.

It is hard to imagine the experience of *nirvikalpa* perception, clear seeing without the mediating presence of mental constructs, until you've actually had it. It is especially hard for those postmodern intellectuals I alluded to earlier; so hard, they don't believe such a thing is possible. Suffice to say, however, that those who have experienced *nirvikalpa* perception will never doubt its reality, since it is an *entirely different order of experience* from any mediated by *vikalpas*. To use words that only approximate it, it is luminous and clear, sharp and vivid, totally present and connected, ineffably beautiful, inexpressibly *real*. It can implode into awareness in a moment, gently or violently, effortlessly sweeping away all that the mind can think. You feel as vulnerable and raw as if your soul has been laid bare, yet invincibly strong. And all these words come only afterward, when you try to explain it. But do not try too hard, lest you objectify the experience; if it becomes another *vikalpa*, you will no longer have access to the power of the experience, it will just be another memory appropriated by your ego.

Let's turn to the exact words of the master. Abhinava writes,

*When a person chooses to gradually purify and refine his mental constructs of reality, as the means for attaining experiential realization of the true nature of things, then he employs a process of contemplation [*bhāvanā*] that presupposes sound reasoning [*sat-tarka*], true scriptures [*sad-āgama*], and instruction by a true Guru [*sad-guru*].*

Tantrasāra: ch. 4

For total stability in this process, we need a threefold support, and that tripod consists of *sat-tarka*, *sad-āgama*, and *sad-guru*. The scriptures (which are, of course, *śuddha-vikalpa*) need the explanation of a true

See page 70

teacher (whose words are also *śuddha-vikalpa*), which together support and empower the development of our own *śuddha-vikalpas* along sound lines when we use proper discernment. "True scriptures" are those that have successfully helped beings to final liberation and have been handed down in lineage transmission. A "true teacher" is one who has a well-contemplated understanding based on his own experience and who speaks for the benefit of all beings (accepting benefit to himself as a mere side effect). A *sadguru*, then, is not a teacher of mere information but a transmitter of the power of experiential understanding. When any teacher speaks a truth that she has full experience of, with clarity and heartfelt conviction, in that moment she embodies the *sadguru*. (However, to be a "full-time" guru, one must have received authorization and empowerment from one's own guru to serve in that role.) Abhinava continues,

Tantrasāra: ch. 4

> *Due solely to the power of differential mental constructs, sentient beings imagine themselves bound, and this very egoic conception is the cause of the repetitive bondage of the cycle of worldly suffering. Hence, when a mental construct that opposes that conception has arisen and become established, it crushes that mental construct that is the cause of saṃsāra; thus it [indirectly] causes salvation.*

Tantrāloka: ch. 15

> *Just as the man who thinks intensely that he is a sinner becomes such, just so one who thinks himself to be Śiva, and none other than He, becomes Śiva. This certainty, which penetrates and affirms itself in our thoughts, coincides with an awareness free of thought-constructs engendered by a series of [refined and purified] differentiated mental representations, the object of which is our identity with Śiva.*[156]

Abhinava then goes on to present an example of a purified thought-form, which if cultivated and deeply internalized, has the power to crush dualistic *vikalpas*. In reading his words, note that *viśva,* here translated as "the universe" also means "all things."

Tantrasāra: ch. 4

That pure unlimited Consciousness—transcending all principles of reality that are limited by nature, from Earth to Śiva—alone is the supreme reality. That is the ground for the establishment of all things. That is the vital essence [ojas] of the universe. By That the universe lives and breathes, and That alone am I. Thus I embody the universe and yet transcend the universe.[157]

Now, if we read this passage just to feel good about ourselves, as an "affirmation," we are cheating ourselves of the power of the practice of *vikalpa-saṃskāra.* Instead, we must take it—or any other passage we wish to work with in this way—through the following steps. This is the *bhāvanā-krama* or stages of contemplation. This could all happen in one day or over many days.

Stages of contemplation

1. Ensure that the passage resonates with you. If not, massage the wording (without changing the meaning) until it does, or find another passage that does.
2. Look up any words that you don't know well; become very comfortable with the meaning of the passage on the *vaikharī* level, the level of the literal words. Traditionally, you would memorize the passage in this stage.
3. Ponder its meaning more deeply; allow your mind to roam through associated ideas. Ask yourself, "How would I experience the world if I felt the truth of this statement fully?" Imagine how you might move through the world if you were living the statement fully. (This is the *madhyamā* level.)

See page 168

4. When you reach a point where you start to become slightly bored with your passage, and think you understand it

thoroughly, sit with it (or part of it, such as the final sentence in the above passage) and meditate. Let it be a mantra. Invoke the power of grace, and ask for deeper understanding than can be gotten through the intellect. Then allow whatever arises to arise. If the meditation becomes stagnant, ask the deeper wisdom, "Is there anything more?" and sit and wait quietly. (This is the *paśyantī* level.)

5. For a few days, go to sleep with the passage, wake up with the passage, and revisit it several times throughout the day. In self-reflection, examine any resistance you have to receiving its wisdom on the deepest level of your being and inquire into the causes.
6. Then let it go, but observe how the wisdom you have internalized shows up in daily life experience.

I could add more stages, but at this point the process becomes highly organic and individual. One may begin the process again with another passage. If this practice, which is sometimes called "insight meditation," is done correctly, it results in the teaching becoming fully assimilated at the deepest level. You know this has happened because you can explain the teaching clearly using language wholly different from that in which you learned it (for example, to a friend or family member who doesn't have a spiritual practice like yours and doesn't know the jargon). As one of my teachers used to say, "If you can't show it, you don't really know it!" If you have deeply assimilated a teaching, you recognize its "energy signature" and can therefore spot the same teaching when it appears in a different religious tradition that uses different language for it. But most significantly of all, an assimilated teaching is a living reality: without having to remember the teaching mentally, it is a pulsing power within you, a power of grace that can open you to experiencing the divinity of any given moment. It is an ally, like a mantra or a deity.

Once you have done the process with a few teachings from this book, try composing your own *śuddha-vikalpa.* Abhinava Gupta teaches us to replace an impure (untrue) *vikalpa* with its opposite. Again, an impure *vikalpa* is one that, if believed, separates us from our essence-nature. To engage the process of removing these *vikalpa*s in the way Abhinava recommends, first identify one of your negative messages or "tapes" that you tend to run when you've done something "wrong" or "bad." For example, when I thought I'd screwed up, I used to punish myself by saying (and believing), "I'm so stupid!" Then one of my teachers said to me, "That's a good way to ensure you keep repeating the behavior." I said, "What? Why?" I thought if I made myself feel badly enough for it, surely I would stop behaving that way. This was in retrospect clearly the internalization of the punishment technique of parenting (which, by the way, is wholly ineffective—virtually everyone uses it, and look at the world we have). My teacher said, "If you convince yourself that you're stupid, then you will obviously keep doing the things that 'stupid' people do. Remember that the ego's priority is to maintain its self-image. It would rather be right than happy, and if you keep repeating the 'stupid' behavior, the ego will have that satisfaction." (Of course, this teaching about relinquishing self-judgment should not be construed to mean that we may thereby relinquish discernment about what constitutes skillful versus unskillful action.)

We all believe things about ourselves that our loved ones find absurd, but we cling to them nonetheless because we believe we have plenty of evidence for them. But our thinking is wrong-headed: it is *because* we believe the self-image that we see the world in such a way that confirms our view. When we ask ourselves, "Would *I* rather be happy or right?" we take a leap of faith. If we wait for enough "evidence" to come in before changing our self-image, we will wait forever, and grow old and petrified in our views in the meantime. So identify one of your negative self-messages now, and compose an antidote for it as Abhinava suggests. Now if, for example, mine is "I'm so stupid," I might think the antidote is "I'm actually really smart!" Unfortunately, such a feeble rejoinder will not be successful in displacing an impure thought-form that has taken deep root and plagued you for years. As Abhinava teaches, the new purified thought-form 1) must be very powerful and 2) must terminate in the ultimate Reality. The only way to make it do that is to take it all the way to God. For example, instead of "I'm actually really smart," I might say, "The divine intelligence that created this whole universe dwells within me as me, and by contacting it, I can understand anything I truly need to know in this life." Now that's something with power that I can work with, and it is a *vikalpa* that can *take me beyond itself,* which if you recall is one definition of a *śuddha-vikalpa.*

If you succeed in finding a true antidote to your negative self-message, you will know because you will probably be uncomfortable repeating it. You might feel silly saying it, or you might start to cry. A student of mine, when working with this technique, identified the negative self-message of "I'm a bad mother." When she came up with the feeble antidote of "I'm a good mother," I challenged her to root her *śuddha-vikalpa* in God. She said, "I am a manifestation of the Divine Mother," and burst into tears. Then she said, "But I don't really believe it." We realized it had to be authentic for her, so we modified the statement to "I am a manifestation of the Divine Mother *in the process of realizing and embodying my true nature.*" You might try something similar so that it challenges you but also rings true for you. Then you might take the ultimate challenge: go to the mirror and look yourself right in the eye and repeat your *śuddha-vikalpa,* no matter how silly you feel, until you get past the point of feeling silly. You may be amazed at what happens. (If the mirror doesn't work for you, you could try using a loved one as your "mirror.")

At the end of chapter 4 of *Essence of the Tantras,* Abhinava offers the following trenchant verses on the practice I have been describing. You might think, by the way, that this practice is startlingly modern in its awareness of human psychology, given that it was taught a thousand years ago in the very different culture of medieval Kashmīr. We may perhaps take it as evidence that the fully awakened and integrated consciousness of a *mahāsiddha* really does transcend its cultural confines, even as it must express itself using the language of that very culture. Abhinava writes,

Tantrasāra: ch. 4

A bound soul has convictions such as "I am only inert matter; I am completely bound by my karma; I am impure; I am a victim." When he succeeds in attaining the firmly rooted conviction of the opposite of these views, he immediately becomes the Lord whose body is the whole universe and whose soul is Consciousness. ||

In whatever manner such a conviction may be attained, a superior yogī must cultivate it at all times. He should not be led into doubt by the mass of foolish teachings in the world; i.e., by any viewpoint not grounded in the real nature of things. ||

He then adds two beautiful, poetic verses, writing not in Sanskrit but rather in the Prākṛt language, which was much closer to the language of the common people:

"I am a filthy sinner," "I am a bound creature," "I am separate from all other beings," or even "I transcend all things"[158]*—when such firm beliefs are innate stains on the heart, how indeed for such a person can the vision of supreme reality flash forth? ||*

In the heart-lotus of consciousness that has blossomed due to an intense Descent of a ray of light from the sun of the Highest Divinity, the phases of awareness emit the exquisite fragrance of the Self, revealing its secret nature: there the bee of Self-

> *Awareness vibrates, cherishing the experience of its own radiant core, humming "I am the divine Lord, overflowing with the reality of all beings!"* ||

The last verse alludes to the other major teaching given under the heading of *śākta-upāya:* the worship of the subtle phases of cognition as twelve aspects of the Goddess Kālī. We will not be examining this secret doctrine of the Krama here. Instead, we will conclude by looking at what Abhinava says about the practices of yoga and *kriyā* in the context of *śākta-upāya.* None of the limbs of yoga (meditation, ritual, the *yamas* and *niyamas*, etc.) can be considered a direct means to liberation, he argues; they have spiritual value only insofar as they contribute to the one and only direct means, which is true insight into reality (*sat-tarka*), an insight that manifests Pure Wisdom (*śuddha-vidyā*). In light of this, he presents the inner, *śākta-upāya* meaning and significance of the most common *āṇava-upāya* practices. In so doing, he means to imply that 1) these are the understandings that can empower those external practices and indeed constitute their very essence for the liberation-seeker, and 2) if these understandings are fully assimilated, we do not necessarily need the external practices (though again, it is a rare being that can do without the external supports).

Abhinava proceeds to list the traditional Indian spiritual practices, describing their significance in a *sādhanā* of Consciousness.

Tantrasāra: ch. 4

> PŪJĀ: *Worship is the offering of all existent things and states of being [bhāvas] into the Highest Divinity, in order to attain the firm understanding that they all subsist within the Highest Divinity alone, and there is nothing other than That.*

> *Because they are pleasing to the Heart, we begin by offering those things that tend to spontaneously dissolve into blissful awareness and are thus easefully offered to God. For this reason, we are taught [in scripture] to use in external practice those things that delight the aesthetic senses, such as flowers, libations of fragrant wine, and scented unguents.*[159]

What does it mean to offer something into the Highest Divinity? It means to dissolve your perception of it as being something other than the one divine Awareness. It means to melt away the thought-constructs by which you see your offering as anything other than God. Now, since some things are easier to see as divine than others, Abhinava suggests that, in the context of ritual, we start by offering objects that are pleasing to the aesthetic sense. When seeing, smelling, tasting, and touching that which is beautiful, it takes little to no effort to repose in awareness. We might take the example of a poem that strikes us as very beautiful: the moment the poem ends, we do not immediately dissect its meaning; rather, for at least a few seconds, we simply rest in the *rasa* or flavor of awareness created by the poem. This repose within innate awareness is called *viśrānti* and is very important in Abhinava's teaching. If the repose is expanded by aesthetic rapture and includes a measure of loving self-awareness, it is called *ānanda*, commonly translated as bliss but actually connoting something much more subtle than excitement or even ecstasy.

Ānanda is unconditional love for one's own power of awareness.

In the state of *ānanda*, one does not differentiate the object of awareness from oneself, and so by loving it, one is loving oneself, one is loving the very power of awareness that is God. So the practice of *pūjā* begins with those things one finds beautiful, so that one can observe what it is like to repose (even for a moment) in a state in which there is no differentiation between the object, one's awareness of it, and the divine Power that makes all awareness possible—with the whole experience englobed by a *love for the sheer fact of being aware.* Notice that when someone smells a sublime scent or tastes sublime food, they close their eyes for a moment; they are savoring consciousness itself, not dwelling on so-called objective reality. This is a tiny kernel of the aesthetic rapture that Abhinava invites us to cultivate.

However, he tells us to offer *all* things into the Highest Divinity, not just the ones we most like. This tells us that the aesthetically pleasing *pūjā* is just a training ground for a more difficult practice. The principle at work here is that of *overspill*—that is, when you cultivate the experience of beauty, you expand your capacity to experience the beautiful. When you cultivate the experience of love, you expand your capacity to love. It's as if you get a kind of momentum of love going, and then it spills over and you find yourself able to love people who previously challenged you. Consciously allowing this overspill is crucial if we wish to become free of our enslavement to the preferences of the mind.

Therefore, after practicing reposing in the sweetness of beauty-flavored consciousness at your altar of worship for some time, begin trying it with other experiences. To do this practice, when you are aware of something that repulses or frightens or bores or amuses you, try bringing your awareness to the fact of your own subjectivity—to consciousness itself, flavored by its object, rather than the illusion of subject-object duality. Become fascinated by the "texture," "color," and "flavor" of a consciousness temporarily imbued with the object in question. Then relish and give thanks for the fact that you are aware at all. In this way, go beyond your superficial like or dislike of the object, and become absorbed by the miracle of consciousness itself. Finally, remember to offer all states of mind and heart into God, by contemplating that they are vibrations of the one energy and realizing their non-difference from That.

Now we may proceed to look at the inner meaning of fire-offerings.

Tantrasāra: ch. 4

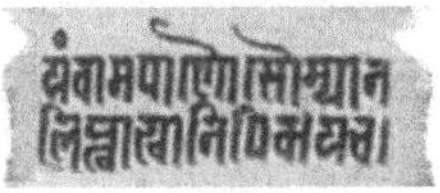

HOMA: *All existent things and states consist of the radiant energy [tejas] of the Highest Divinity. It is to attain a firm understanding of this fact that one makes fire-offerings [homa], which are the dissolution of all existent things and states into the effulgent energy of the Fire of Consciousness that is the Highest Divinity—which longs for the aesthetic rapture of "devouring" all existent things and states—such that all that remains is that energy.*

The same teaching as above, that everything is a form of God, is given here in a different way (it being, after all, Abhinava's central teaching). The key difference is that in the previous practice, there was a remainder of objective awareness; one worked with consciousness flavored by its object. Here, the object is completely devoured in the sense that there is no longer any perception of it as being anything other than the one energy. In this practice then, one does not maintain awareness of difference but rather experiences everything as having the same substance and essence (*sāmarasya*), the blazing effulgence of the all-consuming divine Fire of Consciousness. Thus the previous practice emphasized creation, the Goddess Parā, whereas this one emphasizes dissolution, the Goddess Kālī. (These two goddesses are of course both aspects of each other.) The next practice turns awareness to the ground of both creation and dissolution.

Tantrasāra: ch. 4

JAPA: *In the same way, mantra repetition has the purpose of giving rise to the state of awareness that underlies both [the creating and dissolving functions of Consciousness]. It consists of having the inner awareness: "The supreme Reality that exists as my own innermost essence remains just as it is, unaffected by the differentiated entities or states that constitute the various objects of consciousness, whether internal or external."*[160]

Here the practitioner affirms the understanding that is the true *mantra* (note that the interpretive etymology of *mantra* is "that which protects the one who thinks it"). Even as consciousness is flavored by its objects, there is always an aspect of it that is utterly transcendent, uncontracted by any perception. Affirming this repeatedly with deep conviction can increase our capacity to be connected with that level. As Abhinava says,

> *Though the ultimate reality that constitutes one's own innate nature does not depend upon any vikalpa, it may shine forth by means of the various conceptualizations (described above) that are aspects of Pure Wisdom [śuddha-vidyā].*

Lastly, Abhinava offers us an intriguing and, as far as I know, unique definition of yoga.

> YOGA: *In this context, yoga is a special kind of vikalpa that is in essence an investigation into the true nature of That [Reality], in order to attain nothing less than its constant and uniform manifestation.*

Since "yoga" nearly always denotes a psycho-physical practice aimed at dissolving the mind as we understand it, it is surprising that Abhinava describes it as a "special kind of *vikalpa*." I take him to mean here that yoga entails a particular frame of mind that allows us to experientially enquire into, and realize unity with, the true nature of things. This is the Tantrik paradox: adopting a yogic frame of mind frees us from the belief that we are nothing but the mind. The important point here is that just as physical yoga entails the reconditioning of the body, every spiritual practice, even the transmental ones, must entail the reconditioning of the mind in order to conform it to the deep structure of reality, the innate patterning of Consciousness.

While we might suspect that Abhinava is working to advance his own agenda here by overcoding his mystical gnostic interpretation of these practices, I want to point out that he does in fact have a scriptural basis for this mode of interpretation: the *Vijñāna-bhairava-tantra.* Let us turn to the last verses of that text, where an esoteric reading of ritual and yoga is given that, while much more compressed, parallels Abhinava's quite closely.

See page 242

Vijñāna-bhairava-tantra

> *The revered Goddess said: "If, O Lord, this is the true form of Parā [the Supreme Goddess], how can there be mantra or its repetition in the [nondual] state you have taught? What would be visualized, what worshipped and gratified? And who is there to receive offerings?" The revered Bhairava said: "In this [higher way], O doe-eyed one, external procedures are considered coarse [*sthūla*]. Here 'japa' is the ever-greater meditative absorption [*bhāvanā*] into the supreme state; and the 'mantra' to be repeated is the spontaneously arising resonance [of inner experience] which aligns with that. As for 'meditative visualization,' [*dhyāna*] it is a mind that has become motionless, free of forms, and supportless, not imagining a deity with a body, eyes, face, and so on.* Pūjā *is likewise not the offering of flowers and so on. A mind made firm, which through careful attention dissolves into the thought-free ultimate Void [of pure Awareness]: that is pūjā.*[161]

Such esoteric interpretations serve their function best when they interiorize and deepen already acquired forms of exoteric practice.

While *śāmbhava-upāya* is nonsequential (*akrama*) direct insight, and *āṇava-upāya* involves a process (*krama*) that unfolds in specific stages, *śākta-upāya* is described as "sequential-yet-nonsequential" (*kramākrama*) because it involves gradual cultivation of understanding punctuated by sudden leaps of insight. These leaps take place when the understanding or mental construct we are working with becomes sufficiently close to reality that it suddenly collapses into reality, dissolving into direct (nonconceptual) experience. Just as the *āsanas* of modern postural yoga challenge our bodies, stretching them in new ways, repatterning and creating over time a whole new body, in *śākta-upāya* we hold expanded understandings, "postures of the mind," that function to reshape our consciousness, creating a whole new mind. This mind is fresher, more open and more luminous, with a greater capacity for childlike wonder coupled with mature wisdom. It is also much more flexible and adaptable, responding appropriately to all kinds of situations. It is clear and strong, free of unneeded detritus. To attain this mind, saturate it with the nectarean words of the masters and sages. But do not be content with understanding those words; work them into the very tissues of your being until your whole being vibrates with them!

That comment brings us to the other aspect of *śākta-upāya* work. Once you have worked extensively with the energy (*śakti*) of your own thoughts and feelings, you can tune in more and more effectively to "the powers operating in all of life's activities as particular pulsations (*viśeṣa-spanda*) in the universal rhythm (*sāmānya-spanda*) of the Power of Consciousness."[162] This practice cannot be described in a step-by-step method, for it consists of a deep and grounded attentiveness to the subtle patterns of energy moving in and as all things, patterns that consist both of repeating universals and of unique-to-that-moment particulars. Suffice to say that this practice begins to unfold spontaneously when you have heightened your awareness and slowed down the pace of your life enough to look deeper than the surface of things. When you no longer are projecting your mind-world onto everything, you naturally start to notice the rhythmic dance of life-energy all around you. This integration into the deeper pattern can give rise to astonishing synchronicities, even a sense of magic, as seeing how everything fits with everything else allows your own life to flow more effortlessly.

Integration into the deeper pattern can give rise to astonishing synchronicities.

This whole chapter has itself been an exercise in *śākta-upāya* practice. If you read the words as more than mere information, you are probably not the same person you were at the beginning—and you are now ready to begin again and do your spiritual work with renewed intensity, joy, and faith.

ĀṆAVA-UPĀYA: THE INDIVIDUAL, EMBODIED MEANS

Any spiritual practice that an external observer can see and identify falls under the heading of "the Embodied Means," which thereby covers the great majority of religious acts. For the majority of practitioners, especially those who are just beginning a spiritual practice, *āṇava-upāya* is the most appropriate method. The word *āṇava* ("individual") derives from *aṇu,* a term that refers to an individual embodied soul (= *jīva*), a contracted form of Consciousness. So *āṇava-upāya*, the individual/embodied means, is the appropriate starting place for those who experience themselves in that way: as individuals for whom plurality appears as the most "real" level of reality. In other words, those who see things as concretely differentiated most of the time, i.e., nearly all of us. *Āṇava-upāya* is thus the method that emphasizes objects of awareness (rather than focusing on awareness itself), primarily the body, breath, and centers of the subtle body. It primarily utilizes the Power of Action (*kriyā-śakti*). Therefore, it is the easiest of the three means to understand and practice. It helps to refine awareness, making it more subtle, such that the other two means become more accessible.

Yoga traditionally includes meditation, pranayama, visualization, activating the subtle centers, bodily postures, and mantra.

The techniques of *āṇava-upāya*, conceived generally, are all those usually grouped under the headings of *yoga* and *kriyā*: meditation, *prāṇāyāma*, visualization, mantra repetition, activation of the subtle centers, bodily postures, and meditative ritual performance. Nearly all of these were transmitted into the *haṭha-yoga* tradition (except the last, which was transmitted into Hindu temple culture) and from there into modern yoga. So nearly all of the practices taught under the name of yoga today would be considered *āṇava-upāya.* Since *āṇava* works in the realm of plurality, there is a diverse array of such practices, and the practitioner needs to decide which ones are most effective for her (though traditionally, a guru would assign a practice to a neophyte practitioner, discerning more accurately what will be effective than she can herself). Since these yogic practices are well known, I will not dwell on their basic forms here. Suffice to say that *any* yogic practice, when performed as an integrated part of a Tantrik *sādhanā* grounded in a Tantrik View, automatically becomes a Tantrik practice.

Since you are already familiar with many of the practices of yoga that have survived down to the present, let's look at how these practices are presented in the mature classical Tantra, with reference to Abhinava Gupta's *Light on the Tantras* and *Essence of the Tantras.* There we find much more subtle versions of the commonly known practices. He describes these techniques:

- meditative visualization of the flow of the powers of consciousness through the sense-faculties (*dhyāna*);
- meditation on the flow of the vital energies (*prāṇa-uccāra*);
- meditation on empowered seed-syllables, subtle mantras that are synchronized with the breath (*varṇa-uccāra*);
- performing yogic postures (*karaṇa*);
- performing ritual worship (*pūjā*), in which the divine energy worshipped can be installed in internal substrates, such as the breath, or (more commonly) external substrates, such as *maṇḍalas* or deity images.

We will briefly describe some of these practices. Although Abhinava subordinates them to the higher yoga of the mind, he nevertheless argues that, when approached correctly, they lead to precisely the same result. That is to say, he holds the view that to take any practice to its ultimate conclusion, we must eventually entail and entrain* every part of ourselves in the process. So theoretically, any one practice, thoroughly understood and mastered, could take us all the way to our goal. Most of us, however, are at a distinct advantage if we incorporate a variety of modalities in our spiritual journey. Abhinava writes:

*Entrain means to "incorporate and sweep along in its flow" or "cause (something) to gradually fall into sync," an uncommon but very yogic word.

The Individual Means [āṇava-upāya] is that which is applied in the spheres of imagination, prāṇa, the body, and external things. There is absolutely no difference among these methods in that the practice of any of them may yield the supreme fruit.

Tantrasāra: ch. 5

Dhyāna

Let's explore some of the practices Abhinava describes under the heading of *āṇava-upāya* in his book *Essence of the Tantras* (composed in Sanskrit around the year 1010, here appearing in my translation). The first is a practice of meditative visualization (*dhyāna*) of a kind typical of classical Tantra, though here encoded with deeper spiritual meaning than is commonly found. In this practice, the instrument of imagination (*buddhi*) is predominant. The summary verses that Abhinava composed to describe the practice concisely and poetically are as follows:

Having internalized the triad of knower, knowing, and known, one should meditate on it as the self-luminous Reality that is all, abiding within the radiant abode of bliss in the heart. ||

Tantrasāra: ch. 5

> *One should meditate on that all-pervasive reality in the form of the Fire-Wheel that is Bhairava—with rays of light that are the twelve great Powers of Consciousness—issuing forth from an opening of the body toward an external object, becoming its creation, stasis, and dissolution. ||*
>
> *The yogī should thus contemplate the totality of all external objects and their internal impressions as absorbed into that Wheel, coming to rest in himself as its ground. Thus his real nature will be revealed.*

Of course, the practice needs be described in more practical detail in order to be doable. First I will present a bullet-point summary of the steps, then explain them in detail.

Tantrik *dhyāna* (meditative visualization) as described in *Essence of the Tantras*

1. Center your awareness in the space of the Heart, remembering that therein dwells the divine Light that is the essential nature of all things.
2. Visualize your body as a body of light, focusing your visualization vividly on the three primary subtle channels (*nāḍīs*), breathing out of the solar channel (pingalā), breathing into the lunar (iḍā), and holding the breath in the central channel (suṣumnā) until the three "fuse" in the heart center.
3. Visualize the fused energy as the radiant light of the Deity in the form of a twelve-spoked wheel of fire, rising from the heart, flowing out of one of the sense-apertures, and coming to rest on an external object (actually present or imagined).
4. As the fire-wheel spins, resting on this object, contemplate that the object is created by consciousness alone, that

consciousness alone maintains it, and that consciousness dissolves it back into itself.

5. After the object has dissolved into the fire-wheel, withdraw it back into yourself, reposing in the dynamic stillness of the Absolute ground of the whole process.
6. The process repeats, except now the object is the subliminal impression (*saṃskāra*) of the prior object.

Now that you have an overview, let's explore these steps and the information necessary to apply them. As with all the practices Abhinava offers, you begin by centering your awareness in your heart, which serves as a locus for the contemplation of the ultimate Heart, which is the core of your total being, the one unchanging aspect of yourself: autonomous Consciousness. So bringing attention to "the space of the Heart," to use Abhinava's phrase, does not mean becoming more aware of your feelings. Rather, it is bringing awareness to the fact of awareness itself—the field within which vibrates whatever thoughts or feelings happen to be arising. Abhinava asks us to begin this *dhyāna* practice by "meditating on the self-revealing Light of Consciousness that inheres within all aspects of reality as the power of awareness that is one's own Heart." This sounds terribly lofty but actually points toward something as simple as reminding yourself of that special secret place inside you where you feel the most *you*, that place where you feel the sheer delight of being you, doing your thing. It is the part of you that has remained constant in all experiences throughout your life: the place where you are just yourself, without any effort, beyond any specific thoughts or feelings *about* yourself. It is the place where you feel the very *you-ness* of "you." We might describe it as *the sense of present and loving self-awareness independent of any specific content.* I say "loving," but it's not really as active as that verb implies. It's a place of deep acceptance of what is, simply *because* it is. I am using words here to point to something that words cannot capture, hoping that you will look to where the words point and intuit what they refer to. You already know this inner place I'm talking about, but perhaps you haven't brought as much attention to it as you are now learning to do; or perhaps you have let certain concepts be overlaid upon it and now need to discern the pure essence of it. It is your Heart, which is and always has been an expression of the universal Heart.

The second step in the *dhyāna* involves a technique central to Tantrik *sādhanā*, that of subtle-body visualization. Abhinava asks us to visualize the "triad of fire sun, and moon," known throughout Tantrik literature as the "three lights" or the "triple radiance" (*tri-dhāman*). These terms refer to the three fundamental structures of the subtle body: the central, right, and left channels respectively. The channels or *nāḍīs* of the subtle body are arteries in which *prāṇa*,* life-force energy, is said to flow. There are said to be 72,000 of these channels, but this seems to be hyperbole, for only a few dozen of them (at most) were described or drawn in pre-20th century images. Of these, by far the most important are the three we have mentioned, which are presented in tabular form below.

* Note that the word *prāṇa* can refer to the vital energy in general, or to that of the exhale in particular.

Name	Meaning	Light	Location	Breath	Cognitive aspect
suṣumnā	"graceful"	Fire	Central (spine)	*udāna* (rising)	knower
pingalā	"reddish"	Sun	Right-dominant	*prāṇa* (exhale)	knowing
iḍā	"refreshing"	Moon	Left-dominant	*apāna* (inhale)	known

The lateral *pingalā* and *iḍā nāḍīs* undulate back and forth, crossing the central channel in a caduceus-type pattern. The *pingalā,* which is dominant on the right side, carries the energy of the exhale. It is identified with the sun because (in this yoga of self-awareness) as the breath flows out, consciousness moves outward toward external objects, illuminating them. Just as the sun makes objects manifest to our vision, the Light of Consciousness makes objects manifest in our experience. Therefore the outward-moving warm "solar" breath is identified by Abhinava with the process of cognition, which has its locus in the senses. The idea in the ancient tradition was that consciousness moves out through the various channels of the senses in order to grasp its objects (as opposed to our modern view of the senses as passive recipients of the constantly inflowing data of sense-experience). Understanding this helps the various associations made here make more sense.

The *iḍā nāḍī*, which is dominant on the left side, carries the energy of the inhalation. It is identified with the moon because as the breath flows in, consciousness moves inward, bringing the vibration of the object with it to be savored internally. Just as the moon reflects the light of the sun, but with a very different quality than direct sunlight, the objects of our experience reflect back to us the fact of

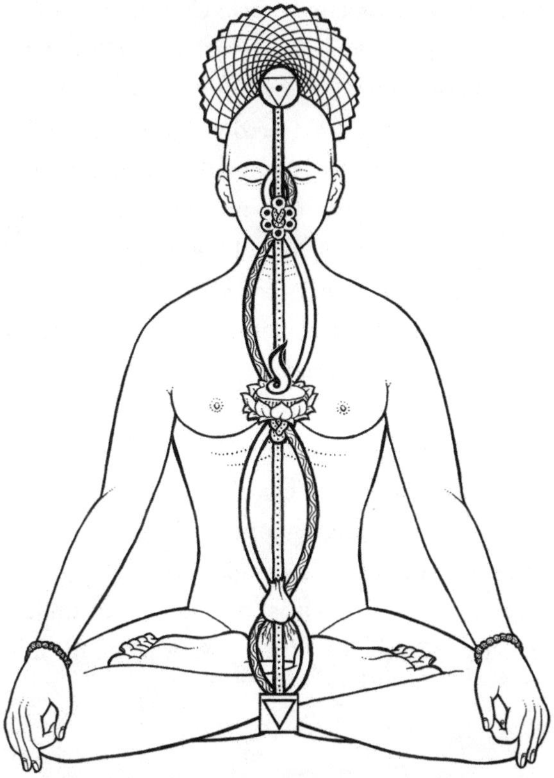

Note that this image depicts the classical Trika system of five *cakras*, which correspond to the five primary elements. The triangles at the bottom and top signify the Lower and Upper Kuṇḍalinī; we also see the *kanda* (bulb), the heart lotus with its "sprout of flame," and the palate *cakra*, surrounded by the six black dots of the wind element.

our consciousness, colored by the particularities of the object doing the reflecting. Additionally, in Indian literature the moon is always thought of as cool, refreshing, and delightful; a blessed relief after the heat of the day. Thus the inward-moving breath is "lunar" both because it is literally cooling, and because it is associated with the internalization of the sense-objects that produces enjoyment.

Note that *prāṇa* is the exhale and *apāna* is the inhale in all the classical Tantrik sources, whereas many modern yoga teachers teach the reverse. Yet the earlier tradition must be regarded as more coherent and logical in its terminology. *Pra + āna* literally means "breathing forth" in Sanskrit and *apa + āna* "breathing down." The inhale is obviously the breath that moves down. But note that this does not necessarily contradict modern yoga teaching that has the body rise up with the inhale—in fact it makes perfect sense to have the body rise up while the *prāṇa* moves down.

We are left, then, with the central channel or *suṣumnā nāḍī.* It is visualized as extending from the pelvic floor to the crown of the head. It is visualized variously as a glowing golden column of light or as cobalt blue and the width of an arrow shaft. The central channel is associated with "the knower" or agent of consciousness. This is a mystical channel, in the sense that when *prāṇa* moves within it, it is solely for the purpose of our spiritual liberation. Originally, this form of *prāṇa* was associated with *udāna-vāyu,* the upward-moving vital energy. The later Tantrik and *haṭha-yoga* traditions call it by the special name of *kuṇḍalī* or *kuṇḍalinī.* The relevant question here is what causes the *prāṇa* to move up the *suṣumnā nāḍī* instead of its usual path of exhalation? To separate the flow of the vital energy from the physical breath to which it is closely linked is not easy. Our vital energy can enter the central channel, says NŚT, because of a yogic practice or a gnostic insight.* The yogic practice in question is alluded to in many primary sources but is little known or understood today, despite its relative simplicity. When you practice for a long time the

* "Gnostic insight" refers to a direct realization of some aspect of the nature of reality that is sufficiently powerful to immediately manifest experientially.

basic but powerful *prāṇāyāma* of lengthening the breaths and making them equal in duration and quality, and retaining the breath after each inhale (for as long as is comfortable), eventually *prāṇa* and *apāna* come into perfect balance. If the breath retention (*kumbhaka*) is done at the same time as vibrating a special seed-mantra (the *kuṇḍalinī-bīja*) in the Heart-space, then something remarkable and mysterious happens. In one of those moments of profound *kumbhaka*-stasis, the energy of the breaths is said to spontaneously "fuse" in a moment of timeless simultaneity and then suddenly surge up the central channel. This is the moment for which the yogī devoutly wishes and practices, for if the *prāṇa* reaches the crown of the head and merges there completely, he has reached the end of his journey.[163]

The gnostic insight that can accomplish the same thing is this: the profound realization that an object known in any cognition—whether it is an external or internal phenomenon—is simply an aspect of your own being, utterly inseparable from the light of your consciousness, which illumines that object, vibrates in sympathy with it, then dissolves it into itself. That is to say, if we truly, experientially realize that the knower, the means of knowing, and the thing known are but three aspects of one dynamic reality, we have accomplished the fusion of the three corresponding subtle channels and breaths by another means. This is what Abhinava means in step 2 of the *dhyāna* instructions when he says, "One should visualize in the Heart the fusion of the triad of fire, sun, and moon, which are forms of the knower, means of knowing, and object known respectively." So, we can take either of two approaches: 1) manipulating the energies of the subtle body to trigger a liberative spiritual experience that results in understanding, or 2) generating an understanding so powerful and so complete that it brings the energies of the subtle body into alignment with it. Both approaches presume a mind-body unity, for the belief that mind and body are but aspects of one another is the driving force of all yogic practices.

So in step 2, if we take the yogic approach, we visualize the three channels of the subtle body vividly while practicing breath extension (*prāṇāyāma*). Imagining that the breath is entering at the third eye or the crown of the head and then moving down toward the base of the heart, you can breathe in to the pearly-white left-dominant lunar channel, seeing it glowing as the *prāṇa* flows along it. The moon sets in the heart center (in the area of the sternum or the xiphoid process), and the breath pauses just before "dawn" in a *kumbhaka* (breath retention), while you experience absolute centeredness. Then the sun rises from the heart center and the *prāṇa* flows up along the reddish right-dominant solar channel and exits out the top of the head. Continue this, gently increasing the time of the pause between the breaths, feeling it as a holding of the solar and lunar vibrations in perfect balance, until a palpable energy (for example, heat or pressure or vibration) arises in the heart center. This is the Fire of Mahābhairava, the one energy that expresses in the three aspects described above. The more you practice the technique, the more powerful it becomes.

Another way of doing this practice, which I discovered through the translation work of Chris Tompkins, is through the following visualization. Vividly imagine the sun rising in the base of the heart center, and slowly exhale it up the central channel until it emerges from the crown of the head. Then visualize the full moon above the head, inhale it down the central channel until it sets in the base of the heart, and hold *kumbhaka.* Then visualize the sun rising once again in the same location. Continue this breath/visualization practice until there comes a *kumbhaka* in which the setting moon and the rising sun are both fully present at the base of the heart in perfect equilibrium; their energies fuse into the Fire of Mahābhairava (white moon + red sun = orange fire).

Now give this energy a form by visualizing it as a Wheel of Fire with twelve spokes representing the twelve *śaktis*. Let the wheel pulse and spin in your heart, then invite it to flow along one of the channels leading to the eye or ear or any other bodily aperture. Visualize it issuing forth from your body and coming to rest on an external object corresponding to the channel it flowed out of—for example, a visual object for the eye, a sound for the ear, a smell for the nose, and so on. (As a beginner, you will have to consciously select an object first, then have the Fire-wheel flow out the corresponding channel; later it will happen more spontaneously.) Work with the sense-field that is strongest for you until you are more experienced. If your imagination is sufficiently vivid, you can work with an object not physically present as well.

In the fourth step, as you visualize the spinning or pulsing Fire-wheel resting on the object of awareness, feel that you are filling the latter with divine energy as you simultaneously contemplate that the object is in fact emitted by your own consciousness. Then hold the object in a state of illumination, in which its true nature as a vibration of energy is manifest. Finally, dissolve the object completely into the Fire-wheel, which then re-enters the body through the relevant

The 12-spoked Wheel of Fire

aperture and rises along the central channel to dissolve in the Void at the crown of the head with a long exhale.

In the fifth step, which occurs when the Fire-wheel has risen to the crown of the head and subsided into the profound silence of the vast space of the crown *cakra*, you simply repose there in the perfect stillness of the Absolute ground of the whole process, which is perfect emptiness.

In the sixth and final step, you repeat the whole process, but this time the Fire-wheel does not leave the body but rather rests on the subliminal impression (*saṃskāra*) of the object that you worked with in steps 1 to 5, which for the purposes of this practice simply means using the memory of the object as the meditational focus.

As with any Tantrik practice, full mastery of this brings about liberation. As Abhinava writes,

Tantrasāra: ch. 5

> *One who meditates thus repeatedly discovers that the cycles of creation, stasis, and dissolution are—in terms of the highest reality—solely one's own consciousness, and thus discovers that the ultimate nature of one's own consciousness is its free and independent exercise of these powers. At the very moment of the full realization of this, he becomes God. So through repeated practice come all desired powers and attainments, as well as liberation.*

Now go back and read the summary verses for the *dhyāna* practice on page 385–6, and they should make perfect sense.

Uccāra

Now we will explore the second practice Abhinava gives under the heading of *āṇava-upāya.* It is called *uccāra*, which can be translated both as "enunciation" and "elevation." In this practice the *prāṇa* is primary. Before we discuss Abhinava's version of *uccāra*, however, we must look at the form this practice takes in the wider Tantrik tradition. In the classical period, *uccāra* played a crucial role in the daily yoga *sādhanā* practiced by nearly all Tāntrikas. The core of *uccāra,* as its name implies, is the raising of an empowered seed-syllable up the central channel of the practitioner to the crown of the head. Though the most common elements of Tantrik practice—mantra, *mudrā*, and visualization—are present in this practice, the *prāṇa* is nonetheless primary, as we will see.

Let's take the example of the seed-syllable **hrīṃ**. When raising this *bīja* up the central channel, the elements of the mantra are arranged along its axis. So, one makes the appropriate *mudrā* at the *mūlādhāra* (which is located, according to the system in question, at the base of the spine, at the perineum or four fingers below the navel) and begins with the enunciation of ***h***, barely audible, raising it (along with the *mudrā* and visualization of a point of brilliant light) to the navel, where the ***r*** sound kicks in; which is then raised to the level of the base of the heart, where it crossfades into the ***ī*** vowel; which is raised to the level of the throat, where the vowel starts becoming increasingly nasalized. At the level of the palate, it becomes a pure nasal, slightly colored by the preceding vowel (***ī***), and vibrates there intensely with a sound similar to that of a swarm of bees. Then it rises still farther, the audible sound tapering off as the subtle vibration continues to rise to the crown of the head and beyond. The whole process is done with a single breath, and is repeated 3, 5, 7, 9, 12, or 108 times (as many times as the practitioner wishes). It may be done with any *bīja-mantra,* such as hauṃ (in which case the *h* sound rises from the lower belly, the vowel *a* kicks in at the base of the heart, *u* at the base of the throat, and the nasal at the level of the palate).

This, then, is the standard form of *uccāra,* in its most basic outline.[164] Notice that the practice involves all the senses: it's synesthetic in the sense that sound, light, and movement are fused, because as the sound of the bīja rises through the central channel, one visualizes it as a brilliant sparkling point of light rising through the central channel and tracks its movement with the rise of the hands and the appropriate mudrā. So in this way, imagination, visual perception, auditory perception, breath, and physical motion all are entrained in this single flow. And this is the key to Tantrik yoga: mantra, mudrā, visualization and breath in a single flow. Note that you are unlikely to practice this successfully without guidance from a teacher or receiving it in a live practice in a live environment. However, in his *Essence of the Tantras,* Abhinava Gupta separates *uccāra* into two practices, one that is more focused on the flow of the *prāṇa* and does not explicitly require mantra, and another (called *varṇa-uccāra*) which does require mantra. We will consider the first of these here, since the second cannot really be taught in a book. Abhinava's *prāṇa-uccāra* is different from mainstream Tantrik *uccāra* in two important respects. First, it utilizes all five of the *prāṇa-vāyus* (aspects of the vital energy), not just the exhale, and second, it is gnostically overcoded, which means it is interpreted in terms of liberative spiritual concepts. It is this form of *uccāra*, developed within the so-called gnostic Trika (which became the most long-lived form of Tantra in Kashmīr), that we will explore now.

Uccāra as Described in *Essence of the Tantras*

This practice might seem conceptually similar to the Fire-wheel *dhyāna* given above, and it is in some ways, for it is meant to accomplish the same goal: the realization of any and every object of experience as a vibration of divine Consciousness, which is identical with your innate awareness. However, in the *dhyāna,* visualization is primary, while in this *uccāra*, the sensation of the rhythmic flow of the breaths is central. For some, this will be easier and more effective to practice, while for more visual people, the *dhyāna* might prove more appealing.

Abhinava gives six steps in his *uccāra* practice, corresponding to the five *prāṇa-vāyus* plus an initial step of centering and opening to grace. I will quote his exact words, explaining where necessary.

1. *In this practice, one who wants to cause the vital energy to rise first reposes in the space of the Heart.*

See page 387 for a discussion of the notion of centering in the Heart-space.

2. *Then, due to exhaling [*prāṇa*], awareness flows through the sense-faculties and rests on an external object.*

The first step of the practice proper is flowing your awareness outward through the "solar" exhale that illuminates a specific object. Beginners should use an external physical object, such as an item on your altar, while more advanced practitioners can use a subtle one (meaning an intangible object). As you direct your exhale toward the object, feel the energy of your consciousness flowing out through your sense-channels and manifesting the object before you.

3. *Then, filling himself with the "moon" that is inhalation [*apāna*], bringing with it the object, he sees himself in all things and thus becomes free from any desire for the other.*

On the "lunar" inhale, allow the vibration or "energy signature" of the object to ride on the breath and enter into your heart center. Experience the inhale as refreshing, carrying with it the realization that the object is and always was a part of you. This is why Abhinava

The practitioner sees himself in all things and thus becomes free from any desire from the other.

says the practitioner *sees himself in all things and thus becomes free from any desire for the other*—for you cannot grasp after something unless you see it as separate from you. So in this practice, you realize any object as a manifestation of your true essence-nature. It is wonderful to do this practice with beautiful symbolic objects on your altar, including deity forms. However, once you have the hang of that, you can graduate to the more challenging practice of doing this type of prāṇa-flow meditation with objects that symbolize a challenging person or situation in your life. By realizing that person as a manifestation of your own essence-nature, you can shift the relationship in a more positive (i.e., productive) direction.

Repeat steps 2 and 3 until the vibration of the object feels fully internalized.

4. *Next, due to the emergence of the equalizing vital energy [*samāna vayu*] in the heart, one experiences repose in the unity.*

The practice of step 4 is one that is central to Tantrik yoga: extending, balancing, and equalizing the in- and out-breaths, while doing breath retention between them. In its simplest form, this means lengthening the two breaths to (say) nine counts each, making them the same in terms of rate and smoothness of flow, and pausing in between, holding the breath for just as long as is comfortable. An intermediate form would be holding the breath for as many counts as the inhale and exhale (e.g., 9-9-9). Advanced forms include adding an exhale pause (e.g., 9-9-9-9) or using a 1-4-2 ratio (for example, 4 count on the inhale, 16 on retention, and 8 on the exhale). But please do not practice these *prāṇāyāmas* on the basis of this paragraph alone; you will need the guidance of a qualified teacher. A friend of mine, Richard Rosen, has a couple of great books on *prāṇāyāma.*

The point of this is that if practiced long enough, the two breaths (*prāṇa* and *apāna*) will spontaneously fuse into *samāna vayu.* You will know when this has happened because, without any conscious effort on your part, the breath will become very subtle, as if it is barely moving, then spontaneously become still for a timeless moment of eternity in which there are no thought-forms: *nirodha*, it's called in some traditions. This is what Abhinava calls *repose in unity.* All the Tantrik and *haṭha-yoga* texts refer to the "unification" of the in- and out-breaths, suggesting the significance of this experience. When breathing continues, after this it is effortlessly balanced and even. Note that step 4 says that *samāna* emerges in the heart; if we understand that term to mean the "core," it could be in the region of the navel as well as the physical heart, or it could be indeed the whole central channel.

5. *Then, when the fire of the up-breath [*udāna vayu*] rises, he absorbs the operations of the perceiver, the perceived, and the process of perception.*

There are two ways of practicing step 5. Following the moment of spontaneous stilling of the breath and mind described above, you can visualize the *prāṇa* rising up the central channel on an exhale, hoping to trigger its actual rise through the power of focused awareness and vivid imagination (which can work, if they are sufficiently developed). Or you can wait until it happens spontaneously of its own accord. That is, when the *samāna* fusion is perfected, the *prāṇa-śakti* may suddenly (and even forcefully) rise up the central channel in the form of *udāna,* in other contexts known as *kundalinī-śakti.*[165] In this moment, Abhinava says, the three aspects of the dynamic flow of consciousness—the knower, act of knowing, and the known—collapse into unity, dissolving into the fire of the Supreme Knower, the ground of all three. This is why there is a spontaneous ascension toward the highest spiritual center, where Śiva eternally dwells in fullness.

6. *When the fire absorbing them subsides and the pervasive vital energy* [vyāna vayu] *emerges, then one shines/vibrates, free of all limitations.*

The final stage of *prāṇa-uccāra* practice cannot be practiced, only experienced. As the fire of reabsorption rises up the central channel, it reaches the Sky of Consciousness (*cidākāśa*) in the crown center, identical with transcendent Śiva. There the fire dies out (for lack of oxygen, as it were) in the vast space of limitless stillness, which is nonetheless pregnant with infinite potential energy. If your practice is sufficiently developed, and you do not become unconscious (i.e., sleepy or numb) in this infinite Void, then the *vyāna* or pervasive vital energy spills forth from the crown center, infusing the blissful nectar of the Absolute into every layer and level of your being, pervading every cell, flowing forth from every pore, and permeating the whole of reality with its coruscating incandescent light. What was previously experienced only as the transcendent Core of your own identity now reveals itself as the totality of all things. *Sphurati,* Abhinava says—*he vibrates and shines* (for the Sanskrit word means both), *free of all limitations,* for he has become all things. The stabilization of this state, called *Mahāvyāpti* or the Great Pervasion (also known as *turyātīta*), is of course liberation and final awakening.

However, if your *saṃskāras* of contracted existence are sufficiently strong, then this experience of the "nectar-pervasion" is incomplete or impermanent and must be returned to again and again through practice until it has obliterated the *saṃskāras* that keep dragging you back into the unawakened state of being. Abhinava writes:

Tantrasāra: ch. 5

> *Having reposed in these levels of uccāra, practicing them one by one, in sets of two, or all together, one reaches that Supreme Reality of grounded and centered awareness, beyond the body, prāṇa, mind, and void.*

You may notice that here Abhinava is referencing the layers of the Five Layered Self that we discussed in Part 1 of the book. And by the way, if the description of this practice is discouraging to you because you aren't much of a one for visionary experiences or mystical experiences or yogic practices of this subtle nature, don't worry. Remember there are several means to liberation. Here we are describing the inner yogas, but you can also attain the same realizations and the same openings through any of the other means described in the previous chapters.

The *uccāra* can also be practiced with *bīja-mantras* or seed-syllables, as Abhinava's next words suggest:

> *That is precisely the secret of performing uccāra with the seed-syllables of creation and dissolution; synthesizing them with the breath, one will refine, purify, and perfect one's mental constructs until they are perfectly aligned with, and thereby dissolve into, the highest nondual nature of reality.*

The seed-syllables in question are the Trika's key mantras, associated with Parā and Kālī respectively; they will not be given here. We can conclude this discussion of Abhinava's nondual gnostic *uccāra* practice by quoting his summary verses for the practice:

> *Reposing first in self-awareness and next on an object, one should completely fill [oneself with] that object. One rests here in the expanded state; then rapidly dissolves the distinction of Knower and Known. Then one reposes in the all-pervasive state. ||*
>
> *These five levels of the uccāra method—six if including [the first step] the space of the heart—are the five prāṇas from the out-breath to the diffuse-breath [*prāṇa *to* vyāna*], which are*

> *associated with the states of consciousness: waking, dream, deep sleep, the Fourth, and Beyond the Fourth. ||*
>
> *One who is committed to this practice quickly ascends to the radiant abode of the awareness of both creation and dissolution. ||*

So in these summary verses, Abhinava specifically associates the five prāṇas (prāṇa, apāna, samāna, udāna, vyāna) with the five states of consciousness we discussed in Part 1 (waking, dream, deep sleep, turya, turyātīta).

Karaṇa: Postures of the Body and Awareness

The final type of yogic practice listed under the heading of the *āṇava-upāya* or Individual/Embodied Means is that of *karaṇa* or postures. We have little evidence of precisely what this term referred to in classical Tantra, apart from a few examples. We will explore these briefly here.

Asana in Tantra usually means 'throne' or the seat of one's Deity in visualization practice.

See page 216

In modern times, the term *āsana* is used to denote all sorts of physical postures intended to stretch and condition the body (and ideally, to help us have an integrated experience of our embodiment). This usage of the term dates from the 18th century. From the point of view of tradition, it is something of a misappropriation of the term. The central meaning of the term *āsana* in Tantra is that of "throne," specifically the throne of the Deity in one's visualization practice. The type of throne visualized is usually a *padmāsana* or lotus throne. By extension, *āsana* came to mean "seat," and any seated posture for meditation can be called an *āsana,* such as *siddhāsana, svastikāsana, or padmāsana* (a sitting posture named after the deity's lotus throne). However, the general term for posture in the tradition is *karaṇa,* which can indicate inversions, dance poses, and subtle internal adjustments as well as "postures of awareness."

What kind of *karaṇa*s do we find in the Tantras? I have not done a thorough examination of the topic, but I will mention a few points of interest. Certainly the most important *karaṇa* described in the Tantras is called the *divya-karaṇa* or "divine posture." This subtle posture of the head, neck, and face is considered crucial for successful meditation. My meditation posture instructions, including the *divya-karaṇa,* go like this:

> Sit on a cushion that elevates the hips so that they are at least as high as the knees. Leaning forward, pull back on the flesh of the buttocks and upper thighs and then sit straight again, creating a gentle rotation in the hips that allows the spine to elongate upward more easily. Let the sit bones ground down firmly, while the crown of the head rises up, creating an elongation in the spine. Let the head float at the top of the spine like a waterlily floating on the surface of a pond. Let the back of the neck be long and let the chin drop gently, unclenching the teeth and releasing the jaw. Let all the muscles of your face soften and release (if necessary, you may wish to use your knuckles to massage your eyebrow ridges and jaw hinge to help them release fully). Now your jaws are hanging on space, the lips almost parting, or perhaps, they do part (either way it's fine). Let the forehead and scalp relax. Let the eyes sink back in the eye sockets. Finally, gently curl the tip of the tongue upward just a little bit and let its tip point toward the crown of the head. All the other muscles of the face and head should be slack.[166]

This simple but significant *karaṇa* can have a profound impact on your ability to let go into meditation. As for the other *karaṇa*s, we know that in the massive Tantrik compendium the *Jayadratha-yāmala-tantra*, there are dance forms called *karaṇa*s that are prescribed for those who are doing a *sādhanā* of Goddess worship that includes dressing as and imitating whichever form of the Goddess is the focus of one's devotion. These passages have never been translated. We might also note that one of the modern-day yoga poses retains this ancient name, specifically the *viparīta-karaṇī*, the simple but powerfully restorative inversion described in classic *haṭha-yoga* texts.

In chapter 32 of his *Tantrāloka,* Abhinava Gupta implies that the words *karaṇa* and *mudrā* are nearly synonymous. For Abhinava (as for the *haṭha-yoga* manuals), *mudrā* means not just "hand gesture" but any posture of the hands, body, or awareness that arises spontaneously in profound meditation or mystical experience. In this definition, Abhinava alludes to the literal meaning of *mudrā* as "seal" or "sign." So, a *mudrā* is a sign of awakened consciousness, and Abhinava advocates that those who wish to awaken adopt and practice the *mudrā*s that *kuṇḍalinī-śakti* has revealed in advanced meditators. Just as a spontaneous *mudrā* is a sign of attainment, one can use a *mudrā* to seal the experience of awakened consciousness. To put it another way, using Abhinava's language, a *mudrā* is both a reflection of an inner state and a means of realizing that state (depending on whether the trajectory is outward or inward respectively).

Mudra is any posture of the hands, body, or awareness which arises spontaneously in meditation, and is considered a sign of awakened consciousness.

The most important *mudrā* for Abhinava is that called *khecarī,* which literally means "moving in the sky [of consciousness]." The real nature of this *mudrā* had been forgotten by the time of the *haṭha-yoga* texts, which describe a very different (and rather bizarre) procedure under that name.[167] Abhinava devotes most of chapter 32 to the *khecarī-mudrā,* which is essentially a name for a procedure of intensifying the "central energy" (a name for *kuṇḍalinī-śakti*) at the base of the spine and raising it to the crown of the head, achieving a higher state of consciousness thereby. As with all forms of Tantrik yoga, this is achieved by a combination of breath control, visualization, and mantra.

Having abandoned the state of the void, he attains pure Being. He abides, having unified the Trident [of Powers], like liquid dissolving into liquid. Experiencing the Trident as a single staff [of energy], rising through the [three] spaces, O Beloved, he adopts the Khecarī Mudrā, meditating on himself as Bhairava, embraced by the [Yoginīs] of the Khecarī circle.

Tantrāloka: 32.18–20

We can tell from the language that here Abhinava is quoting an earlier scriptural source on the nature of *khecarī-mudrā, a* source that is unfortunately now lost to us.

Pūjā: Ceremony of Worship

The final practice of Abhinava's *āṇava-upāya* classification is that of *pūjā*, ritual worship, which Abhinava prefers to call *sthāna-prakalpana*, which he defines as "visualizing [and worshipping] internal structures in external substrates." Though it is specialized, this definition of *pūjā* points us toward the key element of Tantrik worship for all Tāntrikas: it consists in the main of a procedure for summoning the energy of a particular deity into a form that can temporarily house it, then worshipping that energy, that particular vibration of the one Consciousness, never confusing it with the form or image in which it is housed. Though the worship is, of course, the consummation of the rite, the bulk of the *pūjā* ritual is concerned with the purifications and "divinizations" that make it possible to summon the energy of the deity. This makes sense, since it is only our karmic obstacles and contracted perception that hinder us from experiencing the divine power that is in reality present every moment. It is these technologies of divinizing and summoning that are Tantra's unique contribution in the arena of Indian ritual (though the summoning rite is no doubt linked to much older, undocumented forms of shamanism in the subcontinent).

Tantra brought about a paradigm shift in Indian religions, integrating forms of popular religion into a sophisticated yogic practice.

Excursus on Gods, Spirits, and the Traditional Worldview

In articulating these technologies, the Tantra brought about a paradigm shift in Indian religions, integrating forms of popular religion into a sophisticated yogic and ritual practice. You see, by the time of the beginning of the Tantrik movement (c. 5th century), the older Vedic religion had become so mechanized in its ritual that its own authorities believed that the deities named in these rituals had no reality apart from their names. Though their names were mantras, they were not seen by the ritualists as having mystical properties. In fact, at that time the most conservative Vedic authorities were staunchly atheistic. Furthermore, they taught that one must perform the Vedic ritual for no reason other than that the Veda tells you to do so. Nor did these authorities see any truth in the myths and stories of the Veda, which, they said, have the sole purpose of inspiring impressionable people to perform the rituals. All this is very different from the Tantrik View, which is closer to that of folk religion in that it sees the whole world as filled with energies, some of which might be called "spirits," and contends that these spirits can be contacted through the sound vibration of their mantras.

Let us take a moment to explore this often misunderstood view. First, it is important to note that the questions that Westerners have when encountering such a traditional worldview are not necessarily the questions asked by those in the tradition. For example, since the dominant belief system of the modern West is psychology, Westerners want to know if the spirits of the traditional view are thought to have independent agency, because if not, they can be explained in psychological terms as aspects of our own mind—which makes most Westerners quite comfortable and prompts them to nod their heads wisely in understanding and agreement. We love to hear information that confirms and elaborates what we have already decided (or been programmed to believe) is true. Westerners feel very comfortable, if a bit lonely, in their entrenched belief that we humans are the only self-aware beings around and that there certainly are no conscious beings that cannot be perceived with the usual five senses. However, before dismissing all other possibilities, we should first ponder the fact that no traditional society in the world that has ever existed agrees with this materialistic view. Further, we should note that only modern technological societies that are no longer intimately connected to nature hold this view. For the traditional human being, living in nature, the world is absolutely full of seen and unseen beings with whom she must live in a delicate and respectful balance. They form a vast *maṇḍala*-hierarchy of conscious power of which we are only a part. Some of these spirits are seen as the essences of tangible features of nature, such as tree-spirits (*yakṣas*) and snake-spirits (*nāgas*). Others are not connected to a particular natural feature. Now, we are not overly distorting the traditional Indian view if we see these spirits as energies, patterned flows of life-force energy. Though it is true that most traditional people view spirits and gods as having agency (conscious volition), they are less instinctively dualistic than we are in this particular belief. That is, though their ritual interactions with the spirits can look to us like a business negotiation with an independent unseen entity, the people performing the rituals see them as simply part of their role in the natural pattern—their organic response to how the energy flows in their environment. This is substantiated by the fact that Indian villagers who do not believe in the spirits as independent entities perform the same rituals as those who do.

The question of the existence and independence of spirit entities seems significant to Westerners because if the ancient Tāntrikas really believed that "superstitious nonsense," we are tempted to dismiss their worldview altogether. It is also a question of fear—that is, Western materialists often become terribly frightened when confronted with any evidence of the supernatural, which (probably due to the influence of rationalist Protestant Christianity) is instinctively seen as menacing and malevolent. However, the traditional Indian perspective on ghosts and the like is quite matter-of-fact: these unseen spirits are just one more challenge to negotiate in life and are often nothing to be particularly frightened of. If you are in respectful accord with the unseen beings, they don't mess with you. The unseen beings are really just like human beings: a few are benevolent, a few are malevolent, and the great majority couldn't care less about you.

Now that we have touched on the traditional view, let us address the view of a nondualist Tāntrika regarding the unseen world. Being a nondualist, he is also naturally a monotheist—in the sense that he holds that there are not really many gods, but only One. In the Indian context, this does *not* mean that he worships Deity under only one name (which is what it means for Western monotheists). Rather, he pays homage to many deities as expressions of that One. For a follower of Śiva then, all deities are expressions of, and are emanations of, and or servants of Śiva. (Knowing this, you can see how it is easier for an Indian to believe that we are all equally the son of God, all divine incarnations.) The deity that is summoned and worshipped in *pūjā* ritual, then, is always an aspect of the Highest Divinity, but since it possesses its own unique character and qualities, it is propitiated for a purpose and in a manner unique to it.

In his discussion of ritual matters, Abhinava Gupta often emphasizes the nondualist understanding because ritual can seem so dualistic. For example, since Deity—in any of its many forms—is all-pervasive and omnipresent, what is usually called "summoning" is correctly understood as "evoking awareness" of the presence of that form of the Deity. Since performance of a daily ritual was, historically, the most prominent and visible aspect of Tantrik practice, let us investigate this topic more thoroughly, starting with the nondualist theory of ritual.

Only God can worship God: Tantrik ritual theory

When we investigate Tantrik practices of yoga and ritual, the divisions and irreconcilable differences that seemed so clear on the level of doctrine—such as dualism versus nondualism—frequently dissolve. Thus, even though doctrinally the Saiddhāntika dualists hold that the individual soul and God are eternally separate, they also hold, along with the nondualists, that only God can worship God and that, therefore, one must transform oneself into a Śiva in order to worship Śiva. The difference between becoming "a" Śiva versus meditating on your innate universal Śiva-nature, while of importance to philosophers, is likely to seem academic to practitioners, especially when in both cases the forms of the ritual are more or less identical. Remember that the whole Tantrik tradition shares the same ritual structure and types of yogic practice, regardless of doctrine.[168] What defines your lineage as opposed to someone else's is primarily the specific mantra you are initiated into, the form of the Deity to which it corresponds, and that form's retinue of related mantra-deities. Secondarily, what differentiates you from another practitioner is the understanding that underlies and fuels your practice. I say secondarily from the perspective of the practice manuals; but in fact the view you hold of and in ritual performance ends up being crucial, for it directs the energy of your efforts toward one goal or another, to spiritual liberation or to something else.

Here is where the dualists and nondualists really part ways in the ritual arena: the former don't believe that it matters whether ritual brings about an inner experience, whereas the latter hold that ritual is only meaningful and effective to the extent that it successfully brings about an inner experience. In other words, the nondualists rigorously resisted the tendency toward routinization and mechanization that exists in every religion. This is discussed in the masterful and seminal article by Alexis Sanderson, "Meaning in Tantric Ritual." There he explains that ritual can be meaningless, meaningful in a weak sense, or meaningful in a strong sense. It is meaningful in a weak sense if the ritual performer has an intellectual understanding of the symbolic meaning of the ritual and its purpose. It is meaningful in a strong sense, however, if the ritual expresses and evokes in him a liberating awareness of reality as he performs it.[169] Making this liberating awareness possible for the practitioner is precisely Abhinava's goal in the presentation of ritual theory he gives in chapter 15 of his *Light on the Tantras,* which we will discuss below.

First we must understand that for Abhinava, all acts of worship are modes of *samāveśa,* that is, methods of enacting and experiencing the immersion into divine Reality that is both path and goal. The method by which ritual worship accomplishes this immersion, surprisingly, is the same method by which meditative contemplation of the ultimate Truth accomplishes it, that is, through *vikalpa-saṃskāra,* which means "refinement and purification of thought-constructs to bring them into alignment with the nature of reality." (See the section on *śākta-upāya* beginning on page 357.) It may not seem like that is what is happening with all this ritual paraphernalia. But for a nondualist like Abhinava, for whom the basic impurity is not a substance but simply ignorance, ritual *must* be a form of *vikalpa-saṃskāra* if it is even to be included at all in his system. And he could not dispense with the daily ritual, since that was the most well-established form of Tantrik practice, the very base of the tradition. Nonetheless, he did risk controversy by arguing that some rare beings have the aptitude to attain full realization through the power of awareness alone, without recourse to action of any kind, and thus need not perform the practices of yoga and *kriyā* (ritual). This is why Abhinava presents the other *upāyas* before *āṇava-upāya*: there is a slim possibility that you will attain full liberation and awakening through them, without the need for *āṇava* practices. But again, note that other authorities argue that body-based practices are necessary for everyone, and if even if they are not, it could be hazardous to your practice to assume that you are one of the few that can attain complete liberation through reflection and intuition alone. What is certain is that 1) *everyone* benefits from the foundational practices (which include purification and alignment of mind and body), and yet 2) no one attains complete liberation due to those practices unless the practice comes to involve all the levels of being.

Even if you believe that you are one of the rare ones who don't need it, a daily yoga and *kriyā* practice can only benefit you, since it will stabilize, integrate, and enhance the spontaneous realizations of Truth that you have had. If, like me, you have ever had a wonderful spiritual experience and thought that you would certainly dwell forevermore in the awareness it brought, yet found it slipping away in the ensuing days and weeks, that is because you had an insufficient daily practice. You could not hold the energy of the experience because your vessel was weak and leaky. Practice strengthens the vessel and plugs its leaks. The master Abhinava Gupta certainly didn't need a daily yoga/*kriyā* practice, but he did one all the same, either for the joy of it or, perhaps, because even the state of final awakening, which is not static, requires ongoing nourishment.

Let us return now to the notion of meaningful ritual and what sort of understanding we can cultivate through ritual. (I should mention here that I frequently associate yoga and ritual because they *are* closely associated in the tradition. All Tantrik ritual contains yogic elements, and all Tantrik yoga is to some extent ritualized.) In Sanderson's other major article on Tantrik ritual, "Maṇḍala and Āgamic Identity," he explains the way in which ritual performance, properly understood, can be a form of *vikalpa-saṃskāra* (purifying and refining your conceptualization of the nature of reality). In the performance of his daily rites, the Tāntrika is in effect rehearsing the liberating intuition that his true self is the undifferentiated Deity-ground that contains the divine Powers of Consciousness in blissful fusion. Through the internal monologue of the ritual, Sanderson argues, the practitioner erodes his identity in the world of mutually exclusive subjects and objects and uses the mirror of his *maṇḍala* to project the vision of his true identity, an all-containing Self that includes not only the ordinary "I" but *all* "I"s and also the world of objects and values by which they believe themselves to be conditioned. Thus his ritual and his meditation serve to create a domain of awareness in which the boundaries that hem in his lower, public self are absent. Through constant repetition (*abhyāsa*), they transform this visionary projection and creative contemplation (*bhāvanā*) into his fundamental identity, experienced in every moment. As Sanderson concludes: "Thus the scriptural Word-essence which entered him through his initiation speaks with ever increasing clarity and consistency as the continuum of his ritual and meditation until at last it falls silent in unquestioning self-knowledge."[170]

Now that we have Sanderson's beautifully written explanation as a framework to guide our understanding, let us consider Abhinava Gupta's writing on this subject in the middle of *Tantrāloka,* chapter 15, which I was fortunate enough to study with Sanderson himself at Oxford University. Abhinava says that in NŚT, ritual worship brings about "a state of identity of all the factors of action with Śiva," (*Tantrāloka* 15.147).

The factors of action are the ritual agent, the object of his worship, the instrument(s) of that worship, the purpose of the worship, the point from which the worship proceeds, and the locus of the worship (these correspond to the different grammatical cases of the Sanskrit language). So in other words, Abhinava is saying that the correct understanding that ought to be cultivated in ritual performance is this: "I, God, worship God, by means of God, on God, from God, and for the sake of God alone."[171] This is called "the nonduality of the factors of action." It is the realization that all these different elements—cause, effect, agent, instrument, and discursive purpose—are only different from the perspective of the mind. In fact, they are all Consciousness, the one white light diffracting itself as it were into a spectrum of colors to make beautiful art. This viewpoint presents ritual as play, done for no other reason than to express and embody our innate divinity. Not only is this the only possible view for a nondualist to have of ritual, it is a crucial understanding to have if we wish to avoid the strengthening of the *āṇava-mala* (or impurity of individuality) that is caused by ritual performed with the false view "I, a helpless pathetic creature, petition a separate deity for his favor, that I might be blessed with some advantage." Not only is it false view for the obvious reason, but also because the goal of liberation will never be reached by the accumulation of advantages. This view is spiritual materialism, an insidious impostor masquerading as the true spiritual life.

See page 150

Abhinava teaches that ritual with nondual understanding is a practice ground, a rehearsal space for experiencing nonduality in daily life. Ritual worship is a paradigm to be actualized and embodied in one's daily activities. He writes:

Tantrāloka 15.149–150

> *Just as a well-trained horse when loosed from the reins keeps the discipline of his training even in the midst of chaotic battle, in the same way, one for whom all the factors of action have become God through repeated practice of the act of worship dispels the duality of the factors of action even in everyday acts.*

That is to say, by practicing nondual awareness within the intensified and controlled context of ritual action, we pave the way for spontaneously arising nondual awareness in all our mundane activities. In other words, by the "overspill" principle, once we experience the nonduality of the factors of action intensely enough in the context of ritual or yoga, then we start to spontaneously experience the same in everyday life. Washing the dishes or walking down the street, taking care of the children or carrying the laundry: all become the beautiful play of God, the one Actor, the one Light diffracting itself into these various colors. Without duality of action (which is the mind-world of "I need to get this done; if I give this to that person then this will happen; he did this to me and now I have to do this;" etc.) we relax into natural ease and flow, listening to and serving the organic movements of the deeper pattern and surrendering doership. (This sounds like a very high attainment to some, but in fact it is your natural state, revealed when your mental constructs about action are dissolved.) And indeed, if this overspill into everyday life does not take place, you are maintaining the artificial divide between spiritual and worldly life characteristic of dualistic religions. If you notice such a divide, then the Tantra challenges you to erase those artificial boundaries, because the spiritual life is not serving its real purpose if it remains confined to the yoga studio or temple or meditation room.

Abhinava culminates this fascinating and crucial discussion with one of my all-time favorite passages, soaked in the joy of his fully awakened consciousness:

Tantrāloka 15.151ff

> *For one who is dedicated to the constant practice of unity in this way, this whole universe will powerfully explode into life, revealing itself as [it really is:] dancing ecstatically in the intense animation of its all-encompassing and perfect divinity.*[172]
>
> *As my Guru's Guru has said in his Hymn of Worship, "Ah! The extraordinary festival that is worship of God, full of sweet nectar, in which the activation of all thirty-six levels of reality fully unfolds."*[173]

Those who offer worship of this kind, only to attain this state in which they become immersed in the experience of the universe as the perfect fullness of God, are themselves Divine. What goal remains for those who are already perfectly full?[174]

Perhaps inspired by this passage, we find a similar sentiment in Nāga's hymn, *Thirty Verses on True Worship*, a Krama hymn that argues that a rite of worship devoid of spiritual experience hardly deserves the name:[175]

Nāga's *Thirty Verses on True Worship*

What kind of worship is it in which one does not let go of the travails of one's worldly life, gazing at the fullness that, beautiful with the unfolding of the Heart, pervades the Sky of Consciousness as the cycle of its five flows?

What kind of worship is it in which one does not discover the upsurge of expanded consciousness within each and every moment of awareness, taking refuge in sudden meditative awareness [sāhasa-samādhi], flooded with vibrating pure consciousness?

So it is clear that for some lineages of NŚT, ritual worship (*pūjā*) was a mode of bringing about awakened consciousness, just as all the other practices were.

The structure of Tantrik ritual

Now that we have a good sense of why ritual is performed in NŚT, and the attitude to be cultivated in doing it, let us turn to what Tantrik ritual actually looks like. Note that I use the present tense, for this is the facet of Tantra that has most obviously survived the vicissitudes of time and foreign conquest. The forms of ritual preserved in Śaiva and Śākta temples today are thoroughly imbued by elements of the

Tantrik model, even though the performers of these rituals may be unaware of the fact.

However, the heart of Tantrik ritual practice in the classical period had nothing to do with temples and public religion. Instead, it was the rite that initiates performed every day in private with their own small, personal consecrated image as the foundation of Tantrik ritual. When we look at the mainstream of Tantra throughout the era of its flourishing, we see that to be a Tāntrika meant, first and foremost, to be an initiate into the veneration of a specific Tantrik mantra-deity and to do worship of that deity every day.

Deities, or "shining ones," are particular vibrations of the One Light.

What are these "deities" (*devas*) really? The answer to that question varies widely depending on which sect we are looking at. For some, they are considered actual "persons," incomprehensibly powerful beings whom we can enter into relationship with, and who are empowered by our worship even as we are blessed by them. For others, the deities are simply particular vibrations of the One Light (and in fact *deva*, which we translate as "deity" actually means "shining one"), they are harmonic frequencies as it were of the One energy, experienced by us as distinct flavors of exalted Consciousness. What I find interesting is that Tāntrikas on both ends of the spectrum just described agree that the primary mantra of a deity *is* that deity in sound form. Thus, unlike in some other religions, you can (and must) have direct contact with your deity every day: by reciting their mantra, you are caressing their "sonic body" with your very tongue. Of course, you must be initiated into their mantra for it to be alive for you (though on rare occasions, a mantra can spontaneously come to life for someone—if this has ever happened to you, you will not have to ask whether it has). A dead or inert mantra is just a word.

Thus, when we enquire into the nature of a Tantrik deity, we find four aspects in play, three "bodies" (*mūrti*) and one essence (*svabhāva*). From coarse to subtle, less essential to more essential, we have 1) the anthropomorphic, iconographic image of the deity (having so many arms, holding certain symbolic implements, etc.); 2) the *maṇḍala* or mystic diagram of the deity (nowadays also called yantra[176]); 3) the mantra of the deity; and 4) the essence-nature or energy of the deity, which may or may not inhabit any of the previous three bodies. The mantra is the most essential of the three bodies because the deity's energy *always* inheres in it if you received it in an alive state, that is, if you were initiated into it by a qualified guru or *ācārya* for whom the mantra is fully alive. By contrast, the deity must be summoned into the first two bodies (image or *maṇḍala)* on every occasion of worship. This is why we use the phrase "mantra-deity" to refer to the fundamental form of energy that an initiate works with in ritual. Remember that in the classical period Śaiva Tantra's own name for itself was *Mantra-mārga,* "the Way of Mantras." Now you are beginning to see why.

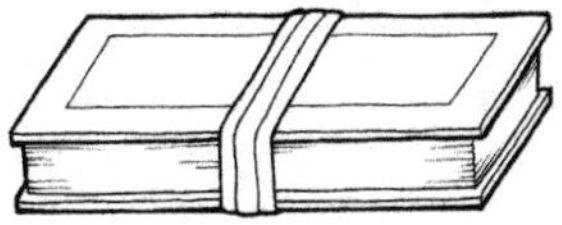

A practitioner may summon the energy of the deity into other prescribed substrates as well. The classical list follows: a smooth, mirror-like surface; a *liṅga*; a rosary; a skull-cup; a skull-staff; a statue of cedar wood, gold, or of fired and painted clay; a sword; a mirror; a Tantrik scripture; a painting of the deity on cloth; or an image incised on a human skull.[177]

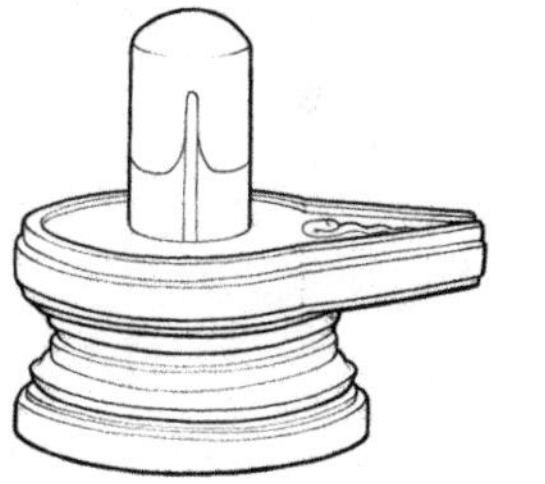

It is crucial to note here that the energy of the deity can equally well be summoned into an *internal* substrate (such as a visualization) as well as an external one (such as a statue, image, or mystic diagram). Indeed, the inner rite is primary, for the external rite cannot be performed without the inner one, but the reverse is not true.

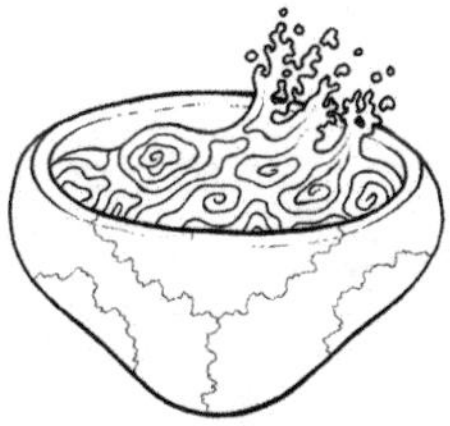

Outline of Tantrik Ritual Based on the Original Sources[178]

Daily Tantrik ritual has these three basic components:

I. Worship of the door-guardians and removal of obstacles
II. Five types of purification/divinization (*pañca-śuddhi*) and inner worship (*antar-yāga*)
III. External worship

External worship can sometimes be omitted (according to some authorities), indicating that the inner worship is the indispensible feature of the daily practice. Even those omitting external worship will always perform it on the days (or nights) sacred to the tradition, such as the eighth and fourteenth nights of each lunar cycle for Śaivas. The second and third items above stand for a complex array of procedures that may be summarized as follows:

II. Five types of purification/inization (*pañca-śuddhi*):
   3. Purification of the site
   4. Purification of one's body and subtle body, followed by a procedure of inner worship (*antar-yāga*) and meditation on oneself as a manifestation of the deity (*śiva-karaṇa*)
   5. Purification of the materials for worship
   6. Purification of the mantras
   7. Purification of the *liṅga* or icon
III. External worship
   4. Worship of the deity's throne (*āsana*)
   5. Installation of the deity's substrate or seed-form (*mūrti*)
   6. Summoning the energy of the deity
      a. *āvāhana* (invoking)
      b. *sthāpana* (establishing)
      c. *sannidhāna* (fixing)

4. Installation of the deity's "limbs" and retinue (as mantras)
5. Worship: offerings of
    a. water for foot-washing and mouth-rinsing
    b. *arghya* (a mixture of water, herbal leaves and fragrant substances)
    c. flowers (*puṣpa*)
    d. incense (*dhūpa*)
    e. flame (*dīpa*)
    f. food (*naivedya*)
6. Showing the *mudrā*
7. *Japa* (repetition of the deity's mantras), offering of the *japa*
8. Circumambulation *(pradakṣiṇa)*, prostration
9. Fire-offerings (*homa*)—optional according to some
10. Offering up of the ritual and its fruit (*karma-nivedana*)
11. Dissolving the *maṇḍala* (*visarjana*)

This list is somewhat abbreviated, but it gives some sense of the complexity of Tantrik ritual. An elaborated version can take almost three hours to perform; a streamlined version of the ritual would take about a third of that time (an hour). It is a ritual that is layered with meaning, though the ritual agent need not understand the specific meaning and function of each given act in order to be moved by the power of the whole. Let's discuss just a few of the salient points; note that this is far from a complete treatment.

1. Worship of the Door-Guardians and Removal of Obstacles

In the ancient Indian view, all kinds of beings are drawn to power-centers, like wild animals to a water hole, and not all of them are benevolent to your practice. Thus the ritual space must be cleared and protected with mantras and visualizations every day. One of the first things one does, before entering the sacred space (*yāga-gṛham*), is to infuse one's weapon-mantra into a flower and cast it into the sanctum. This functions as a kind of flower-grenade, driving out all the various spirits floating around the space. As we have already seen, this is done even if you don't believe in these spirits, beings that can impede your worship; for you certainly believe in the *vighnas*, the "hinderers of yoga": laziness, illness, negligence, apathy, uncertainty, lack of concentration, lack of confidence, depression, distraction, inhibition, and, foremost among them all, carelessness. Now, these states of mind are denoted by the *same word* in Sanskrit as the impeding spirits, *vighna,* which tells us that the former are really the embodiments of the latter. The traditional mind did not see a significant difference between the two uses of the word; and if you do, it is perhaps not so very important. *Vighna*s of whatever kind must be removed before proceeding, and this is why we honor Ganesh, also known as *Vighneśvara*, at the beginning of any undertaking. Note also that making *namas* (activating the feeling of devotion with a reverent bow) itself helps to dispel such obstacles.[179]

II. Five types of purification/ divinization

Having dispelled obstacles and impeders, the space is consecrated and energetically sealed. This is done, like all actions in Tantrik ritual, by a synchronous combination of mantras, *mudrās* (hand gestures), and visualization. This integration of the faculties of body, mind, and spirit in a single action is also crucial for determining how the ritual impacts our being.

In the dualist camp, prior to the ritual one must perform purification of oneself, the site, the ritual implements, the mantras, and the image or substrate. The nondualist performs the same actions but understands them differently. He is purifying his *awareness* of these things, that is, activating his understanding that they are nothing but divine Consciousness, that they are non-different from Śiva. Even though they were just as divine before such "purification," from our non-enlightened perspective this is experienced as an infusion of energy that sanctifies and divinizes the objects in question.

The second of these "purifications," called *ātma-śuddhi* or self-divinization, is the most important. It takes quite a bit more time than the other steps, for it includes the all-important meditative contemplation called *antarayāga* or "inner worship." This consists of the following steps:

1. Elimination of one's conception of the body as gross matter, and also one's identification with it, by incinerating it with psychic fire and blowing away the ashes that represent the subtle impressions of that body-identification (= *deha-śuddhi,* also sometimes called *tattva-śuddhi* or *bhūta-śuddhi* if one purifies the body in the sequence of the five great elements)
2. Creation of a divine energy-body or body of radiant light through the installation and activation of the mantras of the deity and her retinue of emanations
3. Worship of oneself as a manifestation of one's deity, using visualized offerings

After these steps of self-divinization, one proceeds with the inner worship, which is also three steps.

1. Installation of the deity's throne in one's life-force energy (e.g., in the Trika, this would be the trident with three surmounted white lotuses, installed along the central channel)
2. Installation of deity and retinue as mantras and visualizations
3. Worship of the deity's power in the form of this visualized three-dimensional deity-*maṇḍala* made of light and sound

III External worship

Then, having consecrated water (or, in left-hand ritual, wine) and having sprinkled it on the image, the ritual implements, and so on, one proceeds to external worship. Summoning the energy of the deity into the external substrate and fixing it there (using, again, mantra-*mudrā*-visualization), one installs the full retinue of emanations and guardians (the deity's *yāga*) and then offers worship in the form of offerings of elemental substances (water, fire, etc.) in the forms that are presented to an honored guest or king. Tantrik *pūjā* is of course highly sensual: beautiful flowers in abundance, sweet water or wine, herbs, sublime scents of incense and sandalwood paste, bright flames, and delicious food all serve to gratify the goddesses of the senses to repletion.

After all the offerings, there is "showing the *mudrā*," which in the very ancient tradition consisted of imitating the deity in ways that would strike us as bizarre, frightening, amusing, or perhaps "primitive." Sometimes this could take the form of possession-dance. In the mature classical Tantra, however, showing the *mudrā* was entirely internal, a posture (*karaṇa*) of Consciousness. A simple example of this is *śāmbhavī mudrā,* whereby your eyes are kept wide open but your awareness is entirely directed within. In the Trika, this step of the ritual consisted of performing *khecarī mudrā,* which as we have seen, means raising the *kuṇḍalinī* energy up the central channel and then abiding in the pure expansive space of awareness.

After ritually circling the sacred space and bowing, there are fire-offerings to be made on special occasions before one proceeds to offer the fruit of the rite for the benefit of all beings and finally dissolves the *maṇḍala*, releasing the energies that have been bound into the sacred space.

This brings us to the end of our discussion of *āṇava-upāya,* the method that emphasizes the Power of Action, which relies on techniques taught in the scriptures, and utilizes external supports for the development of consciousness, and therefore is appropriate for those who perceive primarily in terms of subject-object duality. Remember that we have only touched on those *āṇava-upāya* practices that are not already well understood; there are of course many more that are commonly taught as yoga today.*

This also concludes our presentation of the *upāyas*, or means to liberation, and of the practice section of the book.

* If by yoga we mean not only what is commonly taught in yoga studios but also what is taught under trademarks like Integral Yoga, Siddha Yoga, Bihar Yoga, and Adi-yoga.

Conclusion

UNDERTAKING A TANTRIK SĀDHANĀ IN THE MODERN WORLD

Having learned in detail about the incredibly rich and powerful array of Tantrik teachings and practices, some are naturally drawn to undertake a Tantrik practice or at least incorporate elements of it into their existing yoga practice. But this is problematic and cannot be done without careful reflection on the various caveats that naturally emerge from a study of the original context of these practices. Indeed, European scholars of the Tantra are incredulous and bemused when they learn of Americans' desire to engage in the practice of this spiritual tradition. This incredulity is not without reason, for they are aware of some of the obstacles that face a Westerner approaching the tradition with this intent. Given that some readers of this book will want to undertake the practice, and given my own belief that a resuscitation of the practice tradition of nondual Śaiva Tantra would be of benefit to all beings, I will here address some of these challenges and how they might be overcome. Even if you disagree that the issues addressed below constitute real hurdles, you are always well served by tempering headlong enthusiasm into careful, responsible, devoted engagement.

Problem of Access

First is the problem of access. Most of the Tantrik lineages have died out, most of the scriptures are unpublished, nearly all of them exist only in Sanskrit, and many of them exist in such a linguistically corrupted* condition that only the best European scholars can repair them (there are sadly virtually no American scholars with adequate linguistic training in Sanskrit and philology to do this). The issue of access is linked to that of secrecy; the tradition has always protected itself from dilution by giving out powerful teachings sparingly and only to those who prove their dedication. Those few remaining Indian Tantrik teachers from India, Nepāl, and Tibet are reluctant to impart their higher teachings to Westerners, and with good reason: talk to any traditional teacher in India—of music, of Sanskrit, of cooking, whatever—and they will tell you that perhaps one percent of their Western students stay long enough to master the discipline. Westerners simply do not (in general) exhibit the patience and staying power these traditions require. The result is they are in real danger of dying out, because young Indians are also not interested in studying them when they can make a lot more money by learning computer programming. Now, this book helps mitigate the problem of access and of secrecy but introduces a further problem: some who read it will believe that they are qualified to undertake the practice by the very fact of having read it. In fact, the tradition is unanimous in declaring that mantras and practices obtained from a book are inert and useless unless activated in relationship with a qualified teacher. Believing otherwise can lead you astray.

* In the discipline of textual criticism, "corrupted" means the text is full of scribal errors due to copying and recopying over centuries (manuscripts don't last very long in the climate of India).

The Role of the Guru

The problem of the role of the guru, discussed briefly above, is also partially a problem of access. We are faced with the choice between Asian masters whose English is frequently not fluent enough for us to determine whether it is their understanding or just their vocabulary that lacks nuance and depth, and Western teachers who are often charismatic and eloquent but grossly premature in their decision to take up the mantle of the teacher. Given the situation, I personally recommend that the interested student of the Tantra follow Abhinava's suggestion and fly like a bee from flower to flower, gathering sweet nectar from all but still always seeking the one flower (teacher) that seems to offer an inexhaustible wellspring of nectar and thus merits a prolonged stay. Later in this section

I name a variety of teachers with whom one might engage this process. Note that it is sitting with teachers in person that I am referring to, not just reading their books. The blueprint of a house is not a house.

See page 436

Exoteric cultural base

Another issue in the potential revival of Śaiva Tantra is the problem of its connection to the culture in which it finds itself. This requires some explanation. Historically, Shaivism spread only to those regions of the world in which the orthodox brāhminical culture of India preceded it—specifically, Southeast Asia and Indonesia. This was because Śaiva Tantra was for the most part inextricably linked to the Vedic religion that it transcended. That is, the initiation ritual that was so central to the Tantra was carefully calibrated to eradicate the sense of egoic identity that was constructed by brāhminical society. You have no doubt gathered by now that the dissolution of self-images or identity constructs is central to the liberative process of Tantrik practice, and this is encoded in its initiation rituals. Now, if these rituals were to be performed in (say) the Judeo-Christian United States, they would have to be rewritten to eradicate the specific identity constructs that are not Veda-determined but Bible-determined (where "Veda" and "Bible" include all the rules, programs, and narratives about reality sanctioned by the orthodoxy of those particular communities).

Now, what is particularly interesting about the Tantra is that in this process it did *not* seek to condemn or repudiate the religious culture it liberated the initiate from. Quite the opposite. A Tāntrika was supposed to maintain his respectable outer civic and religious identity, if only as a kind of costume to conceal an empowered "Tantrik Self" free of all socially-constructed determinants and compulsions. It is this latter Self that the Tāntrika sees as her real identity, so she does not feel bound by the role she plays in normal society. The Tāntrika was not to see the socially sanctioned civic religion as having any spiritual value whatsoever, except where it pointed toward the esoteric Tantrik revelation that alone could lift one out of social and egoic constructs of identity (since actualizing the Tantrik Self was not the mere replacement of one religious identity with another, but rather meant realizing one's essence as the absolutely indescribable, transindividual, transmental, all-encompassing and unlimited Light of Consciousness itself). Thus, a faithful transmission of original Tantra *would have to be tailored to the specific culture that it transcends*. This makes sense if we understand that freedom is not attained by merely asserting it—one must thoroughly see and understand that which is transcended, or the transcendence is illusory, whereby one has merely replaced one identity construct with another, and is therefore equally limited. To live in a *vikalpa* of the Truth is far distant from living in the Truth, though it may feel very good relative to one's previous identity.

Śaiva Tantra as traditionally conceived could not exist without the base of the transcended religious culture, that is, the specific civic cultural and religious identity that it expands out of. To put it another way, there is a strange but true paradox in operation here: you must first have a strong and healthy ego in order to go beyond all ego. There must be a specific identity for you to transcend, otherwise your process of transformation is not sufficiently rooted in the real, one might say. In medieval India, that identity was highly Veda-determined, and thus everyone had more or less the same set of hang-ups. This is not the case in the diverse modern West. This hurdle could be overcome if the guru designed an initiation ritual specific to each individual, but this presupposes that he has a clear grasp of each individual's psychology. You begin to see the problem: in modern America (or England, France, etc.) since traditional societies are now pretty much nonexistent, everyone has a more or less unique set of psychological hang-ups to be overcome. Hence the original purpose of the *dīkṣā* ritual, absolutely central to Tantra, is negated. The enormous challenge that faces the modern Tantrik teacher, then, consists in part of helping students to find ways to release their self-images without knowing what all those self-images are.

Public perception of Tantra as sex

The next problem I wish to address is the public perception of Tantra as primarily concerned with sex. With regard to the Indian tradition, as we have seen, this is manifestly untrue: next to none of the scriptural sources of Śaiva Tantra teach a sexual ritual or sexual techniques of any kind.[180] One of the post-scriptural sources does teach a sexual ritual drawn from the Kaula tradition: this is chapter 29 of Abhinava Gupta's *Tantrāloka*. But this is not the source for modern American neo-tantra, since a) it has never been translated accurately, and b) the meditative rite it describes is almost wholly unlike what is taught in so-called Tantric sex workshops. What, then, is the source for these workshops? Though it remains mysterious, it is likely that all teaching of so-called Tantric sex in North America can ultimately be traced back to Pierre Bernard, a.k.a. "Oom the Omnipotent," who taught a bizarre and idiosyncratic version of yoga and tantra beginning in San Francisco in 1905.* He was the first "spiritual teacher" in America to use Tantrik teachings to satisfy his prodigious sexual cravings (the beginning of a long and sordid history). He received his information from a Bengali immigrant who moved to his native Iowa (not coincidentally, Bengal is the only part of India where Tantra with a sexual dimension survived to the modern period).

* See *The Subtle Body* by Stephanie Syman, *The Great Oom* by Robert Love, and Hugh Urban's detailed article at http://www.esoteric.msu.edu/VolumeIII/ HTML/Oom.html.

For centuries, the Western imagination has been titillated by images of the "exotic Orient" and fascinated by apparent evidence of a much more advanced sexual culture, as exemplified by everything from Japanese geishas to the Indian *Kāma-sūtra*. This helps explain why early Western interest in Tantra focused on rumors of a strange sexual rite. Some, disgusted by the notion, proffered it as evidence of the moral degeneration of India; others, profoundly attracted by the same notion, thought it might be the key to bringing sex out of the realm of sin. But virtually none had any direct experience of the reality behind the rumors. People like Pierre Bernard and Aleister Crowley, lacking access to the original sources, simply invented their own "sex magick" rites, inspired by the little they knew of Tantra, and these have now evolved for over a hundred years. Though there is no direct connection between modern "Tantric sex" and the sexual ritual of original Śaiva Tantra, we will take a moment to describe the latter so that we can see how different it really is. First, this ritual did not have pleasure as its purpose: it was primarily a means to transcend the contracted brāhminical notions around purity and impurity, which were specific to Indian culture. There were two versions of the transgressive ritual. One version focused on the "five jewels," transgressive substances to be used in worship and ingested (at least in small quantities) by the worshipper: these were semen, menses, urine, feces, and phlegm. Small quantities of these substances were used, made palatable by being immersed in a generous portion of wine. These were the most "impure" substances known to Indian culture (anything separated from the human body that originally formed part of the body is considered polluting in the brahmanical view); their consumption, therefore, was considered proof that the practitioner had gone beyond the petty dualistic notion that some things are purer or more divine than others. The second version of the transgressive ritual entailed the use of the "three M's": meat (*māṃsa*), wine (*madya*), and extramarital intercourse (*maithuna*).[181] You may be thinking, that sounds more like neo-tantra. But this second version of the rite is not fundamentally dissimilar from the first, for both were designed to confront the practitioner with substances and acts that were, in that cultural environment, regarded with a horror that a modern "free-thinking" person can scarcely imagine. This confrontation was essentially a challenge to "walk the talk" of the nondual teachings; for after all, these substances in actuality are manifestations of the same divine Light that exists in lovely flowers, puppies, and babies. But if you recoil at the "five jewels," that is taken as evidence that you do not really believe in your heart and gut that all things equally partake of the same divine Light. (If you protest here, saying your concern would be merely hygienic, the Kaula Tāntrikas answer that a strong energy body can digest *anything* without harm to itself.)

The ritual of the "three M's" seems more pleasant than that of the "five jewels," and indeed it was constituted along Kaula lines with the concern for sensual aesthetic beauty central to that lineage. But the real nail in the coffin for those who fantasize about so-called "Tantric sex" is this: as specified clearly in *Tantrāloka* chapter 29, one's partner in the sexual ritual must be someone that you are *not attracted to,* lest the drive of ordinary sexual desire take over, causing you to objectify your partner, which would spoil the liberative purpose of the ritual. (This is why a partner other than one's spouse is assumed as the default. This strikes me as a very generous view of marriage.) Furthermore, if the practitioner is high-caste, the partner (*dūtī*) should be low-caste so as to challenge him to overcome the cultural construct that differentiates caste and social status—since the rite requires him to perceive his partner as an incarnation of the Divine. Therefore, the types of partners that were usually recommended were the most low cast and repellent of women to the high-cast brahminical practitioner. But first and foremost, for Abhinava Gupta anyway, the *kula-yāga* or sexual ritual is a form of meditation. Indeed, he argues that for the advanced and lust-free practitioner, the *kula-yāga* can be a direct means to liberation.

Now you can see that a re-creation of the transgressive ritual would have to be tailored to the culture of the one doing the practice. For example, a student of mine joked, a Californian super-green new age-type person would have to eat a McDonald's hamburger while seeing it as a manifestation of divine Consciousness. While humorous, this is along the lines that we must be thinking if we are serious about the spiritual work that the transgressive ritual represents.

The next problem I will deal with in this section is one that will not concern every reader but still seems worth addressing. This is the problem of whether the tradition itself sanctions the initiation of foreigners or non-Indian "barbarians" (*mlecchas*) into the Tantrik mysteries. After all, would you want to be a member of a religion that doesn't want you? Any Westerner who has been turned away from a Hindu temple on the basis of the color of his skin will realize this is a significant concern. However, we find that, in fact, the Śaiva Tantrik scriptures do approve of the initiation of foreigners in the context of their assertions regarding the nonreality of caste. The primary sources argue, in a manner that is startlingly modern in its critique, that caste is nothing but a cultural construct (*kalpanā*) without basis in fact, and that therefore all devotees of God form a single community regardless of birth. The scripture called *Pauṣkara-pārameśvara* further argues:

Pauṣkara-pārameśvara

> *There is only one caste, that of human beings. No "caste" was ordained for them, nor color such as white. All arise from the union of a linga and a yoni, and thus all souls are one and the same. One who has the eye of wisdom sees God in all of them.*[182]

Though this concept must seem obvious to a modern Western reader, being a fundamental value for us, I cannot begin to communicate how unusual it is to read a statement like this in an ancient Indian source. Seeing it in the original Sanskrit is like recognizing the signature of someone who has travelled back in time from our era. This repudiation of caste was only fully embraced in practice by the left current, in which referring to (let alone disparaging) the former caste of a fellow initiate merited expulsion from the spiritual community. This egalitarianism was remarkably transgressive behavior in the context of medieval India (and, in the end, it was not tolerated). Further, we have two commentators on record saying that it would be better to initiate a sincere foreigner than an insincere brāhmin, supporting my earlier comments that initiation was based, above all, on the sincere longing of the candidate. Since it was the left-current Kaula-influenced lineages that argued this, they would be the most appropriate for Westerners to practice in. A happy coincidence, then, since these are the lineages whose teachings I find Westerners most resonating with.

See page 332

Practice in the 21st century

Lastly, there is the problem of how modern Westerners would like to practice their Tantra. The problem is this: for most of the history of the tradition, the central element of being a Tāntrika was the performance of a fairly involved daily ritual practice and a variety of additional duties modern Westerners would likely find onerous. Fortunately, however, the tradition has provided for a variety of possibilities better suited to the 21st century. For example, in lieu of the involved and expensive *dīkṣā* initiation ritual, Abhinava provides in chapter 30 of *Light on the Tantras* a simple form of Kaula initiation, empowering the recipient with the three Wisdom-Goddess mantras that are thought to be so powerful that recitation of them every day can substitute for a ritual practice.

The Krama tradition, while providing for a detailed ritual life, does not require it, allowing for a practice centering solely on the contemplation and internalization of the compressed power-statements called *chummās* that contain revelatory teachings in seed-form, if these are properly received from a qualified teacher and worked with in the context of a community of initiates (we discussed these chummās in Part 2 of this book). This option makes the Krama the logical school of choice for modern Western practitioners to align themselves with, along with the fact that, as the school that most successfully freed itself from dominant cultural programs we would probably call sexist and racist, it was naturally the most empowering to women and the most likely to initiate non-Indians. I would argue that the Krama is the Tantrik school *par excellence,* the consummation of the tradition, in that it takes dimensions of Tantrik thought that are nascent or partially inhibited in other schools and allows them to come to full development. In other words, of all the Tantrik traditions, the Krama is the most transcendent of the cultural framework that birthed it. Furthermore, it is the most sophisticated in its analysis of Consciousness, articulating a meditation on the process of cognition that is universal, applying as it does to all sentient beings. And finally, it is the Śaiva school most closely aligned with certain Buddhist Tantrik lineages that are still alive today (i.e., Dzogchen and Mahāmudrā), which constitute an allied sister tradition to the Krama. For these reasons and more, to be explored in another publication, the Kaula Krama or Mahārtha presents itself as the school of nondual Śaiva Tantra that 21st century Westerners could practice most authentically (were more sources of it available).

See page 439

Afterword
Modern survivals of Śaiva Tantra; or, "where can I learn more?"

Though Śaiva Tantra is the oldest documented type of Tantra, from which the others clearly derive, it almost did not survive to the present. It is quite amazing that Shaivism, once the dominant religion of all of the Indian subcontinent and much of Southeast Asia and Indonesia, is very nearly forgotten today as a unique tradition, despite its enormous influence on whole cultures (like those in Nepāl and Tibet, as well as in India) and despite the fact that millions still see its beautiful edifices (like Bṛhadīśvara temple in Tamiḷ Nāḍu or Angkor Wat in Cambodia), thousands see versions of its rituals (in temples in Nepāl as well as in the far South and far East of India), and millions in the West know its basic doctrines, if only as clichés—for the influential '60s idea that "it's all one Consciousness" can be traced to spiritual teachers influenced by Tantrik ideas.

Yet Shaivism has passed through the eye of the needle, the point at which it was almost lost and has been regaining ground ever since. That point was the mid-20th century. The last proper Śaiva Tantrik *dīkṣā* ceremonies were performed in Kashmīr in the 1920s, and their purpose had been forgotten well before that. Yet at precisely that time, the Mahārāja of Kashmīr, a Hindu king of an almost entirely Muslim region, saw fit to commission the publication (in the original Sanskrit) of all the major Tantrik texts still existing in the region, which turned out to be quite a lot. And thank God he did—the publication of the hundred-odd volumes of the "Kashmīr Series of Texts and Studies" was the most crucial 20th-century event for the preservation of original Tantra. Wondering what to do with all these books that virtually no one in their own country cared to read, the Kashmīr government gave sets of them to Western university libraries, none of which had the slightest idea initially of what they had received. But some European scholars began to read these texts, and in the 1960s and '70s a few of them (including my mentor, Alexis Sanderson) trickled into Kashmīr to sit with the last remaining teacher of this philosophy in the region, Swāmī Lakṣman Jū of Śrīnagar. He taught them, as well as the young people who were also showing up seeking spiritual understanding in the mysterious East. Lakṣman Jū was familiar with many concepts of Tantrik philosophy, though the rituals and yoga and more transgressive teachings had all been forgotten by this time. By contrast, at the other end of India (in the far South), the rituals and some of yoga had been partially preserved, while the specific Tantrik View teachings were forgotten.

Lakṣman Jū's Western students, and a small handful of Indian scholars connected with him (e.g., Rāmeshwar Jha), began nursing the knowledge of this tradition back to health. For a long time, no one even realized that the gnostic Trika Shaivism of Kashmīr and the ritualized Śaiva Siddhānta of Tamiḷ Nāḍu were two attenuated forms of one and the same tradition, the ancient tradition of Śaiva Tantra. Today, a few dozen scholars are laboring intensively to document the original teachings and practices, though they are sorely overburdened: literally hundreds of key texts are unpublished and untranslated, and of the half-dozen that have been translated, none (!) exists in a version that would suit the general public*. The study of classical Tantra is still a very young field, and one that is in dire need of more scholars.

Scholars of Śaiva Tantra

Though scholarly writing is often difficult and dry, if you are of an academic bent, take note of this list of the few really fine scholars of Śaiva Tantra in North America: Loriliai Biernacki (University of Colorado); John Nemec (University of Virginia); Shaman Hatley (Concordia University, Canada); Gudrun Bühnemann (University of Wisconsin at Madison); Whitney Cox (University of Chicago); and David Peter Lawrence (University of North Dakota). Since the University of Virginia boasts not only John Nemec but also David Germano, a scholar of Tibetan Buddhist Tantra and Dzogchen (see below), it is currently the best place in the United States to study the Śaiva Tantra academically, along with the University of Chicago which has Whitney Cox and Christian Wedemeyer.

* Probably the best English translation of a Śaiva Tantrik scripture available is Lakṣman Jū's *Shiva Sutras: The Supreme Awakening*. My forthcoming translation of *The Recognition Sūtras* is also worthy of note.

It is my hunch, however, that academic study would not "do it" for most readers of this book, who I presume are interested in the actual practice and experience of the Tantrik teachings. If you have been captivated by the subject matter of this book, it's natural to ask how you can learn more, and who among the contemporary teachers of Tantra and Tantrik yoga are "the real deal."

Neo-tantra

First, as noted above, we must confront the sad fact that, in some quarters at least, the word "Tantra" has become almost wholly severed from its original meaning. It is safe to assume that when the word "Tantra" is used in connection with sex and partner work on the New Age and alternative spirituality scene, in almost every case that teacher or workshop has no connection to the original tradition. By making a distinction between something like "original" or "classical" Indian Tantra and what we may call "modern Western neo-Tantra" I do not intend to suggest that the latter is useless or illegitimate. It may be very helpful for some people in improving their quality of life. What I *would* like to challenge is the historical claim some of these teachers make that what they teach is linked in some way—or in *any* way—to the Indian tradition and the contents of these mostly unpublished Sanskrit texts.[183] If what they teach is valuable and effective, no such historical claim is necessary. If it is not, no such claim can render their teaching otherwise.

Finding a teacher

There *are* a few modern spiritual teachers who accurately present some of the teachings and practices of Śaiva Tantra, having received them from a living lineage. It is certainly true that Tantra is still a living tradition, though it is also true that what has survived into the present day is a highly attenuated form of the original tradition. If we seek Tantra's survivors, we must look not to sex manuals but rather to those contemporary spiritual lineages that have studied, practiced, and preserved the original teachings and transmitted those teachings in some form to the West. I will mention a few of these modern teachers, but do not hold me responsible if you have a bad experience with anyone listed here. I tend toward skepticism, and for your safety, I recommend you do the same. Each individual must decide for herself on the basis of her direct experience, ignoring whatever rhetoric is proffered by the promotional literature of a given organization. "The proof is in the pudding" must be our watchword, and we must be very honest with ourselves in assessing the real results we have obtained from following a particular practice. What makes this difficult is the fact that you must give spiritual practice a chance to work, and depending on your level of development, it is hard to be sure that a given practice is *not* working for you in less than six months. But human psychology being what it is, when you have invested as much as six months into a particular path, you might convince yourself that it is working better for you than it actually is because you have become attached to it as part of your identity and don't want to feel that you have chosen wrongly. So what I recommend is this: do some research and use your discernment to choose a practice that is likely to have *some* benefit for you, and after six to twelve months take a break from that practice, a break in which you engage in radically honest reflection about how far you've come. As part of this reflection, to compensate for your own self-denigration or self-aggrandizement you must solicit the input of those who are close to you and can see your changes. Positive changes should be showing up in your day-to-day real life. If you are not getting the results you want, look for another practice and/or teacher.

When you are doing your research, remember that the Internet is, in general, the *worst* research tool you can possibly use to investigate a spiritual teacher or organization. I can't stress this enough. The nature of the Internet is that misinformation is mixed with information in unknown proportions at all times. Even Wikipedia, which has become reliable for certain topics, is so atrocious on everything related to Indian religions that I forbid its use to my university students. And people love to read about scandals on the Internet, so there are endless stories about the misconduct of gurus. Though some may be true, they are no substitute for firsthand experience. For researching gurus, the *only* thing the Internet offers that is of potential benefit is video clips. But even here we must remember that we can only feel the real "energy field" of a human being in his or her physical presence. And unlike with teachers of mere knowledge like university professors, the energy field really matters with a spiritual teacher.

Therefore, you must go to the teacher's āshram or meditation center or retreat yourself. Get a feel for the teacher (without first prejudicing yourself with Internet stories), and more importantly, talk to as many of their students as you can. If a good percentage of a teacher's students are grounded and clear and can relate what they have attained and what shifts they have undergone without glamorizing them, that is your best evidence for a sound path. Don't assume it's a cult based on the use of jargon; after all, look at how many Sanskrit words are in this book. Every spiritual tradition has jargon. Your evaluation should be based on to what extent the practitioners in that community interact with you in a warm, genuine, down-to-earth, and grounded manner.

Spiritual Promiscuity

In the Sanskrit text called the *Guru-gītā,* there is a verse that says, "One God, one religion, one faith is the highest austerity. There is nothing higher than the Guru." Should you gather wisdom-teachings and practices from as many gurus as possible to give you the best chance of attaining the goal? The traditional view is that without having a "root-Guru," this would be spiritually disabling, since, not having a clear outline of the big picture, you will not know how to correctly fit together what various teachers give you. People who "guru-shop" do not go deep with any one system, and thus end up like the proverbial man who dug a dozen holes three feet deep and thus never struck water, as he would have had he dug just one thirty-foot well. Such dilettantish spiritual materialism will not set you firmly on the path. Rather, having gotten a full download from one trustworthy teacher that orients you thoroughly, you may then go to other teachers for unfolding and enhancement of what you have received (not out of any sense of the inadequacy of your root-teacher). This is very different, for you are not sampling different paths, but seeking different ways of understanding the one path to which you have given your heart. On this perspective, you are doing the practice of seeing all authentic gurus as forms of your root-Guru.

The exception to the general rule against spiritual promiscuity is if the teachers you are going to are all in the same order or school, using the same mantras and drawing on the same set of scriptures. Even then, eventually you are supposed to settle on one of them as your root-teacher if you want to get serious. This, at least, is the traditional view, and the primary purpose of this book is to outline the traditional views, but of course, you will find your own way with it, should you choose to practice in this or a related tradition.

There are some authentic teachers of the original Śaiva Tantra who are around, such as Paul Müller-Ortega of Blue Throat Yoga, Swāmī Cetanānanda of the Movement Center in Portland, Dharma Bodhi of Dharma Inc., Swāmī Janakānanda in Sweden, Swāmī Khecaranātha in Berkeley, California, Paṇḍit Rajmani Tigunait in Pennsylvania, and Swāmī Shankarānanda in Melbourne, Australia, and Christopher Tompkins in California. This is a very short list that you can start with. My websites are mattamayura.org and tantrikstudies.org.

My Teachers

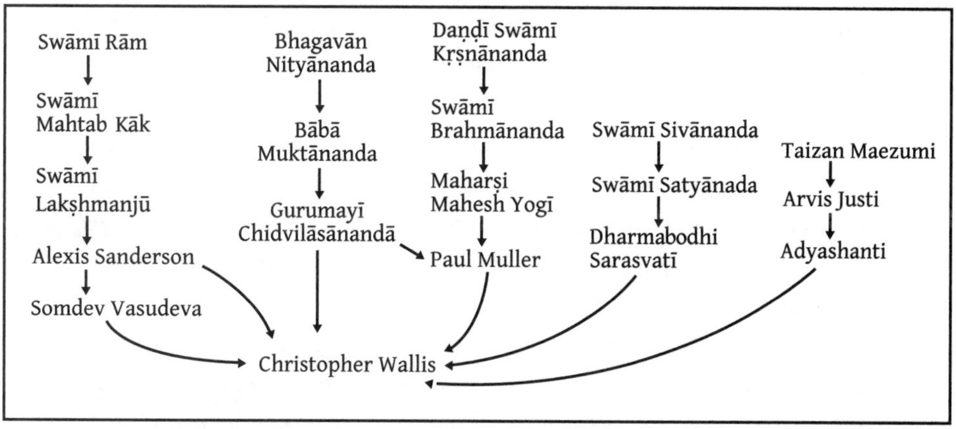

DZOGCHEN: THE TANTRIK YOGA OF THE NYINGMAPAS AND BONPÖS

As long as we are discussing practice gurus, it would be remiss of me to not return to the topic of the similarity to nondual Śaiva Tantra of one of the most remarkable of the Buddhist traditions—that is, Dzogchen. If you have resonated strongly with the teachings in this book, especially those of the Krama, but are more drawn to the aesthetic and culture of Buddhism than that of any of the above practice teachers, then you will feel very much at home with a good Dzogchen teacher. Note that Dzogchen defies easy catagorization as Buddhist Tantra, since it declares itself as being "beyond Tantra" and since it holds views that are not so clearly Buddhist—because they are so close to Śaiva views, and because Dzogchen is taught just as frequently by adherents of the other major Tibetan religion, Bön.

Let's look for a moment at the core Dzogchen teaching, so you can see how similar it really is. It is said that the first to propagate Dzogchen teachings in Tibet was Padma-sambhava himself (c. 8th century), who went there from Uḍḍiyāna. This small kingdom is also, probably not coincidentally, the birthplace of the Krama tradition. Dzogchen, which means "the Great Perfection," teaches that everything is Consciousness. The word in Tibetan is *rigpa*, derived from the Sanskrit *vidyā* (as in *śuddha-vidyā*), but closer in meaning to Sanskrit *cit* or *citi*. *Rigpa* can be translated as awareness, seeing, knowing, the Knower, pure presence, wakefulness, the nondual ultimate nature of mind. Confusion may arise from the occasional translation of *rigpa* as "mind," however, a little investigation reveals that *rigpa* is indeed what the Śaiva nondualists call Consciousness (*cit*) or Awareness (*saṃvit*).

See page 249

Dzogchen teaches that all phenomena arise within consciousness, and thus there is nothing other than consciousness, yet it is itself empty of anything that can be named: it is openness beyond concept. This *rigpa*, though formless and absolute, possesses qualities—namely indestructibility, incorruptible purity, nondiscriminating openness, flawless clarity, profound simplicity, all-pervading presence, and equality within all beings. It is unconditioned, not originated from causes or conditions, and blissful.[184] This is all exactly as in NŚT. In fact, I have not yet been able to identify a significant difference between the two schools (though this may be due to my relative ignorance of Dzogchen), despite the fact that they supposedly belong to two separate religions. Thus we see more evidence that Tantra was and is a spiritual phenomenon that is transreligious.

Though I have no direct experience of them, you might want to check out the following Dzogchen teachers, who trusted friends of mine praise highly: Tsoknyi Rinpoche (www.pundarika.org); Tsultrim Allione, a female lama of Western birth, ordained by the Karmapa (www.taramandala.org); Sogyal Rinpoche (www.rigpa.org); Namkhai Norbu, Lopon Trinley Nyima, and Tenzin Wangyal Rinpoche (of the Bön tradition); and B. Alan Wallace (www.alanwallace.org).

FINAL BLESSING

sarveṣām svastir bhavatu
May all beings be blessed

sarveṣām śāntir bhavatu
May all beings know peace

sarveṣām muktir bhavatu
May all beings be free

sarveṣām pūrṇaṃ bhavatu
May all beings be full

lokāḥ samastāḥ sukhino bhavantu
May everyone everywhere be happy!

Hariḥ Oṃ tat sat

Hariḥ Oṃ tat sat

Hariḥ Oṃ tat sat.

Completed on Aṣṭamī, śukla pakṣa of Śrāvaṇa, Saṃvat 2067 (August 6, 2011)
at Haramara Retreat, Nayarit, México

A NOTE ON SANSKRIT TERMS AND THEIR PRONUNCIATION

Vowels

1 Letter	2 Pron.	3 English Example	4 Sanskrit Example	5 Notes
a	'uh'	sof*a*	anuttara	
ā	'aah'	f*a*ther	ānanda	Quantitatively and qualitatively different from 'a': twice as long and more open sounding
i	'ee'	f*ee*t	icchā	
ī	'eee'	sc*e*ne	īśvara	Only quantitatively different from 'i': twice as long
u	'oo'	fl*u*te	unmeṣa	
ū	'ooo'	p*oo*l	ūrmi	Twice as long as 'u'
ṛ		ch*ur*ch ac*re*	kṛta hotṛ	A vocalic 'r'—position the tongue for an English 'r', but pronounce a neutral 'schwa' vowel. As this is a vowel, not a consonant, there is no contact of the tongue with the palate. The English examples are approximate, as in Sanskrit the vowel sound is heard before, during, and after the 'r' element, whereas in English it is heard before and during but not after. Thus the word Sanskrit word ṛṣi to an English ear sounds halfway between 'ershi' and 'rushi'.
e	'ay'	s*a*ve	evam	As in Fr. *e*tude; long vowel, like ā, ī, ū
ai	'ai'	p*ie*, sk*y*	aiśvarya	Long vowel; note that this is the sound of ā + i, pronounced in rapid succession.
o	'oh'	t*oe*	ojas	Long vowel
au	'ow'	c*ow*	auṣadhi	Long vowel; this is ā + u pronounced in rapid succession.

Vowel modifications

aḥ	'aha'	--	devaḥ	This letter is called *visarga.* The final vowel is repeated lightly, preceded by an 'h' sound; e.g. devaḥ = devaha, taiḥ = taihi.

Consonants

Velars: pronounced in the back of the throat

ka		s*k*ate	kanyā	The letter is unaspirated, i.e., pronounced without a rush of air, like the second *k* in the phrase 'kick it' and *unlike* the first *k.*
kha		*K*ate	khaga	Aspirated as in English.
ga		*g*um	gaja	Never pronounced as in *g*iant.
gha		fo*gh*orn	ghaṭa	Aspirated, as in English compounds like *doghouse* when pronounced quickly. This sound takes practice, as in English it never begins a word.
ṅa		i*n*k, I*n*ga	gaṅgā	This sound never begins a word. It is also heard in English si*ng.*

Palatals: pronounced with the edges of the tongue against the upper molars.

ca	'cha'	--	candra	This sound is 'cha' but without any aspiration. Note that *vāc* is then pronounced 'vaach'.
cha	'chha'	*ch*uck	cheda	As in English (*ch*ip, *ch*ill, etc.). Note that the English word 'church' would be represented in Sanskrit as *chṛc*, with almost exactly the same pronunciation.
ja		*j*ug	jala	Always as in *j*am, never as in French *jour.* Note that the sounds of the English word 'judge' would be written *jaj* in Sanskrit.
jha		he*dgeh*og	jhaṭiti	Only found in compounds in English, as sle*dgeh*ammer. Takes practice.
ña		o*n*ion	ājñā	Before vowels, a *y* sound is heard immediately after the *n*, as in Spanish se*ñ*or.
		pu*n*ch	pañca	Before consonants, there is no *y* insertion.

Retroflex: this class is not found in English. To pronounce, curl the tongue to touch the highest points of the roof of the mouth. The tongue does not need to curl backwards; it should point more or less straight up.

ṭa	ghaṭa	Unaspirated version of following consonant.
ṭha	kaṇṭha	Aspirated version of previous consonant.
ḍa	aṇḍa	Unaspirated version of following consonant.
ḍha	ḍhauk	Aspirated version of previous consonant.
ṇa	kṣaṇa	Retroflex nasal.

Dental: this class sounds like English consonants but are pronounced with the tongue touching the back of the front teeth, almost coming out between them, as in French or Spanish.

ta	*stop*	tathā	Unaspirated, occurs in English only after an *s*.
tha	*top*	ratha	Aspirated t, as in *tank* or an*th*ill, **not** as in thank.
da		danta	As in English, but touching the back of the teeth.
dha		dhana	With aspiration, as in English guil*dh*all (pronounced quickly).
na	*none*	nayana	Dental nasal.

Labial

pa	*spin*	pūjā	Unaspirated; only occurs in English after an s.
pha	*pan*	phala	Aspirated as in English u*ph*eaval; never pronounced as in *ph*rase.
ba	*before*	bāṇa	As in English.
bha	*abhor*	bhaya	Aspirated; unlike in the English example, this is a single consonant.
ma	*mama*	mama	As in English.

Semi-vowels

ya	*yes*	yāmala	As in English.
ra		Hara	A 'tapped' sound, as in Spanish. Different from ṛ.
la	*linger*	lavaṇa	As in English.
va	*vast*	deva	Pronounced as a soft *v* when following

				a vowel or beginning a word.
		s*w*ay	īśvara	Pronounced as an *unrounded* w when following a consonant.
Sibilants				
śa	'sha'	*s*ugar	śakti	
ṣa	'sha'	a*ss*ure	doṣa	A 'sha' sound but with the curled up towards the roof of the mouth without touching.
sa		*s*avor	sakala	As in English.
Aspirate				
ha		*h*and	hasta	As in English.
Conjunct				
jña	'gnya'		yajña jñāna	In this special conjunct consonant, 'j' is pronounced as 'g' (and *only* in this case).

APPENDIX 1: THE OPENING VERSES OF THE TANTRĀLOKA

BENEDICTION HONORING THE SUPREME HEART

vimala-kalāśrayābhinava-sṛṣṭi-mahā jananī
bharita-tanuś ca pañca-mukha-gupta-rucir janakaḥ |
tad-ubhaya-yāmala-sphurita-bhāva-visarga-mayaṃ
hṛdayam anuttarāmṛta-kulaṃ mama saṃsphuratāt || 1 ||

The Mother is She who is the ground of all pure action, radiant with ever-new genesis. The Father is He who is filled (with all the śaktis), maintaining his Light through his five faces. May my Heart, one with the diverse creation flowing forth from the fusion of these two, embodying the nectar of the Absolute, shine forth!
[For the alternate meaning, see page 293]

INVOCATIONS: TO PARĀ (= *SVĀTANTRYA-ŚAKTI* AND *ICCHĀ-ŚAKTI*)

naumi cit-pratibhāṃ devīṃ parāṃ bhairava-yoginīm |
mātṛ-māna-prameyāṃśa-śūlāmbuja-kṛtāspadām || 2 ||

I praise the Supreme Goddess [Parā Devī], the creative inspiration [*pratibhā*] of Consciousness, the yogic consort of Bhairava, who has made her abode the lotus-and-trident-throne, its prongs knower, knowing, and known.

TO APARĀ (= *KRIYĀ-ŚAKTI*)

naumi devīṃ śarīra-sthāṃ nṛtyato bhairavākṛteḥ |
prāvṛṇ-megha-ghana-vyoma-vidyul-lekhā-vilāsinīm || 3 ||

I praise the Goddess in the body of the dancing Bhairava, playful like a streak of lightning in a sky dense with monsoon clouds.

TO PARĀPARĀ AS THE TRIDENT OF WISDOM (= *JÑĀNA-ŚAKTI*)

dīpta-jyotiś-chaṭā-pluṣṭa-bheda-bandha-trayaṃ sphurat |
stāj jñāna-śūlaṃ sat-pakṣa-vipakṣotkartana-kṣamam || 4 ||

May the Trident of wisdom, shimmering as the triad of dualistic bonds scorched by masses of blazing light, be capable of cutting off all that undermines right View.

TO THE TRIAD OF GODDESSES

svātantrya-śaktiḥ krama-saṃsisṛkṣā kramātmatā ceti vibhor vibhūtiḥ |
tad eva devī-trayam antar āstām anuttaraṃ me prathayat svarūpam || 5 ||

The Power of Autonomy, the Will to emit the sequence of creation, and that sequence [itself] are [together] the all-pervasive might (*vibhūti*) of the all-pervasive Lord (*vibhu*). That itself is the triad of Goddesses (Parā etc.)—revealing their ultimate nature to me, may they make their home within.

TO GANESH

tad-devatā-vibhava-bhāvi-mahāmarīci-cakreśvarāyita-nija-sthitir eka eva |
devī-suto Gaṇapatiḥ sphurad indu-kāntiḥ samyak-samucchalayatān mama saṃvid-abdhim || 6 ||

There is only one whose natural state is to behave like the Lord of the Circle, a great ray of light manifesting the majesty of that Divinity: Gaṇapati, the son of the Goddess, shimmering with the splendor of the moon; may he completely uplift the ocean of my awareness.

TO MACCHANDA-NĀTHA, HEAD OF THE KAULA LINEAGE

rāgāruṇaṃ granthi-bilāvakīrṇaṃ yo jālam ātāna-vitāna-vṛtti |
kalombhitaṃ bāhya-pathe cakāra stān me sa Macchanda-vibhuḥ prasannaḥ || 7 ||

May Lord Macchanda, who made the Net, red with passion, stretched and extended, strewn with knots and holes, initiating the immanent powers along the outer path, be pleased with me.

TO THE GURU LINEAGE

traiyambakābhihita-santati-tāmraparṇī-san-mauktika-prakara-kānti-viśeṣa-bhājaḥ |
pūrve jayanti guravo guru-śāstra-sindhu-kallola-keli-kalanāmala-karṇa-dhārāḥ || 8 ||

Triumphant are the ancient masters of the lineage called Traiyambaka, they who share in the exceptional luminosity of the row of pearls in the Tāmraparṇī river. They are the stainless helmsmen who comprehend the play of the mighty billows of the ocean of the Gurus' scriptures.

ABHINAVA HONORS HIS GURUS OF THE PRATYABHIJÑĀ

śrī-Somānanda-bodha-śrīmad-Utpala-viniḥsṛtāḥ |
jayanti saṃvid-āmoda-sandarbhā dik-prasarpiṇaḥ || 10

Triumphant are the compositions—delightfully fragrant with consciousness, spreading in all directions—springing from the reverend Utpala and from the awakened mind of his teacher, the reverend Somānanda.

tad-āsvāda-bharāveśa-baṃhitāṃ mati-ṣaṭpadīm |
guror Laksmaṇaguptasya nāda-saṃmohinīṃ numaḥ || 11

We praise the bee-mind of the Guru Lakṣmaṇagupta, its enchanting resonance intensified by its total immersion in relishing that (Lotus, i.e., his teacher Utpala).

HIS SADGURU AND CONSORT

Jayatāj jagad-uddhṛti-kṣamo 'sau bhagavatyā saha śambhunātha ekaḥ |
yad-udīrita-śāsanāṃśubhir me prakaṭo 'yaṃ gahano 'yaṃ śāstra-mārgaḥ || 13 ||

May the unique Śambhunātha, together with his consort, capable of rescuing the whole world, be triumphant! |
This impenetrable path of scripture was made clear for me through the rays of his amplified teaching.

AUTHORSHIP

śrībhaṭṭanātha-caraṇābja-yugāt tathā
śrībhaṭṭārikāṃghir-yugalād guru-santatir yā |
bodhānya-pāśa-viṣanut-tad-upāsanottha
bodhojjvalo'bhinavagupta idaṃ karoti || 16 ||

The transmission of the Guru lineage from the lotus feet of the reverend Bhaṭṭanātha and from the lotus feet of the reverend Bhaṭṭārikā (i.e., Śambhunātha and consort) is the antidote to the poison of the bonds of what [seems] other than Awareness. Ablaze with the awakening arising from adoration of that [lineage-transmission], Abhinavagupta performs this work.

APPENDIX TWO: THE STRUCTURE OF KRAMA WORSHIP

A central text of the Krama explains:

Mahānaya-prakāśa 1.22–23

> *...the nature of the Self dawns through the method of worshipping the goddesses of cognition that shine forth in every state of mundane experience, flowing outwards and inwards with each successive object of awareness, their contraction dissolved as they merge with the Great Void.* (Translation Sanderson)

This passage simultaneously refers to two important doctrines: First, that the opportunity to realize the nature of the Divine, and oneself as a condensed expression thereof, exists in every single perception and cognition—for each cognition reproduces in microcosm the pattern by which divine Consciousness creates all reality, and then comes to rest in the one ground of all reality (called "the Great Void" above). Secondly, if one is not able to grasp this realization through a contemplation of the flow of cognition itself, one should worship the goddesses that embody the phases of cognition through external ritual, until such patterned action is sufficiently ingrained to make possible a deep insight into the nature of reality.

Exactly what form, then, did this esoteric Krama worship take? There were two primary cycles of worship. The first was articulated as ten stages, divided into two sets of five, with an additional preliminary stage at the beginning. Here is an outline of these phases of worship:

0. Worship of the **SACRED SITE**, i.e., Uḍḍiyāna, the origin place of the Krama revelation; the site and its deities (*ḍākinīs* and so on) are worshipped in the microcosm of one's one body, thus this phase is also consecration of the worshipper's body.

1. Worship of the circle of **THE FIVE FLOW GODDESSES:**
    1) She Who Emits the Void (*Vyomavāmeśvarī*), understood as the inner ground of pure potential before the arising of object-cognition;
    2) She Who Moves in the Sky (*Khecarī*);
    3) She Who Moves in All Directions (*Dikcarī*);
    4) She Who Devours Dissolution (*Saṃhārabhakṣiṇī*); and
    5) the Fierce Goddess (*Raudreśvarī*).

    The first of these is especially emphasized, for Vyomavāmeśvarī is the ground of the following process; thus the worship of the other four here is a foreshadowing of that process.
2. Worship of the circle of **ILLUMINATION** (consisting of 12 goddesses, understood to be aspects of Khecarī and embodying the five sense-capacities, the five action-capacities, and the mind's faculties of attention and discernment). This is the phase of the sense faculties reaching out to the object of awareness and thus illuminating it; it is associated also, therefore, with the exhale and the sun.
3. Worship of the circle of **BLISS** (16 goddesses, understood to be expressions of Dikcarī, embodying the 10 capacities, the mind's faculty of attention, and the 5 subtle elements). This is the phase in which the sense faculties incorporate the object of awareness; associated also, therefore, with the inhale and the moon.
4. Worship of the circle of **EMBODIMENT** (17 goddesses, understood to be expressions of Saṃhārabhakṣiṇī, embodying the 10 capacities, the subtle elements, and the mind's faculties of discernment and identity-construction). This is the phase of subjective awareness of self as perceiver.
5. Worship of the circle of the **MULTITUDE**, also called the **CELESTIAL ORDER** (the 64 Yoginīs with their leader, the supreme Goddess Mangalā). In this stage the Yoginīs dissolve the subtle

traces of the preceding process, and self-awareness reverts fully to its enlightened core. This phase subdivides into six as follows, with worship of

a) the 16 Yoginīs who dissolve the subtle traces (saṃskāras) remaining from phase 4,
b) the 24 Yoginīs who dissolve the saṃskāras of phase 3,
c) the 12 Yoginīs who penetrate the field of consciousness with pure nondiscursive awareness,
d) the 8 Yoginīs who purify the traces of the eightfold subtle body,
e) the 4 Yoginīs who purify the impression of the sensation of contact of the three aspects of mind with the object of cognition, and
f) Mangalā as the nonrelational ground of the 64 Yoginīs

Pristine consciousness follows.

The foregoing is the iteration of the process on the introversive level. Then the worshipper explores a similar pattern extroversively; or, to put it another way, the five Flow Goddesses express a similarly patterned pulsation of energy on the extroversive level. This phase involves worship of

6. the **GURU-LINEAGE** as embodiments of the realization of the foregoing process[185]
7. the circle of **CREATION** (of a cognition)
8. the circle of **STASIS**
9. the circle of **WITHḌRAWAL**
10. the circle of the **NAMELESS**—in this final phase, perfect interpenetration and balance of the inner and outer states is fully realized

The circle of the Nameless constitutes the final iteration of the process of cognition plus its ineffable ground. This is worshipped as twelve forms of the goddess Kālī, plus a thirteenth, who embodies the unity of the other twelve. The twelve Kālīs are discussed at the end of part 1 of the book.

The complexity of the foregoing compressed outline might seem intimidating. Remember that none of this was necessary for those who could have a direct, non-discursive, intuitive insight into the nature of reality triggered by a transmission of power from the guru or sparked by one of the revealed teachings that, though seemingly partial, mystically point to the whole pattern. For others, though, this process of worship was considered necessary to imprint the brain with the pattern of the deep structures of both consciousness and manifest reality (for they are of course the same in this nondualist system). We might compare the complexity of this course of worship to the level of detail given on the workings of the physical body that is taught in a modern 500-hour yoga teacher training; it is not, then, as unmasterable as it might at first seem.

APPENDIX THREE:

TEXTS (WITH COMMENTARIES AND AUTHORS) SORTED BY SAMPRADĀYA

This list is collated from the articles of Alexis Sanderson. Though it is not complete, it gives a sense of the substantial scope of textual production in Śaiva Tantra. Key texts of each school appear in bold.

Śaiva Siddhānta

Demonstrably early tantras (in approximate chronological order):

Niśvāsatattva-saṃhitā (divides into 5 parts; chronologically, Mūlasūtra comes first [around 450 CE], then Uttarasūtra and Nayasūtra, then Guhyasūtra and Niśvāsa-mukha)

Kālottara (many recensions, starting in the early 7th cen., incl. 350v recension, Sārdhatriśati-kālottara, with the *vṛtti* of Bhaṭṭa Rāmakaṇṭha [which includes the Nādakārikā])

Rauravasūtra-saṅgraha (early 7th cen., with *vṛtti* by Sadyojyotis, c. 700 CE),

Pārameśvara (= Pauṣkara-pārameśvara, early 7th cen. [earliest MS 810 CE]),

Kiraṇa (8th cen., with vṛtti by Bhaṭṭa Rāmakaṇṭha)*

Svāyambhuvasūtra-saṃgraha (7th cen., with *-uddyota* by Bhaṭṭa Rāmakaṇṭha, and *vṛtti* by Sadyojyotis translated by Filliozat)

Sarvajñānottara (7th cen.)

Niśvāsakārikā, incl. the Dīkṣottara (8th cen.)

Mataṅgapārameśvara (mid-8th cen., with *vṛtti* by Bhaṭṭa Rāmakaṇṭha)

Parākhya (9th cen.)*
Mṛgendra (9th cen.), with vṛtti by Nārāyaṇakaṇṭha
Bṛhatkālottara (a.k.a. Śaṭsahasra-)

* Edited and translated by Dominic Goodall

<u>Exegetical texts</u> (9th cen. onward, excepting those of Sadyojyotis [c. 675–725 CE]; these are in Sanskrit alphabetical order):
Kriyākramadyotikā of Aghoraśiva (1158 CE)
Jñānaratnāvalī of Jñānaśiva
Tattvatrayanirṇaya of Sadyojyotis with commentaries by Bhaṭṭa Rāmakaṇṭha and Aghoraśiva
Tattvaprakāśa of Bhoja (12th cen. or earlier)
Tattvasaṅgraha of Sadyojyotis
Nareśvaraparīkṣā of Sadyojyotis with the -**prakāśa** of Bhaṭṭa Rāmakaṇṭha
Paramokṣanirāsa-kārikā-vṛtti of Rāmakaṇṭha (see the Rauravavṛtti below)
Prāyaścittasamuccaya of Hṛdayaśiva (12th cen. or earlier)
Bālabodhinī of Jagaddhara with *-nyāsa* by Rājānaka Śitikaṇṭha (1471 CE)
Bhāvacūḍāmaṇi of Vidyākaṇṭha (II)
Bhogakārikā of Sadyojyotis
*Mantravārttika-ṭīkā of Rāmakaṇṭha
Mahotsavavidhi of Aghoraśiva (1157 CE)
Mokṣakārikā (see the Rauravavṛtti below)
Ratnatrayaparīkṣā of Śrīkaṇṭha with *-ullekhinī* by Aghoraśiva
Rauravavṛtti-viveka of Bhaṭṭa Rāmakaṇṭha (commentary on the vṛtti by Sadyojyotis, surviving incomplete in the form of several sub-headed works, i.e., the the Mokṣakārikā, the Bhogakārikā, and the Paramokṣa-nirāsa-kārikā with upanyāsa of Rāmakaṇṭha)

Vyomavyāpistava of Rāmakaṇṭha (authorship uncertain)
Śivapūjāstava of Jñānaśambhu
Śaivabhūṣaṇa of Pañcākṣarayogin (17th cen.)
*Sarvāgamaprāmāṇyopanyāsa of Rāmakaṇṭha

* Now lost.

Paddhatis (ritual manuals), consisting in the main of Saiddhāntika ritual prescriptions (most based on the Kālottara)

Agnikārya-paddhati
Aghoraśivācārya-paddhati / Kriyākramadyotikā (1158 CE)
Ātmārthapūjā-paddhati
Īśānaśivagurudeva-paddhati (after 14th cen.)
Karmakāṇḍakramāvalī of Somaśambhu (a.k.a. Kriyākāṇḍa-padakramāvalī a.k.a. Śaivakarmakramāvalī a.k.a. Somaśambhupaddhati, 1096 CE, commissioned by Kalacuri monarch Yaśaḥkarṇa), with *vyākhyā* by Trilocanaśivācārya
Kalādīkṣāpaddhati of Manodaguru/Manodadatta (c. 1336), expanded by Śivasvāmin. A Mantrapīṭha guide to the ceremonies of Śaiva initiation (dīkṣā) and consecration (abhiṣeka) as practiced in Kashmīr until recent times. Draws on the Svacchanda and Netra as well as Saiddhāntika texts. A late (17th cen.?) insertion includes several hymns: the Bhairava-stotra of Abhinavagupta, the Bhairava-daśaka, the Aparādha-sundara-stava ascribed to (a) Śaṅkarācārya, the Bhairavastotra of Śaṅkara-kaṇṭha, and the Śambhu-kṛpā-manohara-stava of Ratna-kaṇṭha.
Jñānaratnāvalī (12th cen.)
Nityādisaṃgrahapaddhati of Takṣakavarta (after 11th cen.)
Naimittikakarmānusaṃdhāna of Brahmaśambhu. The codex unicus of part of the earliest surviving Saiddhāntika Paddhati (939 CE).

Prāsādapaddhati of Prāsādaśiva
Mṛgendrapaddati of Aghoraśiva (12th cen.), with *-ṭīkā* by Vaktraśambhu
Śāradātilaka (12th cen.; mainly *dhyāna-ślokas* with a chapter on yoga)
Śivanirvāṇapaddhati (on Śaiva cremation)
Siddhāntaśekhara (prob. 13th cen.)
Siddhāntasāra-paddhati of Bhoja (1050 CE)
Siddhāntasārāvalī (prob. 13th cen.) with comm. of Anantaśambhu

Amṛteśvara / Mṛtyuñjaya

Netratantra (c. 800 CE [between 700 and 850]; a.k.a. *Sarva-srotaḥ-saṅgraha-sāra*), with *-uddyota* by Kṣemarāja (in Kaula Trika school)
Amṛteśvaradīkṣāvidhi of Viśveśvara. A guide in verse to the performance of initiation into the cult of Amṛteśvara.
Amṛteśvaradhyāna-vivaraṇa of Lakṣmīrāma a.k.a. Lasakāka (c. 1800)
Amṛteśvarapūjā-paddhati

Vāma

Vīṇāśikhā (7th cen.; only complete text to survive)

Mantrapīṭha

Svacchandabhairavatantra (with uddyota by Kṣemarāja, of the Kaula Trika school); earliest MS 1068 CE
Bhairavānukaraṇastotra of Kṣemarāja [hymn giving nondualistic reading of the symbols and attributes of Svacchandabhairava]
Bahurūpagarbhastotra, with commentary *–viṣamapadasaṅketa* of Anantaśakti [hymn to Svacchandabhairava (and Aghoreśvarī); its recitation is a standard preliminary to Śaiva ritual in Kashmīr]
Niṣkala-svacchanda-dhyāna-vivaraṇa of Lakṣmīrāma a.k.a. Lasakāka (c. 1800)
Svacchanda-maheśvarāṣṭaka (late hymn – 17th cen.?)

Yāmala

Brahmayāmala (early 8th cen.)
Matasāra
*Rudrayāmala, *Viṣṇuyāmala, *Skandayāmala, *Umāyāmala
* Lost.

Trika

Kularatnamālā
Tantrasadbhāva
*Trikasadbhāva
*Trikasāra/Trikahṛdaya
*Triśirobhairava/Anāmaka
*Devyāyāmala
Parātrīśikā with the *-vivṛti of Somānanda, the -vivaraṇa by Abhinavagupta, -laghuvṛtti (a.k.a. Anuttaravimarśinī and Trīśikāśāstravimarśinī) attributed to Abhinava (before 12th cen.; with vyākhyā by Kṛṣṇadāsa), and –vivṛti by Lakṣmīrāma (a.k.a. Lasa Kāka), 1811
Bhairavakula
Mālinīvijayottara [7th cen.]
Vijñānabhairava with the –vivṛti of Kṣemarāja (vv. 1–23 only) and Śivopādhyāya (mid-18th cen.) and the *–kaumudī* of Bhaṭṭāraka Ānanda (a Traipura; text dated 1672)
*Vīrāvalī
Siddhayogeśvarīmata (= Triśūla) [early 7th cen.]

Trika/Pratyabhijñā Guru lineage

[Govindarāja? ->] Somānanda (c. 900–950; he knew Pradyumnabhaṭṭa below) -> Utpaladeva (c. 925–75) -> Rājānaka Rāma & Lakṣmaṇagupta (c. 950–1000) -> Abhinavagupta (c. 975–1025) -> Kṣemarāja (c. 1000–1050) -> Yogarāja (c. 1025–75)

Spanda (Trika/Krama) Guru lineage

Vasugupta (c. 825–875) -> Kallaṭa (c. 850–900; Kalhaṇa puts him in the reign of Avantivarman) -> Pradyumnabhaṭṭa (c. 875–925) -> Prajñārjuna -> Mahādevabhaṭṭa -> Śrīkaṇṭhabhaṭṭa -> Bhāskara (c. 975–1025)

Exegetical works on the Trika (see below for the Pratyabhijñā)

Tantrāloka by Abhinavagupta [early 11th cen.], with viveka by Jayaratha [mid-13th cen.]

Paramārthacarcā of Abhinavagupta

Paramārthasāra of Abhinavagupta (loosely based on the exoteric text of the same name by Śeṣamuni) with comm. by Yogarāja

Bodhapañcadaśikā of Abhinavagupta

Mālinīślokavārtika of Abhinavagupta

Śivasūtra of Vasugupta with -vārtika by Bhāskara (c. 925–75), vimarśinī by Kṣemarāja (the latter summarized twice: by Varadarāja/Kṛṣṇadāsa in his Śivasūtravārtika and also the anonymous Śivasūtravṛtti).

Śivāṣṭaka of Yogarāja (11th cen.)

Spandakārikā by Vasugupta or Kallaṭa (9th cen.), with these seven commentaries: the *-vṛtti* by Kallaṭa, *-sandoha* by Kṣemarāja (on the first verse only but summarizing the whole text), *-nirṇaya* by Kṣemarāja, *-nirṇaya* by Vāmana/Vīravāmanaka, *-pradīpikā* of Bhāgavatotpala (a Vaiṣṇava, c. 950–1000), *-vivṛti* by Rājānaka Rāma, and *-pradīpikā* of Bhaṭṭāraka-svāmin (a Traipura; 17th cen.?)

Pratyabhijñā

Ajaḍapramātṛ-siddhi of Utpaladeva

Īśvara-pratyābhijñā-kārikās of Utpaladeva with two auto-commentaries, the *-vṛtti* and *-*vivṛti* (a.k.a. *-ṭīkā*); also the *-vimarśinī* by Abhinavagupta (with sub-commentary *-vyākhyā* by Bhāskara-kaṇṭha, c. 1700) and *-vivṛti-vimarśinī* by Abhinavagupta (1015 CE, on Utpala's *-vivṛti)

Īśvarasiddhi of Utpaladeva with auto-*vṛtti*
Pratyabhijñā-hṛdayam of Kṣemarāja
Śivadṛṣṭi of Somānanda with the *-vṛtti* (a.k.a. Padasaṅgati) of Utpaladeva
Sambandhasiddhi of Utpaladeva

Kālīkula, esp. Krama

Scriptural texts:
Ūrmikaulārṇava (a.k.a. Bhogahasta), teaches a Kaula form of the Kālīkula related to the Krama, revealed by Lord Macchanda in Kāmarūpa]
Kālīkākramapañcāśikā (allegedly revealed to Vidyānanda by a disembodied voice belonging to Niṣkriyānanda when the former was propitiating the Goddess in a cave in the mountains of the *pīṭha* Śrīśailam in Andhra)
Kālīkulapañcaśataka (a.k.a. Devīpañcaśataka; revealed by Jñānanetra)
Kālīkulakramasadbhāva (revealed by Jñānanetra; partially lost)
Kālīmukha
Kaulasūtra of Bhaṭṭaśrī Śitikaṇṭha (transmits oral teachings of the Krama)
Chumāsaṅketaprakāśa of Niṣkriyānandanātha (transmits oral aphorisms of the Yoginīs in Old Kashmīrī with Sanskrit commentary)
Jayadrathayāmala (a.k.a. Tantrarājabhaṭṭāraka) in 24,000 verses (Book 1 = Śiraccheda, originally a separate work); the bulk of the work composed prior to 800 CE (the approximate date of its partial redaction into the Buddhist Laghusaṃvaratantra). The principal deities of its four ṣaṭkas: 1. Kālī Kālasaṃkarṣaṇī, 2. Siddhalakṣmī, 3. Sāraśakti, 4. Siddhayogeśvarī & the Śāktam Cakram)

Devīdvyardhaśatikā (paraphrased as the Siddhakhaṇḍa of the Manthānabhairava)
Mahākaravīrayāga
Mādhavakula
Yonigahvara (shares much material with the Devīdvyardhaśatikā and some with the Kālīkulakramasadbhāva)
Vātulanāthasūtra attributed to "the Yoginīs" with the *-vṛtti* of "Someone," a.k.a. Anantaśakti (oral transmission; 13 sūtras of unknown provenance with commentary)

Exegetical texts and philosophical poems (Krama)
Aṣṭikā of Prabodhanātha
Kālīkulakramārcana of Vimalaprabodha (Nepāla, c. 1200)
Kramavilāsastotra
*Kramastotra of Eraka (a.k.a. Saṃvitstotra; given the authority of a scripture) with the *-*vivaraṇa* of Hrasvanātha and a *-vivṛti* titled *Kramakeli by Abhinavagupta
Kramastotra of Abhinavagupta (991 CE)
Caryāmelāpaka-pradīpa
Ciñciṇīmatasārasamuccaya (including two short texts, the Kālīkākramaślokadvādaśikā and the Kālīkramapañcāśikā)
Cittasantoṣa-triṃśikā of Nāga
Cidgaganacandrikā of Śrīvatsa (12th–13th cen.)
Jayadrathayāmala-prastāra-mantra-saṃgraha / Jayadrathayāmala-mantroddhāra-ṭippaṇī, decodes mantras and diagrams of the Jayadratha-yāmala
Tantrarāja-tantrāvatāra-stotra of Viśvāvarta, on the transmission and deities of the Jayadratha-yāmala
Triṃśaccarcā-rahasya / Chummāsampradāya of Niṣkriyānanda
Dvayasaṃpatti-vārtika a.k.a. Bodhavilāsa of Vāmanadatta (= Hrasvanātha?)

Paramārcana-triṃśikā of Nāga

Bhuvana-mālinī-kalpa-viṣamapada-vivṛti of Śrīvatsa, a commentary on a chapter of the JY that gives the worship of Bhuvanamālinī (11th cen. or later)

Mahānaya-prakāśa of Arṇasiṃha

Mahānaya-prakāśa in Old Kashmīrī with Sanskrit commentary of Śitikaṇṭha (before the 13th cen.)

Mahānaya-prakāśa (Anonymous)

Mahārthamañjarī in Prākṛt, attributed to a Yoginī, with extensive Sanskrit commentary (-parimala) by Maheśvarānanda (c. 1300, Cidambaram)

Śrīpīṭhadvādaśika of Cakrabhānu

Subhagodayavāsanā of Śivānanda (13th cen.)

Svabodhodaya-mañjarī of Vāmanadatta [inspired by the Vijñānabhairava and Krama sources; though 'exegetical' it is considered as the work of a Siddha and therefore scripture]

<u>Some texts significantly influenced by the Krama:</u>

Advayadvādaśikā/Paramārthadvādaśikā of Ramyadeva

Jñānakriyādvayaśataka (probably by Sillana)

Tantrāloka and *-viveka*

Pratyabhijñā-hṛdayam of Kṣemarāja

Bhāvopahāra-stotra of Cakrapāṇinātha with the *–vivaraṇa* of Ramyadeva

Śivarātrirahasya of Śiva[rāma]svāmin Upādhyāya II (early 19th cen.)

Śivasūtravimarśinī

Spandanirṇaya

<u>Kaubjika</u>

Kubjikāmata

Manthānabhairava (trans. by Dyczkowski)

Kulālikāmnāya
Nityāhnika-tilaka (exegetical)

Śrīvidyā

Guru-lineage

First propagated in Kāshmīr in the 11th cen. by Īśvaraśivācārya and Śaṅkararāśi. Most important South Indian lineage is as follows: Dīpakācarya aka Dīpakanātha (mid 11th cen.) [Siddha and lineage-founder] -> Jiṣṇudeva (late 11th cen.) -> Mātṛgupta (c. 1075–1125) -> Tejodeva (early 12th cen.) -> Manojadeva (mid-12th cen.) -> Kalyāṇadeva (late 12th cen.) -> Ratnadeva (c. 1175–1225) -> Vāsudevamahāmuni (early 13th cen.) -> Śivānanda (mid-13th cen.) -> Mahāprakāśa (late 13th cen.) -> Maheśvarānanda (c. 1275–1325) [also a Krama initiate]

Early Texts

Nityākaula, teaching an early form of the Tripurā cult with eleven Nityās plus Kāmadeva
Nityāṣoḍaśikārṇava/Vāmakeśvarīmata, with -*vivaraṇa* by Jayaratha and –*artha-ratnāvalī* by Vidyānanda, and -*ṛjuvimarśinī*) by Śivānanda (13th cen.), and -*setubandha* by Bhāskararāya
Yoginīhṛdaya (12th cen.?) with –*dīpikā* by Amṛtānandayogin (14th cen.)

Later texts

Kāmakalāvilāsa of Puṇyānandayogin (early 14th cen.)
Cidvilāsastava of Amṛtānandayogin (14th cen.)
Jñānadīpa-vimarśinī a.k.a. Tripurasundarīvyākhyā of Vidyānanda-nātha
Tripurasundarī-daṇḍaka-stotra of Dīpakācārya (13th cen.)
Śrīvidyā-nityapūjā-paddhati of Sāhib Kaul (17th cen.)
Saṅketapaddhati of Jiṣṇudeva
Saubhāgyasudhodaya of Amṛtānandayogin (14th cen.)

Some of Abhinavagupta's Gurus

Guru	Lineage	Sect
Vāmanātha	Āmardaka	Saiddhāntika
Bhūtirāja	Siddha	Krama
Lakṣmaṇagupta	Traiyambaka	Trika
Śambhunātha	Half-Traiyambaka	Kaula Trika
Maheśvara	Śrīsantāna	Unknown

The Four Original Śakti Pīṭhas (sacred power-centers)

1. Uḍḍiyāna (aka Wuzhangna [Ch.], Ujōna [Jap.], O rgyan [Tib.], and scripturally known as Uttarapīṭha, Praṇavapīṭha, Oṃkārapīṭha, Udgītthapīṭha): a small kingdom located north of Peshawar in modern Pakistān, with a capital on the river Swāt (150 mi. as the crow flies from Śrīnagar) called Mangora [from Maṅgalāpura]. East of the town was the Karavīra cremation ground, the birthplace of the Krama. Deity: Maṅgalā. Site-guardian: Balotkaṭa. Esoterically associated with the ear, oral transmission, and the vibration of Oṃ. Associated with the *brahmarandhra* in the Yoginīhṛdaya.

2. Jālandhara; cremation ground: Laṅkuṭa; deity: Jvālā. Esoterically associated with the mouth and speech. Associated with the eyebrow-center in the Yoginīhṛdaya.

3. Kāmarūpa (the Western half of modern Assam). Birthplace of Macchanda Esoterically associated with the eye and seeing. Associated with the *mūlādhāra* in the Yoginīhṛdaya.

4. Pūrṇagiri / Pūrṇapīṭha (prob. in Mahārāṣṭra, in the Sahya mountains, in the northern part of the Ghats). Associated with the heart in the Yoginīhṛdaya.

ENDNOTES

This book is not footnoted or referenced with the same kind of thoroughness as an academic work. If any scholar or student of the tradition wishes to contact me for precise textual references, I will attempt to answer all such requests. More adequately referenced writing is available on my website, christopherwallis.org. Of course, any beginning student of Śaiva Tantra must become acquainted with Sanderson's work, beginning with the easier introductory pieces: "Shaivism and the Tantric Traditions," "Power and Purity among the Brahmins of Kashmir," and "EPHE Lectures: Long Summary," all available on alexissanderson.com.

1. See especially his Nothing Exists That is Not Śiva and Secret of the Siddhas.
2. I will substantiate this claim with reference to the three books that might appear to challenge it. Georg Feuerstein's Tantra: The Path of Ecstasy presents us with an overview not of the unique philosophical system of classical Tantra, but rather of those elements of Tantrathat were incorporated into Hinduism. Thus his book may be seen as a good introduction to the post-classical Hindu Tantra of the 13th century onward. As you will discover, the classical Tantrik philosophy presented here is related, but considerably different. The second book I am thinking of is Kamalakar Mishra's Kashmir Shaivism: The Central Philosophy of Tantrism. This covers much classical Tantrik philosophy but does not cover the history and social context of the religion which gave rise to it. So Mishra perpetuates the now almost century-old misunderstanding that this tradition was a phenomenon of the region of Kashmīr, whereas as we shall see, it was a pan-Indian (and eventually pan-Asian) spiritual movement. Thirdly, we have Swāmī Shankarānanda's book Consciousness is Everything: The Yoga of Kashmir Shaivism. This is a fine book for contemplative practitioners, however, as the author himself admits, not being able to read Sanskrit has limited him to the handful of Tantrik texts translated into English, none of which are translated all that well.
3. Philip Goldberg's American Veda (2010) identifies the following as the foremost doctrine of the Vedānta philosophy acquired by the U.S.: "Ultimate reality is both transcendent and immanent, both one and many..." This is a key teaching of the Tantra, but not at all a doctrine of Vedānta, except the highly syncretic version of Vedānta taught in the last two centuries—a version very much influenced by Tantra. Another teaching Goldberg gives in the same list that is not at all Vedāntic but very Tantrik: "Individuals can awaken to their divine nature through any number of pathways and practices; no single one is right for everyone."

This misunderstanding whereby Tantrik teachings are credited to other schools is widespread.

4. In other words, Buddhist Tantra is essentially Mahāyāna Buddhism remodeled along Tantrik Śaiva lines. This is bound to be a controversial claim in some quarters: many Buddhist scholars and practicing Buddhists will immediately deny it, since new scholarly findings that go against what has been generally accepted are always denied at first, however sound the evidence. But that evidence has been amassed in incredible quantity and detail by Professor Alexis Sanderson, primarily in his 300-page masterpiece, "The Śaiva Age," published in *Genesis and Development of Early Tantrism* and available from his website. For an important and much briefer presentation of evidence, download Sanderson's Gonda Lecture, as well as the handout "How Buddhist is the *Herukābhidhāna-tantra*?" For those readers who ask why the historical priority (and predominance) of Śaiva Tantra over all other forms of Tantra was not previously common knowledge, the answer is that in previous generations of scholars there were many scholars of Buddhism and virtually none of Śaivism.

5. In other words, though this is a simplification, where Buddhist Tantra articulates a philosophy distinct from the Mahāyāna, that philosophy corresponds closely to nondual Śaivism, especially that of the mature Krama school (which is, as we shall see, far distant from the Veda-congruent Śaiva orthodoxy). This near identity of the Śaiva philosophy of the far left (this term is explained later) with the Dzogchen and Mahāmudrā lineages of Buddhism will become more clear when scholars have correctly transposed the relevent technical terms from Tibetan to Sanskrit and vice versa. (A start in this direction has been made by scholar David Germano.) As I point out, unlike in the case of the Tantrik practices, scholars are not yet proposing a direction of transmission for this philosophy, which for the present we may regard as coming out of the shared milieu of nondualist thought in the Himālayan region.

6. This can also be seen in the fact that Dzogchen is not only a Buddhist phenomenon but equally belongs to the Bön religion of Tibet.

7. Cabezón, José. "The Discipline and Its Other: the Dialectic of Alterity in the Study of Religion," *Journal of the American Academy of Religion,* 74:1, 2006.

8. As we will see, the widespread notion in both the modern West and India that modern yoga came from (or is even connected to) the pre-Tantrik tradition of Patañjali's *Yoga-sūtra* is false. That text give nearly no specifics of practice (except for concentrative meditation), as opposed to the vast literature on yogic practices in the Tantrik tradition. Apart from the 20th-century revival of Patañjali, it is safe to say that whatever of his thought we find in the *haṭha-yoga* tradition was transmitted there through the Tantrik tradition. More will be said on this.

9. Unfortunately, this cannot be taken to imply that all effective practices survive. Due to historical discontinuities (such as the Muslim conquest) many powerful teachings are lost. This contraction of tradition is particularly tragic in the Indian case, because due to cultural attitudes around the transmission of knowledge, it will not generally be admitted that something has been lost. This explains why virtually no effort is being made by modern India to recover one of the most extensive, beautiful, and effective spiritual traditions of its long history, that of Śaiva Tantra.

10. Though it is true that black holes cannot be seen in the visible spectrum, their existence can be proved by the orbits of nearby stars in a binary system or by their radiation of x-rays.

11. To give one brief example, however, we may cite the fact that Alexis Sanderson, based on the model of Shaivism he had evolved, predicted that goddess worship must have been a part of the pre-Tantrik Śaiva tradition, though there was no known evidence of it. Such evidence did indeed come to light, in the form of

newly discovered inscriptions and manuscripts.

12. *Tanoti vipulān arthān tattva-mantra-samanvitān | trāṇaṃ ca kurute yasmāt tantram ity abhidhīyate ||*
13. That is, my teacher Somadeva Vasudeva (Columbia University), who brought this passage to my attention.
14. *Sārdhatriśati-kālottara-vṛtti,* p. 5. This is necessarily a paraphrase, as the formal and culturally-specific style of the Sanskrit bars a literal translation here. Note that this definition can be equally well applied to Buddhist Tantra, if we replace the word "God" with "the Bodhisattva(s)." The original Sanskrit reads: *tantraṃ ca—parāpara-puruṣārthādhikāriṇāṃ viśiṣṭa-saṃskāra-pratipādana-pūrva[ka]m īśvarārādhanāya niyata-vidhi-niṣedhaṃ tadājñātmakaṃ vākya-jātam.*
15. With the exception of the *Vijñāna-Bhairava Tantra,* which is the only original Tantrik scripture from the Śaiva tradition in general circulation in English, and even then not in quite correct translations. Though the *Vijñāna-Bhairava* is a remarkable text, it should be noted that its contents are atypical of Tantrik scriptures. There are other scriptures available in partial English translation, though they are extremely scholarly and quite difficult to get hold of. Examples are the *Mālinī-vijayottara Tantra* (trans. S. Vasudeva) the *Kiraṇa Tantra* and the *Parākhya Tantra* (trans. D. Goodall), all published by the Ecole Française d'Extreme Orient / Institut Français de Pondichéry in India.
16. This naturally suggests to us the possibility that there could be a Tantrik version of other religions, for example a Tantrik inflection of Christianity, in which the mantras and visualizations would pertain to Christian forms of Deity. A start has been made in this direction by former Jesuit John Dupuche, who recently published *Towards a Christian Tantra.* This is possible because Tantrik practice can be conceived of as a "way of doing religion": a structure that can contain any content. As we shall see, the content is the energy of Deity in whichever flavor is evoked by the sect in question.
17. Of this list, the first four are the indigenous Indian religions. They are each named after either their founder or their central deity (i.e., the primary name they use for God). Thus the names of the religions are derived from Śiva, the Buddha, Viṣṇu, and the Jina (a.k.a. Mahāvīra). The second and fourth have both atheistic and polytheistic forms. The first and third have both polytheistic and monotheistic forms. These two, Shaivism and Vaishnavism, are today part of what is called "Hinduism." This misnomer will be explained below. There was also another thoroughly Tantrik religion, that of Shāktism (named after the Goddess or Śakti), which I am here treating as part of Shaivism, even though it later developed forms that are separate. For evidence that Tantra infiltrated even Islām in India, see Shaman Hatley's article "Mapping the Esoteric Body in the Islamic Yoga of Bengal."
18. This fact remains not commonly known even amongst scholars, though as mentioned in an earlier endnote, more than enough evidence to substantiate it has been presented by Prof. Alexis Sanderson in a number of articles.
19. Williams, Paul and Anthony Tribe, *Buddhist Thought,* pp. 197–202.
20. This discussion is necessarily a simplification. In fact, not only Europeans but also early Muslim and Chinese sources used the term Hindu. The term was widespread because it was originally a geographical one, referring to all the people living in the area of the river Sindhu and east of there. While the term 'Hindoo' is first documented in the early 1600s, 'Hindooism' only followed in the late 1700s, though the derogatory reductionism of all indigenous Indian traditions to a single category (e.g., "idolatry") began with the usage of the earlier term. See Will Sweetman's important discussion at www.soas. ac.uk/southasianstudies/keywords/file24805.pdf
21. The Indian tradition did not prefer the suffix –ism (or the Sanskrit equivalent *-tva*) for its religious tradi-

tions. Their indigenous names are: Vaidika-dharma, Śaiva-dharma, Śākta-, Vaiṣṇava-, Bauddha-, and Jaina-dharma, where the word "dharma" (= religion, code of conduct, and way of life) could also be replaced in the compound by the word "śāsana" (= teaching), as in Bauddha-śāsana, the teachings of the Buddhist way. Note also that there were three nonindigenous religions in India from an early period, represented in small numbers: Christians, Jews, and Parsīs or Zoroastrians.

22. It is not a coincidence that the first documented Indian to use the term Hinduism was Western-educated and Westernized, and furthermore (with the best of intentions) he created a new "sanitized" version of Indian religion that won the approval of his European rulers. His name was Rammohun Roy (1772–1833), and his new sect was the Brahmo Samāj.

23. I speak here of classical Shaivism, i.e., before 1300. After that time, Shaivism increasingly adapted itself to Brāhmanism, giving rise to Vedic-Tantrik syncretism.

24. This process, which also has included a massive reduction of the complexity of Indian religious culture, especially in its intellectual dimension, is largely the result of the loss of state patronage for indigenous Indian religions. That is to say, the complex and detailed teachings and practices of the Indian religions were sustained by monasteries, educational institutions, and thousands of dedicated full-time teachers that were only possible with large amounts of funding. When the Muslims conquered north India (beginning around the 13th century and complete by the 16th), this funding evaporated, causing the total disappearance of Buddhism from India as well as the simplification and merger of the remaining traditions. It was really the arrival of the Muslim "others" that created the specifically Hindu identity—the earliest uses of the term "Hindu" as a self-designation (among the Vaiṣṇavas of eastern India, 16th cen.) are specifically in contrast to "Muslim". This modern Hindu identity centers on the devotionalism, temple culture, and the simplified reproductions temple rites in Hindu homes.

25. Though I would be remiss if I failed to note that historically, if one wished to receive Tantrik initiation after having made vows of commitment in any other religious tradition, one first had to undergo a ritual to remove that earlier religious identity. This ceremony (called the *liṅgoddhāra*) was *not* deemed necessary in the case of the one who grew up in a particular religious context but never committed to its practice (like someone from a Catholic family who never received confirmation).

26. We find the first point made in one of the earliest Śaiva scriptures, the *Niśvāsa-kārikā* (12.161–67) and the second made by early commentators Vāladhārin and Jayaratha. See Sanderson, "The Śaiva Age," note 691.

27. Note that many Śaiva Tantrik lineages, especially of the dualistic schools, would *not* have been willing to initiate non-Indians (i.e., people without caste). However, the lineages we are most concerned with here were willing to initiate anyone with a sincere and sustained interest.

28. For this see the recent work of Mark Singleton, the first scholar to successfully identify the forces at work in the formation of modern yoga, revealing it to be definitively a product of globalization. The indigenous Indian element in its formation was *haṭha-yoga*; the primary synthesizers of the modern discipline were three men working in the 1920s and '30s, Kuvalayānanda and Śrī Yogendra of the greater Bombay area, and Kṛṣṇamāchārya of Mysore.

29. Some philosophers argue that no experience is immediate (= unmediated), that all religious experiences are mediated to us (= shaped and determined) by language and culture. To put it simply, Śaiva Tantra's viewpoint is that while language shapes our experience of reality, it cannot create an artificial experience. The fact that tools such as language are used to bring about an experience does not thereby invalidate it.

The important question is which aspect of reality do you wish to experience? How do you want to experience it? You can use divine language to bring about an authentic divine experience. This viewpoint is further rooted in the Tantrik notion that the structures of language express (on a superficial level) the structures of reality itself. Therefore, you are not so much using religious language to *construct* an experience of reality but rather to *access* an aspect of reality previously unavailable to you. Finally, Shaivism argues, you are firmly anchored in the knowledge that your experience expresses a *transpersonal* reality (rather than, say, solipsistic delusion) by the fact that it corresponds to divinely revealed scripture.

30. This definition is partially inspired by the definition of Tantra as a general category offered by David White in his introduction to the book *Tantra in Practice:* "Tantra is that body of beliefs and practices which, working from the principle that the material universe is nothing other than the concrete manifestation of the divine energy of the godhead that creates and maintains that universe, seeks to appropriate and channel that energy, within the human microcosm, in creative and emancipatory ways." This definition in fact only holds for nondual Śaiva Tantra, not Tantra in general, but in that context serves well, though it is perhaps too broad. It emphasizes Tantra as a ritual technology that allows us to access *śakti* (divine power) and use it to attain the twin goals of Tantra mentioned earlier in the main text.
31. I am paraphrasing a remarkable passage from Spencer Brown's *Laws of Form,* already noticed by Ken Wilber in the latter's early work.
32. *ātmā prakāśa-vapur eṣa śivaḥ svatantraḥ | svātantrya-narma-rabhasena nijaṃ svarūpam | saṃchādya yat punar api prathayeta pūrṇam.*
33. *ajñānaṃ kila bandha-hetur uditaḥ śāstre malaṃ tat smṛtaṃ | pūrṇa-jñāna-kalodaye tad akhilaṃ nirmūlatāṃ gacchati | dhvastāśeṣa-malātma-saṃvid-udaye mokṣaś ca tenāmunā.*
34. Consciousness does not really count as a "layer," for reasons we will come to, which explains why some sources call this the four-layered self. Note that this schema is similar yet different to the the "sheaths" [*kośa*] of Vedānta philosophy.
35. *mukhyatvaṃ kartṛtāyās tu bodhasya ca cid-ātmanaḥ / śūnyādau tad-guṇe jñānaṃ tat-samāveśa-lakṣaṇam ||* Īśvara-pratyabhijñā-kārikā 3.23
36. To be more precise, all the layers except the Void are ever-changing, but the changeless Void cannot be your ultimate identity because it is wholly transcendent.
37. We may draw a parallel to a concept in quantum physics, in which an electron is said to not so much have a specific location as a "probability waveform": if measured, the electron could turn out to be in any one of a number of locations, and it doesn't bother to have a location until it is measured. Though the probability is low, it is theoretically possible for an electron attached to an atom in your body one moment to be hundreds of miles away in the next. In the same way, though anything could arise out of the infinite field of pure Consciousness within, it is most likely that thought-forms will arise that are repetitions or slight variations on previous thought-forms (which is called conditioning).
38. We see in Dr. Oliver Sacks' famous essay "The Man Who Mistook His Wife for a Hat" (in the book of the same name) the bizarre result of a failure of this process by which the mind synthesizes an object out of various ābhāsas (Dr. Sacks, of course, does not use that language—the reader will have to decide for herself whether I am correct in identifying the neurological deficit he describes in this way).
39. I give the example "justice," but of course there is no such thing as an object of awareness that is purely abstract such as the concept of "justice" in general. All concepts used by real individuals are highly specific, such as, say, the specific concept of justice in the mind of Felix Frankfurter when he wrote his analysis of the

Sacco-Vanzetti case, which was unique to him and that moment in history. That specific concept of justice may be analyzed in terms of the various *ābhāsas* that comprise it; but an abstract concept like "justice in general" may not, for it *does not really exist* except as a linguistic construct.

40. Though this teaching is explicitly given in the original sources, my understanding of it is influenced by the writing of a great meditator Swāmī Anantānanda in his book *What's on My Mind?*, published by the SYDA Foundation.
41. The astute reader will have noticed that I say "commonly used" as if there are other, more esoteric or accurate *bīja* mantras for the five great elements. There are; the commonly known *bījas* are, it turns out, simplifications or possibly even erroneous misreadings of the original Tantrik mantras. This has been confirmed by the pioneering work of Christopher Tompkins in this field, and I will leave it to his forthcoming publication to reveal what the Tantrik mantras for the five great elements are.
42. More accurately, the formula is: Śiva – all powers + *kañcukas* = *jīva*.
43. Sanderson's translation.
44. In some accounts of the *kañcukas*, the order of #10 and 11 is reversed (*niyati* then *kāla*). In other (very early) accounts, they are not found at all, the first three *kañcukas* being the important ones. The fact that our scriptural sources are not all in agreement supports the notion that they are evolved out of the contemplated spiritual experience of real men and women, whose articulation of their insights—descending to the approximate level of the spoken word—will never be in perfect accord.
45. I here follow the *Pratyabhijñā-hṛdayam*, which differs from the earlier *Īśvara-pratyabhijñā-kārikā* in placing the level of equal apposition on *Īśvara-tattva* rather than *Śuddhavidyā-tattva*. In the *-hṛdayam*'s schema, there is a neater progression from the embryonic germ of universe held within Sadāśiva, to equal apposition with Īśvara, to full expression (as a pattern of energy, not yet physical matter) on the level of Śuddhavidyā.
46. Literally, "He exists in every sphere, and in all objects of the senses: wherever one may look, that which is not God is found nowhere." *viṣayeṣu ca sarveṣu indriyārtheṣu ca sthitaḥ | yatra yatra nirūpyeta nāśivaṃ vidyate kvacit || Svacchanda-tantra 4.314 || We could also translate śiva in its common meaning as "auspicious" or "blessed," yielding the meaning "nothing that is not a blessing can be found."*
47. As far as the Trika tradition is concerned, one of the most important examples of this is the reification of the simple phrase "I see a pot." That is to say, since the linguistic construction contains three separate elements (a first-person agent, a verb denoting perceptive process initiated by that agent, and a direct object of that verb) we believe that there *are* three separate things: a person who sees, the act of seeing, and an object seen. However, careful reflection reveals that there is one unified process with three aspects. The perception "pot" is simply a particular vibration within consciousness, inseparable from the observer, who is inseparable from the process by which objects of consciousness are created (in this case, seeing). If there really were three separate and distinct things, they could never be meaningfully related in such a way as to give rise to any valid form of knowledge.
48. The language of this paragraph (and certain other points throughout this section) draws on the excellent article by Italian scholar Rafaelle Torella called "The Word in Abhinavagupta's Bṛhad-vimarśinī."
49. *The Aphorisms of Śiva*, p. 33.
50. When we occasionally enter the waking state while still occupying the subtle body, we find that we are paralyzed for a few moments before we can transit awareness to the physical body. This is known in the West as "sleep paralysis."
51. If we are making comparisons, note that though Abhinava the theologian can be compared to Thomas

Aquinas, Abhinava the philosopher must be compared to Hegel and Kant, not only in significance and influence but even in some of the content of his thinking.

52. From "Maṇḍala and Āgamic Identity," p. 170.
53. The Order of Āmardaka = the Śaiva Siddhānta, described in the next section of the book; the Order of Śrī is an ancient lineage that is the forerunner of the Krama, also detailed later; the Order of Tryambaka = the Trika; and the Order of the Half-Tryambaka (or the Three-and-a-half), founded by Tryambaka's daughter, is the Kaula Trika, that is, the Trika incorporating the nonsectarian spiritual tradition of Kaulism, revealed in the present age by Lord Macchanda.
54. Thanks to Sanderson's article on "The Doctrine of the Mālinīvijayottaratantra" for this phrasing (p. 295)
55. The translation is a modified version of Sanderson's, from his "Commentary on the Opening Verses of the Tantrasāra."
56. Abhinavagupta's commentator Jayaratha adds, "He means that in the Kula or Kaula system, there is a prohibition of wearing matted locks, ashes, and the rest, as taught [in the scripture that says]: 'He should not associate in act, thought or speech with anyone who wears such insignia as matted locks and ashes, the banner, the [human bone] ornaments of the Kāpālika observance, the trident and the terrible skull-staff. For in this [nondual system] is taught a method of realizing one's identity with Śiva easily, without effort, even while one is immersed in [the experience of] the objects of the senses, as taught in [the Svabodhodaya-mañjarī of Hrasvanātha]: "The ancients taught cessation [of contracted awareness] by means of yogic practice and detachment. But I teach now that this cessation may come about effortlessly."'" (Trans. Sanderson, slightly modified) Here we see the tension that the doctrine of Supreme Nonduality seeks to resolve.
57. I first read this passage with Somdev Vasudeva, and my translation (like all those in this section) is indebted to him and Prof. Sanderson.
58. Learn more about the physical properties of waves and the beautiful patterns that they create when they combine ("interfere" in physics language) by going to http://en.wikipedia.org/wiki/Interference_(wave_propagation). "Constructive interference" is the Parā aspect of the supreme Goddess; "destructive interference" is the Kālī aspect. Note that the dark places in the interference patterns are not a lack of energy (*śakti*) but rather *the product of energy waves combining to create space.*
59. My understanding of this teaching is deeply indebted to Sanderson's "Meaning in Tantric Ritual" and Paul Muller-Ortega's unpublished work on the 12 Kālīs.
60. To get a complete picture of this dissemination, one would have to read several hundred pages of very dense academic prose including many citations in Sanskrit. However, I encourage the dedicated reader to obtain copies of "The Śaiva Age" and "History through Textual Criticism" (both showing how Buddhist Tantra derives from Śaiva sources), as well as "The Lākulas" (on the connections between pre-Tantrik and Tantrik Śaivism), and "Śaivism among the Khmers" (on its propagation in Southeast Asia, especially the Śaiva kingdom of Angkor Wat), all available from alexissanderson.com. You can also find there some more readable introductory articles, such as "Śaivism and the Tantrik Traditions" and "Power and Purity among the Brahmans of Kashmīr".
61. Though if they came from the background of another religion, they would have to go through a ritual that stripped them of their (attachment to their) previous religious identity. Note that those whose background was Brāhmanism did not have to undergo this ritual, which shows that Śaivas did not consider Brāhmanism a religion as much as a culture (similar to some forms of Hinduism today).
62. This description is drawn from Sanderson, *Religion and the State: Initiating the Monarch in Śaivism and the Buddhist Way of Mantras,* p. 9.

63. The first complete Buddhist tantra is the *Mahāvairocanābhisaṃbodhi-tantra,* dating from the 7th century. The dates of the Buddhist texts can be ascertained quite precisely by their Chinese translations; the dates of the Śaiva texts cannot. However, the early 6th century date for first Śaiva Tantrik text, the *Niśvāsa* (see below), was arrived at by the most careful scholars and skilled Sanskritists in the field.
64. *Mañjuśriyamūla-kalpa* 47:53–54, translation by Sanderson, p. 130 of "The Śaiva Age."
65. That is, this appearance and these accoutrements are reserved in the law books for anyone convicted of murdering a brāhmin priest. These murderers were forced to wander in this way, announcing their abhorrent presence with the ringing of a bell. Yet these Atimārga ascetics called Kāpālikas, innocent of any crime, *voluntarily* adopted this mode of conduct in their seeking of transcendence. This is especially impressive when you remember that as they themselves were brāhmins, they were voluntarily casting themselves down from the most respected position in society to the least. It strikes me as an unparalleled act of courage.
66. I was fortunate to read this passage with a master scholar specializing in this very early Tantrik literature, Dominic Goodall of the French Institute in Pondicherry, Tamiḷ Nāḍu.
67. If we continue with the Christian parallel, the NŚT groups are similar to what we might imagine the 2nd and 3rd century Gnostic Christians might have been like if they had survived to become more successful. I am thinking of the latter's nondualist teachings, their anti-institutional emphasis of personal mystical experience, their empowerment of women, etc.
68. The complexities of the sectarian relations of the various groups of the left current are beyond the scope of this book. It is not entirely accurate for all periods to use the term Kaula so broadly, but it does allow us to name and distinguish the dominant streams of the tradition, and it is true that "Kaula" can be used as a synonym for Śākta (Goddess-worshipper). By the end of the classical period, the word Kaula had a very broad semantic reach. I tend to say Kaula when focusing on the practice and culture of the left current, and NŚT (nondual Śaiva Tantra) when focusing more on the philosophy, because it transcends sectarian affliation (though its primary authors were all Kaula-influenced if not Kaula initiates).
69. See, e.g., Sanderson's "Purity and Power among the Brahmans of Kashmir," pp. 201–202.
70. Several sentences in this paragraph are paraphrased from Sanderson 1988:680.
71. See www.tantricart.net. This website features the work of the last living lineage of authentic Tantrik artists (as far as I am aware), members of the Newārī clan of the Kāthmandu valley. They are to be congratulated, in my view, for incorporating Western artistic advances (such as perspective and three-dimensionality) without in the least compromising the traditional nature of their subject. One of the extremely talented artists on the website, Dinesh Shreṣṭha, is a teacher of this book's artist, Ekabhūmi Ellik, for whom see endnote 74 below.
72. By "charismatic" gurus, I mean those who possess an impressive degree of personal power and attainment, mere contact with whom can trigger an awakening or bring on the next stage in one's spiritual development. Charismatic gurus are a fascinating and problematic feature of Indian religions (and religion in general), for on the one association with them speeds up one's process considerably, but on the other hand, their personal power can translate to a cult of personality which poses many dangers to the seeker. For more on the role of the guru, see Part 3 of the book.
73. The doctrine of nonduality in a coherent and fully explicit form is found only in the furthest left groups. Though it would seem to us that professing duality or nonduality must be an either/or proposition, there are some (usually early) texts on the spectrum that mix dualist and nondualist elements in a way that is logi-

cally incoherent but not necessarily ritually incoherent (e.g., the *Svacchanda-tantra* of the Dakṣiṇa school, the *Mālinīvijayottara-tantra*, etc.).

74. Charles Ekabhūmi Ellik is an artist of singular talent, who has studied both Western and Indian (especially Himālayan) artistic conventions extensively. He is, in my experience, able to discern something of the energy of each deity and depict them accordingly. It is a matter of good fortune for lovers of Tantrik art that he is available for hire. Love for the tradition is his primary motive, infusing all his work. You can find out more about him at www.ekabhumi.com.

75. Relativism is the idea that everyone's point of view is equally valid, and no one viewpoint can negate any other. It sounds very nice and tolerant: the only problem is it is totally incoherent. The only way every point of view can be equally valid is if *none* of them have any truth-value, so popular relativism is just nihilism in disguise. This is why I say we must have a hierarchy of truth if we wish to avoid relativism; but it can be an inclusivist hierarchy, one that allows lower (provisional) truths their own sphere of validity. Since they are true as far as they go, there is no need to intolerantly force their adherents to give them up, since if those seekers proceed in their inquiry, they will necessarily eventually come to see that there are "higher," i.e., more all-encompassing, truths.

76. *Mataṅga-pārameśvara-tantra*, Yoga section, 1.12; following Sanderson's unpublished translation.

77. This discovery was made by Christopher Tompkins, a colleague of mine and scholar of early Śaiva Tantrik Yoga. Note the major difference between this teaching and that of the later Haṭha-yoga tradition: here *kuṇḍalinī* does not lie dormant at the base of the spine. Rather, she must be summoned from her natural home at the crown of the head in order to rescue the individual soul (*jīva*). Hence she is brought to the heart, or whatever center individuated awareness is occupying; there she begins to feel a longing (as it were) to be reunited with Śiva at the crown. The soul is able (with practice) to cling to her coattails (as it were) when she surges back up the central channel to her Beloved. This, at least, is my understanding of the explanation given to me by Tompkins based on the *Kālottara* and related sources.

78. Translation by Christopher Tompkins, modified slightly by myself.

79. Due partially to its antiquity, the text is extremely corrupted, which means filled with scribal errors, indicating to us that it was transmitted for a unknown number of generations beyond the point that its practice was followed (for, if the scribes copying it understood what they were reading, they would not have made so many errors). Much meaning can still be extracted by the astute linguist, however, and this work has been done by two scholars of my acquaintance. One of them, Shaman Hatley (of Concordia University), has written a remarkable dissertation on the *Brahma-yāmala.* The translation here follows that of Shaman Hatley in his Ph.D. dissertation.

80. The translation here follows that of Shaman Hatley in his Ph.D. dissertation.

81. That of William Arraj from the University of Chicago, 1988.

82. Translation Sanderson, "The Śaiva Age," pp. 293–94.

83. This explanation of Abhinava's schema is simplified from Sanderson's "Maṇḍala and Āgamic Identity."

84. Translation based on that of Sanderson, "Meaning in Tantric Ritual," p. 65.

85. In some accounts; in others she is depicted as exactly the same as the terrifying Aparā, though with a reddish body rather than a red-black body as the sole difference. See Sanderson's "Visualisation of the Deities of the Trika."

86. Here I use phrases from Sanderson's masterful article "Maṇḍala and Āgamic Identity," (pp. 192–193) which I have been contemplating for many years and still have not learned everything it has to offer.

87. Abhinava Gupta, *Essence of the Tantras* chapter four: *"The whole of reality is encompassed by three basic Powers. She by whom the Highest Divinity supports, perceives, and manifests all this—from Śiva down to Earth—as pure undifferentiated Consciousness, is his sacred Transcendent Power, the Supreme Goddess [*Śrī Parā-śakti*]. She by whom [he supports, perceives, and manifests all] as diversity within unity is his sacred Intermediate Power [Śrī Parāparā-śakti]. She by whom [he supports, perceives, and manifests all] as entirely differentiated, characterized by [apparent] mutual separation, is his sacred Lower Power [Śrī Aparā-śakti]. She by whom he devours this three-fold process, embracing it to himself alone as unitary awareness, is simply his Blessed Goddess Śrī Parā [in her higher all-encompassing form], denoted by other names [in the scriptures], such as Mātṛsadbhāva 'Mother Existence/The Essence of Knowers], Kālakarṣiṇī [The Projector and Withdrawer of Time] or Vāmeśvarī [The Goddess who Emits Reality]."*
88. Thanks to Judit Törzsök for providing this reference, which is to *Siddha-yogeśvarī-mata* 28.41–42.
89. Note that the book published by Lorin Roche under the name *The Radiance Sutras* cannot claim in any sense to be a translation of the *Vijñāna-bhairava,* or even a rendering, since Roche does not read Sanskrit at all. It is, rather, poetry inspired by a rendering of a translation, and thus is at several removes from the original. This of course has nothing to do with the quality of the poetry.
90. This long section on the Krama is even more indebted to Sanderson's work than other sections of the book, because no one really understood anything about the Krama before his work (despite the publication of a poor and confusing study by N. Rastogi called *The Krama Tantricism of Kashmir*). Thus this section draws heavily on materials in Sanderson's *magnum opus,* "The Śaiva Exegesis of Kashmir."
91. Parapharased from Sanderson 1988:675.
92. Translated by Sanderson from the Old Kashmīrī *Mahānaya-prakāśa* ("Śaiva Exegesis," p. 265).
93. Sanderson's translation from "Śaiva Exegesis," p. 322, except that I have replaced "enlightenment" with the more literal "awakening" (*bodha*).
94. It has been translated by Rafaelle Torella and by Christopher Tompkins, though the former's is difficult to find and the latter's is unpublished.
95. "Śaiva Exegesis," p. 277, emphasis mine. The reader may notice a similarity to Buddhist language here, and indeed the Krama is the most "Buddhistic" of the Śaiva schools, though it is more accurate to say that they both emerged out of the same Himālayan cultural milieu, which fostered an interest in nondualist meditation in this period.
96. Following Sanderson's emendation of *surata* from the manuscript's *svarata.* If the latter reading is correct, it would imply self-pleasuring instead of lovemaking.
97. Note that the King did not give him the punishment for sexual misconduct, which would have been the brand of a vulva. We can therefore suppose that he did not disapprove of that aspect of the "circle gathering." See "Śaiva Exegesis," p. 281.
98. Closely following Sanderson, "Śaiva Exegesis," p. 291.
99. Or, "...identical with the ground of their innate I-sense." (*sahajāhaṃbhāva-bhūmiḥ*) Translation follows Sanderson, "Śaiva Exegesis," p. 327.
100. Translation closely follows Sanderson, "Śaiva Exegesis," pp. 365–6.
101. This verse was discovered by Sanderson in the commentary on the *Vijñāna-bhairava* by Śivopādhyāya, where it is quoted. Its original source is lost. See "Śaiva Exegesis" pp. 294-5.
102. Translation Sanderson, "Śaiva Exegesis," pp. 293–4.
103. In fact the later Krama went by many names: those meaning "the Krama teaching, viewpoint, or way," i.e., *krama-śāsana, kramārtha, krama-darśana,* and *krama-naya*; those meaning "the Great teaching, way, or tradition," *mahārtha, mahānaya, mahāmnāya,* and *mahā-śāsana*; those meaning "the way of the Goddess or the way of Kālī," *kālī-naya, kālikā-krama, devatā-naya,* and

devī-naya; one meaning "the tradition of the Ecstatic Gathering," *melāpa-darśana*; and finally one meaning "the secret (or esoteric) tradition": *rahasyāmnāya*.

104. Following Sanderson, "Śaiva Exegesis," p. 350.
105. Sanderson, "Śaiva Exegesis," p. 309.
106. I am thinking here of Whitney Cox, whose fine dissertation is on this text. He is currently at the School of Oriental and African Studies, University of London. The two sample verses following are adapted from his translations.
107. Abhinavagupta and Kṣemarāja both criticize Brāhminical culture for its *śaṅkā* or paralyzing inhibition that results from belief in hierarchical purity laws. See, e.g., *Pratyabhijñā-hṛdayam* sūtra 12, part one.
108. See Sanderson's "Śaiva Exegesis," pp. 335–7, 366.
109. Translation Sanderson, "Śaiva Exegesis," p. 335.
110. Translation Sanderson, "Śaiva Exegesis," p. 334, modified slightly.
111. Adapted from the translation in "Śaiva Exegesis," p. 296.
112. This whole passage comes from the original unpublished Sanskrit manuscript of the *Chummā-saṅketa-prakāśa* kindly furnished to me by Prof. Sanderson; and my explanation, as with everything in the Krama chapter, draws on his detailed analysis in "The Śaiva Exegesis of Kashmir".
113. Indeed, the Newars of the Kāthmāndu valley sometimes worship Svacchandabhairava as a consort of Kubjikā. See Mark Dyczkowski's *A Journey in the World of the Tantras*, chapter 6, "The Cult of the Goddess Kubjikā."
114. In the world of modern (Western) postural yoga, the term *kuṇḍalinī-yoga* has unfortunately become associated in the minds of many with a system of practice propounded by the Sikh entrepeneur Harbhajan Singh Puri, known as "Yogi Bhajan." The original forms of *kuṇḍalinī-yoga* were not concerned with physical postures or movements at all but rather with visualizations and energy practices of the subtle body utilizing secret Tantrik mantras and *prāṇāyāmas* quite unlike the collection of practices presented by Yogi Bhajan, who, evidently lacking access to the original sources, appears to have fabricated a number of unprecedented techniques intended to arouse the *kuṇḍalinī*. That does not in itself imply that his techniques have no intrinsic merit.
115. For the myth of Kubjikā, see Mark Dyczkowski's "Kubjikā, the Androgynous Goddess" in *A Journey in the World of the Tantras*.
116. *Kularatnoddyota* ("Illuminating the Jewel of the Kula") 1.78–79.
117. See Csaba Kiss's 2009 Oxford D.Phil. thesis, "Matsyendranātha's Compendium," a major contribution to the field.
118. This Matsyendra must be different from the much earlier Macchanda (a.k.a. Matsyendra), the founder of Kaulism, but is clearly a figure modelled on the latter.
119. As clearly seen in the *Nityākaula* text discovered by Sanderson; see "The Śaiva Age."
120. Two important works of this Vedānta/Tantra hybrid were produced in the late Middle Ages, the *Saundarya-laharī* and *Ānanda-laharī* ("Waves of Beauty" and "Waves of Bliss"), still much studied and recited today. They are not, of course, authored by the original Śaṅkara, who does not exhibit any Tantrik influence.
121. After the Muslim conquest of Kashmīr (1339), when Shaivism lost its institutional base, the tradition began to contract, and study of the original scriptures slowly disappeared, leaving a gnostically-oriented and trimmed-down version of Śaiva Tantra based on the exegetical writings referred to here. For a more complete explanation of this process, see Sanderson's "Swāmī Lakshman Joo and his Place in the Kashmīrian Tradition."
122. My translation follows that of Sanderson in "Śaiva Exegesis," p. 404.
123. The former commentary has been translated by Mark Dyczkowski, the latter by Swāmī Lakṣman Jū.
124. The last great Kashmīrī Guru of Śaivism, Swāmī

Lakṣhman Jū, left his body in 1991. His Western disciples have continued to publish his work, including his commentary on the *Śiva-sūtras* and on the *Vijñāna-bhairava*, which are currently the best available translations of those works. Published in an imperfect but useful translation by Jaidev Singh, under the title *A Trident of Wisdom;* note that Singh's other translations are *not* useful and not recommended, having all been superseded by substantially superior work.

125. Published in an imperfect but useful translation by Jaidev Singh, under the title *Trident of Wisdom;* note that Singh's other translations are *not* useful and not recommended, having all been superseded by substantially superior work.

126. Popular American scholar David White would have us believe that power-seeking sinister yogis were always the majority and argues this thesis in his recent book *Sinister Yogis*. That book, like *Kiss of the Yoginī*, suffers from the serious scholarly defect of "confirmation bias," research carried out with a predetermined thesis in mind (the more time-consuming and accurate method of research is reading a wide and diverse range of sources without any specific idea of what one will find). For evidence that White's work suffers from the skewed perspective generated by confirmation bias, see James Mallinson's new review of *Sinister Yogis.*

127. James Mallinson wrote to me in an email in May 2011, "I'm not certain that the *Amṛtasiddhi* was a 'Nāth' text. It may be more closely connected to the [Śaiva] Kālamukha lineages found at Shringeri/Vijayanagara, the latter having Virūpākṣa as its tutelary deity."

128. It is important to note that there was another major branch of the *haṭha-yoga* tradition, a Vaiṣṇava branch that paralleled its Śaiva counterpart (because it was based in Tantrik teachings that ultimate derive from Śaiva sources). The progression of this branch goes like this: the first text to teach something explicitly named *haṭha-yoga* is the 13th-century *Dattātreya-yoga-śāstra* or *Scripture on Yoga by Lord Dattātreya.* Dattātreya was said to be an *avatāra* (incarnation of God) who was claimed by both the Śaiva Dasnāmīs and the Vaiṣṇavas, though he eventually become more associated with the latter. From the *Dattātreya-yoga-śāstra* flowed a series of *haṭha-yoga* treatises that were copied throughout India. The practices taught in these texts influenced the Rāmānandī lineage (which survives to the present) and the Śrī-vaiṣṇava lineage (a tradition with its roots in Vaiṣṇava Tantra; note that one of the latter's 11th-century scriptures, the *Vimānārcanākalpa,* is the first text to teach non-seated *āsanas*). So it is important to note that the founder of modern postural yoga, Śrī Krishnamāchārya, was a member of the Śrī-vaiṣṇava lineage (see p. 319 for more on him).

129. To be more accurate, we cannot be sure that Gorakṣa's source is the *Sārdhatriśati-kālottara,* since that text was copied and paraphrased by several other Tantrik scriptures, such as the *Svacchanda-tantra.* What Tompkins has proven is that the author of *The Hundred Verses of Gorakṣa* had some Tantrik texts in front of him (or in his head) while writing, and the earliest known source for many of these specific ideas is the *Sārdhatriśati-kālottara.*

130. To complicate the picture, there were other classifications of yoga practice that were more popular in the Tantrik scriptures than the *aṣṭāṅga-yoga,* such as the *ṣaḍaṅga-yoga* or six-limbed yoga that we see also in the *Maitrī Upaniṣad.*

131. In a provocative and impeccably researched article in the Journal of Indian Philosophy ("Haṃsamiṭṭhu: 'Pātañjalayoga is Nonsense'"), my teacher Somdev Vasudeva traces the various sources of the additional *aṅgas* presented in this schema. The importance of the 18th-century writing of Haṃsa-miṭṭhu is that it shows both that Patañjali was known and cited in early modern India (prior to Western interest in the text) and that Tantrik sources were cited more often and in the same context. For example, Haṃsa-miṭṭhu says that the value of Patañjali's yoga of eight limbs is that

it frees one from *karma,* and then he cites as evidence not the *Yogasūtra* but rather the *Kulārṇava-tantra!* Then he goes on to present the 15-*aṅga* yoga listed here. This implies to us that the *aṣṭāṅga-yoga* did not survive separately from the Tantrik yoga that had absorbed it.

132. You can study the Yogasūtra in an engaging format of short video presentations by going to my website learnyogasutras.com. The interpretation of each sūtra is inspired by the Tantra without diverging too much from Patañjali's original intention.
133. See Sanderson, "Swāmī Lakshman Joo and his Place in the Kashmīrīan Tradition," pp. 118–19.
134. See his groundbreaking book *Yoga Body: The Origins of Modern Posture Practice* from Oxford University Press.
135. Since View and practice must be in alignment to bear their fruit, yogic practice cannot be arbitrarily joined with any philosophy. From a traditional perspective, then, the View that is taught in conjunction with yogic practice must be one that was evolved in direct organic connection to yogic practice.
136. The difference between these two terms is that *dāna* refers to a regular (e.g., monthly) donation to a temple, āshram, or guru, while *dakṣiṇā* refers to a financial offering made in exchange for the guru's teaching or ceremonial performance. Today these two terms are more or less interchangeable.
137. Here are the primary rules of the code of conduct (*samaya*) that Samayins would adopt, using the *samaya* code of the Kaula Trika as an example (source: *Tantrasāra* 13):
    1. The initiate should be devoted and loyal, with his whole being, to his guru, the teachings, the form of the Deity s/he has been linked to, and the corresponding mantra with which s/he has been initiated.
    2. S/he should nonjudgmentally turn away from those people who are opposed to these four [guru, teachings, deity, and mantra].
    3. Just as he venerates the guru, he should venerate those "sons" of the guru who have been initiated before him (i.e., senior guru-brothers and -sisters), his kin through the tie of wisdom (*vidyā*). He should also venerate the family of the guru, not because they have special status, but in order to pay tribute to him.
    4. Women must be treated with reverence. The initiate must avoid any action which might cause him to feel disgust for a woman.
    5. The name of his Deity, his guru, or his mantra should not be uttered in casual conversation but only at the time of worship.
    6. The initiate should not look on anyone in the world as superior to himself except for his guru.
    7. He should honor the lunar days on which special worship is required (e.g., the full moon, the new moon, and the 8th and 14th lunar days).
    8. If members of his *kula* (spiritual community) visit his home, he should practice with them to the best of his ability.
    9. He should avoid excessive social contact with followers of other traditions during this probationary period; if he becomes the pupil of someone from another tradition, out of curiosity to learn his doctrine, he must give up that teacher as soon as the instruction is complete.
    10. He should honor *sādhus* (homeless mendicants), but not practice with them.
    11. He must give up all inhibitions, anxieties, and doubts (concerning caste differences, purity laws, what is proper to eat, etc.).
    12. The only temple or pilgrimage site he may reverence is that of his own body.
    13. He should maintain awareness of the Heart-mantra as much as possible.
138. This is drawn almost verbatim from a description was written by my teacher Prof. Sanderson, drawing on accounts in the *Netra-tantra* (ch. 18), the *Hara-carita-cintāmaṇi* (ch. 31), the *Jayadratha-yāmala,* and the

Siddhānta-sāra-paddhati, one of the most important ritual manuals of the Śaiva tradition. These sources are not published in English.

139. I have read the Sanskrit sources that give us this information, but I should note that my understanding was greatly enhanced by Prof. Sanderson's unpublished summaries of the relevant data in the *Tantrāloka, Mṛgendra-tantra,* and *Siddhānta-sāra-paddhati.*
140. This section draws almost verbatim on unpublished writings by and conversations with Prof. Sanderson, whose expertise in the area of Śaiva ritual is far beyond mine, and due to whom I know what little I do of this ritual world. However, I should note that my knowledge has more recently been augmented by the work of my colleague Christopher Tompkins, who has been translating sections of the *Siddhānta-sāra-paddhati,* which was also Sanderson's source.
141. Sound and sensation are offered to Brahmā, taste is offered to Viṣṇu, vision and odor are offered to Rudra, intellect and ego to Īśvara, and mind to Sadāśiva. These are the eight parts of the eightfold subtle body that transmigrates from one life to another.
142. The dualistic Saiddhāntikas admit that there is often no perceptible effect of fusing the soul with Śiva; while the nondual Kaulas or Kaula-influenced lineages claim that their initiation frequently triggers a strong *śaktipāta.*
143. Some confusion has arisen due to the use of the term "Rājānaka" by Douglas Brooks to denote his body of teachings. There is not any documented lineage called Rājānaka; in the original sources it simply denoted a Kashmīrī Tantrik scholar who had received official recognition and/or an endowment from the king, much like a knighthood in England. In time the title became hereditary. I have not yet seen it used in non-Kashmīrī sources.
144. In modern lineages influenced by Śaiva Tantra, such as that of Siddha Yoga, the concepts of *śaktipāta* and *dīkṣā* have fully merged, and the phrase *śaktipāt-dīkṣā* is used.
145. See Sanderson's "Commentary on the Opening Verses of the Tantrasāra," p. 84, where he explains that the Guru lineage is to be seen as a single state of being, identical with the Deity, in which individual identities are irrelevant.
146. I owe this phrase to my friend Dharmabodhi Sarasvatī, whose explanation of Guru-yoga made all that I had previously learned about it finally click into place.
147. This fact is complicated by the *avadhūta* type of Guru, who exists in perfect union with the divine but whose behavior takes no account of the rules of propriety of the society in which he lives. A classic 20th-century example is that of Bhagavān Nityānanda of Gaṇeshpurī.
148. There is a strange misconception held by many of the students I have worked with in regard to the concept of unconditional love. When exhorted to cultivate unconditional love for all beings, especially the actual people in one's life, students often object, "But then I will be taken advantage of!" or "I don't want to be a doormat!" When I hear this, I am just flabbergasted. There is simply no logical reason to suppose that having unconditional love for someone means that you do everything they tell you do, or fail to voice your own opinion, or fail to maintain your independence in any way. Though I do not yet understand why Westerners think otherwise, there is clearly a connection between this way of thinking and the total fiasco of guru-disciple relationships that we have seen in recent history when Westerners are the disciples. From the traditional perspective, you practice seeing and treating your Guru as God, and maintain commitment to that practice regardless of what he does or says, all the way up until you abandon him if you have decided that his conduct is sufficiently in conflict with your beliefs that you will likely not be successful in your guru-yoga. Then you would simply walk away and never look back. You do not spend years bemoaning how wronged you were on the Internet. You simply find another guru whose conduct is not such a bar to the guru-yoga, and if you are very lucky, that person has an attainment that will

make your guru-yoga relatively easy (though it's never easy). After all, the whole reason guru-yoga can work regardless of the guru's "level" is because he—and everyone—really *is* God! And, finally, nothing says that you have to practice guru-yoga at all. But for someone who really gets it, it's one of the most efficient means to liberation.

149. These three levels or centers are not immediately comprehensible to the Westerner who is likely to divide up the human being differently. As discussed earlier in the book, the Western dichotomy of heart versus mind is not operative in the Asian context, which views thoughts and emotions as inextricably linked—"heart" and "mind" are the same word in Sanskrit (e.g., *citta*). The heart-mind center is also the hub of the subtle body, and thus it is sometimes referred to as the "energy" center. The issue of correctly identifying these centers in English is further confused by the fact that the highest center, here called "spirit," is named as Mind in some Buddhist sources. Both "spirit" and "higher Mind" refer to the spacious clarity of pure Awareness.
150. Dyczkowski, Mark. *The Doctrine of Vibration.* SUNY Press, 1987, p. 172.
151. TĀ 1.146–7; translation follows Dyczkowski 1987:180.
152. Note that Zen—which derives from Ch'an Buddhism, which derives in part from Buddhist Tantra— emphasizes *śāmbhava-upāya* to the extent that it sometimes excludes the other *upāyas* entirely, which is precisely why it is only appropriate and effective for a certain type of practitioner.
153. My translation of this verse was improved by Professor Sanderson, and the wording of the last phrase is his.
154. Here I am arguing that all stories have their roots in conditioning, but note that it does *not* follow that everything about a person's individual makeup can be explained in terms of psychology and their past history. In fact, sometimes we experience what might be called *existential* fear, anger, or joy that is not linked to our psychology but is spontaneously arising as a natural expression of embodied consciousness that cannot and need not be interpreted or explained. These existential emotions may (or may not) be a manifestation of your connection to the "collective unconscious"; at any rate, they are not a problem to be solved.
155. *Nirvikalpa* does not here mean having no thoughts, but rather that thoughts are not in the slightest degree taken to be reality, and therefore they no longer interpose themselves and filter reality to the experiencer.
156. *Tantrāloka* 15.269–71a; translated by Dyczkowski (1987:192).
157. The last phrase, *viśvottīrṇo viśvātmā cāham* could be used as a mantra. It admits of several translations, specifically in its second word. *viśvātmā* can mean "I am one with the universe," "I embody the universe," "I am one with all things," "I embody all things," or "I am the essence of the universe." This connects to the teaching given in Śiva-sūtra 1.13, *dṛśyaṃ śarīram,* "All that is perceptible is my body."
158. This alternate translation of the third phrase was suggested by Prof. Sanderson; the statement is delusional because of its implied dualism.
159. In the parallel passage in *Tantrāloka,* Abhinava makes the unorthodox move of arguing that anything can be used in worship if it elevates and expands awareness, not only the prescribed substances:

> *Therefore, whatever in this world evokes heightened awareness, even a little bit, because it is graced by consciousness, it is enlivened and thus completely suitable for worship in our system. ||164c-5b||*
>
> *Whatever effectively causes one's submerged consciousness to emerge is suitable for an offering, because it is this emergence of Awareness that is called bliss* [ānanda]. *||167c-8b||*

This is the basis of his argument in favor of the use, by qualified practitioners, of the sexual fluids for worship. These are considered power substances with semimagical properties in the Kaula Trika, but Abhinava reveres them because they are produced only in heightened states of consciousness. And if one's sexuality has itself become a spiritual practice, as he teaches in chapter 29, the substances produced thereby are very sacred and powerful. One is thus to offer them in divine worship, not caste them away as waste products. If one cannot see sexual fluids as completely pure and divine, one is not a *vīra,* an adept ready for this level of practice. But this is just one special application of the theory. It is equally unorthodox (from the perspective of conservative Śaivas) to suggest that you can improvise in your *pūjā* and utilize whatever heightens your awareness and gives you a sense of the sacred. But this is of course the norm in a spiritual culture that has no orthodoxy, such as American alternative spirituality.

160. My understanding of the Sanskrit of this passage is due to Prof. Sanderson's assistance.
161. My translation in some places follows that of Sanderson's: see "Visualization of the Deities of the Trika," pp. 74–76.
162. Dyczkowski, Mark. *The Doctrine of Vibration.* SUNY Press, 1987, p. 190.
163. The clarity and precision of this description is very much due to the recent scholarly work of Christopher Tompkins, who is specializing in the yogic practices of Śaiva Tantra. The brief description given here is of great significance, for the commonly known *haṭha-yoga* materials that treat this subject (using the later *kuṇḍalinī* terminology) can now be seen to have classical Śaiva Tantra as their source and antecedent.
164. My understanding of *uccāra* is primarily due to the work of Christopher Tompkins and to a lesser extent that of Richard Davis (see his *Ritual in an Oscillating Universe*).
165. We should note that the functions of the five *prāṇa-vāyus* as described here in the context of mystical yoga practice are distinct from the functions described in the context of the medical liturature. There, for example, *samāna* governs balance and digestion, *udāna* governs coughing, vomiting, and speaking, and *vyāna* governs distribution of nutrients, movement of the limbs, and sensation in extremities. The medical functions are certainly known to the Tantras. They are linked to the mystical functions in certain ways; for example, *udāna* is associated with speech, and the power of speech derives from *Parā-vāk,* the Goddess of the Supreme Word, who is identical with *kuṇḍalinī-śakti,* universally identified as a "phonemic" or mantric power in the earliest sources. Eventually *kuṇḍalinī-śakti* comes to designate the innate intelligence of embodied consciousness. However, we should note that in none of the Tantrik sources is *kuṇḍalinī-śakti* described as lying dormant at the base of the spine. This idea, found in *haṭha-yoga* sources, would have been absurd to the Tāntrikas, for if *kuṇḍalinī* was dormant, you would be in a coma. Rather, in the Tantrik sources, *kuṇḍalinī* dwells in the crown of the head, for the Goddess is eternally inseparable from her other half. In Tantrik yoga-sādhanā, she is invited to descend to the relevant *cakra* (often the heart, sometimes the *kanda*), creating a rubber-band like tension that then can be used to catapult the soul (individual consciousness) up to the highest center. This revolutionary scholarly discovery made by Christopher Tompkins was obvious to all initiates of classical Tantra, but since forgotten.
166. I first learned about *divya-karaṇa* from my teacher Dr. Somdev Vāsudeva (Columbia University), and my knowledge of it was recently enhanced by Christopher Tompkins.
167. I refer to the mechanical stretching of the tongue and severing of the frenulum in order to insert the tongue tip into the pharynx and up into the nasal cavity. This is done in imitation of a spontaneous (involuntary) *kriyā* that can happen as a result of *kumbhaka* (breath retention) practice, in which the tongue turns back and enters the pharynx and the practitioner tastes "divine nectar." Though its occurance is well documented among yogīs (and even occasionally among

long-distance swimmers), there is not yet scientific understanding of how it happens.

168. One of my graduate school professors, Śrī Padmanabh Jaini, liked to compare India with the West with the words, "In India everyone can think differently as long as they all act the same, whereas in the West everyone is free to act differently as long as they all think the same."
169. Sanderson, "Meaning in Tantric Ritual," (1995), pp. 24–25.
170. Paraphase of "Maṇḍala and Āgamic Identity," pp. 171–2 and quote from p. 173.
171. This reminds me of the beautiful teaching of the early Sūfī woman saint Rābi'a of Basra. She was seen walking through town carrying a torch and a bucket of water. The people asked her why, and she replied, "I am going to burn down heaven and extinguish the fires of hell so that people will worship God for the sake of God alone!"
172. *tathaikyābhyāsa-niṣṭhasyākramād viśvam idaṃ haṭhāt | saṃpūrṇa-śivatā-kṣobha-narīnartad iva sphuret || 15.151* My translation is of course influenced by Sanderson, and I would not have understood the sense of the word *kṣobha* (which usually means "agitation," here translated [following him] as "intense animation") without his aid.
173. Abhinava is here quoting from Utpaladeva's *Śivastotrāvalī,* hymn 17. The fact that he seems to be quoting from memory corroborates my vision of the present passage as being dictated while in an exalted state.
174. *tadetādṛk-pūrṇa-śiva-viśvāveśāya ye 'rcanam | kurvanti te śivā eva tān pūrṇān prati kiṃ phalam ||* We could also translate *pūrṇa-śiva-viśva* as "the universe as Śiva in his fullest expansion" following Sanderson. The phrase "this state in which they enter into and become immersed in the experience..." translates the various nuances of the single word *āveśa.*
175. My translation closely follows that of Sanderson, Śaiva Exegesis, p. 295. The term *sāhasa-samādhi* is unique to the Krama and means something like "a sudden and intense plunge into a mystical state of consciousness." Sanderson translates "the trance of sudden enlightenment" or "sudden immersion in the dynamic purity of consciousness." The word *sāhasa* usually means an aggressive, violent assault (!).
176. Originally *maṇḍala* meant a temporary large-scale Tantrik diagram used for meditation and initiation rites, and *yantra* meant a small magical diagram or symbol for controlling energy, sometimes written on a scroll and buried or placed in a locket for protection. Now the terms are used almost interchangeably.
177. See "Maṇḍala and Āgamic Identity," p. 170, note 3. The list comes from *Tantrāloka* chapter 27.
178. Adapted from the authoritative 11th century manual, the *Somaśambhu-paddhati.* This book, written by the equivalent of an archbishop of Śaivism named Somaśambhu, has been translated into French by the late Helene Brunner.
179. For more information on this subject, see the first few pages of Sanderson's "A Commentary on the Opening Verses of the Tantrasāra," especially note 7, and also page p. 174 of "Maṇḍala and Āgamic Identity."
180. There is one sexual rite recorded in the literature, of a very different character. This is the "Razor's Edge Observance" recorded in chapter 39 of the *Brahmayāmala* (see p. 223–5). Here an otherwise celibate homeless Śākta Śaiva ascetic obtains a beautiful girl "eager for good sex," giving her as much jewelry as he can afford, and couples with her every day for one to six months *without ejaculating* in order to obtain special powers through this Herculean effort, said to be "hard to practice even for gods." If he ejaculates accidentally (e.g., at night or because she makes him), he must do 10,000 repetitions of his mantra; if he does so on purpose, he must start all over. Clearly, this also bears no real resemblence to American "Tantric sex," though refraining from ejaculation also appears as a theme there, though this probably derives from the

influence of the so-called "Taoist sexuality" taught by Mantak Chia and others, not from awareness of the unpublished Brahmayāmala.

181. People familiar with the extant popular literature on Tantra will have heard of the "five M's" rather than the three. This is because the post-classical Tantra of east India is better known than classical Himālayan Tantra. The Bengalis, being great fish-lovers, added *matsya* to the list, but then needed a fifth because four is not a sacred number, so they cast about and added *mudrā,* fried grains, despite the fact that it is not a transgressive substance. This has led to comical speculations by under-informed Western scholars that perhaps the grain in question had a psychedelic mold growing on it (!).

182. *Manuṣya-jātir ekaiva...na jātir vihitā tatra varṇam vāpi sitādikam, yoni-liṅgodbhavāḥ sarve jīva ekaḥ samaḥ sthitaḥ. Tatra sarvagato Devo dṛśyate jñāna-cakṣuṣā.*

183. A few teachers of American neo-Tantra have now become acquainted with one or two of the published texts, such as the *Vijñāna-Bhairava Tantra,* and use them in their teaching. While this attempt to connect to the original tradition is commendable, to my mind it in no way substitutes for a thorough and sustained engagement with a wide range of primary sources and published material by accomplished scholars on the philosophy and development of the Tantrik traditions. Only such an engagement, in my view, qualifies a teacher to claim to represent an ancient tradition accurately, especially when that tradition is rooted in such a different cultural matrix as medieval India.

184. See *Unbounded Wholeness: Dzogchen, Bön, and the Logic of the Nonconceptual* in the Bibliography. For more on Dzogchen, especially as interpreted within Bön, see Namkhai Norbu, Samten Karmay, Per Kvaerne, and David Snellgrove.

185. With one exception: the sexual rite taught as the "Razor's Edge Observance" in chapter 39 of the *Brahmayāmala* (see p. 223). Here, an otherwise celibate homeless Śākta Śaiva ascetic obtains a beautiful girl "eager for good sex," giving her as much jewelry as he can afford, and couples with her every day for one to six months without ejaculating in order to obtain special powers through this Herculean effort, said to be "hard to practice even for gods." If he ejaculates accidentally (e.g., at night or because she makes him), he must do 10,000 repetitions of his mantra; if he does so on purpose, he must start all over. The explicit purpose of this rite is to gain magical powers. Clearly, this bears no real resemblance to American "Tantric sex," since its purpose is neither increasing intimacy nor maximizing pleasure. Refraining from ejaculation does sometimes appear as a theme in American neo-tantra; this probably derives from the influence of the so-called "Taoist sexuality" taught by Mantak Chia and others, not from awareness of the unpublished *Brahmayāmala.*

BIBLIOGRAPHY

Books

Alper, Harvey, ed. *Mantra.* (Also published as *Understanding Mantras.*) SUNY Press, 1989.

Anantānanda, Swāmī. *What's on My Mind?: Becoming Inspired with New Perception.* SYDA Foundation, 1996.

Bailly, Constantina Rhodes. *Śaiva Devotional Songs of Kashmir: A Translation and Study of Utpaladeva's Śivastotrāvali.* SUNY Press, 1987.

Brooks, Douglas. *The Secret of the Three Cities.* University of Chicago Press, 1990.

Davis, Richard. *Ritual in an Oscillating Universe.* Princeton University Press, 1991.

Dyczkowski, Mark. *The Aphorisms of Śiva: the Śivasūtra with Bhāskara's Commentary.* SUNY Press, 1992.

________. *The Doctrine of Vibration: An Analysis of the Doctrines and Practices of Kashmir Shaivism.* SUNY Press, 1987.

________. *A Journey in the World of the Tantras.* Indica, 2004.

________. *The Stanzas on Vibration.* SUNY Press, 1992.

Isayeva, Natalia. *From Early Vedanta to Kashmir Shaivism.* SUNY, 1995.

James, William. *The Varieties of Religious Experience: A Study in Human Nature.* Penguin, 1982. Full text: http://openlibrary.org/books/OL6359268M/The_varieties_of_religious_experience

Klein, Anne Carolyn and Geshe Tenzin Wangyal Rinpoche. *Unbounded Wholeness: Dzogchen, Bon, and the Logic of the Nonconceptual.* Oxford University Press, 2006.

Lakṣman Joo, Swāmī. *Shiva Sutras: The Supreme Awakening.* AuthorHouse, 2007.

________. Vijñāna-bhairava: *The Practice of Centring Awareness.* Indica, 2007.

Mishra, Kamalakar. *Kashmir Shaivism: the Central Philosophy of Tantrism.* Rudra Press, 1993.

Muktānanda, Swāmī. *Nothing Exists That is Not Śiva.* SYDA Foundation, 1997.

Padoux, André and Lilian Silburn. *La lumière sur les tantras: chapitres 1 à 5 du Tantrāloka.* Collège de France, 1998.

Shankarānanda, Swāmī. *Consciousness is Everything: The Yoga of Kashmir Shaivism.* Shaktipat Press, 2003.

Singh, Jaideva. *A Trident of Wisdom.* SUNY Press, 1989.

Singleton, Mark. *Yoga Body: The Origins of Modern Posture Practice.* Oxford University Press, 2010.

Torella, Raffaele. *The Īśvarapratyabhijñākārikā of Utpaladeva with the author's vṛtti.* Motilal Banarsidass, 2002.

Watson, Alex. *The Self's Awareness of Itself: Bhaṭṭa Rāmakaṇṭha's Arguments against the Buddhist Doctrine of No-self.* Wien, 2006.

White, David, ed. *Tantra in Practice.* Princeton University Press, 2000.

Williams, Paul and Anthony Tribe. *Buddhist Thought.* Routledge, 2000.

Articles

A. Aspect, P. Grangier, and G. Roger. "Experimental Realization of Einstein-Podolsky-Rosen-Bohm Gedankenexperiment: A New Violation of Bell's Inequalities," Physical Review Letters, 49:2, 1982.

Brunner, Hélène. "Ātmārthapūjā versus parārthapūjā in the Śaiva tradition," in *The Sanskrit Tradition and Tantrism*, Teun Goudriaan, ed. Brill, 1990.

Cabezón, José. "The Discipline and Its Other: the Dialectic of Alterity in the Study of Religion," Journal of the American Academy of Religion, 74:1, 2006.

Davis, Richard. "Becoming a Śiva, and Acting as One, in Śaiva Worship," in *Ritual and Speculation in Early Tantrism. Studies in Honour of André Padoux*, T. Goudriaan, ed. SUNY Press, 1992.

Hatley, Shaman. "Mapping the Esoteric Body in the Islamic Yoga of Bengal," History of Religions 46, 2007.

Heilijgers-Seelen, Dory. "The doctrine of the Ṣaṭcakra according to the Kubjikāmata," in *The Sanskrit Tradition and Tantrism*, Teun Goudriaan, ed. Brill, 1990.

Mallinson, James. "Haṭhayoga," in *The Brill Encyclopedia of Hinduism*. Forthcoming.

Muller, Paul. "Tantric Meditation: Vocalic Beginnings," in *Ritual and Speculation in Early Tantrism. Studies in Honour of André Padoux*, T. Goudriaan, ed. SUNY Press, 1992.

________. "'Tarko Yogāṅgam Uttamam': On Subtle Knowledge and the Refinement of Thought in Abhinvagupta's Liberative Tantric Method," in *Theory and Practice of Yoga*, Knut Jacobsen, ed. Brill, 2005.

Sanderson, Alexis. [All articles except "Śaiva Exegesis" available from alexissanderson.com]

________. "Purity and Power among the Brahmans of Kashmir," in *The Category of the Person: Anthropology, Philosophy, History*, M. Carrithers, S. Collins and S. Lukes, eds. Cambridge University Press, 1985.

________. "Maṇḍala and Aagamic Identity in the Trika of Kashmir," in *Mantras et Diagrammes Rituelles dans l'Hindouisme*, ed. A. Padoux. Éditions du Centre National de la Recherche Scientifique, 1986.

________."Saivism and the Tantric Traditions," in *The World's Religions*, edited by S. Sutherland, L. Houlden, P. Clarke and F. Hardy. Routledge and Kegan Paul, 1988. Reprinted in *The World's Religions: The Religions of Asia*, edited by F. Hardy. Routledge and Kegan Paul, 1990.

________. "The Visualization of the Deities of the Trika," in *L'Image Divine: Culte et Méditation dans l'Hindouisme,* edited by A. Padoux. Éditions du Centre National de la Recherche Scientifique, 1990.

________. "The Doctrine of the Mālinīvijayottaratantra," in *Ritual and Speculation in Early Tantrism. Studies in Honour of André Padoux*, T. Goudriaan, ed. SUNY Press, 1992.

________."Meaning in Tantric Ritual," in *Essais sur le Rituel III: Colloque du Centenaire de la Section des Sciences religieuses de l'École Pratique des Hautes Études*. A.-M. Blondeau and K. Schipper, eds. Peeters, 1995.

________. "A Commentary on the Opening Verses of the Tantrasāra of Abhinavagupta," in *Sāmarasya: Studies in Indian Arts, Philosophy, and Interreligious Dialogue in Honour of Bettina Bäumer*, Sadānanda Das and Ernst Fürlinger, eds. D.K. Printworld, 2005.

________. "The Lākulas: New evidence of a system intermediate between Pāñcārthika Pāśupatism and Āgamic Śaivism." Indian Philosophical Annual 24 (2003-2005).

________. "Swami Lakshman Joo and His Place in the Kashmirian Śaiva Tradition," in *Samvidullāsaḥ*, Bettina Bäumer and Sarla Kumar, eds. D.K. Printworld, 2007.

________. "The Śaiva Exegesis of Kashmir," in *Mélanges tantriques à la mémoire d'Hélène Brunner / Tantric Studies in Memory of Hélène Brunner*, Dominic Goodall and André Padoux, eds. Institut français d'Indologie / École française d'Extrême-Orient, 2007.

________. "The Śaiva Age," in *Genesis and Development of Tantrism*, Shingo Einoo, ed. Institute of Oriental Culture, University of Tokyo, 2009.

Torella, Rafaelle. "The Kañcukas in the Śaiva and Vaisnava Tantric Tradition: A Few Considerations Between Theology and Grammar", in *Studies in Hinduism II, Miscellanea to the Phenomenon of the Tantras*, G. Oberhammer, ed. Wien, 1998.

Vasudeva, Somdev. "Haṃsamiṭṭhu: 'Pātañjalayoga is Nonsense'," Journal of Indian Philosophy, 2011.

Illustrator's Bibliography

Beer, Robert. *The Encyclopedia of Tibetan Symbols and Motifs*. Shambhala, 1999.

Bühnemann, Gudrun. *Mandalas and Yantras in the Hindu Tradition*. DK Printworld, 2007.

Dehejia, Vidya and Thomas B. Coburn. *Devi: The Great Goddess : Female Divinity in South Asian Art*. Smithsonian Institution in association with Mapin Publishing and Prestel Verlag, 1999.

Huntington, Susan. *The "Pala-Sena" Schools of Sculpture*. Brill, 1984.

Jackson, Janice and David Jackson. *Tibetan Thangka Painting: Methods & Materials*. Snow Lion Publications, 1984 (second edition, 2006).

Jansen, Eva Rudy. *The Book of Hindu Imagery: Gods, Manifestations and Their Meaning*. New Age Books, 2005.

Johari, Harish. *Tools for Tantra*. Destiny Books, 1988.

Khanna, Madhu and Ajit Mookerjee. *Yantra: The Tantric Symbol of Cosmic Unity*. Inner Traditions, 2003

Kossak, Steven M. and Jane Casey Singer. *Sacred Visions: Early Paintings from Central Tibet*. Metropolitan Museum of Art, 1999.

Pal, Pratapaditya. *A Collecting Odyssey: The Alsdorf Collection of Indian and East Asian Art*. The Art Institute of Chicago, 1997.

Rhie, Marilyn M. and Robert Thurman. *Wisdom and Compassion: The Sacred Art of Tibet Harry N. Abrams*; expanded edition, 2000.

Sakya, Jnan B. *Short Description of Gods, Goddesses and Ritual Objects of Buddhism and Hinduism in Nepal*. Handicraft Association of Nepal / Subhash Printing Press, 1989.

INDEX

Page numbers in **bold** refer to illustrations.

Photo: Christine Mason

Christopher D. Wallis (Hareesh)
was introduced to Indian spirituality at the age of six and initiated into the practice of meditation and yoga at sixteen. While traveling around the world in his early twenties, he felt an inner inspiration to study, teach, and practice Indian spirituality as the focus of his life.

A highly decorated scholar with a Masters of Philosophy in Classical Indian Religions from the University of Oxford, he is currently a Ph.D. candidate in Sanskrit at the University of California, Berkeley. He has received traditional yogic education at ashrams in India, Thailand, and New York. Hareesh teaches internationally on meditation, yoga philosophy, Sanskrit, and chanting, and he also offers spiritual coaching. He is the founder of the Mattamayūra Institute for Studies in the Tantrik Arts and Sciences: mattamayura.org

Christopher's teaching balances accuracy with accessibility, profundity with clarity, and intellectual integrity with heart-expanding inspiration.